Presidential
Decisions for War

THE AMERICAN MOMENT

Stanley I. Kutler, Series Editor

Presidential Decisions for War

*Korea, Vietnam,
the Persian Gulf, and Iraq*

Second Edition

Gary R. Hess

The Johns Hopkins University Press
Baltimore

The Johns Hopkins University Press
2715 North Charles Street
Baltimore, Maryland 21218-4363
www.press.jhu.edu

ISBN-13: 978-0-8018-9123-6 (hc)
ISBN-10: 0-8018-9123-X (hc)
ISBN-13: 978-0-8018-9124-3 (pbk)
ISBN-10: 0-8018-9124-8 (pbk)

Library of Congress Control Number: 2008930595

A catalogue record for this book is available from the British Library.

Special discounts are available for bulk purchases of this book. For more information, please contact Special Sales at 410-516-6936 or specialsales@press.jhu.edu.

The Johns Hopkins University Press uses environmentally friendly book materials, including recycled text paper that is composed of at least 30 percent post-consumer waste, whenever possible. All of our book papers are acid-free, and our jackets and covers are printed on paper with recycled content.

To Bernie Sternsher—a dedicated historian, superb friend, and loyal Red Sox fan

Contents

Series Editor's Foreword

PRESIDENT GEORGE W. BUSH'S decision to force regime change in Iraq marked a departure for American foreign policy. Congress readily supported his decision to attack Iraq, but it reflected a momentary public consensus, orchestrated by the administration, that the war was just and vital to American security. Earlier presidential decisions to use force in Korea, Vietnam, and the Persian Gulf responded to the use of force by perceived, dangerous enemies. But for Iraq in March 2003, the president invoked a newly declared doctrine of preemptive war.

Americans were told that Saddam Hussein and the Iraqi government possessed weapons of mass destruction (WMDs)—meaning nuclear and chemical weapons—and that Iraq had links with the notorious al-Qaeda, the perpetrator of the World Trade Center destruction in 2001. The president and his advisers assured Americans that the Iraqi people would greet American soldiers as liberators, welcome them with flowers, and, with our aid, establish a democratic government that would inspire political change throughout the Middle East. No WMDs were ever discovered, and no links between the Iraqi regime and al-Qaeda ever existed. The Middle East remains safe for autocracy.

War followed and the president triumphantly declared "Mission Accomplished" on May 1, 2003, two months after hostilities had begun. But after more than five years of fighting and occupation, the United States found itself bogged down with 140,000 troops in Iraq, confronting a violent sectarian and civil conflagration that the president and his advisers had in no way anticipated and saddled with an Iraqi government that had neither the will nor the capability to govern effectively. The president increased the commitment in 2007, saying that we could not withdraw because there was too much violence. A year later, his commander in Iraq testified that violence was down, but he reversed his own promise to draw down American forces that year. Those decisions largely assured that Bush's successor would be bound to maintain the commitment. Meanwhile, more than four thousand military fatalities had occurred in Iraq, nearly thirty thousand had been wounded and maimed, more than one million Iraqis had been reported killed, and millions of Iraqis had become displaced refugees.

The president's allegations and promises regarding Iraq proved empty and exaggerated; indeed, the evidence is overwhelming that the administration "cooked" the intelligence to support their case. In short, it was a presidential decision, unilaterally based on his word, without any real debate.

Gary Hess's case studies of presidential decisions to go to war in Korea, Vietnam, and earlier in the Persian Gulf offer no evidence that Presidents Truman, Kennedy, Johnson, and George H. W. Bush came to office determined to launch an attack on some perceived enemy. George W. Bush and his advisers, on the other hand, provided ample evidence of their intention to force regime change in Iraq.

Hess's work usefully reminds us how power and decision making are balanced and considered within a wide array of interests. Our system provides for a president to share power with Congress, and a president who ignores the congressional role assumes greater risks for failure. Woodrow Wilson in 1919 tried to "go it alone" at the Versailles Conference, with disastrous results. The president also must moderate conflicting views among his advisers, consider the views of potential allies, and finally consider and then harness, if he can, that amorphous, ever-changing—but always very real—force of public opinion.

War on the scale that occurred in 1941–45, now a nostalgic memory, seems unlikely in the foreseeable future. But we can expect moments when presidents will seek intervention abroad, whether in pursuit of the national interest, some historical principle, humanitarian concerns, or even vague notions of nation building. Interests vary. For Iraq, how can we ignore George W. Bush's obvious concern about oil and the need to protect oil resources? Or how he was influenced by a powerful sway of neoconservative ideology?

Presidents seem powerfully tempted to pursue such adventures, believing that war will add luster to their historical legacy. But a careful reading of history betrays such assumptions. Presidents who conducted massive, total wars, notably Abraham Lincoln and FDR, indeed are honored and revered as great crisis leaders. Gary Hess's depiction of the adventures conducted abroad by presidents of the past six decades offers a more mixed, questionable record. His work is a thoughtful reminder of a president's choices and burdens in an ever more complex, contentious world.

STANLEY I. KUTLER
Madison, Wisconsin

Preface to the Second Edition

THIS BOOK HAD ITS ORIGINS in a conversation with Stanley Kutler during which he mentioned the possibility of including, in the American Moment Series, a book examining U.S. foreign interventionism. After further discussion and correspondence, we settled on a study of how Presidents Harry Truman, Lyndon Johnson, and George Bush took the United States to war in Korea, Vietnam, and the Persian Gulf. Having long been interested in the powers of the presidency and the means of decision making, I found this project to be as fascinating as it was challenging. I tried to reconstruct, succinctly but with attention to important issues and developments, the historical moments when presidents moved through the fog of crises and ultimately decided on the necessity of war. I then examined each president's leadership during the ensuing war, with the objective of comprehending how he responded to military, diplomatic, and political challenges. The second edition adds two chapters on George W. Bush and the Iraq War, in which I follow the same approach as for the earlier presidents and their wars.

My fellow historian Warren Kimball describes Franklin Roosevelt's World War II leadership as that of a "juggler," a word that describes Presidents Truman, Johnson, Bush I, and Bush II as well. Each of those presidents was constantly juggling as he weighed advice from civilian and military officials, the pressures of domestic politics, the actions of other nations, and his obligations under the Constitution. As these four cases illustrate, reaching sound decisions and providing strong leadership require that a president utilize the formal and informal powers of his office. In the end, I tried to balance the contexts of the decision for, and the waging of, war against what seem to be reasonable expectations of presidential leadership. Thus, I reach judgments on the performances of Presidents Truman, Johnson, Bush I, and Bush II. In the last case, I recognize the problems of writing contemporary history, but I am confident that the evaluation of Bush II's leadership will be substantially justified once the American troops withdraw and Iraqis settle their own fate. I hope that readers will find the judgments on all four presidents to be fair-minded and thoughtful, or at least worthy of debate.

Several research assistants at Bowling Green State University helped immensely: Bill Remle, Bill Allison, Doris Chang, Mike Evans, Matt

Young, and Pete Genovese. I am also indebted to Bowling Green's Institute for the Study of Culture and Society, in particular its director, Dr. Vivian Patraka, for a semester's research leave that facilitated the completion of the first edition.

At the Johns Hopkins University Press, I appreciate the support and advice of Henry Y. K. Tom, Executive Editor, who suggested moving forward with a second edition; Stanley Kutler, Editor of the American Moment Series; Suzanne Flinchbaugh, Assistant Editor; and Linda Forlifer, Assistant Managing Editor.

Presidential
Decisions for War

Introduction

Presidential Leadership and International Crises

A GOVERNMENT'S MOST MOMENTOUS DECISION is to take its people to war. In the American political system, the president is at the center of the movement toward war. The Constitution confers upon the president the power to define and implement foreign policy. In his classic 1908 study of the American constitution, Woodrow Wilson, the scholar who became president, wrote that "one of the greatest of the president's powers is his control, which is very absolute, of the foreign relations of the nation. The initiative in foreign affairs, which the president possesses without any restriction whatever, is virtually the power to control them absolutely."

This power is especially impressive during periods of international crises. The president sets American objectives and has a wide range of political, economic, and military means by which to exert pressure on a rival nation. The president may align U.S. interests with those of other peoples or nations. For instance, in the crisis with Spain that led to war in 1898, President William McKinley made the cause of Cuba's independence an American objective. On a larger scale, Presidents Wilson and Franklin D. Roosevelt, in facing the international crises of 1914–17 and 1939–41, respectively, effectively aligned American interests with nations already at war whose survival they deemed vital to U.S. security. Among several examples that could be drawn from the cold war are three presidents who, in confronting the Soviet Union over a divided Germany, committed the United States to the defense of a vulnerable West Berlin. To achieve objectives, the president can exert economic pressure on a rival. By freezing Japan's assets in 1941 and thus cutting off trade, Roosevelt endeavored to restrain Japan from further aggression. This tactic was emulated by President Jimmy Carter against Iran during the 1979–81 hostage crisis.

Foremost among the instruments of power is military force. The president, as commander in chief of the armed forces, can deploy the military in ways that directly affect relations with adversaries. In 1846 President James K. Polk, in perhaps the most controversial example of that power, ordered U.S. troops into disputed territory with Mexico, thus provoking a Mexican attack that Polk then used to justify a declaration of war.

A century later, President Roosevelt deployed the U.S. Navy in 1941 to protect the shipment of goods across the Atlantic to beleaguered Great Britain—an action that brought undeclared naval warfare with Nazi Germany.

Beyond formal powers, the president enjoys the authority of the "bully pulpit"—the unique capacity inherent in the presidency to speak directly as the nation's leader to the American public, which naturally rallies around presidential leadership in times of crisis. Enhancing that bond with the public is the president's capacity to cast his objectives in terms of the ideals and traditions that Americans associate with their role in the world. During the events leading to both World Wars I and II, Presidents Wilson and Roosevelt used the persuasive authority of their office to gain popular and congressional support for policies that they justified, in large part, by relating them to the vision of a better world based on liberal values.

The power of a president, however, has its limits. Congress, interest groups, the press, and other media respond to initiatives, so that every step toward involvement in a foreign crisis risks domestic criticism. A president thus must combine boldness with political sensitivity, being cautious not to lead where the public will not follow. Some of the president's measures for pressuring adversaries may require congressional approval, as was the case when President Wilson wanted to increase the size of the navy in 1916 and when President Roosevelt sought to implement the nation's first peacetime draft in 1940 and, a year later, to provide all-out support, short of military intervention, to the victims of Axis aggression through what became the Lend-Lease Act. At times, Congress has been more inclined toward belligerency than has the president. In the events leading to both the War of 1812 and the Spanish-American War of 1898, majorities in Congress pushed the seemingly reluctant James Madison and William McKinley toward conflict, but in the end both presidents accepted the imperative for war. While a president must be attentive to domestic restraints and pressures, the constitutional authority and the informal powers of his office enable him to set the terms of debate and to garner popular support.

The president thus clearly can take the country to the brink of war, but the Constitution mandates that the final step requires congressional action. Article I, Section 8, of the Constitution grants to Congress the power "to declare War, grant Letters of Marquee and Reprisal, and make Rules concerning Captures on Land and Water." The reservation of this power to Congress reflected the strong convictions of the framers of the Constitution that executive power had to be restrained and that a decision for war ought to be undertaken only after careful legislative deliberation. From the establishment of the Federal Republic in 1789 until 1950, presidents on five occasions requested that Congress declare war, which it did against England in 1812, Mexico in 1846, Spain in 1898, Germany in 1917, and Japan in 1941. In every instance except World War II, when the vote (with only one dissenting voice) was taken the day after Japan's attack on Pearl Harbor, congressional debate was extensive; in those cases, 10 to 40 percent of the members of Congress voted against the war declarations.

In the middle of the twentieth century, Americans expected that at some time in the near future a president would call upon them to wage another world war. Representative of the midcentury anxiety was an influential book by the renowned scholar-diplomat George Kennan. In the modestly titled *American Diplomacy, 1900–1950*, Kennan addressed the question: "How has the United States—so secure in the world of 1900—become so insecure today?" With the cold war now a part of history and the prospects of a major war no longer a great concern, those insecurities seem remote. Yet the threat to the nation's security at that time seemed formidable and unrelenting. The cold war had led to tensions with the Soviet Union in the Middle East and Europe, most recently a crisis over Berlin in 1948–49. Adding to the insecurity, the Soviet Union in late 1949 tested an atomic bomb, thus ending sooner than expected the American atomic monopoly. Finally, the ascendancy of the Chinese Communists in their civil war against the American-supported government of Chiang Kai-shek brought a communist movement to power in the world's most populous country and seemingly foreshadowed the further advance of what was then seen as Soviet-directed communism in Asia.

Kennan's book placed those anxieties within the context of what he considered the misguided nature of U.S. foreign policy during the first half of the century, and he argued for a more realistic and less moralistic approach to the world's problems. Whether readers accepted his analysis, few disagreed with his observation: "A country which in 1900 had no thought that its prosperity and way of life could be in any way threatened by the outside world had arrived by 1950 at a point where it seemed to be able to think of little else but this danger."

The threat indeed seemed imminent. In an April 1950 public opinion poll, 67 percent of Americans said that they expected another world war within the decade. In this tense atmosphere, officials in the U.S.

government quietly redefined national security policy. The National Security Council approved NSC-68, a massive top-secret document that spoke ominously of America being "in greater jeopardy than ever before in its history." A hostile Soviet Union sought domination of the world and viewed the United States as "the principal enemy whose integrity and vitality must be subverted or destroyed by one means or another." The United States had to respond with a "rapid build-up of political, economic, and military strength. . . . It is necessary to have the military power to deter, if possible, Soviet expansion and to defeat, if necessary, Soviet or Soviet-directed actions of a limited or total character." In sum, NSC-68 concluded that the resources of the United States had to be mobilized to wage a many-faceted, long-term global struggle against the Soviet empire.

World War III—anticipated by the American public and planned for by its leaders—never occurred. Instead, during the last half of the twentieth century, the United States fought three wars against unexpected enemies, each a minor power, in areas seemingly remote to American interests. In responding to crises in Korea in 1950, Vietnam in 1964–65, and the Persian Gulf in 1990–91, Presidents Harry Truman, Lyndon Johnson, and George H. W. Bush believed that American national security necessitated the use of force. Their decisions, reached after extended discussions and considerable advice from various sources, took Americans to war against North Korea, North Vietnam, and Iraq. These wars against lesser enemies were related, in the minds of U.S. leaders, to that unfought larger war, for Truman, Johnson, and Bush believed that waging these smaller wars would avert a larger one. In the new millennium, President George W. Bush led Americans into a war very different in rationale and objectives. The doctrine of "preventive war" guided the war against Iraq that was launched in March 2003; it was intended to eliminate weapons of mass destruction (WMD) before Iraq could arm terrorist groups or intimidate its neighbors, which necessitated ending the regime of Saddam Hussein. In its place, a democratic Iraq would emerge, which would become a model for political change throughout the Middle East.

Each of these decisions for war and the ensuing conflicts had controversial aspects at the time, aspects that have been the subject of continuing debate involving participants, journalists, and scholars. The purpose of this study is to evaluate the leadership of Presidents Truman, Johnson, Bush I, and Bush II in meeting the crises in Korea, Vietnam, the Persian Gulf, and Iraq. How effectively did each president respond to the challenges presented by prewar tensions? Context is vital, so in examining the decisions for war, an attempt will be made to recreate the sense of crisis—the "historical moment" when issues of war and peace were in the balance—as seen from the perspectives of the four presidents—and to recount their actions within the context of unfolding events and antici-pated contingencies. This will involve a discussion of the origins of each crisis and its international ramifications, the president's decision-making style, the influence of domestic politics on policymaking, and, above all, how the presidents and those advisers closest to him defined U.S. na-tional security concerns and options and how they concluded that war was necessary.

After that effort to recapture the "historical moment," the decision for war will be assessed in terms of several related questions. First, and most basic: how compelling was the case for war? (How strong was the consensus for war among those advising the president? Were there un-explored, or insufficiently explored, alternatives?) Second, were political objectives and military means understood and coordinated? (Were there reasonable prospects that the anticipated deployment of military power could achieve objectives?) Third, how fully and effectively had the presi-dent adhered to the constitutional process and built congressional and popular support for war? (Had the president explained his decisions to Congress and the public? Had he secured their backing? Did he have congressional authorization?) Fourth, did U.S. actions have international support? (Had efforts been made to solicit the advice of America's ma-jor or regional allies? Were they supportive? Did the United States have support in, or of, the United Nations?) There is, of course, no perfect decision; the process is always untidy and circumstances often demand hurried calculations on the basis of incomplete information. The litera-ture on warfare talks about the "fog of battle"—that is, the inability of commanders to comprehend fully all that is happening as armies are fighting. The same is true during a crisis, for it too has an uncertainty or "fog" that precludes a firm grasp of its many dimensions. That is why an evaluation of presidential leadership must take into account the full context of the unfolding crisis.

The quality of the decision for war is bound to influence the problems that a president faces during the war itself. The president's powers here are broad. The Constitution leaves no doubt that the Founding Fathers thought it essential that, once the nation was committed to war, full au-thority to direct military operations had to be vested in the president. His designation as commander in chief ensured, in the words of the authors of the *Federalist Papers*, that "of all the cares or concerns of government, the direction of war most peculiarly demands those qualities that distinguish the exercise of power by a single hand." The Constitution also underlined the principle of civilian control of the military. The relationship between the president and military leadership in wartime is almost always riddled with tensions. The president's concern with integrating the political and military aspects of the war conflicts with the military leadership's focus on the battlefield. The inherently broad powers of the president during wartime notwithstanding, the president remains a domestic leader, who must sustain popular support for the war. At the same time, the president also functions as a diplomat and must deal with other countries, cultivating the support of allies and perhaps international organizations, responding to proposals from third parties or adversaries on ending the war, and deciding when to take his own initiatives for peace.

Beyond the problems facing all presidents in wartime, Truman, Johnson, and Bush I each confronted the special difficulties posed by waging "limited" wars. While they were convinced that U.S. security required the use of force in the Korean, Vietnam, and Persian Gulf crises, the three leaders were equally determined to make certain that their actions did not lead to a larger war. As a result, these wars were limited in objectives and scope. Unlike World War II, which in many ways shaped the way that Americans look upon warfare, these conflicts were not waged with the objectives of destroying enemies and forcing their "unconditional surrender." Rather, in each of these cases, the U.S. objective was limited to forcing the enemy's acceptance of the integrity of another government: South Korea, South Vietnam, and Kuwait.

In limited wars, presidents must seek to build popular support without generating demands for victory. They must call for sacrifice on behalf of a cause that does not stir a deep sense of outrage and commitment. The popular emotions are different from the patriotism triggered by events like the destruction of the battleship *Maine* in 1898 ("remember the *Maine* and to hell with Spain!"), German submarine warfare on U.S. ships in 1917, and the Japanese attack on Pearl Harbor in 1941 ("remember Pearl Harbor!"), which assured broad support for the Spanish-American War and World Wars I and II. Rather, in these late-twentieth-century conflicts, presidents were asking Americans to defend distant, small countries, not to react against a direct assault on the United States, and to fight on behalf of peoples with whom Americans had little sense of identity (unlike those involved in the Spanish-American War and the two world wars) against an equally remote enemy (which was, in the case of divided Korea and Vietnam, differentiated from the American ally only by arbitrary cold war dividing lines).

In contrast with the other three wars, Bush II's war against Iraq involved conquest and postwar occupation with a broad political objective of democratizing the country. These characteristics made the Iraq campaign closer to World War II, with its elimination of enemy governments and the transformation of the German and Japanese political systems. The military challenge in Iraq, of course, did not approximate what the United States faced at the beginning of World War II. As expected, the Iraqi armed forces were no match for the Americans, and "mission accomplished" was proclaimed after six weeks of combat, but the postwar objective proved illusive and far more costly in terms of American lives. So, in contrast to the other three wars, the study of the Iraq War concentrates on the occupation, which found Americans involved in combating an "insurgency" in a confusing civil war.

As with the decision for war, a measured assessment of presidential leadership during wartime requires an understanding of context. The ways that Presidents Truman, Johnson, and Bush I and Bush II juggled the demands of leadership as they responded to unfolding military, political, and diplomatic events—many, of course, unforeseen—provide an essential appreciation of the inevitable difficulties of waging war. With that context in mind, each can be assessed in terms of several basic questions. First, did the president coordinate military means with political ends? (Did the president have clear political objectives? How effectively did he manage civilian-military relations?) Second, was the president an effective domestic leader? (How well did the president communicate the U.S. objectives and was he able to sustain popular and congressional support?) Third, was the president a good diplomat? (Was he able to win international support for U.S. objectives? Did his conduct of the war strengthen or weaken the U.S. position internationally? How effectively did he manage, or provide direction to, opportunities to end the war?)

For Truman, Johnson, Bush I, and Bush II, the wars proved to be the defining events of their presidencies. Their records in meeting the challenges presented by the crises in Korea, Vietnam, the Persian Gulf, and Iraq overshadowed other international and domestic problems and accomplishments. Each left office remembered mostly as a wartime president.

"We can't let the U.N. down"

HARRY S. TRUMAN WAS VACATIONING in his hometown of Independence, Missouri, on the last weekend of June 1950 when he received the startling news that the North Korean army had invaded South Korea. An urgent phone call from Secretary of State Dean Acheson at 11:20 P.M. on Saturday, June 24, told Truman that forces of the Communist government of North Korea had crossed the thirty-eighth parallel that divided Korea. The attack threatened the American-supported government of South Korea. Quickly, Truman and Acheson agreed that the United States should request an emergency meeting of the United Nations Security Council. Three hours later, Acheson called again and gained Truman's approval of a draft resolution to be presented to the Security Council, charging North Korea with a "breach of the peace" and an "act of aggression" and calling upon the Security Council to take action that would end the fighting.

The fragmentary first reports had left uncertain the dimensions of the attack, but by Sunday morning the news from Korea left no doubt that the North Koreans had launched an all-out invasion and that the outmanned South Korean army could offer little resistance. The North Korean forces were advancing on the South Korean capital of Seoul, and the government headed by Syngman Rhee was preparing to flee. In New York City, the U.N. Security Council met at 2:00 P.M. and passed the American resolution condemning the North Korean attack and calling for the withdrawal of their forces from below the thirty-eighth parallel. Ordinarily, the Soviet Union would have exercised its power as a permanent member of the Security Council to veto a resolution directed against one of its allies. In this instance, the United States benefited from the Soviet Union's decision six months earlier to boycott the United Nations in protest of the denial of membership to the recently established Communist government in China. So the U.S. resolution passed 9-0 (with one abstention).*

---

*The Security Council in 1950 included the five permanent members (the United States, the Soviet Union, the United Kingdom, France, and the Chinese Nationalist government) and nonpermanent members India, Egypt, Yugoslavia, Cuba, Ecuador, and Norway. On this resolution, Yugoslavia abstained (and the Soviet Union, of course, did not vote).

As the U.N. Security Council was meeting, Acheson and Truman again conferred by phone and agreed that the president should return immediately to Washington. On his flight that Sunday afternoon, Truman resolved that the United States had to provide international leadership. In his memoirs, Truman recalled what went through his mind:

> I had time to think aboard the plane. In my generation, this was not the first occasion when the strong attacked the weak. I recalled some earlier instances: Manchuria, Ethiopia, Austria. I remembered how each time that the democracies failed to act, it had encouraged the aggressors to keep going ahead. Communism was acting in Korea, just as Hitler, Mussolini, and the Japanese had acted ten, fifteen, and twenty years earlier. I felt certain that if South Korea was allowed to fall, Communist leaders would be emboldened to override nations closer to our own shores. If the Communists were permitted to force their way into the Republic of Korea without opposition from the free world, no small nation would have the courage to resist threat and aggression by stronger Communist neighbors. If this was allowed to go unchallenged it would mean a third world war, just as similar incidents had brought on the second world war. It was also clear to me that the foundations and the principles of the United Nations were at stake unless this unprovoked attack on Korea could be stopped.

Upon arriving in Washington, Truman vowed to the awaiting Acheson and other advisers, "By God, I'm going to let them have it!" What it meant to "let them have it" was uncertain, for there were many imponderables: No one knew the strength of the North Korean forces; no one knew the role of the Soviet Union or the Chinese People's Republic in the attack; no one knew whether the members of the United Nations would support a strong stand against North Korea; no one knew whether ending the North Korean advance would require U.S. military support of the South Korean army. And, most ominously, no one knew whether the Korean crisis would trigger World War III.

Truman was beginning a week of intense decision making that would take the United States into war in a country that few Americans could have located on a map. The Korean peninsula, jutting like a dagger off the Asian continent toward Japan, is surrounded on three sides by the waters of the Yellow Sea and the Sea of Japan. Small geographically (approximately equivalent to the state of Idaho) and in population (about twenty-seven million people at the end of World War II), Korea had long been a point of rivalry for the major powers, and, after 1945, that pattern continued as the United States and the Soviet Union occupied the country, ending forty years of Japanese domination.

The interaction of Korean nationalism with the emerging cold war triggered a persistent crisis on the peninsula. Japan's defeat in World War II brought Soviet and American forces to Korea; the two powers agreed to divide their military occupation at the thirty-eighth parallel, which cuts across the middle of the Korean peninsula. It was assumed that this arbitrary division would be temporary because the United States, the Soviet Union, and the other Allies had earlier endorsed the objective of Korean independence "in due course."

The major powers paid scant attention to the dynamics of Korean nationalism, for all political groups, from radical to conservative, demanded immediate independence. As World War II ended, it seemed that the communists enjoyed the greatest popularity throughout the country. In the southern zone, the American military government, headed by Lt. Gen. John Hodge, fostered the political ascendancy of conservatives under the leadership of the seventy-year-old Syngman Rhee, who returned to Korea in late 1945 after thirty years in political exile. Having fled Korea to escape Japanese persecution, Rhee had worked tirelessly overseas, principally in the United States, for the Korean cause. Meanwhile, in the northern zone, the Soviets worked with the Korean Communist Party (KCP) under the leadership of the thirty-three-year-old Kim Il-sung, who had been trained in the Soviet Union. Korean national integrity was compromised as the military occupation reflected the hardening of major-power conflict.

In the early years of the cold war, however, Korea seemed to be one of the less important points of Soviet-American tension. As the United States in 1947 embarked upon a policy of containment of the Soviet Union, its focus was on European economic recovery. To the extent that Asia entered into strategic thought, America's principal concerns were the occupation of Japan and the Chinese civil war.

These priorities left few resources for places like Korea, yet the Truman administration moved toward solidifying the U.S. position there. The Joint Chiefs of Staff (JCS) questioned the strategic significance of Korea in the event of general war and favored a withdrawal of military support, even if it led to communist domination of the entire country. Truman, however, agreed with the State Department's recommendation that the United States should strengthen the South Korean government, thereby helping to counter the impression that communism was the wave of Asia's future. Such thinking was reinforced by the steady advance of Communist armies in the Chinese civil war, which foreshadowed their eventual 1949 victory.

To gain legitimacy for U.S. objectives, American officials took the Korean problem to the United Nations. In late 1947 the United States gained U.N. General Assembly endorsement of a resolution calling for the Soviet Union and the United States to hold elections in their respective zones, under the supervision of the United Nations Temporary Commission on Korea (UNTCOK), for the formation of a national assembly. American officials recognized that the Soviets would not accept United Nations–supervised elections because the international body was at that time dominated by the United States and because the southern zone, which had about two-thirds of the Korean population, would have a predominant influence in any national assembly. Predictably, the Soviets rejected the proposal and instead called for the mutual withdrawal of troops, which would work to Soviet advantage, since they had trained and equipped a large army in the northern zone.

Facing an impasse, the United States appealed to UNTCOK to conduct elections "in such parts of Korea as might be accessible to the Commission." Although some U.N. members hesitated before holding elections in only part of the country, in May 1948 UNTCOK supervised national assembly elections in the American-occupied area that resulted in a substantial victory for Rhee's party. This provided the basis for the establishment of a government under his leadership. A legislative committee quickly drafted a constitution, which the national assembly approved in July; it then elected Rhee as president of the Republic of Korea (ROK), the official name of what was commonly called South Korea. In December 1948 the U.N. General Assembly declared the ROK the lawful government in the part of Korea where UNTCOK had observed elections and that it was the "only such government in Korea." The United States quickly extended diplomatic recognition to the ROK and launched a program of economic and military assistance. Rhee moved to consolidate his position, including among his tactics the suppression of communists and other political rivals.

Paralleling these developments in the south, the Soviet Union and the KCP completed the establishment of a Communist-dominated regime in the north. In 1948, the Korean Democratic People's Republic, the technical name of what was commonly called North Korea, was established and Kim Il-sung became premier. His commitment to unification was reinforced by Communist leaders who had fled from the south. Amply supplied by the Soviet Union, whose troops were withdrawn in 1948, the North Koreans built a strong army of about 125,000 men. The United States delayed the withdrawal of its troops from South Korea until June 1949. By that time, it had built a ROK army of some fifty thousand men, which was considered adequate to deter an attack.

The tensions in Korea were part of a global scene in which Americans felt increasingly insecure. In late 1949, the international balance of power seemed to be shifting. America's atomic monopoly ended when the Soviet Union successfully tested its first atomic bomb. The Chinese civil war culminated with Mao Tse-tung's proclamation of the Chinese People's Republic (CPR) and the flight of the remnants of Chiang Kai-shek's Nationalist government and army to the island of Taiwan. To American officials, the Communist victory in the world's most populous nation constituted "a grievous political defeat." The CPR's alliance with the Soviet Union, it was feared, would provide the base for further expansion of communist influence in Asia.

In this unnerving situation, the Truman administration in early 1950 redefined American national security policy. On January 12, Secretary of State Dean Acheson delivered a major speech intended, in part, to respond to critics' charges that the United States lacked a coherent Asian policy. Acheson identified American interests with Asian aspirations for freedom and, in the most important part of the speech, endeavored to clarify U.S. military commitments. He outlined a "defensive perimeter," affirming that the United States would fight to hold the island chain stretching from the Aleutians to Japan and the Ryukyus and on to the Philippines. With respect to the rest of Asia, Acheson's statement was ambiguous. "[To] guarantee these areas against military attack . . . is hardly sensible or necessary," he stated, which seemed to indicate that the United States was writing off the other non-Communist states. Yet Acheson did not suggest indifference in the event of aggression outside the "defensive perimeter." In that case, "the initial reliance must be on the people attacked to resist it and then upon the commitments of the entire civilized world under the Charter of the United Nations which so far has not proved a weak reed to lean on by any people who are determined to protect their independence against outside aggression." Finally, in a closing discourse Acheson stressed, among other objectives of U.S. assistance programs, the determination to foster a strong government in South Korea.

Meanwhile, the National Security Council (NSC), under the leadership of Paul Nitze, whom Acheson had named director of the State Department's Policy Planning Staff, began a comprehensive overview of U.S. policy. Ultimately, this review took the form of a sixty-page top-secret document—NSC-68: "United States Objectives and Programs for National Security."* This sweeping statement extended the containment doctrine to global dimensions and called for a greater commitment of resources and manpower to waging the cold war. Casting the Soviet-American rivalry as a "polarization of power which inescapably confronts the slave society with the free," NSC-68 described the Soviet Union as "animated by a new fanatic faith, antithetical to our own . . . [and seeking] absolute authority over the rest of the world." Soviet efforts at the moment were "directed toward the domination of the Eurasian land mass." No compromise was possible: "The assault on free institutions is worldwide and in the present polarization of power a defeat of free institutions anywhere is a defeat everywhere." To meet this monumental challenge, the United States "must lead in building a successfully functioning political and economic system in the free world . . . [for] the absence of order among nations is becoming less and less tolerable." The United States had to mobilize its economy to build a position of military superiority, increasing drastically the size of its conventional forces and accelerating the development of the hydrogen bomb to offset the recent Soviet atomic capacity. While some officials regarded the assumptions and recommendations of NSC-68 as unduly alarmist and financially crippling, Nitze and Acheson gained wide support from civilian and military leaders before the document was sent to Truman in April 1950.

Acheson's public statement on the "defensive perimeter" and the secret formulation of NSC-68 reflected the Truman administration's adaptation to domestic, as well as international, pressures. Conservative

*The NSC had been established in 1947 as part of the National Security Act, which was intended to provide for effective coordination of the diplomatic, military, and fiscal aspects of U.S. foreign policy. The NSC's responsibilities included advising the president "with respect to the integration of domestic, foreign, and military policies relating to the national security" and assessing and appraising "the objectives, commitments, and risks in relation to our actual and potential military power," with authority to make recommendations in such matters. In 1950, the membership of the NSC included the president, secretary of state, secretary of defense, and chairman of the National Security Resources Board (positions mandated by law) and others invited by the president: the director of the Central Intelligence Agency (also established by the National Security Act), the chairman of the Joint Chiefs of Staff, and the director of the Atomic Energy Commission.

Republicans castigated Truman and Acheson for the "loss" of China caused by their failure to "save" Chiang Kai-shek's government. Some critics, led by Wisconsin senator Joseph McCarthy, went so far as to claim that communist agents in the State Department had traitorously "sold out" China. Although such criticism regarding China policy lacked any basis in fact, it gained notoriety at a time when a few celebrated cases of alleged Soviet espionage undermined public confidence in the integrity of national leaders. Truman and Acheson were unquestionably correct in their assertions that the Chinese civil war was determined by Chinese, not external, forces and that the United States could not have saved Chiang from defeat. Still, the criticisms put them on the defensive. Any appearance of weakness in the face of a communist challenge would further undermine Truman's leadership.

In this intense international and domestic situation, the Truman administration, in early 1950, strengthened the U.S. position in Asia by accelerating the economic revitalization of Japan, expanding economic and military assistance programs to the Philippines and Thailand, and supporting the French in their war against the Communist-led nationalist insurgents in Vietnam. U.S. officials became increasingly concerned about South Korea. Despite American assistance and support, Rhee's hold on power weakened as arrests of opponents failed to end protests and as deficit financing produced rampant inflation. In the May 1950 elections for the National Assembly, Rhee's supporters won only 48 seats while opposition groups won 168 seats.

Meanwhile, in Pyongyang, the capital of North Korea, Kim Il-sung sought to exploit his military superiority and the chaos in South Korea. In early 1950 the North Koreans secretly began planning an all-out invasion of South Korea. Kim believed that the peoples of South Korea would rally to the support of the Communist "liberators" and that the unification of Korea would be quickly accomplished.

Since the North Koreans were dependent upon the Soviet Union, Kim sought Premier Josef Stalin's approval of his plans. Stalin was cautious, fearing that the Americans would "never agree to be thrown out" of Korea and risk losing "their reputation as a world power." It took repeated pleas from Kim and his assurance that the invasion would bring a quick victory before Stalin gave his assent. Even then Stalin attached conditions. First, the Soviet Union would supply the North Korean army, but it would not send troops if the North Koreans ran into unexpected difficulties. Second, Kim needed the approval of the Chinese People's Republic for his plans and should look to China for military support if necessary. So Kim sought and gained the endorsement of Mao Tse-tung, who saw an opportunity to support "revolutionary" forces against "imperialists" in a neighboring country. The ambitions of Mao paralleled those of Kim, for Mao was also planning an invasion, in his case of Taiwan, to achieve national unification. With the approval of the larger communist powers, the North Koreans thus launched their offensive across the thirty-eighth parallel. The leaders in Pyongyang, Moscow, and Beijing, however, had miscalculated the American response.

THE RESPONSIBILITY for America's reaction to the North Korean invasion rested with Harry S. Truman, who, at age sixty-six, had been president for five years. Immediately seeing the Korean crisis as the most important challenge of his presidency, Truman took strength from what he considered to be the lessons of standing firm in previous cold war confrontations. Indeed, his stature as president was derived principally from his foreign policy leadership, despite his scant earlier interest or experience in dealing with international problems.

Born in 1884 to a Missouri farm family of modest means, Truman's formal education had ended with his graduation from high school, but throughout his life he was an avid reader, especially of history. He worked on the family farm and failed in a couple of business ventures. At the age of thirty-three, he experienced his first unqualified success when he volunteered for service in World War I, became an artillery captain, and proved a brave and effective leader in combat. When he eventually decided to pursue a political career, Truman again found success; he was an adept campaigner and an efficient administrator, and he earned a reputation for honesty and integrity (despite his association with the notorious political machine that dominated Missouri politics). Elected to the U.S. Senate in 1934, Truman became an ardent supporter of Franklin Roosevelt's New Deal reform program. During World War II, he gained national renown by chairing a Senate committee that investigated the efficiency of military expenditures. When the ailing Roosevelt ran for a fourth term as president in 1944, he found in Truman—a respected senator from an important state who was acceptable to important constituencies within the Democratic Party—a logical choice for the vice presidential nomination. Vice president for just twelve weeks, Truman was suddenly thrust into the presidency upon Roosevelt's death on April 12, 1945.

Truman initially felt overwhelmed by the immense challenges he faced, but he quickly evidenced a confidence in his ability. "I am here to make decisions," Truman told a visitor, "and whether they prove right or wrong I am going to make them." From his study of American history, Truman believed that the president needed to be in firm control and to provide strong leadership. Hence, he sought to coordinate policy-making by establishing a highly structured means of administration that contrasted sharply with the loose, informal arrangements of his predecessor. At the top of the system was Truman, whose desk was adorned with a famed sign: "The buck stops here." Truman's no-nonsense style of leadership, reinforced by his industriousness and self-confidence, helped to steer U.S. foreign policy through the postwar tensions with the Soviet Union.

Truman, however, was never a very popular president and was in some ways his own worst enemy. His approval ratings, as measured by periodic samples of public opinion of his presidential performance, generally were below 50 percent. He suffered from comparisons with his illustrious predecessor, but many of the problems were of his own making. Truman was a mediocre public speaker, whose shrillness and stridency rarely inspired audiences. He often acted in undignified ways, reflecting his pettiness, short temper, and partisanship. He also harbored a good deal of resentment, believing that he was not taken seriously and that his hard work was not appreciated. When Truman unexpectedly won election to the presidency in 1948 in the greatest political upset in American history, his "give 'em hell Harry" style of partisanship (as well as an ill-conceived campaign by his overconfident Republican challenger) served him well. The results, rather than en-couraging Truman to reach out and seek compromise with his oppo-nents, seemed to make him more snappish and cocky. In fairness to Truman, the Republican Party's bitterness over their 1948 loss, its harsh criticism of Truman's Asian policy, and its charges of communist influ-ence in his administration made problematic any presidential calls for reduced partisanship.

Throughout his often beleaguered presidency, Truman's foreign pol-icy reflected his deference to the two men whom he held in the highest regard, George C. Marshall and Dean Acheson. In early 1947, after unsatisfactory experiences with two earlier secretaries of state, Truman prevailed upon General Marshall, who as chief of staff in World War II had guided the Allied victory, to take that office. When poor health forced Marshall to resign, Truman named Acheson as his successor. Acheson, whose advice and loyalty as under secretary of state from 1945 to 1947 had earned the president's respect, took office in January 1949.

By the time of the Korean crisis, the Truman-Acheson working relationship was well established. Acheson—the Ivy League–educated lawyer, whose appearance and haughty demeanor embodied the Eastern establishment—came from a different world than Truman, but the two men developed a profound mutual respect that facilitated decision making. Truman appreciated Acheson's loyalty, deference, and concise advice, while Acheson admired Truman's directness, character, and decisiveness. They met regularly, Acheson presenting recommendations that Truman discussed and then almost invariably approved. Thus, Acheson, while never forgetting that ultimate authority rested with the president, enjoyed wide discretion, a power that he used shrewdly. Acheson himself relied for advice on a well-qualified staff; of particular importance on Asian policy was Dean Rusk, the assistant secretary of state for Far Eastern affairs.

Unlike several later secretaries of state, Acheson was not challenged, in his direction of foreign policy, by the secretary of defense— a position that had just been created by the National Security Act of 1947 and that was held in 1950 by the politically ambitious and temperamental Louis B. Johnson. Acheson loathed Johnson, with whom he clashed over numerous issues, most notably NSC-68's call for a drastic increase in defense spending, which Acheson considered essential for national security and which the fiscally conservative Johnson vehemently opposed as unnecessary and wasteful. Truman had appointed Johnson as a reward for his important role in the 1948 presidential campaign but never held him in high regard.

Upon his return to Washington late in the afternoon of June 25, 1950, Truman began extensive discussions of the unfolding crisis and requested that Acheson assemble high-ranking State and Defense Department officials that evening. The group assembled for dinner at Blair House. (While the White House was undergoing extensive renovations, Blair House—located across the street—was being used as the temporary presidential home; White House offices were still available to the president and his staff for official duties.) Talking informally over dinner, the thirteen officials who gathered that evening shared the conviction that the United States had to respond to a blatant act of aggression. They saw parallels with Hitler's piecemeal aggression of the 1930s and believed that the appeasement of that decade could not be repeated. They all believed that the Soviet Union was testing the resolve of the United States and the United Nations. One official recalled Truman repeating, half to himself, "We can't let the U.N. down. We can't let the U.N. down." While agreeing that some response was necessary, the advisers also feared that the Korean invasion might be a diversionary maneuver on the part of the Soviet Union, intended to draw U.S. resources away from other areas that would be left vulnerable to intimidation or attack. No one was certain what ultimately might be required, but all recognized that inaction was not an alternative. The prevailing sentiment was that the time had come to "draw the line."

Once the formal meeting began after dinner, Acheson dominated the ensuing decisions. He summarized developments, including a recent report from Ambassador John Muccio in Seoul that the North Koreans were engaged in a full-scale attack and had issued a proclamation tantamount to a declaration of war. Acheson recommended that American power be projected into the unfolding crisis by instructing Gen. Douglas MacArthur, Commander in Chief Far East, based in Japan, to supply South Korea with additional arms, ammunition, and equipment and to provide air cover for the evacuation of civilians from Seoul. After others at the meeting supported these initiatives, Truman authorized their implementation.

Truman, never doubting that the North Koreans would ignore the U.N. Security Council resolution, anticipated additional measures. He pressed military leaders about the likelihood of the Soviet Union pushing the crisis to a general war and for estimates of the relative strength of the Americans and Soviets in the region. He instructed the Joint Chiefs of Staff to prepare for reinforcing U.S. forces and to have MacArthur send a survey team to Korea to assess the military situation. After nearly four hours, the meeting adjourned at 11:00 P.M.

The next morning, Monday, June 26, the reports from Korea were ominous. Ambassador Muccio described a situation of "rapid deterioration and disintegration" and began evacuating U.S. Embassy personnel. The South Korean National Assembly appealed to the United

States and United Nations for assistance. President Rhee and his Cabinet fled Seoul. From the Embassy in Moscow, Ambassador Alan Kirk advised that "determined countermeasures will deter the Soviets who are not prepared to risk the possibility of global war." To provide an opportunity for a graceful Soviet disengagement, Kirk urged that the United States should downplay Moscow's role in the invasion and avoid public condemnation.

Truman and other officials began the day by maintaining normal schedules, but the crisis was all-absorbing. Newspapers throughout the country reported the worsening situation in Korea, and editorials called for action. According to the *New York Times*, the fighting was forcing "upon the United States the necessity for a decisive and unequivocal policy. . . . We can lose half a world at this point, if we lose heart."

That was exactly how Truman saw the situation. He shared his thinking that morning with an administrative assistant. Walking to a large globe in the Oval Office, Truman pointed to the Middle East. He recalled meeting Stalin at the Potsdam conference in 1945 and Stalin's remark regarding the Soviet military's dependence on oil imports. Putting his forefinger on Iran, Truman said, "Here is where they will start trouble if we aren't careful." He believed that his experience in dealing with the Soviet Union was instructive: "Korea is the Greece of the Far East. If we are tough enough now, if we stand up to them like we did in Greece three years ago, they won't take any next steps. But if we just stand by, they'll move into Iran and they'll take over the whole Middle East. There is no telling what they'll do, if we don't put up a fight now."

Just before noon Truman issued his first public statement on the crisis. In a brief press release, he affirmed the determination to counter "unprovoked aggression" and promised that the United States would "vigorously support the effort of the Security Council to terminate this serious breach of the peace." Truman's resolve did not silence his critics. When the Senate convened a few minutes later, Republicans exploited the crisis to renew their assault on Truman's "appeasement" in Asia, which they charged had "lost" China and had led to the crisis in Korea. Actually, some of the rhetoric of Truman's critics paralleled the statements of officials at the Blair House meeting the previous evening. During his tirade, Styles Bridges (New Hampshire) repeatedly stated that the time had come to "draw the line." The words of William Knowland (California) might well have been those of Truman:

Korea stands today in the same position as did Manchuria, Ethiopia, Austria and Czechoslovakia at an earlier date. In each of those instances a firm stand by the law-abiding nations of the world might have saved the peace. . . . The destruction of the Republic of Korea would be catastrophic. . . . If this nation is allowed to succumb to an overt invasion of this kind, there is little chance of stopping communism anywhere on the continent of Asia.

Knowland and the other conservative Republicans were not engaged in an act of bipartisanship. Rather, they were indicting Truman and Acheson for political gain. Bridges spoke absurdly of "some of our leaders appear[ing] not to be interested [and] . . . shrug[ging] their shoulders," while Knowland criticized the United Nations, saying that "the free people of Korea may lose their liberty while the diplomats are talking."

Truman needed no one to remind him of the urgency of the Korean situation. From Tokyo, MacArthur cabled that North Korean military superiority was overwhelming and that the South Koreans could offer no effective resistance. He concluded that "the complete collapse is imminent." At Blair House later that afternoon, a tearful John K. Chang, the South Korean ambassador, presented appeals from Rhee and the National Assembly for "effective and timely aid." Truman tried to reassure Chang, reminding him that other peoples had survived even worse situations.

Whatever comfort they may have offered Chang, Truman and Acheson realized that time was running out for the South Koreans. Returning to the State Department, Acheson began to discuss the situation with several subordinates and then abruptly terminated the meeting, saying that he wanted to be alone and to put his thoughts in writing. As additional reports underscored the desperation of the South Koreans, Acheson called Truman and suggested that another meeting of high officials be convened immediately.

Accordingly, the same group of officials who had gathered twenty-four hours earlier met again at Blair House on Monday evening. After Gen. Omar Bradley, chairman of the JCS, presented MacArthur's dire assessment, it was again Acheson who cut through a rambling discussion and presented a clear course of action, which was endorsed by others, although with some reservations from the military leaders. The most urgent recommendation was that the navy and air force be ordered to give full support to the South Korean forces south of the thirty-eighth parallel. Acheson coupled that step with additional recommendations intended to strengthen the American strategic position in Asia by increasing U.S. forces in and military assistance to the Philippines and accelerating military assistance to the French in Indochina. At the same time, he sought to defuse the situation between the Chinese People's Republic and the Nationalist government on Taiwan; he proposed that the U.S. Navy's Seventh Fleet patrol the Taiwan Straits to prevent either a CPR invasion of Taiwan or Nationalist raids against the mainland. Last, Acheson recommended that the United States present a resolution to the U.N. Security Council, when it would meet the next day, calling on members to provide military support to South Korea.

These monumental military and diplomatic steps raised several questions. Would the Soviet Union send its representative to the Security Council meeting and veto any further U.N. action? The Soviet experts in the State Department advised Acheson that the cumbersome Soviet bureaucracy would be unable to act quickly in the face of the unexpected developments in Korea, so it seemed unlikely that the Soviet delegate would suddenly appear at the Security Council. Would U.S. air and naval power be sufficient, or would combat troops be required to resist the North Koreans? The leadership of the army was skeptical of navy and air force claims that they could handle the situation. Acheson responded that the United States had to act even if the effort was unavailing. Reinforcing the army's concern, Bradley and army Chief of Staff Gen. J. Lawton Collins urged that, if ground forces were required, Truman should order mobilization. Should Congress be consulted? Truman decided that he, Acheson, and Johnson should meet the next morning with congressional leaders, but they made no plans to seek any formal authorization.

Truman approved Acheson's recommendations. Based on his understanding of the "lessons" of the 1930s and on his experiences in dealing with the Soviet Union, Truman was convinced that the United States and the other democratic members of the United Nations had to demonstrate resolve. During the meeting, he drew parallels between the Korean crisis and the early aggression of Germany, Japan, and Italy during the 1930s. He went on to observe how the determined application of power had forced the Soviet Union to back down during the Greek crisis of 1947 and the Berlin blockade of 1948–49.

The actions taken at Blair House on the evening of June 26 meant that, within forty-eight hours of the North Korean attack, Truman had committed U.S. air and naval forces to the defense of the beleaguered South Koreans. While hoping that such support would enable the South Koreans to resist the invaders, the officials at Blair House recognized that U.S. ground troops might be required. They were prepared to risk Soviet or Chinese intervention. Truman stated several times that he did not want a war, but he was determined to resist aggression. To Truman, circumstances demanded quick action, but still, his commitment of U.S. military forces was taken without congressional authorization and before the U.N. Security Council had called for military sanctions. Nonetheless, the Department of Defense sent word to MacArthur that his "mission [was] to throw the North Koreans out of South Korea."

By the conclusion of that second Blair House meeting, Truman and his advisers had implicitly embraced a set of operating assumptions that guided their thinking and actions throughout the crisis.

First, the Soviet Union directed the attack, but it wanted to avoid a major war. No one questioned Soviet responsibility for the North Korean invasion, but estimates of Soviet objectives varied. Three hypotheses were advanced to explain the Soviet Union's behavior: it was "testing" Western resolve by "probing" a "weak spot"; it was engaging in a "diversionary" tactic by engaging the United States in Korea while planning action against another point of vulnerability; it was initiating an "East Asian strategic move" aimed at reducing U.S. influence throughout the region. Accordingly, American officials assumed that Moscow anticipated multiple benefits from a North Korean victory. They also believed, however, that Stalin had expected an easy conquest, but when faced with the resistance of a United States–led United Nations, he would conclude that Korea was of limited significance and not worth the risk of a general war.

Second, the aggression challenged the security of the United States. Whatever the Soviet motivation, the attack was on a government that was dependent on the United States and a symbol of the American position in Asia. "Credibility" was on the line: Failure to respond to aggression would cause allies to lose confidence in American promises and would embolden adversaries to challenge the United States in other ways. The "lessons" of the 1930s had taught that appeasement would lead to more aggression. In his memoir, Acheson reflected that, "to back away from this challenge, in view of our capacity for meeting it, would be highly destructive of the power and prestige of the United

States. By prestige I mean the shadow cast by power, which is of great deterrent importance."

Third, the aggression also challenged the integrity of the United Nations. The United Nations, having given international legitimacy to the South Korean government, had special responsibilities for upholding it. More importantly, if American aspirations for an effective United Nations were to be realized, it had to meet this challenge. The Korean crisis tested whether the United Nations could avoid the fate of the League of Nations, which had fallen into insignificance because of its irresolution in the 1930s.

Fourth, the United States had to provide strong but restrained leadership. While taking the initiative in the United Nations in denouncing aggression and planning for sterner measures, the United States had to avoid provocation of the Soviet Union. Truman, Acheson, and others were profoundly angered by the Soviet Union for what they believed was its role in directing the North Korean invasion, but that emotion had to be tempered by the recognition that the Korean situation presented the great danger of escalating into a major war. American officials assumed that the Soviet Union did not want a larger war, but they knew that, if threatened, it would fight.

Fifth, in view of the possibility that the Korean assault was but the first phase of coordinated communist offensives, the United States had to strengthen its positions elsewhere while taking measures to prevent other crises. This was underscored in the effort to stabilize the three Asian flash points—Vietnam, the Philippines, and the Taiwan Straits—and, more generally, to strengthen the U.S. military position globally.

Sixth, once American determination was evident and power properly employed in Korea, the adversary would back down. Seeing Korea as another "test" posed by the Soviet Union, like those in Greece in 1947 and in Berlin in 1948–49, Truman and other officials implicitly believed that, as in those cases, the communists would retreat in the face of American resolve.

Thus, on Tuesday, June 27, U.S. air and naval forces undertook direct support of the South Korean army. That day, in Washington and New York, the Truman administration sought congressional and U.N. support for the decisions reached the previous evening.

At 11:30 A.M., Truman, Acheson, and Johnson met with the Democratic and Republican congressional leaders, all of whom strongly endorsed his actions. When one congressman inquired whether the

United States was now committed to the defense of South Korea, Truman said yes, both as a member of the United Nations and in response to Security Council resolutions. Acheson discussed the resolution calling upon members to aid South Korea, which the United States was presenting to the U.N. Security Council that afternoon, but cautioned that little help could be expected from America's allies. Truman promised to keep Congress apprised of developments. At the conclusion of the meeting, the White House released a statement justifying the expanded U.S. military role in terms of upholding the United Nations. Truman explained that, because the North Koreans had ignored the U.N. Security Council resolution of June 25, he had "ordered United States air and sea forces to give the Korean Government cover and support." The most strongly worded passage followed:

> The attack upon Korea makes it plain beyond all doubt that Communism has passed beyond the use of subversion to conquer independent nations and has defied the orders of the Security Council. . . . In these circumstances they will now use armed invasion and war. Its occupation of [Taiwan] by Communist forces would be a direct threat to the security of the Pacific area and to United States forces performing their lawful and necessary functions in that area. Accordingly I have ordered the Seventh Fleet to prevent any attack on [Taiwan]. As a corollary to this action I am calling upon the Chinese Government on [Taiwan] to cease all air and sea operations against the mainland. The Seventh Fleet will see that this is done.

Word of Truman's military commitment spread quickly and received wide acclaim. In both the House of Representatives and the Senate, members stood and cheered. Republicans joined Democrats in praising Truman's decision. Senator Knowland, long one of the outspoken critics of Truman's Asian policy, now proclaimed that Truman "had drawn the line in the Far East . . . [and deserved] the overwhelming support of all Americans, regardless of their partisan affiliation." Governor Thomas Dewey of New York, Truman's opponent in the 1948 presidential election and the titular head of the Republican Party, telegraphed his approval of a decision that "was necessary to the security of our country and the free world."

Meanwhile, at the United Nations, the Security Council—with the Soviet seat still empty—met at 3 o'clock. Warren Austin, the U.S. ambassador to the United Nations, had returned hurriedly from a vacation that had prevented his participation in the June 25 emergency meeting.

Austin spoke briefly but cogently of the North Korean invasion as "an attack on the United Nations itself. . . . It is difficult to imagine a more glaring example of disregard for the United Nations and for all the principles which it represents." He then called for sanctions, explaining that "it is the plain duty of the Security Council to invoke stringent sanctions to restore international peace. The Republic of Korea has called on the United Nations for protection. I am happy and proud to report that the United States is prepared as a loyal Member of the United Nations to furnish assistance to the Republic of Korea." Finally, Austin introduced the resolution, which called upon U.N. members to "furnish assistance to the Republic of Korea as may be necessary to repel the armed attack and to restore international peace and security in the area." The U.N. Security Council adjourned at 5:10 P.M. so that representatives could consult with home governments before voting on this historic resolution.

At 10:25 that evening, the U.N. Security Council reconvened for further deliberations. Shortly before midnight the council adopted the resolution by a vote of seven in favor and one (Yugoslavia) opposed. With the Soviet Union absent, no major power exercised its veto power. The Egyptian and Indian representatives, in the absence of instructions from their governments, abstained. (On June 28 Egypt announced that it would not support the resolution, and on June 29 India indicated its support. This meant that, in effect, the resolution was approved by an eight-to-two margin.)

Hence, by midnight Wednesday, a little more than seventy-two hours after the North Koreans had launched their attack, the Truman administration had pieced together an international commitment to the defense of South Korea. U.S. air and naval power, sanctioned by the United Nations and backed by strong support at home, was deployed in a desperate move to avert what American officials saw as an impending disaster that would destroy U.S. prestige in Asia.

Wednesday, June 28, was a relatively quiet day in Washington, as Americans anxiously watched developments in Korea to see whether the limited deployment of U.S. military power could reverse the tide. Throughout the country, newspaper editorials praised Truman's decisions, as did most of the European press and the leaders of Britain, France, and other countries. Great Britain became the first country to offer military assistance, as Prime Minister Clement Attlee placed British naval vessels in the Pacific area at American disposal. Truman received a thunderous ovation when he spoke that afternoon at a convention of reserve military officers. In a speech to the same group, Secretary Johnson extravagantly praised Truman, calling his decisions "the finest hour in American history to date" and declaring that "the occasion has found the man in Harry Truman."

On the floor of the U.S. Senate, however, an influential Republican challenged the constitutionality of Truman's actions. While supporting the decision to stand by South Korea, Senator Robert Taft of Ohio, whose stature as a voice of conservatism had earned him the distinction of being called Mr. Republican, questioned the means by which Truman was involving the nation in the conflict. A few members of Congress had raised this issue earlier, but Taft developed fully the argument that Truman had done "the right thing the wrong way." Contrary to the provisions of the Constitution, Truman had bypassed Congress in committing U.S. forces in Korea. Had the administration asked Congress to authorize intervention, Taft would have voted for it. That authorization, however, was a constitutional requirement. Taft maintained that Truman's

> action unquestionably has brought about a de facto war with the Government of northern Korea. He has brought that war about without consulting Congress and without congressional approval. . . . [This] seems to me . . . a complete usurpation by the President of authority to use the Armed Forces of this country. If the incident is permitted to go by without protest . . . we would have finally terminated for all time the right of Congress to declare war, which is granted to Congress alone by the Constitution of the United States.

The Truman administration ignored Taft's challenge, but it could not avoid the somber news from Korea. Early in the day, Americans learned that Seoul had fallen to the North Koreans. Roads were clogged by the retreating South Korean army and tens of thousands of fleeing civilians. Ordered to provide air and naval support to help South Koreans, MacArthur dispatched all available bombers and fighters to attack North Korean troops, tanks, planes, and supply lines below the thirty-eighth parallel.

Truman was aware of dangers inherent in the bold measures that had been taken to halt the North Koreans. At a National Security Council meeting, Acheson foresaw the erosion of international and domestic support if the military situation worsened and intervention involved substantial sacrifice. Vice President Alben Barkley noted that many senators were skeptical of support from European allies. Truman said that he was determined to hold South Korea but conceded that he might have to rethink that commitment if a more serious crisis forced action elsewhere. Those uncertainties added to Truman's determination to obtain as much help as possible from other U.N. members.

On Thursday, June 29, the South Korean cause became more and more desperate. In the morning, reports reached Washington that the South Korean army had tried but failed to halt the North Koreans at the Han River south of Seoul. Brig. Gen. John Church, whom MacArthur had sent to Korea to report on the situation, cabled Washington that only the commitment of U.S. combat troops could prevent a North Korean conquest of the entire peninsula. MacArthur decided to inspect the front personally and left Japan aboard his plane *Bataan*. During the early Thursday morning flight (Wednesday night in Washington), MacArthur conferred with Rhee and Church, observed the fighting south of Seoul, and met with U.S. military and diplomatic personnel; he quickly concluded that a U.S. troop commitment was needed. During his four-hour flight back to Tokyo, MacArthur, pad in hand, prepared his report and recommendations; he arrived Thursday evening Tokyo time (Thursday morning in Washington), but it was nearly sixteen hours before he cabled his report to Washington.

Before MacArthur's findings were known, Truman and Acheson made important public statements on the unfolding American commitment to South Korea's survival. In a press conference that afternoon, Truman conveyed forcefully his determination to resist aggression. While being peppered with questions, however, Truman allowed a reporter to put words in his mouth, words that seemed to trivialize any military measures. A reporter had inquired, "Everybody is asking in this country, are we or are we not at war?" Truman responded that "we are not at war" and added that "the members of the United Nations are going to the relief of the Korean Republic to suppress a bandit raid." Then a reporter asked, "Mr. President, would it be correct, against your explanation, to call this a police action under the United Nations?" Truman quickly replied, "Yes. That is what it amounts to." Truman undoubtedly thought of the U.S. role as part of an international police action, but this proved to be an unfortunate choice of words, which took on negative overtones as it became embedded in the national consciousness. Later, with casualties mounting in an indecisive war, critics would refer derisively to Truman's "police action."

In a speech that same day to the American Newspapers Guild, Acheson clarified the limited objective of the unfolding U.S. commitment against "a cynical and brutal act of aggression" that was "a direct challenge to the United Nations." U.N. support of the South Koreans was "solely for the purpose of restoring the Republic of Korea to its status prior to the invasion from the north and of reestablishing the peace broken by that aggression."

When the National Security Council gathered that evening for a momentous meeting, Acheson captured the thinking of those assembled: "It was essential to give [MacArthur] whatever he needs to stop a disaster." With a draft directive from the Joint Chiefs of Staff to MacArthur as the basis of discussion, Truman agreed to authorize air and naval operations north of the thirty-eighth parallel and to permit the introduction of ground troops for essential support purposes. The imperatives of the Korean situation left the president no choice. Yet Truman and Acheson were also determined to limit the U.S. role only to those measures necessary to restore the prewar division of the country. Thus, Truman approved a recommendation that air and naval operations could be extended against military targets in North Korea only when, in MacArthur's estimation, "serious risk of loss of South Korea might be obviated thereby." Truman wanted to restrict actions to those necessary to "keep the North Koreans from killing the people we are trying to save. You can give [MacArthur] all the authority he needs to do that, but he is not to go north of the 38th degree parallel." To halt the North Korean advance, the JCS planned to establish a beachhead on the southeastern coast around the port city of Pusan. Toward that end, Truman also approved the dispatch of American troops to Korea for the servicing of aircraft and runways and for the protection of airfields.

Truman's apprehension about triggering a larger war was evident in his concern over a section in the JCS draft directives that dealt with the possibility of the Soviet Union's intervention. Truman was adamant: "I do not want any implication . . . that we are going to war with Russia at this time." He added that "we must not say that we are anticipating a war with the Soviet Union. We want to take any steps we have to to push the North Koreans behind the line, but I don't want to get us over-committed to a whole lot of other things that could mean war." Truman's outburst revealed understandable anxiety in an inherently risky situation. In fact, the JCS directive to MacArthur indeed anticipated, quite appropriately, the contingency of Soviet intervention, ordering, in that event, only defensive operations while awaiting instructions from Washington.

Truman and other officials were encouraged by the relative moderation of the Soviet Union's response to the crisis. The American Embassy in Moscow interpreted early statements in the government-controlled newspaper *Pravda* as indicating a "wait-and-see" posture. In response to a U.S. note of June 25, the Soviets predictably blamed the outbreak of war on South Korea but added that they would not interfere in the internal affairs of North Korea. The State Department interpreted this statement as signaling the Soviet Union's disinclination to commit its own forces to the conflict. Truman added presciently that the "Russians are going to let the Chinese do the fighting for them." Indeed, the Chinese Communist reaction to U.S. policy troubled American officials. From Beijing, Foreign Minister Zhou En-lai charged that the imposition of the Seventh Fleet in the Taiwan Strait constituted "armed aggression against Chinese territory." Acheson feared that the Chinese People's Republic might use the Taiwan impasse as a pretext for involvement in Korea.

The complications presented by the two Chinese governments prompted Acheson to return to the White House later that evening for a personal conference with Truman. He reported that Chiang Kai-shek had offered thirty-three thousand seasoned Chinese Nationalist forces to join the U.N. operations in Korea. Truman wanted to accept the offer, since he was determined to line up strong international backing for both military and symbolic purposes. Yet the introduction of Chinese Nationalist forces into Korea, Acheson warned, would enrage the Chinese Communists and might provoke their intervention. Acheson also stressed that Chinese Nationalist troops were needed to defend Taiwan. Truman deferred his decision.

The orders to MacArthur, cabled to Tokyo at 6:59 P.M., were immediately overtaken by events. Six and a half hours later, at 1:31 A.M. Friday morning, the Defense Department finally began receiving MacArthur's urgent recommendation for the use of U.S. combat troops. He had found the South Korean army in disarray and "incapable of gaining the initiative over such force as embodied in the North Korean Army." The North Korean army, which "obvious[ly] . . . has been built as an element of Communist military aggression," was poised to overrun the entire peninsula. "The Korean Army is entirely incapable of counter-action," MacArthur continued. "The only assurance for the holding of the present line is through the introduction of U.S. ground combat forces into the Korean battle areas." MacArthur requested two divisions. Anything less would be either "needlessly costly in life, money, and prestige . . . [or] doomed to failure."

As the Pentagon received MacArthur's cable, General Collins, the army chief of staff, was awakened in the JCS office, where makeshift sleeping arrangements had been set up during the crisis. He immediately gathered other military and diplomatic officials for a teleconference with MacArthur, which began at 3:40 A.M. Collins told MacArthur that Truman's approval would be necessary before combat troops could be committed, but he authorized, as provided in the directives that Truman had approved a few hours earlier, the dispatch of a regimental combat team (RCT) to the Pusan beachhead. MacArthur responded tersely: "Your authorization, while establishing basic principle that U.S. ground combat forces may be used in Korea, does not give sufficient latitude for efficient operation in present situation. . . . Time is of the essence and a clear cut decision without delay is imperative." Collins promised an early decision on whether the RCT could be moved into combat. He also told MacArthur that meetings at the White House had "clearly indicated to me that the President would wish carefully to consider with his top advisors before authorizing introduction of American combat forces into battle areas."

The urgency of MacArthur's request, which was supported by Collins and Secretary of the Army Frank Pace, compelled an immediate decision, but Truman refused to be rushed. When he was awakened at 4:57 A.M. and informed of MacArthur's recommendation, he asked, "Do we have to decide tonight?" He approved the combat commitment of one RCT but deferred action on the commitment of additional combat troops. As word reached the Pentagon of Truman's decision, Collins informed MacArthur: "Your recommendation to move one RCT to combat area is approved. You will be advised later as to further build-up." Hence, in the early hours of Friday, June 30, an American ground unit was committed to a combat role.

The flurry of urgent communications throughout the night led Truman to summon key military and civilian officials to meet with him early Friday morning. With time being of the essence, Truman sought advice on how he should respond to Chiang Kai-shek's troop offer and MacArthur's request. Truman still wanted to accept the troops, which he viewed as impressive evidence of U.N. support. No other government had yet offered ground forces; since the British naval offer, four other countries—Australia, Canada, the Netherlands, and New Zealand—had promised air and naval support. Acheson and the JCS, however, pointed out that the introduction of Chinese Nationalist forces into Korea could provoke Chinese Communist intervention, and they ultimately prevailed upon Truman to decline Chiang's offer.

Then Truman moved to the most momentous decision of this critical week, perhaps of his entire presidency. The JCS had drafted a new directive to MacArthur, authorizing the dispatch of two combat divisions. MacArthur's urgent assessment was reinforced by a report from Ambassador Muccio describing a demoralized South Korean government and army on the verge of disintegration. Truman announced that he would give MacArthur authority to deploy, as he deemed necessary, any ground forces under his command. Truman also authorized a recommendation that the navy impose a blockade of North Korea. No one questioned Truman's decisions. Having seen the Korean crisis worsen each day since Sunday, Truman and his advisers had realized that this fateful step might be necessary. They believed that, if a combat role were to be undertaken, MacArthur should be given wide latitude to assure the attainment of U.S. objectives. These decisions, made in a matter of minutes, took the United States to war.

Ninety minutes later Truman met for the second time with congressional leaders. After reviewing the military reports, he informed the congressmen of his order that ground troops be sent to Korea. They strongly supported Truman's action, with only a few raising questions about its implications and constitutionality. Senator Chan Gurney (R.-S.D.) asked whether Truman realized that the United States was now wholly committed to defend South Korea; Truman replied, "I certainly do understand that." Senator Kenneth Wherry (R.-Nebr.), was upset that Congress had not been consulted. Truman defended his actions on the grounds that an emergency had not left time for talk. Wherry said he "understood" but pressed that "Congress ought to be consulted before any large-scale actions are taken again." Truman replied that, if congressional action was necessary, he would ask for it, adding that he hoped "we can get those bandits in Korea suppressed without that."

As in the previous meeting, Truman read the leaders a brief press statement that was to be released at the conclusion of the meeting. After mentioning the "full review of the intensified military activities" given congressional leaders, the statement concluded:

> In keeping with the United Nations Security Council's request for support to the Republic of Korea in repelling the North Korean invaders and restoring peace in Korea, the President announced that he had authorized the U.S. Air Force to conduct missions on specific military targets in Northern Korea wherever militarily necessary and had ordered a Naval blockade of the entire Korean coast. General MacArthur has been authorized to use certain supporting ground units.

The closing sentence was, in the words of one Truman biographer, "grossly obscure and did not convey the scope of Truman's decision on the commitment of ground forces." Security considerations dictated the vagueness of the statement, as Washington did not want to complicate MacArthur's discretionary authority to move troops into combat. Thus, the full implications of the commitment would be understood only when large numbers of U.S. troops were sent, over the next several days, into combat in Korea.

TRUMAN ALWAYS CONSIDERED the decision to intervene in Korea as the most important of his presidency. The case for intervention was compelling: to have permitted the North Korean military conquest of South Korea would have weakened the stature of the United States and would have undermined the United Nations and the international order that it was established to preserve. None of Truman's advisers questioned whether the United States had to come to South Korea's aid. Members of Congress, the nation's press, and the general public almost universally concurred. To Truman and others of his generation who could vividly remember the international disintegration of the 1930s, the North Korean invasion immediately brought to mind the actions of the Germans, Japanese, and Italians that had led to World War II. The appeasement of aggressors, so the "lessons of the 1930s" seemingly taught, led eventually to all-out wars.

Until 1950, the expansion of communist power had been more opportunistic than aggressive and, in some ways, had a degree of legitimacy. The extension of Soviet influence over eastern Europe had been a function of the capacity of the Red Army, as it pursued retreating German forces, to bring to power local Communist parties, which had often been leaders in the anti-German underground. Non-Communist parties in areas under Soviet influence were gradually eliminated as tensions with the United States mounted in the postwar period. In the Czechoslovakian coup of 1948—the most notorious power play in the establishment of the Soviet bloc—Moscow exploited the relative strength of Czech communism and the disarray of non-Communist leaders. In Asia, communist advances had resulted from identity with nationalism. The communist victory in China, as American leaders recognized, resulted from indigenous factors beyond the control of outside powers. In Vietnam and Korea, communist movements likewise owed their vitality and appeal to their leadership in opposing foreign domination.

It has been argued that Koreans, free from outside interference, would have embraced communism. Had the North Koreans not resorted to armed force, it is conceivable that the communist capacity to exploit unrest in South Korea and the widespread dissatisfaction with the Rhee government could have led to civil war and eventual communist control of the entire country. The United States would have been hard-pressed to "save" South Korea in such circumstances.

The critical point, however, was not the relative strength of Korean communists and conservatives. To the United States as well as most non-Communist nations, what mattered was that the North Korean army had crossed a cold war dividing line. Its objective was the elimination of a government recognized by the United Nations. Whatever its defects, the Rhee government was a victim of aggression.

The North Koreans, armed and equipped by the Soviet Union, were presumably acting at Moscow's direction. U.S. officials were unaware that Kim Il-sung had instigated the war, that Stalin had been a reluctant supporter and had sent Kim to Mao Tse-tung for Chinese backing; a more sophisticated knowledge of relations among the communist powers, however, would not have altered the U.S. response. The distinction between a Soviet-directed and a Soviet-supported invasion was insignificant. From Washington's perspective, the North Korean attack clarified the international situation. No longer was the United States dealing with intractable matters like the piecemeal spread of an "iron curtain" in eastern Europe, the coup in Czechoslovakia, or the communist victory in the Chinese civil war. Korea presented a simpler problem than the crisis in Greece or the Berlin blockade. There was no ambiguity in this case: aggression had to be resisted. Joseph Harsch, a correspondent with twenty years' experience in Washington, observed about that last week in June 1950: "Never before in that time have I felt such a sense of relief and unity pass through the city."

The case for war was enhanced by strong international backing. Taking the issue immediately to the United Nations was not without risks. Yet the blatant aggression facilitated the Truman administration's determination to build a coalition of allies and emerging nations in Asia and the Middle East. The historic U.N. Security Council resolutions enabled the United States to integrate its purpose with that of the United Nations and to wage war with an unprecedented degree of international authority.

Truman's movement toward war, however, was not without its shortcomings. First, by taking the country into war without congressional approval, he missed an opportunity to assure broad bipartisan support based on the constitutional process. He also invited charges of abusing presidential power. That criticism began on June 27, when a few Republican senators questioned whether Truman, by his first minimal step to aid South Korea, was acting with disregard for the constitutional provision that gives Congress the power to declare war. The criticism continued on the following day, when Senator Taft charged "a complete usurpation by the president of authority to use the armed forces of the country."

Truman's failure to seek congressional authorization resulted from a combination of constitutional, political, and strategic considerations. He believed that his power as commander in chief and the obligations of U.S. membership in the United Nations provided sufficient authority to send American forces to Korea. He was determined to uphold the prerogatives of his office and believed that an effective foreign policy depended on strong presidential leadership. The counsel that he received during the crisis reinforced his thinking. On June 26, Truman asked Democratic Senator Tom Connally of Texas, the chairman of the Foreign Relations Committee, for advice on the matter of a war resolution. Connally warned that a request for a war declaration "might run into a long debate by Congress, which would tie your hands completely." Instead, Connally advised, "You have the right to [send forces] as commander in chief and under the U.N. Charter."

Truman's public statements about supporting the United Nations implicitly argued that U.S. membership in the international organization transferred war making under certain circumstances to the Security Council. The U.N. Charter, which the Senate had overwhelmingly approved in 1945, provided that the Security Council, in cases of threats to peace or acts of aggression where lesser measures have failed, "may take such action by air, sea or land forces as may be necessary to maintain or restore international peace and security." The Security Council resolutions on Korea were the first application of this collective coercive power.

It was not until July 3—as U.S. troops were engaging in combat—that Truman gave full attention to the constitutional issue. In a meeting with his Cabinet and the Democratic Party leader in the Senate, Scott Lucas of Illinois, the president sought advice on a State Department proposal that Truman go before a joint session of Congress and review the developments in Korea, basing his decisions on his powers as commander in chief. Rather than Truman requesting a war resolution, Acheson proposed that administration officials work behind the scenes with congressional leaders to have them introduce a resolution supporting the president's action. Hence, both the president's powers as commander in chief and Congress's power to authorize war would be upheld. Indeed, Acheson had prepared a draft resolution that affirmed a "sense of Congress that the United States continue to take all appropriate action . . . in support of the Charter of the United Nations and of the resolutions of the Security Council." Acheson and other State Department officials at the meeting argued that the involvement and support of Congress would be helpful internationally, especially if problems developed in Korea.

Senator Lucas, however, was reluctant. Rather than upholding congressional prerogatives, as might have been expected, he foresaw political problems with the State Department's proposal. He feared that, if Truman went before Congress, he would appear to be asking for a "declaration of war." While believing that Truman enjoyed overwhelming support, assuring eventual passage of the proposed resolution, Lucas foresaw a lengthy debate, as Republicans would seize the opportunity to renew their familiar criticism of Truman's Asia policy. Lucas added that some members of Congress did not want Truman to involve them in the process and suggested that Truman explain his decisions to the American public via radio and television. Significantly, no one at the meeting argued that congressional authorization was constitutionally necessary. So the meeting ended indecisively, and never again did Truman focus on the issue.

Truman and Acheson had no doubt that congressional authorization was not necessary. On the same day as the White House meeting, Acheson released a lengthy memorandum that the State Department had hurriedly prepared, which justified Truman's intervention in Korea on the basis of his powers as commander in chief and historical precedent. To make the case, the State Department cited eighty-five instances between 1812 and 1932 of presidents dispatching troops abroad without congressional authorization. Moreover, the State Department memo added that, in the world of 1950, the "preservation of the United Nations for the maintenance of peace is a cardinal interest of the United States."

Besides constitutional considerations, domestic politics influenced Truman's position regarding congressional authorization in two distinct ways. First, the fact that Congress's support was Truman's for the asking ironically became a reason for not seeking it. The extent of the backing that he enjoyed in Congress and among the public added to Truman's conviction that a war resolution was unnecessary. When one adviser asked why he was not rushing to Congress for support, Truman responded, "They are all with me." Another aspect of the political context, however, troubled Truman and his advisers. While not questioning a favorable vote, they feared that the price would be a prolonged debate in which Republicans would renew their assault on Truman's Asian policy. Influential senators like Connally and Lucas warned Truman not to go to Congress for this reason.

Finally, on the strategic level, Truman engaged in "wishful thinking" that also seemed to render congressional authorization unnecessary. Implicit in Truman's decision for war was the expectation that, once American resolve was demonstrated, the crisis would quickly end. Believing that the Soviet Union had directed the invasion and having seen the Soviets back down in earlier crises, Truman anticipated that Moscow would call off the campaign in Korea or, at least, not give much support to the North Koreans, who, left to their own resources, would be repelled. Especially revealing of his thinking are Truman's public references to the North Koreans as "bandits" and to intervention as a "police action." The expectation of a brief conflict, of course, made it easier to ignore Congress. The fact that neither congressional leaders nor Truman thought it necessary to cancel the July 4–10 congressional recess underlines the extent to which the movement to war had not altered Washington's "business as usual" mentality.

Ultimately, the rationales for Truman's refusal to go to Congress are not persuasive. Constitutionally, his case was weak. With respect to the State Department's claim of historical precedent for the Korean intervention, the constitutional historian Edward Corwin wrote at the time that it had compiled a "lengthy list of fights with pirates and bandits." Indeed, virtually all of the eighty-five cases involved brief interventions for minor purposes (most commonly protecting American lives and property in revolutionary situations) and did not directly engage other armies. "The list," constitutional scholar Louis Fisher has written, "contains not a single military adventure that comes close to the dimensions of the Korean War." Sending U.S. troops to resist an act of aggression by a force of ninety thousand men some ten thousand miles from the mainland United States was an unprecedented level of overseas involvement without congressional authorization.

Likewise, Truman's contention that membership in the United Nations gave the president authority to send U.S. forces into combat lacked substance. Congress had addressed this issue in passing the United Nations Participation Act, which Truman had signed in 1945. It affirmed that U.S. troops could be committed to support United Nations–sanctioned military actions only if authorized by Congress. When this measure was being considered, Acheson, then under secretary of state, had testified before a congressional committee that a president could commit troops requested by the U.N. Security Council only after he had received approval of Congress. Taft's argument that the congressional war-making power could not be compromised—"There is no authority to use armed forces in support of the United Nations in the absence of some previous action by Congress dealing with the subject and outlining the general circumstances and the amount of force that can be used"—was sound.

Among the factors influencing Truman's decision, the fear of prolonged congressional debate was the least persuasive. In his memoir, Acheson argued that, once U.S. forces were committed and then were forced to retreat during the first weeks of fighting, the time for seeking a congressional resolution had passed: "Congressional hearings on a resolution of approval at such a time, opening the possibility of endless criticism, would hardly be calculated to support the shaken morale of the troops or the unity that, for the moment, prevailed at home. The harm it could do seemed to me far to outweigh the little good that might ultimately accrue." Acheson's argument was disingenuous. It is inconceivable that Congress would have engaged in "endless criticism" of Truman's actions when American troops were in combat against an unexpectedly difficult foe. And the "unity that . . . prevailed at home" would unquestionably have been reflected in Congress; one can only imagine the adverse public reaction had Congress failed to act quickly.

Finally, while "wishful thinking" is common among leaders taking their countries to war, it was unrealistic in Korea in 1950. The lack of preparedness of U.S. forces, the weakness of the South Korean army, the limited support from other countries, and the strength of the North Koreans meant that expectations of a quick victory were ill-founded. Military leaders recognized that the Korean intervention would require considerable sacrifice.

A resolution of congressional support would not have precluded eventual criticism of the war, but it would have put some constraints on that opposition. As the war became more controversial, Truman could have always pointed to Congress's endorsement, while critics in Congress (assuming they had voted for the war resolution) would always have to explain why they no longer supported Truman's policy. In sum, Truman could have preempted some eventual opposition and largely precluded the charge that Korea was Mr. Truman's War. Most importantly, he would have taken a more united nation into combat, with his leadership solidified by having adhered to the constitutional process.

Related to the failure to gain congressional backing was the ambiguity in U.S. objectives. A congressional resolution might have forced clarification. The United States was clearly committed to restoring the division of Korea. This was explicit in Truman's public statements of June 26, 27, and 30, with their references to North Korean withdrawal and U.S. assistance to South Korea. Acheson's June 29 speech limited the military objective to the prewar status quo. And Truman's "police action" statement—however inappropriate in some ways—implied the restoration of a divided Korea. On the other hand, the commitment of U.S. forces was based on the Security Council resolution of June 27, which requested support of the South Koreans "to repel the armed attack and to restore international peace and security in the area"—language that could be construed as setting broader objectives.

Even within the Truman administration the objective was far from clear. At the State Department, a quiet but sharp debate divided officials who advocated reestablishment of the division of Korea from those who favored unification under U.N. auspices. By declining to settle the question at the time of intervention, Truman and Acheson set the administration on a course whose objectives would ultimately be determined by military operations overseas and political considerations at home.

Besides the ambiguity of objectives, the manner in which Truman took the United States to war also suffered from uncertainty as to how the crisis in Korea related to American security. Americans generally accepted the proposition that it was necessary to resist North Korean aggression, but Truman's explanation for his decision was insufficient. He persistently related the defense of South Korea to U.S. obligations as a member of the United Nations, a reflection of his view that the crisis was principally a test of the five-year-old international organization's capacity to succeed where the League of Nations had failed. This rationale continued after troops had been in combat. In a national radio and television address on July 19, he offered his fullest statement yet on the reasons for fighting. "Korea is a small country thousands of miles away," Truman began, "but what is happening there is important to every American." The North Korean "act of raw aggression" had violated the U.N. Charter, and American forces, constituting the "principal effort," were fighting under U.N. command and a U.N. flag, making this "a landmark in mankind's long search for a rule of law among nations."

Clearly, the vast majority of Americans shared his hopes for an effective United Nations, but what Truman failed to convey was that the nation's security was served by both a strong United Nations and an independent South Korea. The United States had fundamental interests in preserving international stability, assuring the survival of a government that it had supported, and preventing its adversary from a strategic advance. The administration's statements did not talk in those terms. As a consequence, much of the public came to see the conflict as more of a United Nations, rather than an American, war. That perception, heightened by Truman's characterization of the war as a U.N. police action, also worked against him in the long run. What was lost in the rhetoric was that U.S. leaders would have concluded that the nation's interest in Korea necessitated intervention in 1950 even if there had not been a United Nations. So the commitment of U.S. troops was accompanied by incomplete consideration of constitutional, political, and strategic issues, which added to the challenge of waging war.

Those shortcomings of Truman's path to war reflected, in part, the unparalleled urgency faced by him and his advisers during the last week of June 1950. Never before had a president confronted a crisis where an unexpected act of aggression against an American-backed government necessitated immediate action to prevent that ally from being overwhelmed. What Truman did right was more important than his mistakes.

His political and constitutional miscalculations ought not to obscure the decisiveness with which Truman, with the close counsel of Acheson, took the United States into what seems, in retrospect, as then, a "necessary" war. Considering the heightened international tensions of 1950 and the blatant North Korean aggression, Truman had to act. Cast against the common belief in the "lessons" of the 1930s and the related hopes for a strong international organization, the decision to intervene in Korea took on an added imperative. Never far from the consciousness of Truman and his advisers were the shrill criticisms of Republicans denouncing "appeasement" in Asia and the internal "coddling" of communists. Intervention provided an opportunity to demonstrate resolve and strength.

Above all, a North Korean victory bringing the nation's unification under a communist government would have constituted a significant gain for the communist powers. The ever cautious Stalin recognized that the Americans would instinctively try to hold their position in Korea, which is why he reluctantly approved the North Korean attack and sent Kim Il-sung assurances of Chinese support should it be necessary. America's allies generally shared the American anxiety about the consequences of a communist victory in Korea. More significant, however, was the fact that the emerging nations of Asia and the Middle East, mostly neutral and unconcerned about cold war gains and losses, also opposed the North Korean aggression. Truman's and Acheson's decision to take the issue to the United Nations helped to assure the support of allies and neutrals. At the same time, they tempered their disgust with the Soviet Union with determination to avoid a major war. In the end, Truman led a substantially unified public into a war that had strong international support, sanctioned by and fought under the auspices of the United Nations.

Decision by Indecision

HAVING MADE THE DECISION to intervene in Korea, Harry S. Truman became the only American president to be commander in chief in two major wars. Unlike his experience during the last triumphant weeks of World War II, Truman found mostly frustration in the Korean War. In some ways, Truman's difficulties reflected the inherent difficulties of waging a limited war. leaders, especially in democracies, face the unique challenge of calling for popular support and sacrifice for objectives that are short of a decisive victory. To some extent, Truman's problems were derived from the shortcomings of the way that he took the United States to war. The failure to enlist congressional authorization, to present the war to the public as important to U.S. security, and to define a clear political objective also undermined his leadership during the war.

Yet Truman's problems as commander in chief might have been mitigated had he acted with greater political acumen and had he received better advice. Truman reviewed and approved, rarely with much questioning, the recommendations of military and civilian officials. As always, Truman relied heavily on the counsel of a few key officials, above all Secretary of State Dean Acheson, but the war altered their relationship. Acheson, who had tightly controlled the decision-making process that led to U.S. intervention, deferred to the military leadership once the fighting began. This reflected in part the importance that Acheson attached to lines of authority; he was protective of his role as the principal adviser on foreign policy issues and likewise was not inclined to challenge the secretary of defense or the Joint Chiefs of Staff (JCS) on military matters. "In some respects," two scholars have written, "Acheson was in awe of military strategists and appeared reluctant to challenge their judgments directly, even when military decisions had significant diplomatic consequences." The effect of this deference was to yield much authority to the commander of U.N. forces, for American tradition followed the practice of giving wide latitude to the field commanders. Truman himself accepted this proposition: "You pick your man, you've got to back him up. That's the only way a military organization can work."

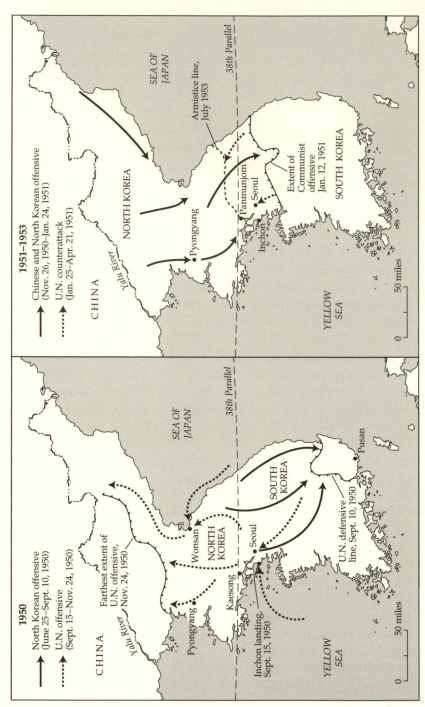

THE KOREAN WAR: Campaigns of North Korean, Chinese, and U.N. Forces

Truman's first decision—picking that man—underscored his deferential style. On July 7, 1950, the U.N. Security Council passed a resolution calling upon U.N. members to provide "military forces and other assistance" in the defense of South Korea and establishing a "unified command under the United States [which would] designate the commander of such forces." With the authority to appoint the commander of the United Nations Command, Truman asked the JCS for a nomination and they quickly suggested Gen. Douglas MacArthur. Truman, without hesitation, approved. Given MacArthur's renown as a commander in the Pacific during World War II and subsequently as commander in chief of U.S. forces in the Far East and of the Allied occupation of Japan, the JCS saw "only one conceivable choice." Ignored were reasons for looking elsewhere: MacArthur was seventy years old (past the military's statutory retirement age) and was increasingly bothered by health problems; moreover, he had a long record of acting impulsively. His considerable ego and flare for self-promotion made him a poor team player. *New York Times* columnist James Reston observed that "diplomacy and a vast concern for the opinions and sensitivities of others are the political qualities essential to his new assignment, and these are precisely the qualities General MacArthur has been accused of lacking in the past."

As the U.N. Command was established, Truman tolerated prolonged discussion within his administration about the United Nations' political objective and, in the process, allowed that objective to shift from a "limited" one (restoring the prewar status quo) to "victory" (defeating North Korea and unifying the country). As U.S. forces began to engage in combat, the "limited" objective seemed clear from the language of the U.N. Security Council resolutions that Truman said guided American commitment, as well as from his own description of a "police action" against "bandits" and Acheson's statement that intervention was "solely for the purpose of restoring the Republic of Korea to the status prior to the invasion from the North."

During the first weeks of the fighting, the U.N. forces were on the defensive before finally halting the North Korean advance and building a narrow foothold at the southeastern tip of the peninsula around the port city of Pusan. Under those conditions, reversing the military situation and forcing the North Koreans back across the thirty-eighth parallel seemed like a formidable and distant challenge. Several military and civilian officials, however, anticipated that an eventual counteroffensive would provide the opportunity for a decisive military victory over North Korea, which would lead to the unification of Korea under U.N. auspices. As early as July 1, John M. Allison, director of the State Department's Office of Northeast Asian Affairs, urged that the United States should plan to occupy North Korea and have the United Nations supervise national elections. MacArthur never doubted that the war should be carried into North Korea; he told the army and air force chiefs of staff, when they visited him in Tokyo, that he intended to destroy the North Korean army and to unite Korea.

The objective of "victory" gained considerable support within the Truman administration. It was based on several assumptions. First, the alternative—a restoration of the status quo—would renew the instability of the Korean peninsula. As was observed by John Foster Dulles, the respected Republican diplomat who was then serving as a State Department adviser, division would provide "asylum to the aggressor" and would result in either the "exposure of the Republic of Korea to greater peril than preceded the June 25 attack or the maintenance by the United States of a large military establishment to contain the North Korean army at the 38th parallel." The JCS added that "from the point of view of military operations . . . [the 38th parallel] has no more significance than any other meridian." It offered no natural barrier, and allowing the North Koreans to retreat behind it would provide an opportunity for them to rearm and renew warfare in the future.

Second, U.N. movement into North Korea offered a unique opportunity to achieve a victory over communism. The JCS contended that it provided "the first opportunity to displace part of the Soviet orbit" and thus disrupt "the strategic complex which the USSR is organizing between its own Far Eastern territories and the continuous areas." In the process, Korean unification would undermine the impression that communism was the wave of the future in Asia; the JCS maintained that, "throughout Asia, those who foresee only inevitable Soviet conquest would take hope." Still another political benefit was the potential role of an independent Korea in fostering a "wedge" between the Soviet Union and China. Chinese commercial and other contacts with Korea could reduce its dependence on the Soviet Union; the JCS contended that, "skillfully manipulated, the Chinese Communists might prefer different arrangements and a new orientation."

Third, a decisive victory would enhance the purpose of the United Nations by punishing North Korea for its aggression and the hardship and suffering that its army had inflicted upon the South Koreans. To the State Department's Allison, this moral dimension was compelling: "I fail to see what advantage we gain by a compromise with clear moral principles and a shirking of our duty to make clear once and for all that aggression does not pay—that he who violates the decent opinions of mankind must take the consequences and that he who takes the sword will perish by the sword. . . . When all legal and moral right is on our side, why should we hesitate?"

Fourth, the military conquest of North Korea did not seem to risk a larger war. By late August, most U.S. officials had become convinced that the Soviet Union would not intervene in Korea. Soviet actions during the first two months of the war were restrained and conciliatory. The Soviet Union ended its boycott of the United Nations in August and, when its representative Jacob Malik returned to the U.N. Security Council, he endorsed India's proposals for an end to the war in Korea through a conference of both Korean governments followed by the withdrawal of all foreign troops.

While most U.S. officials convinced themselves that Korean unification was feasible, a few questioned the prevailing assumptions and urged caution. In particular, Soviet specialists George Kennan and Charles Bohlen warned that Moscow would react unfavorably to the presence of U.N. forces on Korea's northern border. The State Department's Policy Planning Staff added that any military advance into North Korea risked Soviet or Chinese intervention and the erosion of support for the United States in the United Nations. Kennan was the most persistent advocate of restraint. He urged Acheson to ignore those who were "indulging themselves in emotional moralistic attitudes" that could take the United States to "real conflict with the Russians." In sum, what these officials urged was an understanding of the Korean conflict from the perspective of the major communist powers. If the United States had acted to prevent the "loss" of South Korea, why would the Soviet Union and the Chinese People's Republic (CPR) not act to prevent the "loss" of North Korea?

Dismissing such concerns, the National Security Council (NSC) recommended planning for a cautious military move into North Korea whenever the military situation permitted. Without raising any questions, Truman on September 11 approved NSC-81/1, which authorized such an advance if there seemed to be no obstacles. A final decision was to be made in the light of "the action of the Soviet Union and the

Chinese Communists, consultation, and agreement with friendly members of the United Nations, and appraisal of the risk of general war."

These plans were soon to be tested, for the war changed dramatically on September 15, when U.S. and South Korean forces launched an amphibious landing at the port city of Inchon on the west coast of Korea. MacArthur masterminded this daring invasion, which Truman and the JCS had authorized despite doubts about its feasibility. Its objective was to exploit the North Korean army's vulnerability resulting from overextended lines of supply. The gamble paid off, as the assault on Inchon caught the North Koreans by surprise and enabled the United Nations to take the initiative. The war changed overnight. After securing Inchon, marines advanced on Seoul, some twenty miles away. Overcoming strong resistance, they took control of the capital by September 28, and the next day Syngman Rhee and his government returned. Meanwhile, to the south, other U.N. forces, spearheaded by the U.S. Eighth Army under Gen. Walton H. Walker, broke through the North Korean lines. Suddenly the North Korean army was in retreat and the deferred question of the United Nations' objective had to be resolved.

No longer was that issue discussed in confidential memorandums; now it was a matter of public debate. Americans, who had been dispirited by the retreat and losses in the early weeks of the war, quickly embraced the objective of victory. Congressional leaders and newspaper editorials throughout the country endorsed unification and discounted the possibility of Soviet or Chinese intervention. The esteemed columnist Walter Lippmann, who had criticized much of Truman's foreign policy since 1947 for being too strident and uncompromising, argued that reestablishment of the prewar status quo would be unacceptable. Other widely read columnists also urged victory. Joseph Alsop said Truman should stop "shilly-shallying," and David Lawrence wrote that failure to defeat the North Koreans and unify the country would constitute appeasing an aggressor. Congress also was awash in hawkish sentiment, with Democrats vying with Republicans in issuing strident calls for victory. Republicans, who had vocally criticized Truman's "loss" of China to the Communists, repeatedly equated hesitancy to pursue the war into North Korea with the "rewarding" of aggression.

Although Truman had already substantially decided to pursue the course now being urged upon him, he declined to acknowledge it publicly. At his press conference of September 21, Truman was asked whether he had decided to send U.S. troops across the thirty-eighth parallel. His reply was disingenuous: "No I have not. That is a matter for the United Nations to decide. That is a United Nations force, and we are one of the many who are interested in that situation. It will be worked out by the United Nations and I will abide by the decision that the United Nations makes."

Truman's buoyancy was enhanced by his appointment of George C. Marshall as secretary of defense. Truman prevailed upon the ailing Marshall to return to the Cabinet during this critical period, which meant that the two men whom he trusted above all others—Acheson and Marshall—would now be his principal advisers on the political and military aspects of the war. Marshall had earned immense prestige as a military leader, particularly for his service as U.S. chief of staff during World War II, and as secretary of state from 1947 to 1949. His appointment as secretary of defense helped to give still greater influence to the military leadership; even Acheson was in awe of Marshall and did not challenge his judgments. This final assignment of Marshall's distinguished career, however, may have been one too many, for poor health limited his effectiveness. He never took the firm direction of the war that was needed, given MacArthur's headstrong behavior and the complex political situation facing the United States in Korea.

When Acheson and Marshall jointly recommended on September 27 that MacArthur be directed to undertake military operations north of the thirty-eighth parallel, Truman immediately assented. To reduce the possibility of provoking either of the major communist powers, the directives to MacArthur specified that no non-Korean forces were to be employed in the areas near the Korean border with China and the Soviet Union. The contingency of intervention by the major communist powers was also addressed: if by the Soviet Union, then MacArthur was to assume a defensive stance, avoid any provocative action, and report to Washington; if by the Chinese, then MacArthur was to continue military operations so long as they offered a reasonable chance of success.

Truman next gave quick approval to MacArthur's military plans. The Eighth Army was to continue its advance in the west toward the North Korean capital of Pyongyang and beyond, while the X Corps (comprising one marine and one army division) would be separated from the Eighth Army and moved by sea for an amphibious landing on the east coast at Wonsan, about one hundred miles north of the thirty-eighth parallel, from which it would launch a northeastward movement. MacArthur envisioned having U.S., South Korean, and other U.N.

forces moving quickly to cut off the North Koreans before they could retreat across the Chinese border. Reflecting the tradition of giving field commanders considerable latitude in carrying out orders, Marshall cabled MacArthur: "We want you to feel unhampered strategically and tactically to proceed north of the 38th parallel." MacArthur interpreted the directive as negating the earlier limitations on non–South Korean forces near the Korean-Chinese border; he replied to Washington that he saw "all of Korea open for our military operations unless and until the enemy capitulates." Thus, Truman authorized military operations north of the thirty-eighth parallel without prior U.N. sanction and in ways that gave wide discretion to MacArthur.

Having decided to carry the war into North Korea, the Truman administration now sought the approval of the United Nations. Acheson and other U.S. officials, working closely with British colleagues, prepared a resolution that authorized U.N. forces to enter North Korea— "all appropriate steps be taken to ensure conditions of stability throughout Korea"—in order to achieve Korean unification. Since the Soviet Union's delegation had returned to the United Nations and could now veto any Security Council resolution, the United States took this new resolution to the General Assembly, where all members were represented, the major powers had no veto power, and American allies were in the majority. For tactical reasons, the United States did not sponsor the resolution; ultimately, the "eight-power resolution" authorizing military operations in North Korea was introduced by Britain and seven other nations.

During the last days of September and the first week of October, as the Americans and British refined the wording of the eight-power resolution and lined up support, the Chinese People's Republic warned that it would intervene if U.N. forces crossed the thirty-eighth parallel. On September 25, a Chinese official told India's ambassador in Beijing that the Chinese would not "sit back with folded hands and let the Americans come up to their border." A week later Foreign Minister Zhou En-lai stated that, if U.S. troops entered North Korea, China would intervene.

For the first time, international support for U.S. policy weakened. European allies and neutral countries took China's threats seriously and feared a larger war. American officials, however, dismissed the warnings, with Truman calling them "a bald attempt to blackmail the United Nations." In a meeting with British officials, Acheson likened the situation to a "poker game" and saw the Chinese "bluffing." Whatever the risk of Chinese intervention, Acheson contended, "a greater risk would be incurred by showing hesitation and timidity." It was too late to stop the movement into North Korea. Even officials who took Chinese threats seriously thought that the United States should not be intimidated. For instance, China specialist O. Edmund Clubb, who was director of the State Department's Office of Chinese Affairs, argued fatalistically that, since Soviet or Chinese intervention meant a willingness to risk World War III, "we cannot avoid danger either by retreating from it or by surrendering to the [Chinese] threat; either move would increase, not diminish, the danger inherent in the situation for us."

In disregarding China's threats and employing military force to achieve unification, the United States rejected several proposals for a negotiated settlement and began to lose the confidence of many of the nations that had supported the initial resistance to North Korean aggression. At the United Nations, America's allies as well as Asian and Middle Eastern neutrals urged restraint. On October 2, the Soviet Union advanced a proposal that several U.N. members believed provided the basis for a settlement.* American officials dismissed it. Some believed that the Soviet Union had been intimidated by the United Nations's intervention in Korea and was acting from a position of weakness. One wrote that the "failure of [the] Soviets to intervene openly in Korea, and [the] mild tone of their recent notes . . . their attempts, half-hearted as they may appear, to seem co-operative in U.N. . . . may be early ephemeral fruits of policy of containment and building of areas of strength." On the other hand, leaders of several important nations looked more sympathetically upon the Soviet Union's initiatives. Most prominently, India's Prime Minister Jawaharlal Nehru announced opposition to military operations in North Korea "until all other means of settlement have been explored" and proposed the establishment of a special committee to seek a compromise between the Soviet proposal and the eight-power resolution. The Soviet Union responded favorably to the Indian proposal, but the United States opposed it. Defeating it was not easy, however, for many of America's allies questioned what they saw as the headlong pursuit of military victory. After considerable lobbying of its

---

*The Soviet proposal called for a cease-fire in Korea, withdrawal of all foreign troops, free elections throughout the country arranged by the two Korean governments, and the establishment of a U.N. committee (to include nations bordering on Korea, i.e., the CPR and the Soviet Union) to observe the process.

allies, the United States prevailed; the Indian resolution was narrowly defeated in the U.N. General Assembly with twenty-four in favor and thirty-two opposed.

The General Assembly on October 7 then passed the eight-power resolution authorizing operations north of the thirty-eighth parallel; the vote was forty-seven to five, with seven abstentions. That substantial majority belied the misgivings of America's European allies and others about the broadening of objectives and the attendant risk of a larger war. European support reflected mostly a sense of loyalty to the United States and determination not to undermine the Atlantic alliance.

The passage of the eight-power resolution did not end efforts to reverse the American course. Canada and the Netherlands advanced informal proposals to end the war by giving North Korea an opportunity to accept peacefully the reunification plan of the eight-power resolution, either through the dispatch of a U.N. diplomatic mission to North Korea or through delay in the movement of U.N. troops into North Korea. Neither of these approaches challenged the objective of Korean unification, but the United States, determined to press its military advantage, dismissed both as giving respite to the retreating enemy.

This combination of warnings from China and diplomatic initiatives in the United Nations ought to have given Truman reason to reflect on the magnitude of his decision to send U.S. forces into North Korea. Moreover, the proposals showed that the issue was not between stopping militarily at the thirty-eighth parallel and thus restoring the prewar status quo or continuing militarily into the north and achieving unification. The various schemes advanced at the United Nations seemed to promise, at the least, the reduction of North Korean power and even the opportunity for unification through electoral means.

The lack of direct diplomatic relations between the United States and the Chinese People's Republic hampered the prospects for mutual understanding. China's warnings reflected a mounting insecurity. Diplomatically, the CPR faced unrelenting U.S. hostility—the refusal to extend recognition, the opposition to its U.N. membership—which challenged its international legitimacy. Militarily, the steps taken by the United States to "draw the line" against communist expansion in Asia—beginning to assist the French in Indochina, shielding Taiwan by the Seventh Fleet, and dispatching troops to Korea—threatened encirclement. The *People's Daily* spoke of American "designs for a blockade

... taking shape in the pattern of a stretched-out snake; starting from South Korea, it stretches to Japan, the Ryuku Islands, Taiwan and the Philippines and then turns up at Vietnam." To defend its borders and to intervene in Korea, if necessary, China began as early as July to augment its military strength by stationing a 200,000-man force in Manchuria, its large province just across the Yalu River from Korea.

North Korea's survival and China's security became intertwined. Desperate to avoid annihilation, North Korean Premier Kim Il-sung appealed to Soviet Premier Josef Stalin on September 29 for "direct military aid," but Stalin, while promising further arms and weapons, said that additional armed forces should be in the form of "people's volunteers" from China. As it contemplated its course in Korea, the CPR also launched a massive internal propaganda campaign that generated popular hostility toward the United States and patriotic sentiment to protect the homeland.

Ignorant of the interactions among the communist states and indifferent to the warnings emanating from China, the United States led the movement of U.N. forces into North Korea. Truman and Acheson were sensitive to the concerns of other U.N. members, but MacArthur was not and quickly added to the mounting tensions in Korea and to the annoyance of allies by broadcasting an ultimatum that extended his authority beyond that intended in the eight-power resolution. While the resolution called upon the military to "ensure conditions of stability" that would lead to a political settlement, MacArthur demanded that the North Koreans "lay down [their] arms and cease hostilities ... [and] cooperate fully with the United Nations in establishing a unified, independent and democratic government of Korea." Kim Il-sung responded in his own radio broadcast: "The Korean People are not standing alone in our struggle and are receiving the absolute support of the Soviet Union and the Chinese Republic." And in Beijing, Foreign Minister Zhou En-lai warned that "the American war of invasion in Korea has been a serious menace to the security of Korea from its very start.... The Chinese people cannot stand idly by with regard to such a serious situation." Indeed, the day before, Premier Mao Tse-tung had ordered Chinese "volunteers" to enter Korea "to resist U.S. imperialism."

With military momentum in America's favor but with disquieting signals from China, Truman decided that he wanted to meet directly with MacArthur. In his memoir, Truman explained that "I thought he ought to know his Commander in Chief, and that I ought to know the senior field commander in the Far East." The two men had never met. The idea of a conference with MacArthur had originated in early September among members of the White House staff who believed it would help Truman politically to be associated with the revered MacArthur. At first, Truman demurred because the meeting would appear blatantly political, but when it was suggested again in late September—after MacArthur's spectacular success at Inchon—Truman endorsed it. Notably, neither Acheson nor Marshall favored the meeting, and both declined to join the president. Truman's motivation blended politics with policy; he certainly recognized the potential gain of identifying with MacArthur, whose stature had soared after the Inchon landing, just three weeks before congressional elections, but he also seriously sought reassurances from the commander that the war would soon end victoriously.

For these varied reasons, Truman summoned MacArthur, and the two men met on Sunday, October 15, at Wake Island, a tiny speck in the middle of the Pacific Ocean, which necessitated a 7,500-mile journey for the president and a 2,000-mile trip for the general. MacArthur seized the opportunity to ensure Washington's support for his military plans. It was not an occasion for memorable words. Arriving early in the morning, Truman told the waiting MacArthur, "I've been a long time meeting you," to which the general replied, "I hope it won't be so long next time."

The Wake Island conference was brief. The two men met privately for a half-hour, during which MacArthur assured Truman that the Chinese would not attack and that victory was imminent. Then they adjourned to a longer session with the small staffs that had accompanied each of them. MacArthur dominated the meeting, telling the president and his entourage what they wanted to hear. He promised that resistance would end by Thanksgiving. When Truman inquired again about the possibility of Soviet or Chinese intervention, MacArthur replied that neither would "endeavor to throw good money after bad." He was contemptuous of China's capabilities, contending that "they would have the greatest difficulty getting more than fifty or sixty thousand [troops] across the [Yalu] river into North Korea. They have no air [force]." He added that, "if they tried to get down to Pyongyang, there would be the greatest slaughter." When pressed, at the end of the meeting, to account for China's warnings, MacArthur replied that he "did not fully understand why they had gone out on such a limb and that they must

be embarrassed by the predicament in which they now find themselves." In sum, MacArthur embodied utter confidence that the United
Nations controlled the situation.

Altogether the Wake Island conference lasted barely three hours.
Upon his return to the American mainland, Truman told reporters "I've
never had a more satisfactory conference since I've been president" and
praised MacArthur as a "very great soldier." Actually, the meeting at
Wake Island—as Truman must have realized—had accomplished little.
Without giving the meeting much forethought and lacking an agenda
to guide discussion, Truman had made no effort to impress upon Mac-
Arthur his determination to direct the war or to force full consideration
of Chinese intentions and capabilities. Instead, Truman had allowed
MacArthur to dominate the discussion and had questioned none of his
assertions. Many topics were raised, but none was discussed thoroughly. Late in the meeting, one of his aides sent a note to Truman
advising him to slow things down; Truman scribbled a response: "Hell,
no! I want to get out of here before we get into trouble." In the end, the
meeting at Wake Island reinforced the assumptions and directions of
U.S. policy, which, because they seemed to be working, Truman saw no
reason to question. "There had been no discussion of basic U.S. and
U.N. policy objectives," two historians have written, "and thus no opportunity to reach a real meeting of the minds between the President
and the General—or, alternatively, to bring into the open their disagreement. Such discussion did not take place because there seemed no need
for it."

The failure of the Wake Island conference was arguably more the
responsibility of Marshall and Acheson than of Truman. The presence
of one or both could have forced a more deliberative discussion; the
lower level officials who were present recognized that Truman was
rushing matters, but they could not restrain him. In declining to accompany the commander in chief to Wake Island, Acheson and Marshall
showed a certain contempt for Truman. Once Truman made the decision to meet with MacArthur, he deserved their support. In his memoir,
Acheson expressed his disdain for the enterprise: "I begged to be excused. While General MacArthur had many of the attributes of a foreign sovereign, I said, and was quite as difficult as any, it did not seem
wise to recognize him as one. . . . The whole idea was distasteful to me.
I wanted no part in it, and saw no good coming from it." So Truman,
despite his pride in presidential prerogatives, permitted his two chief

Cabinet officers to absent themselves from what he considered—for good reason or bad—to be an important conference. Acheson's smug self-righteousness about the conference explained but did not excuse his absence.

MacArthur was by no means alone in discounting the Chinese threats. U.S. diplomatic and military officials, with few exceptions, were convinced that China's interests and capabilities precluded its intervention. Their reasoning seemed airtight. First, the Chinese government's overriding priority was internal: to recover from more than a decade of warfare and to launch the communist program of reform. Second, the Chinese army, which (according to a U.S. military analysis) had never met "a well trained force with high morale equipped with heavy weapons and possessing the will and the skill to use those weapons," lacked the resources to fight effectively against U.N. forces. Third, the Chinese People's Republic wanted to be seated in the United Nations, and that objective would be undermined by intervention. Fourth, Moscow's evident disinterest in Korea was a restraint on China, since the Chinese, if they intervened, would need Soviet air and naval support and that would risk the larger war that Moscow seemed determined to avoid. Fifth, North Korea was a satellite of the Soviet Union and a government with which the CPR had limited contact, so it lacked an imperative to "save" North Korea.

The conclusion to a Central Intelligence Agency (CIA) report reflected the prevailing American thinking: "Despite statements by Chou En-lai, troop movements to Manchuria, and propaganda charges of atrocities and border violations, there are no convincing indications of an actual Chinese Communist intention to resort to full-scale intervention in Korea." If the Chinese intended to intervene, U.S. officials believed, they would have done so when the North Koreans were on the verge of victory. Had Chinese troops been thrust into the war in July, an American analysis observed, "the influx of overwhelming numbers of Chinese ground forces would have proved the decisive factor."

During the three weeks after the Wake Island conference, operations in Korea entered a bizarre phase. On one level, the advance of the U.N. force fulfilled the optimism of the conference. On October 19, South Korean forces captured the North Korean capital, Pyongyang, forcing the government of Kim Il-sung to flee farther north. The next day, Mac-

Arthur's headquarters announced that "organized resistance on any large scale has ceased to be an enemy capability." The dual offensive moved forward, with the Eighth Army advancing in the west and the X Corps in the east.* By October 26, a South Korean reconnaissance platoon, operating under General Walker's command, reached the Yalu River at Chosan. The war seemed to be won.

In the midst of what seemed to be the closing phase of the war, however, the Chinese threat moved to the battlefield. Beginning in early October, the Chinese had surreptitiously moved forces into Korea. In two separate incidents on October 25, South Korean units encountered the Chinese army, and in one case substantial fighting ensued, with the South Koreans absorbing heavy losses. Chinese forces—described by General Walker as "well organized and well trained"—next engaged American and South Korean armies, leading to more heavy fighting that lasted several days. Such clashes continued intermittently. A few captured Chinese soldiers told of the movement of a large number of troops into Korea.

U.S. officials refused to believe the implications of the Chinese actions. The prevailing assumption—at MacArthur's headquarters no less than at the Defense Department, State Department, and CIA—was that China had nothing at stake in Korea and, had it intended to fight there, intervention would have occurred earlier. So the United States dismissed the call of allies and neutrals for restraint.

Washington's control over MacArthur, never firmly established, began to unravel. When he learned that more Chinese men and materiel were crossing into Korea over the Yalu River and that Soviet fighter airplanes—MIG-15s—had begun operating near the river in support of Chinese forces, MacArthur took matters into his own hands. Without consulting the Joint Chiefs of Staff, he ordered a massive bombing campaign—"combat crews are to be flown to exhaustion if necessary"—against North Korean lines of communication, factories, and other installations, including the Korean side of Yalu River bridges. When the commanding general of the Far Eastern air force reported the order to

*The U.N. Command comprised principally U.S. and South Korean forces; by this time, five other nations—Great Britain, Australia, Turkey, the Philippines, and Thailand—had contributed some nine thousand ground, air, and sea troops. Another twenty-seven thousand men had been offered by U.N. members, but the United States, believing that they would not all be needed, had decided to accept only an additional six thousand troops.

his superiors in Washington on November 6, it alarmed officials of the State and Defense Departments, who feared that the bombing could lead to attacks on Chinese territory.

MacArthur's planned bombing campaign came at a delicate diplomatic moment. America's allies were alarmed by reports of Chinese forces operating in Korea and feared that the United States was blundering into a larger war. Acheson had promised to consult with Great Britain regarding any military operations that might threaten China and was also seeking support for a proposed U.N. resolution calling for the Chinese to withdraw their forces from Korea. Any provocative action by the United States threatened the fragile international coalition and prospects for exerting diplomatic pressure on China. At Acheson's suggestion, Truman ordered that the bombing campaign be deferred, with MacArthur being instructed to "postpone all bombing of targets within five miles of the [Chinese] border."

MacArthur—with "the gravest protest I can make"—challenged Truman's order. With Chinese troops and equipment "pouring across all bridges over the Yalu" and "threaten[ing] the destruction of the forces under my command," MacArthur pleaded for authorization to destroy the bridges. Delay would "be paid for dearly in American and other United Nations blood." The responsibility would be Truman's: "Your instructions may well result in a calamity of major proportion for which I cannot accept the responsibility without [your] permission and direct understanding of the situation." Truman relented. It was difficult to resist such an emotional and strategic appeal. He authorized the bombing of the Yalu bridges. In transmitting Truman's approval to MacArthur, however, the JCS stressed concern over provoking a wider war: "It is vital in the national interest of the United States to localize the fighting in Korea . . . [and] that extreme care be taken to avoid violation of [Chinese] territory."

The fear of a larger war was enhanced by a CIA report that China, with perhaps as many as 40,000 men already in Korea and at least 200,000 regular forces stationed across the Yalu River, was capable of not only halting the U.N. advance but also launching a major counteroffensive. Since the Chinese intervention presumably was sanctioned by the Soviet Union, it indicated a willingness on the part of both communist powers to risk a general war.

The situation soon became further confused. On November 7, China's forces abruptly disengaged from conflict with U.N. forces and vanished into the mountainous regions of North Korea. No one knew whether this was a temporary or permanent withdrawal from fighting.

Alarmed by this unpredictable military situation, the JCS alerted MacArthur that "your objective . . . 'the destruction of the North Korean armed forces' may have to be reexamined." He refused, however, to reconsider his strategy and replied that he planned to launch his attack to complete the destruction of North Korean forces "on or about November 25 with the mission of driving to the border and securing all of North Korea."

Truman requested that the National Security Council reassess U.S. objectives and strategy. Truman, however, did not attend the NSC meeting of November 9, which considered a JCS report expressing alarm about the "heavy drain on our military potentialities . . . [of a] sustained military campaign in Korea" and urging that "every effort should be expended as a matter of urgency to settle the problem of Chinese Communist intervention in Korea by political means, preferably through the United Nations." The JCS saw three alternatives: (1) continuing the pursuit of the campaign aimed at the defeat of North Korean forces, (2) halting the advance and "maintain[ing] a defensive position on a line short of the Korean border," or (3) withdrawing from Korea. The third option was obviously out of the question, but the second had much to recommend it; such a course was "apparently feasible now and it might be a temporary expedient pending clarification of the military and political problems raised by Chinese intervention which are as yet unanswered." Elaborating on that alternative, Acheson advanced the possibility of an agreement with the Chinese for a demilitarized zone along the Korean-Chinese border. In the end, however, no one at the NSC meeting recommended modifying the existing objective, only that it "should be kept under review." So the NSC, essentially by default, reaffirmed the victory option. When informed afterward of the NSC discussion, Truman did not question the recommendation.

Yet Truman and his advisers were sufficiently concerned that they tried to reassure China that the impending defeat of the North Koreans and the reunification of Korea under the United Nations were no threat to its security. The lack of direct diplomatic relations between Washington and Beijing hindered communications, so U.S. officials had to rely on intermediaries and public pronouncements. Most importantly, Truman, at a press conference on November 16, stated that the Americans "never at any time entertained any intention to carry hostilities into

China." He promised "every honorable step to prevent any extension of the hostilities in the Far East."

Truman's reassurances were directed not only to China but also to allies and neutral countries. At the United Nations, the British and others pressed the United States to delay further military advance and to negotiate a buffer zone along the Korean-Chinese frontier. There were voices of caution in Washington as well. Concerned about the erosion of international support and the prospects for a larger war, the State Department's Policy Planning Staff recommended on November 17 that U.N. forces should pull back to a defensible line at the "narrow neck" of the Korean peninsula. Recognizing that the military leadership would reject any such move, Acheson gave scant consideration to this option and discouraged the British from pursuing their initiative, a decision he came to regret. In his memoir, Acheson reflected on this episode and the inadequacy of his counsel throughout this period: "All the President's advisers in this matter, civilian and military, knew that something was badly wrong, though what it was, how to find out, and what to do about it they muffed. . . . I have an unhappy conviction that none of us, myself prominently included, served him as he was entitled to be served."

In the end, Acheson, Marshall, and the JCS substantially deferred to the judgment of MacArthur, who dismissed all suggestions to modify established objectives. It would be fatal, he cabled, "to weaken the fundamental and basic policy of the United Nations to destroy all resisting armed forces in Korea and bring that country into a united nation." Failure to maintain the offensive would "destroy the morale of my forces." He urged "no weakening at this critical moment and that we press on to complete victory which I believe can be achieved if our determination and indomitable will do not desert us."

So, when he met with Marshall and other Defense Department officials on November 21, Acheson did not urge restraint. In the end Washington did not modify its directive to MacArthur other than to suggest that he consider two alternatives: (1) halting his offensive ten to twenty-five miles south of the Yalu River (which would have, in effect, established a neutral zone along the border) or (2) after having completed the advance to the Yalu, withdrawing all but South Koreans to such a line (thus eliminating a Western-dominated international army on China's frontier). Since these were only suggestions, MacArthur predictably disregarded them.

In their failure to restrain MacArthur, Truman and his advisers ignored evidence of Chinese intent and capabilities. On the eve of the "final offensive," another CIA report warned that the Chinese "have the capability of forcing [the U.N. army] to withdraw to defensive positions for prolonged and inconclusive operations, which, the Communists might calculate, would lead to eventual U.N. withdrawal from Korea."

Undeterred, MacArthur, from his headquarters in Tokyo, confidently announced on November 24 the launching of the "United Nations massive compression envelopment . . . [which] should for all purposes end the war." He then journeyed to Korea, where he visited the front and said that he "hoped to have the boys home by Christmas."

On the night of November 25, these expectations were shattered as some 300,000 Chinese troops attacked the U.N. forces. MacArthur urgently cabled Washington: "We face an entirely new war. . . . Our present strength is not sufficient to meet this new undeclared war." Suddenly, the U.N. forces were in full-scale retreat. MacArthur's ill-considered division of his forces into two widely separated units, which civilian officials ought to have questioned, left the soldiers isolated and vulnerable in the mountainous terrain near the Chinese border.

The Chinese intervention was the most shocking assault upon U.S. forces since the Pearl Harbor attack nine years earlier. The situation called for decisive presidential leadership, and Truman recognized the enormity of this unexpected challenge. He told the Cabinet: "This is the worst situation we have had yet. We'll just have to meet it as we've met all the rest."

The Chinese assault enhanced the risks of a general war and weakened America's stature. A virtual state of panic prevailed at the United Nations. Unlike earlier cold war crises, however, when the United States had enjoyed considerable international support, much of the world now blamed American leaders for having blundered into a military and diplomatic disaster. With its steadfast rejection of all overtures for restraint, the United States had undermined the international stature that it had earned by responding quickly to the North Korean attack. After the Chinese intervention, politics at the United Nations changed as the United States no longer dominated the making of U.N. policy in Korea but was instead increasingly restrained by pressures from its allies and neutrals.

In responding to this crisis, Truman and his advisers confronted difficult questions: What were the Chinese capabilities and objectives?

Could the Americans and South Koreans halt the offensive? Would the Soviet Union also intervene? Could the United States retain the support of allies and neutrals who had been urging restraint beforehand?

Initially Truman seemed to meet the challenge. He quickly accepted the necessity of redefining the war's objective. Within hours of learning of the Chinese attack, he chaired a hurriedly called meeting of the National Security Council. Marshall and Acheson were the dominant figures in the discussion, from which emerged a consensus to scale back objectives and to wage a limited war. There was no choice: the United States could not match the Chinese capacity to commit forces to Korea, and if it carried the war directly to China through bombing or other means, the Soviet Union would intervene. Overall, the NSC concluded that its purposes were "to fulfill [its] U.N. obligations but not to become involved in a general war in China with the Chinese Communists." To achieve that objective, it was essential "to find a line that we can hold, and hold it" and to work through the United Nations for a settlement that would end the fighting. Although prepared to condemn China publicly for its "aggression," the United States "should use all available political, economic, and psychological action to limit the war." Throughout this discussion was implicit an agreement that the war would be "limited" not only in its military scope, but also in its political objective, for there was no mention of unification, but rather of allowing a "zone in North Korea."

Underlying the NSC discussion on the "entirely new war" in Korea were calculations about the Soviet Union's role and objectives. U.S. officials assumed that the Soviet Union was behind the Chinese attack and would welcome seeing American resources drained in an all-out war with China, which would facilitate communist advances elsewhere. The United States must not "fall into a carefully laid Russian trap [in Korea]." No one questioned that U.S. security dictated a substantial military buildup of its forces and those of its allies in Europe.

Having agreed privately to a cautious and reasoned strategy, Truman quickly lost control of the situation through ill-considered public comments. During the NSC meeting, Averell Harriman, the veteran diplomat whom Truman had recently named a special assistant, had urged that Truman assert leadership in ways that would reassure allies. At a press conference on Thursday, November 30, Truman did exactly the opposite. After affirming determination to hold on in Korea and announcing plans to increase spending on national defense, Truman allowed himself to be drawn into a series of questions about the possible use of atomic weapons in Korea. Truman would have been well advised to avoid commenting at all on the subject, but evidently he wanted to warn the Soviet Union and China against further escalation. Whatever his motivation, the president answered one question after another, and the more he said, the more damaging were the results. The sequence culminated with a reporter asking: "Mr. President, did we understand you clearly that the use of the atomic bomb is under consideration?" Truman replied: "Always has been. It is one of our weapons." As reporters followed up with other questions, Truman added: "It's a matter that the military people will have to decide. I'm not a military authority that passes on those things. . . . The military commander in the field will have charge of the use of weapons, as he always has."

By this unfortunate digression, Truman allowed a press conference that had been intended to show statesmanlike resolve to degenerate into nuclear saber-rattling. He had not only said that atomic weapons were under active consideration (to the extent that U.S. officials had looked at that alternative in Korea, they had considered them impractical), but also indicated that MacArthur could unleash them (when, in fact, legislation signed by Truman himself provided that only the president could authorize their use).

The international reaction was overwhelmingly unfavorable. Truman was denounced in the press throughout Europe, Latin America, the Middle East, and Asia. Headlines in newspapers around the world told millions of people that America was prepared to employ atomic weapons. America's allies, no less than neutral countries, were horrified by what they saw as American recklessness. The headline in a leading newspaper in India captured the international mood: "NO! NO! NO!" So egregious was Truman's misstatement that the White House found it necessary to "clarify" what he had said; a subsequent press release averred that the president had not authorized the use of atomic weapons.

The controversy stirred by Truman's comments occurred as the U.N. military position in Korea deteriorated. Amid turbulent snow with temperatures as low as twenty-five degrees below zero, American and South Korean forces, encircled in the mountains south of the Yalu River, were reeling under the Chinese onslaught. It was uncertain whether the retreating forces would be able to establish a defensive line. At the White House on the evening of December 2, Truman, Marshall, and

JCS Chairman Gen. Omar Bradley discussed the possibility of having to undertake a quick and risky evacuation of U.S. troops; afterward, Truman wrote in his diary: *"It looks very bad."*

The situation brought out the worst in many people. Several Republicans charged that Truman was responsible for the military disaster; Senator Joseph McCarthy led the attack, calling for the resignations of Acheson and Marshall and the impeachment of Truman. Other critics in Congress and the press used the Korean debacle to urge either a return to isolationism or, among so-called Asia-firsters, greater priority to Asia and "winning" in Korea. MacArthur, whose views reflected an "Asia-first" position, defied the chain of command and played to Truman's critics by issuing a public statement blaming his predicament on restrictions imposed by Washington that were "without precedent."

On the international front, an alarmed British Prime Minister Clement Attlee insisted on an immediate consultation with Truman. He rushed to Washington for four days of meetings beginning on December 4. Attlee pressed the concerns of European allies that the United States was being dragged into an Asian war that would prevent it from strengthening the North Atlantic Treaty Organization, thus leaving Europe vulnerable to attack or intimidation by the Soviet Union. Truman refused to back away from his determination not to allow the Chinese to drive Americans out of Korea but agreed that China's intervention necessitated a change in war aims—a cease-fire that restored the division of Korea at about the thirty-eighth parallel. On the atomic bomb question, Truman assured Attlee that he was responsible for its use and promised consultation with the British before any such decision. Truman and Acheson, however, rejected British suggestions that the West tie a Korean settlement with China to other issues (i.e., China's admission to the United Nations and the withdrawal of the U.S. protection of Taiwan). Unwilling to become involved in negotiations that might suggest concessions to the Chinese as reward for ending their "aggression" in Korea, the Americans insisted that other issues had to be deferred until the war ended.

Besides trying to repair America's international stature, Truman needed to reassure a shaken public. As a State Department official observed, "The American people are getting the impression that their Washington leadership is utterly confused and sterile. They are saying in effect: 'Don't just sit there, do something.'" Indeed, Truman had to "do something" because, despite all of the talk of holding the line against the Chinese, the Americans and South Koreans continued their bloody retreat. Although he was determined to avoid a larger war, circumstances dictated the imperative of preparing for that contingency.

So, on the evening of December 15—almost three weeks after the Chinese attack—Truman addressed the American public. Speaking from the White House, Truman warned that the country was "in great danger" because "the rulers of the Soviet Union have been waging a relentless attack . . . [and in Korea] have been willing to push the world to the brink of a general war." The United States "must act calmly and wisely and resolutely . . . [and would] continue to take every honorable step to avoid general war." Toward that end, Truman announced plans for a significant increase in military spending and declared a state of national emergency. That step permitted government controls over production, prices, and wages and various other measures that would strengthen national security. He closed with an appeal that, "in the days ahead, each of us should measure his own efforts, his own sacrifices, by the standard of our heroic men in Korea."

Those brave words notwithstanding, Truman could do little more than hope for a reversal of the military situation, and for the next month, the news from the front remained ominous. The Eighth Army virtually fell apart as a fighting force and retreated before the Chinese and reinvigorated North Korean onslaught. To the east, the X Corps fought more effectively and executed an orderly withdrawal to the coast for evacuation by sea.

With the military advantage, the Chinese dismissed cease-fire appeals. Their position paralleled that of the United States a few months earlier: they were under pressure from their Korean ally to achieve total victory, they faced what appeared to be a defeated enemy, and they feared that any halt in their military advance would give the enemy an opportunity to recover and launch a counteroffensive. So the imperative of "victory" was as compelling in Beijing in December as it had been in Washington in September. By Christmas—when MacArthur had predicted victory—the Communist forces had pushed the Eighth Army back nearly three hundred miles, almost to the thirty-eighth parallel.

In the harrowing days of the longest retreat of an American army in the nation's history, military fortunes changed once again. Gen. Matthew Ridgway took command of the beleaguered Eighth Army, replacing General Walker, who had been accidentally killed. Rarely in military history has a change in command brought such dramatic results as was the case with Ridgway's leadership in Korea. Initially, he had no choice but to continue the withdrawal, as the Chinese and North Koreans pushed across the thirty-eighth parallel and, early in the new year of 1951, captured Seoul and continued their southward advance. Ridgway, however, steadily rebuilt the Eighth Army into an effective fighting force. Providing forceful leadership epitomized by a visible presence at the front, Ridgway inspired a dispirited force, attended to its basic needs, and modified its tactics, notably in exploiting its advantage in firepower to offset the Communist numerical superiority. By the middle of January 1951, a transformed Eighth Army halted the Chinese advance by building a solid defensive line about fifty miles south of Seoul. The overextension of Communist lines of supply left them vulnerable to American aerial attack. The reversal on the ground was facilitated by the fighting qualities not only of Americans but also of other supporting U.N. members, especially Turkish and British units. By January 25—a month after Ridgway's arrival—the Eighth Army began, in his words, "rolling forward."

This stabilization of the front meant that the U.N. forces were not going to be driven out of Korea. It undercut MacArthur's claims of impending defeat unless Truman approved his strategy of carrying the war directly against China. Toward that end, MacArthur wanted Truman to authorize a naval blockade of China's ports, the bombing of China's industrial center, the use of Chinese Nationalist forces in Korea, and Chinese Nationalist attacks on the Chinese mainland. He put the onus on Truman for continued loss of American life. A MacArthur message in January 1951 was unusually blunt: "Under the extraordinary limitations and conditions imposed upon the command in Korea its military position is untenable, but it can hold for any length of time up to its complete destruction if overriding political considerations so dictate." After the rejuvenation of the Eighth Army, however, such dire predictions and urgent recommendations, in the words of two historians, "no longer commanded the respect that they had once enjoyed."

The change on the battlefield encouraged diplomats at the United Nations to seek a negotiated end to the war, but America's indignation over China's intervention initially threatened such initiatives. The Truman administration had come to accept the necessity of a compromise settlement, but it was also profoundly angered by China's intervention. Reflecting public sentiment, both houses of Congress passed a resolution calling upon the United Nations to brand China as an "aggressor" in Korea. Truman and Acheson likewise believed that the integrity of the United Nations demanded that China be condemned for its actions in Korea.

At the United Nations, opinion was divided. Many allies, as well as some members of the Arab-Asian bloc, shared the American indignation over China's "aggression." Yet most U.N. members were skittish about taking any step that would put the Chinese on the diplomatic defensive and reduce the prospects for negotiations. Unlike their actions in earlier deliberations over the war, allies forced modification of an "aggressor" resolution to include provisions for United Nations–sponsored negotiations. Still, it took a great deal of American pressure to keep its allies in line (including "reminders" that Congress would remember which countries supported the United States when it came time to authorize foreign assistance) before the U.N. General Assembly, on February 1, passed a resolution condemning China as an "aggressor" in Korea.

However great the Chinese annoyance over being branded an "aggressor," Beijing, no less than Washington, could not ignore the imperative of negotiations. The changed course of fighting in Korea reinforced international pressures on both sides for a settlement. The reinvigorated Eighth Army pushed back the Communist forces, retaking Seoul on March 15, and approached once again the thirty-eighth parallel. Restrained by international sentiment and chastened by the folly of the previous fall's campaign, no one in the Truman administration contemplated another effort at conquering North Korea.

No one, that is, except MacArthur, who refused to compromise the objective of Korean unification. Frustrated and bitter over Washington's refusal to authorize the blockade and bombing of China, MacArthur increasingly aired his differences publicly. On March 7, he told the press that, unless his forces were strengthened and restrictions were removed, a bloody stalemate would ensue. Eight days later, he told a reporter that a defensible line could not be established in the vicinity of the thirty-eighth parallel and warned that his superiors in Washington "must not ignore the heavy cost in allied blood which a protracted and indecisive campaign would entail." A triumphant march to the Yalu, he argued, was still militarily attainable.

MacArthur's open questioning of directives from Washington now moved to defiance of civilian authority, clearly constituting insubordination. At Truman's instruction, the Defense and State Departments carefully crafted a cease-fire proposal. Upon learning of the initiative and before it was publicly enunciated, MacArthur sabotaged it. Truman had tolerated earlier indiscretions by MacArthur but nothing that approximated this act. In a bizarre move that astonished all parties to the war and triggered outrage in Washington, MacArthur on March 24 issued a statement that denigrated China's military capabilities and threatened to expand the war: "The enemy . . . must by now be painfully aware that a decision of the United States to depart from its tolerant effort to contain the war to the areas of Korea, through an expansion of our military operations to his coastal areas and interior bases, would doom Red China to the risk of imminent military collapse." Rather than risk such a defeat, China should send its military commander to surrender to MacArthur. "I stand ready at any time to confer in the field with the commander of the enemy forces in an earnest effort to find any military means whereby the realization of the political objectives of the United Nations in Korea . . . might be accomplished without further bloodshed." In sum, China should abandon Korea or risk an American assault against its homeland.

MacArthur's insubordination challenged Truman's authority. Meeting with advisers, Truman showed "disbelief with controlled fury." He had no choice but to abandon the cease-fire initiative. He also had no choice so far as MacArthur was concerned. In his memoirs, Truman stated the situation bluntly: "[MacArthur's ultimatum] was in open defiance of my orders as President and as Commander in Chief. This was a challenge to the President under the Constitution. . . . By this act MacArthur left me no choice—I could no longer tolerate his insubordination."

Yet Truman did not face up to the imperative to dismiss MacArthur. Instead, he authorized the mildest of reprimands—a reminder to MacArthur of an earlier order that public statements had to be approved by authorities in Washington. Truman's backing away from a showdown with MacArthur was principally a political calculation. MacArthur remained very popular with Americans, and his ultimatum had received a favorable public response. Meanwhile, Truman's own stature was at a terribly low point: his "job approval" rating had fallen to 26 percent, which was principally attributable to the unpopularity of the war. Yet Truman must have recognized that chastising MacArthur would not change his behavior. In effect, Truman postponed an inevitable decision, one that was bound, whenever it happened, to have serious domestic political consequences. In the process, he weakened the stature of the presidency and added to the widespread international disappointment in U.S. leadership.

Within a matter of days, MacArthur again challenged Truman's authority even more directly and defiantly, creating an extraordinary moment in the House of Representatives. On April 5, the Republican leader, Congressman Joseph Martin of Massachusetts, read to his colleagues a letter that he had received from MacArthur, which argued the case for "victory" in Korea. In a unique bit of strategic reasoning, MacArthur argued that the war in Korea would determine the fate of Europe and the outcome of a global struggle with communism. "It seems strangely difficult for some to realize that here in Asia is where the Communist conspirators have elected to make their play for global conquest, and that we have joined the issue thus raised on the battlefield: that here we fight Europe's war with arms while the diplomats there still fight it with words; that if we lose the war to communism in Asia, the fall of Europe is inevitable, win it and Europe most probably would avoid war and yet preserve freedom." He concluded with what was to become a favorite refrain: "There is no substitute for victory."

Truman confided in his diary that "this looks like the last straw. Rank insubordination." He now accepted the inevitable decision. While keeping his own position to himself, Truman sought the advice of officials directly responsible for the war as well as from congressional leaders and longtime political associates. Everyone recognized the political ramifications of firing the widely revered general. On the other hand, they also could not ignore the growing perception among much of the public that Truman had lost control of the situation and that he was afraid to confront MacArthur. They were also aware that MacArthur's erratic behavior unnerved other U.N. members and undermined the widespread international sentiment for a negotiated settlement. Over the course of a few days of intense and highly secret discussions, a consensus emerged, most notably among those most responsible for the conduct of the war—Acheson, Marshall, Harriman, Gen. Omar Bradley (and through him the unanimous recommendation of the Joint Chiefs of Staff)—that MacArthur had to be relieved of his command. When they informed Truman of their recommendation, Truman said that it was the course he also favored. So, on April 11, 1951, Truman, at last, fired MacArthur, with Ridgway replacing him as U.N. commander.

In a national radio address that evening, Truman explained fully the rationale of waging a limited war in Korea. This was the clearest statement he had yet made connecting the intervention in Korea to U.S. security. Carrying the war against China, he said, risked drawing the United States into "a vast conflict on the continent of Asia" and rendering "our task . . . immeasurably more difficult all over the world." Continuing the war in Korea and the overall buildup of U.S. military strength would enable the United States to blunt aggression in Korea and discourage it elsewhere.

A public stunned by MacArthur's dismissal was little influenced by Truman's measured defense of a limited war. For the next several days, Truman was subjected to ridicule and criticism perhaps without parallel in the history of the presidency. Truman and his advisers had anticipated a political firestorm, but nothing had prepared them for the emotional outpouring and partisanship that accompanied MacArthur's triumphant return to the United States. As Republicans in Congress and much of the press condemned Truman's decision, MacArthur was greeted by enthusiastic and overwhelming crowds in Honolulu, San Francisco, and New York, where he was feted with the largest ticker-tape parade in the city's history. The popular response was driven in large part by MacArthur's unique stature as a military hero who had been out of the country for fourteen years waging war against Japan and then rebuilding postwar Japan and who had now been fired by an unpopular president for trying to do his job in Korea. Partisan politics heightened the triumphant return, for MacArthur had always been a favorite of conservative Republicans and his dismissal gave the party an issue on which to savage the Democrats. Adding to the hysteria was the fact that MacArthur's promise of "victory" had appealed to a public that was disenchanted by the frustrating war.

In an emotional and eloquent televised address to Congress on April 19, MacArthur directly challenged Truman's strategy of a limited war. His words resonated with millions of Americans who could recall the great victories of World War II: "Once war is forced upon us, there is no other alternative than to apply every available means to bring it to a swift end. War's very object is victory—not prolonged indecision. In war, indeed there can be no substitute for victory." He promised a strategy that would bring "victory"—unifying Korea—by carrying the war against China through a naval blockade, air reconnaissance, and Chinese Nationalist operations against the mainland. The alternative to "victory" would be "an indecisive campaign, with its terrible and constant attrition upon our forces." In his most emotional passage, MacArthur talked of the men at war: "Why, my soldiers asked of me, surrender military advantages to an enemy in the field? I could not answer." Then, after referring to an old army ballad titled "Old Soldiers Never Die, They Just Fade Away," he ended with a memorable peroration: "I now close my military career and just fade away—an old soldier who tried to do his duty as God gave him the light to see that duty." It was a defining moment: a revered commander promising "victory" without much sacrifice and challenging an unpopular president's "limited war" with its endless indecision.

Truman could do little more than allow the emotional homecoming to run its course. Even at the height of the MacArthur hysteria, however, much of the mainstream press, several leading columnists, and virtually all Democrats and even some Republicans in Congress praised Truman for asserting civilian control of the military. Further, even among those Americans who cheered MacArthur or those politicians who exploited his dismissal for partisan advantage, few actually favored his military strategy.

Indeed, an unintended consequence of MacArthur's recall was that it forced the Truman administration to present to the American public its case for a limited war. The forum was a joint congressional committee that conducted hearings into the war and questioned MacArthur as well as Acheson, Marshall, Bradley, and other administration officials. In the process, the public learned of the shallowness of MacArthur's strategy. The measures that he proposed would not bring victory; rather, military action against China would greatly increase the risk of a third world war. Of particular significance was the testimony of the military leaders, as Bradley and the other members of the Joint Chiefs of Staff criticized MacArthur's conduct of the war and his "victory" strategy. Officials of the Truman administration argued that, through a limited war, the United States could uphold the original objective of repelling aggression without being drawn into a larger war on the Asian continent, which would divert American resources from Europe. Most telling were the words of Bradley, who said that, "frankly, in the opinion of the Joint Chiefs of Staff, [MacArthur's] strategy would involve us in the wrong war, at the wrong place, at the wrong time and with the wrong enemy." While much of MacArthur's appeal quickly faded, that did not translate into a rise in American popular support for Truman (his approval rating never again going above 33%) or for the war (over 50% of Americans seeing it by this time as a "mistake").

The dismissal of MacArthur nonetheless had a liberating effect. Truman was able to pursue an armistice in Korea without hindrance from an obstreperous commander. With neither side able to achieve a victory and with their armies again dividing the Korean peninsula after nearly a year of warfare, many nations believed that it was time for a truce. Other parties to the war were less enthusiastic. Neither the North Koreans nor the South Koreans were prepared to abandon their objectives of dominating the entire peninsula. The Chinese also approached negotiations cautiously, as their leaders anticipated that protracted warfare in Korea could work to their long-term advantage. The Soviet Union had conflicting interests: playing the role of peacemaker in Korea would enhance its international stature, but it also gained certain strategic advantages in having Americans and Chinese tied down by the fighting in Korea.

The international pressures for ending the war mounted during intense fighting in the spring of 1951. On April 22, the Chinese and North Koreans launched a two-phased "spring offensive," which the U.N. forces withstood before beginning a counteroffensive that, by the end of May, had pushed the Communist armies north of the thirty-eighth parallel. The U.N. army did not continue its advance, however, partly because the enemy's defense strengthened, but also as a means of facilitating negotiations.

Truman pursued that path. Calculating that the Soviet Union shared an interest in ending the war, the State Department instructed U.S. officials in Paris and at the United Nations to engage in behind-the-scenes discussions with their Soviet counterparts. On June 1, Trygve Lie, the secretary-general of the United Nations, stated that a cease-fire line in the vicinity of the thirty-eighth parallel would vindicate the objectives of the United Nations. The Soviet Union then took an important initiative when, on June 23, Jacob Malik, its delegate to the United Nations, announced support for negotiations "for a cease-fire and an armistice providing for the mutual withdrawal of forces from the thirty-eighth parallel." Truman seized the opening and, with the Chinese and North Koreans quickly giving their assent, truce talks began on July 10, 1951, at Kaesong, a village in the vicinity of the thirty-eighth parallel.

The negotiations between the United Nations and the North Koreans–Chinese (conducted by military representatives on both sides) were frustratingly extended. Just getting the two sides together was difficult: after seven weeks of meetings at Kaesong, the Communist side abruptly broke off the talks. After an interlude of two months, they were renewed on October 25 at Panmunjom, another village in the same area.

In the end, two issues—establishing a cease-fire line and exchanging prisoners of war (POWs)—were central to ending the war. On the first, the North Koreans and Chinese wanted a restoration of the thirty-eighth parallel, while the United States sought a dividing line (and demilitarized zone) north of the parallel, which would be more defensible. The United Nations prevailed, as eventually the negotiators agreed to a dividing line that would follow the military front at the time of the cease-fire. The point of contact in late 1951 found U.N. forces controlling areas that were mostly just north of the parallel; both sides thereafter engaged in relatively small-scale fighting and concentrated on strengthening the defense of areas already under their control.

The POW issue proved the most intractable. At the beginning of the war, both sides had announced adherence to the Geneva Convention of 1949, which included the provision that POWs should be "released and repatriated without delay after the cessation of hostilities." Such an "all-for-all" exchange meant that the United Nations would return about 150,000 North Korean and Chinese POWs while the Communist side would repatriate some 12,000 U.N. POWs. Some U.S. officials questioned whether "all-for-all" served U.S. interests. Strategically, it meant that North Korean and Chinese armies would be strengthened in ways that might destabilize the balance of power on the Korean peninsula. More important, however, was a moral concern. The Chinese "volunteers" included Chinese Nationalist troops who had been forced into service, and the North Koreans had impressed South Korean soldiers as well as civilians into their army. The "all-for-all" practice would have obliged the United Nations to practice "forcible repatriation"—sending thousands of men, estimated at almost one-third of the United Nations–held POWs—to "return" to governments for which they had fought involuntarily. The moral concern merged with a psychological one. If repatriation of POWs were "voluntary," it was expected that tens of thousands of Chinese and North Korean POWs would refuse to return to their governments, which would be a significant propaganda victory for the United Nations.

U.S. officials were deeply divided. While many believed that the moral and psychological benefits should lead the United States to insist on voluntary repatriation of the POWs, others, including (at least initially) Acheson and Ridgway, favored the all-for-all approach, even if it meant forcible repatriation. They gave priority to effecting a cease-fire quickly and, in the process, getting American and other U.N. POWs released as soon as possible.

On this issue, Truman's position was decisive. He opposed forcible repatriation on moral grounds. He stated publicly that it "would be unthinkable. It would be repugnant to the fundamental moral and humanitarian principles which underlie our actions in Korea." This stance won popular support.

With the United States insisting on the principle of voluntary repatriation, the POW issue prolonged the negotiations. When Truman left office on January 20, 1953, the war still had not ended. Six weeks later, the death of Stalin brought to power a new leadership in Moscow, which undertook a "peace offensive" to improve relations with the West and, as part of that campaign, renewed pressure on the Chinese and North Koreans to bring the Korean conflict to an end. Also, Truman's successor, Dwight Eisenhower, threatened through diplomatic channels to broaden the war against China directly (implicitly including nuclear weapons) unless the Communist negotiators accepted new proposals to resolve the POW issue. In any event, the Chinese and North Koreans accepted the U.N. position on repatriation. The conflict finally ended with the signing, on July 27, 1953, of an armistice that divided Korea at the cease-fire line and provided for the voluntary repatriation of POWs. The American insistence on that principle protected from forced repatriation 22,600 Chinese and North Korean prisoners held by the U.N. Command (and 359 U.N. prisoners held by the Communists), who chose not to be repatriated.*

So, THREE YEARS after he had taken the United States to war in Korea, the now retired Truman saw his objectives realized. Americans do not usually think of the Korean stalemate as a victory, but limited wars must be measured by their modest objectives. The restoration of the division of Korea constituted victory as U.N. objectives were defined

---

*In the end, the United Nations returned 75,823 North Korean and Chinese POWs in exchange for 12,773 United Nations–held POWs (including 3,597 Americans). The vast majority of nonrepatriates were Chinese. Among the 359 U.N. prisoners held by the Chinese or North Koreans who declined repatriation were 23 Americans.

in the June 1950 U.N. Security Council resolutions and then restated after the Chinese intervention. As Truman calculated in taking the country to war, the Korean War had broad international implications, and
on that level the United States secured a strategic victory as well. According to the historian William Stueck:

> That victory extended well beyond Korea itself, as the demonstration of
> willingness and an ability to combat "aggression" combined with the mili-
> tary build-up at home and in western Europe to deter such action elsewhere.
> For the long term, the strains placed on the Sino-Soviet alliance could not
> help but benefit the United States. In its competition with the Soviet Union,
> the United States certainly emerged the overall winner.

The strengths of Truman's leadership were in the decisions for war
itself and for a restoration of the prewar division of the peninsula.
Those were sound decisions. The failures were in prolonging the war
by the movement of U.N. forces across the thirty-eighth parallel, disregarding diplomatic concerns and initiatives at the United Nations, and
dismissing China's warnings and show of force. Had Truman embraced
any of several alternatives to the pursuit of unification through military
means, China's intervention would probably have been averted and the
objectives incorporated in the July 1953 armistice could well have been
attained by the fall of 1950.

At every step as commander in chief, Truman allowed decisions to
flow from the course of events. The price for this reactive decision making was not only an extended war but also the diminishing of America's
international stature. Truman's decision to advance into North Korea
and to pursue unification was driven by the success of the Inchon landing and reinforced by pressures from within his own administration
and strong popular sentiment. To have halted the U.N. army at the
thirty-eighth parallel or, later, to have stopped the U.N. advance short of
the Yalu River and accepted a buffer of some sort would have required
courage based on a sensitivity to international opinion and to China's
understandable concerns. The situation called for statesmanship and a
willingness to risk criticism at home for exercising restraint. Truman
lacked the political insight and failed to receive the advice that would
have led him to approach this important decision with a full appreciation of its international ramifications.

Truman's decision to accept a limited war was determined by the
startling Chinese intervention, which American officials had managed

to convince themselves would be irrational, despite abundant evidence throughout October and November of 1950 that the Chinese thought otherwise. The decision to dismiss MacArthur was taken only after repeated acts of insubordination; delay only postponed an unpleasant political episode as the world's wariness of American leadership intensified. Truman's most significant public acts—the Wake Island conference of October 15 and the threat of atomic weapons at the November 30 press conference—showed an impulsiveness that was no substitute for measured leadership.

Throughout much of the war, Truman suffered from poor advice, notably from Acheson (who acknowledges the point in his memoir) and Marshall. They and others shared Truman's tendency to avoid difficult questions and (until the Chinese intervention) to trust MacArthur's judgment. The result was that it was not until MacArthur's dismissal that Truman asserted firm diplomatic and military direction to the war. By that time, however, his credibility had suffered irreparable damage at home and the United States had lost considerable stature internationally.

The perspectives of several decades have diminished the international and domestic disappointments of the last two years of the Truman presidency. Eventually, historians and the American public came to hold Truman in higher esteem than did his contemporaries and to see the Korean War, despite all the inconsistencies and indecision, as necessary and successful. Those judgments are sound. Yet more prudent leadership from the White House would have achieved comparable results in Korea at far less human cost and without the erosion of international confidence in American leadership.

"America keeps her word"

LYNDON B. JOHNSON, from the grim day when the assassination of John F. Kennedy thrust him into the presidency, confronted a crisis in Vietnam. Had he lived, Kennedy would have told a Dallas audience on November 22, 1963, that Americans "dare not weary of the task [of assisting peoples] confronted directly or indirectly with the threat of Communist aggression." His undelivered text went on to list nine vulnerable "key countries"—headed by Vietnam. There the American-fostered government of South Vietnam was threatened by a communist-led insurgency, which received support from North Vietnam.

To Americans, the world seemed as dangerous in 1963 as it had been in 1950 when the Korean crisis had led to an agonizing three-year war. Indeed, the cold war had entered what can now be seen as its most dangerous phase. The Soviet-American crises over Berlin in 1958 and 1961, which had led to the construction of the Berlin Wall, had been followed by a tense showdown in October 1962, resulting from the U.S. determination to prevent the deployment of Soviet missiles in Cuba. To American officials, the most intractable threat posed by the Soviet Union and the Chinese People's Republic (CPR), under the leadership of Premiers Nikita Khrushchev and Mao Tse-tung, respectively, was the capacity of the communist powers to exert influence in developing nations. There the challenge to Western political and economic interests went beyond diplomatic initiatives, economic assistance, and propaganda; it included communist-led guerrilla movements—"wars of national liberation"—against established governments.

South and Southeast Asia—the vast area surrounding much of China and stretching from the Indian subcontinent in the west to the Philippine Islands in the east and the Indonesian archipelago in the south—had become a focus of this struggle. U.S. policy was driven by the assumption that a stridently anti-Western and bellicose Chinese People's Republic—always labeled Communist China at the time—was poised to expand its influence over the region. Ever since the Korean War, the United States had sought to isolate the CPR diplomatically, economically, and militarily. The United States refused to recognize the CPR as the legitimate government of China, thus precluding formal diplomatic relations, and steadfastly opposed its admission to the United Nations. Instead, the United States maintained diplomatic relations with the Chinese Nationalist government that had taken refuge on the island of Taiwan when the communists seized control of the mainland in 1949. The United States imposed a boycott on trade with the CPR and built a system of military alliances with nations on its periphery; Pakistan, Thailand, the Philippines, Taiwan, South Korea, South Vietnam, and Japan were all linked to the American security system.

By the 1960s, the struggle in Vietnam was seen as the test of whether the United States could meet the challenge of a "war of national liberation" and hold its position in the developing world. As in Korea, a relatively small country—Vietnam is about the size of the state of New Mexico—took on global significance. American officials believed that Vietnam, which is located on the east coast of the Indochinese peninsula, with China on its northern frontier, was the vital link in determining the future of South and Southeast Asia.

Like the crisis in Korea, that in Vietnam had its origins in the great changes of the mid–twentieth century: World War II, the rise of nationalism, and the cold war. As a prelude to its conquest of Southeast Asia after the attack on the U.S. base at Pearl Harbor, Japan had occupied French Indochina, which included Vietnam, Laos, and Cambodia. During World War II, the communist-led Viet Minh emerged as the dominant expression of Vietnamese nationalism. When Japan abruptly surrendered in August 1945, the Viet Minh quickly asserted control over the country. On September 2, 1945, Ho Chi Minh, the longtime leader of the Vietnamese communist movement, proclaimed independence in the name of the Democratic Republic of Vietnam (DRV). France, however, attempted to restore its authority, ultimately resorting to force.

In the ensuing eight-year war, the Viet Minh relied on guerrilla tactics to counter the better-armed French. During that conflict, the United States first became involved in Vietnam as it began to provide equipment and funding for the French military effort and recognized the legitimacy of the French-controlled, nominally independent government, which was intended to draw support away from the Viet Minh. Despite substantial U.S. support, France failed to defeat the elusive Viet Minh and, facing war weariness at home, sought to negotiate an end to its Indochina venture. An extended Viet Minh siege of the French outpost at Dien Bien Phu in the mountainous terrain of northern Vietnam led to a humiliating French surrender in May 1954.

At a conference in Geneva that summer, the major powers reached agreements that ended the war and the French empire in Indochina. Laos, Cambodia, and Vietnam were granted independence. Vietnam, however, was temporarily divided: the DRV (which came to be commonly called North Vietnam, with its capital at Hanoi) was restored to power north of the seventeenth parallel, while the remnants of the French regime controlled the south. Reunification elections, under international supervision, were to be held in 1956. Those elections would certainly have resulted in unification under the communists, for the Viet Minh had led the struggle for independence and the vast majority of Vietnamese looked upon Ho Chi Minh as the preeminent voice of their aspirations.

Into this situation stepped the United States, which had declined to endorse the Geneva agreements.* Determined to "hold the line" against further communist advance, President Dwight D. Eisenhower and Secretary of State John Foster Dulles supported the establishment of an independent, noncommunist government in the southern zone and of a multinational regional alliance, the Southeast Asia Treaty Organization (SEATO).

Through extensive military and economic assistance as well as covert operations undertaken by the Central Intelligence Agency (CIA), the United States committed its resources and prestige to the Republic of Vietnam (commonly called South Vietnam, with its capital at Saigon), which was headed by Ngo Dinh Diem, an anticommunist nationalist who had a scant following among Vietnamese. By the late 1950s, a renewed communist-led insurgency, commonly called the Viet Cong, challenged the authority of the Diem government and gained strength in the rural areas of South Vietnam. To Ho Chi Minh and other North Vietnamese leaders, unification remained the overriding objective. Ac-

---

*The major decisions at the Geneva conference were made by France, the United Kingdom, the Soviet Union, and the Chinese People's Republic. Although represented at the conference, the United States distanced itself from the negotiations because it feared a settlement that would lead to a communist-dominated Vietnam and it wanted to keep the communist powers uncertain of its plans. At the end of the conference, the United States issued an ambiguous statement, pledging that it would "refrain from the threat or the use of force to disturb the agreements" and support the unification of nations "divided against their will . . . through free elections supervised by the United Nations [to] insure that they are conducted fairly." Then, after noting the opposition of the remnants of the French regime in the south to the agreements, the United States "affirmed its traditional position that peoples are entitled to determine their own future." This seemed tantamount to a rejection of the Geneva settlement.

cordingly, they supported the Viet Minh and the establishment of the National Liberation Front (NLF) as the communist-led political movement. To assist the southern insurgency, North Vietnam sent supplies and cadres across the demilitarized zone, which divided the two Vietnamese governments, and down a series of paths and trails that wound through the mountains and jungles of Laos and Cambodia into South Vietnam, which came to be known as the Ho Chi Minh Trail.

By the time that John F. Kennedy became president in 1961, the American nation-building effort in South Vietnam was unraveling. Kennedy responded by dramatically increasing American presence and power. He authorized an increase in the number of U.S. military advisers from fewer than six hundred in 1960 to more than sixteen thousand by 1963. The American effort concentrated on support of an expanded South Vietnamese army counterinsurgency campaign. Kennedy's determination was unequivocal. In his 1962 State of the Union address, he asserted that "the systematic aggression now bleeding that country is not a 'war of national liberation'—for Vietnam is already free. It is a war of attempted subjugation—and it will be resisted." Although Kennedy increased U.S. involvement substantially, he rejected recommendations for a direct U.S. military role. As he stated publicly: "It is their war. They are the ones who have to win it or lose it. We can help them . . . but they have to win it—the people of Vietnam—against the Communists."

Despite U.S. support, the Diem government steadily lost ground, and not just to the Viet Cong. Diem's authoritarianism led to protests and a simmering rebellion in Saigon, Hue, and other cities, which was led, not by communists, but by the Buddhist community, the largest religious group in the country. When Diem suppressed Buddhist protests, American officials came to believe that fresh leadership could salvage a stable South Vietnam. With Kennedy's tacit approval, CIA agents provided covert support to military officers, led by Gen. Duong Van Minh, who plotted Diem's overthrow. Hence, it was with American complicity that a military junta engineered a coup in early November 1963, which ended with the assassination of Diem. Three weeks later, another assassination made Johnson president.

Beginning in 1950 as modest diplomatic and financial support of France and growing into a substantial commitment by 1963, the U.S. involvement in Vietnam that Johnson inherited was based on three related assumptions. First, Vietnam was considered vital to shielding South and Southeast Asia from Chinese-Soviet expansion. This belief found expression in the often-cited "domino theory." Communist control of Vietnam, it was believed by U.S. officials, would trigger a chain reaction, resulting in the ascendancy of communism throughout the region. President Eisenhower offered the classic statement of this reasoning when he talked of "falling dominoes" in Asia. Speaking in 1954, Eisenhower foresaw that communist control of Indochina would lead to the "loss . . . of Burma, of Thailand, of the [Malay] Peninsula, and Indonesia . . . [and] the loss of materials, sources of materials [and] . . . millions and millions of people. The possible consequences of the loss are just incalculable to the free world." Americans did not anticipate a military conquest, but rather a political one, in which pro-Western and neutral countries would come to see communism as the wave of the future and thus would turn toward communist leadership. Such a shift of the political balance in South and Southeast Asia would benefit the Soviet Union and the Chinese People's Republic and would deprive the United States, its European allies, and Japan of access to an important source of raw materials and a potentially profitable market. That communist victory in Vietnam would necessarily have such dire implications beyond that country was, of course, uncertain, but U.S. officials refused to risk that it would not tip the scales in the region against the West.

Reinforcing the imperative of preventing "falling dominoes" was a second assumption: American "credibility" was on the line. Once the United States established its foothold in South Vietnam, holding that position became an end itself and was justified as a test of American will and determination. Whenever the United States increased its assistance or sent more advisers, it also put more of its prestige on the line, making it more difficult to withdraw. Vietnam as a measure of credibility was thus far more important in 1963 than it had been a decade or even three years earlier. "Credibility" had global significance. Failure to stand by an ally, policymakers feared, would erode America's international stature, for adversaries would be emboldened to act aggressively and friends would lose confidence in America's word.

Finally, linked to the "domino" and "credibility" assumptions was a third: that U.S. resistance to communist expansion would "nip aggression in the bud" and prevent a larger war. Like Truman in confronting the Korean and other crises, his successors saw communist advances within the framework of the powerful "lesson" of the 1930s: that the failure to halt the initial phases of aggression by Nazi Germany, Japan, and Italy had only encouraged further aggression and ultimately led to World War II. The containment of the Soviet Union and the Chinese People's Republic, the sending of troops to fight in Korea, the firm stand during crises over Berlin and Soviet missiles in Cuba, and other cold war measures all were seen by Americans as avoiding the mistakes of the past. In this way of looking at the world, Ho Chi Minh's movement to unify Vietnam was considered not an expression of nationalism, but rather another instance of piecemeal communist aggression, which required a firm U.S. response. Adlai Stevenson, the two-time Democratic Party presidential candidate and ambassador to the United Nations from 1961 to 1965, stated it succinctly: "The point is the same in Vietnam as it was in Greece in 1947 and Korea in 1950."

Johnson accepted these assumptions about Vietnam's strategic importance. While vice president, Johnson visited South Vietnam in 1961 and strongly identified with the American mission. His report to Kennedy linked "domino" and "credibility" thinking, as he warned that "the basic decision in Southeast Asia is here. We must decide whether to help these countries to the best of our ability or throw in the towel in the area and pull back our defenses to San Francisco and a 'Fortress America' concept. More important, we would say to the world in this case that we don't live up to treaties and don't stand by friends."

AS HE ASSUMED the presidency, Johnson quickly took control of Vietnam policy. That Johnson asserted strong leadership on Vietnam (and other issues inherited from his predecessor) was not surprising to anyone who had followed his rise in American politics. When he became president upon the death of his predecessor, he had none of the self-doubt and sense of being overwhelmed by problems that Truman had expressed under similar circumstances eighteen years earlier. Indeed, the fifty-five-year-old Johnson was remarkably self-confident, an outgrowth of a quarter-century's political success driven by the single ambition of one day becoming president.

He had come a long way from his modest origins in the hill country of central Texas. After graduating from Southwest Texas State Teachers College and briefly teaching high school speech, he went into politics, beginning as secretary to a congressman and, within a few years, winning, at age twenty-nine, his own seat in the House of Representatives. Aside from military duty during World War II, he served in Congress from 1937 until he became vice president in 1961. After being elected to the Senate in 1948, he became one of the dominant figures in that body, serving as majority leader during the last six years of the Eisenhower administration. After Kennedy won the 1960 Democratic Party presidential nomination, which Johnson had also sought, Kennedy unexpectedly offered Johnson the vice presidential nomination and Johnson, just as unexpectedly, accepted it.

Throughout his career, Johnson combined strong, at times impassioned, convictions with the art of compromise. He identified with the liberal reform tradition of one of his mentors, Franklin D. Roosevelt, and mastered the give-and-take of politics. In his successful legislative career, Johnson had a remarkable capacity to cajole, intimidate, and compromise to attain his objectives. He had come to believe that all problems were subject to rational discourse. One close adviser later observed: "LBJ really believed that if he applied his total intellect and concentration to a problem and if there was any alternative possible, he would find a way to an agreement. In all his career his reliance on reason and face-to-face challenge had never failed. He had no doubts that it would succeed in Vietnam."

Upon becoming president, Johnson kept the team of foreign policy advisers that he inherited from Kennedy. Most influential were Secretary of State Dean Rusk and Secretary of Defense Robert McNamara. Behind the deliberative and low-keyed style of Rusk, a Rhodes Scholar who had served as assistant secretary of state for Far Eastern affairs during the Korean War and as director of the Rockefeller Foundation before Kennedy named him secretary of state, was a steely determination. Coming from a humble Southern background like Johnson's, Rusk earned Johnson's respect; "He's a damned good man," Johnson said, "hard-working, bright and loyal as a beagle. You'll never catch him working at cross purposes with his president."

At the beginning of his presidency, Johnson held McNamara in similar esteem. Kennedy had tapped the brilliant president of the Ford Motor Company to revolutionize the cumbersome Defense Department through the application of management principles drawn from the business world. With the technocrat's faith in precise measures of performance, McNamara had masterminded the growing U.S. involvement in Vietnam during the Kennedy administration and confidently told a reporter in 1963 that "every quantifiable measurement we have shows that we're winning the war."

In addition to Rusk and McNamara, Johnson also relied heavily on the advice of McGeorge Bundy and Maxwell Taylor. Renowned as one of Kennedy's "action intellectuals," Bundy had left a deanship at Harvard to serve in the key position of the president's special assistant for national security affairs. Taylor, the chairman of the Joint Chiefs of Staff (JCS), enjoyed similar renown. His influential book, *An Uncertain Trumpet*, which criticized Eisenhower's national security policy, helped elevate Taylor to the distinction of being known as Kennedy's "favorite general."

In formulating his foreign policy, Johnson typically relied a good deal on informal consultation with these officials and a few others. He rarely summoned the National Security Council. Johnson's decision making was paradoxical in that it was both open and controlled. He seemed to be solicitous of advice, seeking a wide range of opinions. In some situations, he had a tendency to say what a particular individual or group wanted to hear—a practice that may be attributed to his skills in the art of compromise. At other times, especially with his staff, he would become an intimidating figure, and those around him learned that challenging his position required courage and risked chastisement.

While Johnson publicly made "let us continue" the dominant theme of his early presidency, in the case of Vietnam he immediately asserted privately what one adviser saw as a "Johnson tone"—a shift from a political and toward a military emphasis. Meeting with several advisers two days after the assassination, he criticized U.S. complicity in Diem's overthrow, which he characterized as part of a mistaken effort to remake Asians "in our own image" through emphasis on "so-called social reforms." Rather, he insisted that the principal effort needed to be military: "to win the war." Toward that end, he demanded a united "country team" of military and political officials in Vietnam with the ambassador firmly in charge; he wanted none of the "serious dissensions and divisions . . . [and] bickering" of the previous administration. Shortly afterward, he approved a program of expanded covert military operations and intelligence gathering directed against North Vietnam.

Johnson considered Vietnam "our most critical military area right now," a situation aggravated by the "indecision and drifting" of the new South Vietnamese leadership. Johnson and other U.S. officials welcomed a second coup in January 1964, which brought to power another group of generals headed by Gen. Nguyen Khanh. Johnson seized upon Khanh as the leader who would stabilize South Vietnam and reinvigorate the counterinsurgency campaign. Telling advisers that "we must make General Khanh 'our boy' and proclaim the fact to all and sundry," he instructed them to give "prompt and sympathetic responses" to requests for more assistance to South Vietnam and to speed up "contingency plans for pressures against North Vietnam."

As he pressed the South Vietnamese for a more vigorous military course, Johnson rejected the alternative of a negotiated settlement. The growing number of critics of U.S. involvement believed that Johnson should be working toward withdrawal from a chaotic political situation. Johnson's successor as Senate majority leader, Mike Mansfield (D.-Mont.), who enjoyed wide respect on foreign policy issues, wrote to Johnson on several occasions, consistently urging the pursuit of an international agreement providing for the neutralization of Vietnam, Laos, and Cambodia. Mansfield warned Johnson that the United States was drifting toward a land war on the Asian mainland and a substantial risk of conflict with China. Meanwhile, on the international front, French President Charles DeGaulle and Prince Norodom Sihanouk of Cambodia proposed a diplomatic initiative leading to the neutralization of Vietnam. Johnson, along with nearly all of his advisers, however, dismissed such suggestions, believing that American withdrawal would inevitably lead to communist domination.

Domestic political considerations also influenced Johnson's determination to prevent a communist victory in Vietnam. He feared that a "loss" in Vietnam would trigger a conservative backlash; he was haunted by memories of how charges of "losing China" had contributed to Truman's political demise. Johnson anticipated that the presidential election of 1964 would give him a mandate for the most far-reaching domestic reform since Roosevelt's New Deal. He needed to make certain that the problems in Vietnam did not destroy the consensus for civil rights legislation, the war on poverty, and the building of what he would term the Great Society.

So, as Johnson concentrated on the domestic agenda, he never equivocated on his commitment to the survival of South Vietnam. Before various audiences, he spoke of a critical U.S. interest, typically dwelling on the commitment that he had inherited from Eisenhower and Kennedy, which recognized Vietnam's global implications in terms of preventing "falling dominoes," meeting the challenge of counterinsurgency, and upholding credibility. He summarized the essential argument succinctly: "It may be helpful to outline four basic themes that govern our policy in Southeast Asia. First, America keeps her word. Second, the issue is the future of Southeast Asia as a whole. Third, our purpose is peace. Fourth, this is not a jungle war, but a struggle for freedom on every front of human activity."

As political chaos enveloped Saigon and the communist insurgency gained ground, Johnson compulsively sought a solution. In the spring of 1964, he repeatedly dispatched high-ranking officials to South Vietnam. Rusk went twice, as did the team of McNamara and Taylor, and each mission provided grim assessments. The CIA added its stark projection of an "extremely fragile" South Vietnam where, "if the tide of deterioration has not been arrested by the end of the year, the anti-Communist position in South Vietnam is likely to become untenable."

A depressed Johnson lamented privately to his longtime friend and mentor, Democratic Senator Richard Russell of Georgia, that Vietnam was "the biggest damn mess I ever saw." He dreaded sending young men to fight in Vietnam, but he said there was no choice but to persevere. His dilemma was simple: "I don't think it's worth fighting for, and I don't think we can get out."

As both his public utterances and private ruminations pointed toward a direct U.S. military role, Johnson contemplated whether congressional authorization would be necessary. The State Department assured him that his powers as commander in chief enabled him to deploy forces overseas and that membership in SEATO obliged the United States to defend South Vietnam.* While contending that the president could act on his own, the State Department nonetheless drafted a congressional resolution—for presentation if deemed appropriate—that would authorize the president to take any measures to prevent the loss of South Vietnam.

To underline his commitment to South Vietnam, Johnson strengthened the U.S. political-military leadership in Saigon, beginning with the appointment of General Taylor as ambassador. Taylor replaced Henry Cabot Lodge, who had returned to America to pursue the Republican Party's presidential nomination. While Lodge's resignation deprived Johnson of the political advantage of having a prominent Republican identified with U.S. policy in Vietnam, it also enabled him to

---

*Whether membership in SEATO in itself committed the United States to the defense of South Vietnam was unclear. The terms of the 1954 agreement establishing SEATO provided that, in the event of aggression against any member or any other country protected by SEATO (which included South Vietnam), each member would "act to meet the common danger in accordance with its constitutional processes." That would seem to suggest that congressional authorization was necessary before U.S. forces could be committed.

appoint a renowned military officer to this key position, which showed his determination to carry the war to the enemy. Johnson believed that Taylor would provide strong "country team" leadership. The other essential part of the "team" was Gen. William Westmoreland, whom Johnson named commander of the U.S. Military Assistance Command. Shortly after his arrival in Saigon, Taylor, at Westmoreland's request, urged increasing the number of U.S. military advisers in South Vietnam by about forty-two hundred over the next several months, which would bring the total of American "advisory" personnel to twenty-two thousand. Johnson quickly approved.

Then, as the U.S. military presence was quietly escalating, a "crisis" in the Gulf of Tonkin electrified Americans. On the afternoon of Sunday, August 2, three North Vietnamese patrol boats fired upon the U.S. destroyer *Maddox* in the Gulf of Tonkin off the coast of North Vietnam. The *Maddox*, which (according to the official explanation) was on "routine patrol," sustained negligible damage, but it returned fire, and together with aircraft from the nearby carrier *Ticonderoga* sunk one and damaged two of the patrol boats.

Johnson summoned Rusk, McNamara, and JCS Chairman Gen. Earl Wheeler for a tense meeting at the White House. They agreed to issue a strongly worded protest note to North Vietnam, which warned of "the grave consequences which would inevitably result from any further unprovoked offensive military action against United States forces." Johnson also decided to enlarge naval patrols in the Gulf of Tonkin; another destroyer, the *C. Turner Joy,* was ordered to join the *Maddox.*

Then, on the evening of August 4, the North Vietnamese seemingly engaged in another "unprovoked military action." In the darkness of the Gulf of Tonkin, the *Maddox* reported an imminent attack from nearby vessels and radar detected unidentified surface vessels and aircraft. Fighter aircraft took off from the USS *Ticonderoga* to protect the *Maddox* and *C. Turner Joy.* Shortly afterward, the *Maddox* indicated that the aircraft had disappeared from the radar screen and that the surface vessels were at a distance.

When classified reports reached Washington (the second "incident" not yet being publicly known), they touched off a frantic day of meetings and hurried decisions. Johnson and his advisers agreed that the United States had to react militarily with a "firm, swift retaliatory strike" against North Vietnam. As the JCS prepared for an attack, a cautionary report from the commander of the *Maddox* suggested a "'complete evaluation' of the situation be undertaken before any further action," since his review of the evidence raised questions of whether there had been any contacts with North Vietnamese ships and whether any torpedoes had been fired at the *Maddox*. After a cursory review that fell far short of a "complete evaluation," McNamara concluded that there was sufficient evidence of an attack. He glossed over any questions regarding the "incident" when he later met with the National Security Council and then with congressional leaders. At the latter meeting, Johnson gained unequivocal backing for military retaliation and for a congressional resolution supporting his actions.

After word reached Washington at 11:20 P.M. that planes had taken off to carry out the attack on North Vietnam, a solemn Johnson spoke to the American public from the White House. As millions watched on television, he summarized the events in the Gulf of Tonkin and the response: "Air action is now in execution against gunboats and certain supporting facilities in North Vietnam." He cast the attack on U.S. vessels within the framework of the struggle for South Vietnam: "Aggression by terror against the peaceful villagers of South Vietnam has now been joined by open aggression on the high seas against the United States." American determination to support South Vietnam would be "redoubled by this outrage," Johnson said, and the response, "for the present, will be limited and fitting. . . . We still seek no wider war."

Still, Johnson had widened the war. As he spoke, the United States unleashed, for the first time, direct military power in Vietnam. From the aircraft carriers *Ticonderoga* and *Constellation*, bombers flew sixty-four sorties against four North Vietnamese patrol boat bases and oil storage facilities.

The next day, Johnson sent Congress the grandiosely labeled Joint Resolution to Promote the Maintenance of International Peace and Security in Southeast Asia. It quickly became known simply as the Gulf of Tonkin resolution. A revised version of the draft resolution that the State Department had prepared a few weeks earlier, it was brief, simple, and open-ended. Charging North Vietnam with having "deliberately and repeatedly attacked US naval vessels lawfully present in international waters" and that "these attacks are part of a deliberate and systematic campaign of aggression that the Communist regime of North Vietnam has been waging against its neighbors," the resolution affirmed that Congress "approves and supports the determination of the president, as Commander in Chief, to take all necessary steps to repel any armed attack against the forces of the United States and to prevent further aggression." Finally, the resolution authorized the president "to take all necessary steps, including the use of armed force, to protect any [SEATO] member or protocol state . . . requesting assistance in defense of its freedom."

In the crisis atmosphere that gripped the nation, Congress hastily and uncritically approved the resolution. With Johnson urging congressional leaders to act quickly to assure the maximum international effect, Senator J. William Fulbright (D.-Ark.), the powerful and respected chairman of the Foreign Relations Committee, and other leaders in the Senate and House of Representatives guided the measure through Congress.

There was no challenge to the White House version of events in the Gulf of Tonkin, and only a few members of Congress questioned the necessity of giving the president the authority to wage a wider war. Republican Senator John Sherman Cooper of Kentucky asked pointedly: "Then, looking ahead, if the president decided it was necessary to use such force as could lead to war, we will give that authority by this resolution?" Fulbright replied: "That is the way I would interpret it." Senator Gaylord Nelson (D.-Wis.) futilely proposed an amendment indicating that Congress opposed extending the conflict or sending U.S. forces into combat. The most outspoken critics were Democratic Senators Ernest Gruening of Alaska and Wayne Morse of Oregon. Gruening warned of "sending our boys into combat in a war in which we have no business. . . . I am opposed to sacrificing a single American boy in this venture. We have lost far too many already." And in a strident statement, Morse foresaw "that history will record that we have made a great mistake in subverting and circumventing the Constitution of the United States. . . . We are in effect giving the president . . . war-making powers in the absence of a declaration of war. I believe that to be a historic mistake."

In the end, Congress swept aside such concerns and overwhelmingly embraced Johnson's request to send an unequivocal warning to North Vietnam. The Gulf of Tonkin resolution was approved unanimously (416 to 0) by the House of Representatives and nearly so in the Senate, where only Gruening and Morse cast negative votes while eighty-eight of their colleagues voted in favor.

Besides congressional support, Johnson also received strong popular backing. Opinion polls revealed that 85 percent of the public supported the air strikes against North Vietnam. Editorials in newspapers throughout the country praised Johnson. Johnson's "approval rating" soared by thirty points to 72 percent—his highest since the early days of his presidency.

Unknown to Congress and the public, which uncritically supported Johnson, were the details of the Gulf of Tonkin incidents. The Johnson administration concealed the context of these bizarre events. Earlier in 1964, Johnson had sanctioned secret operations against North Vietnam. The U.S. Navy and CIA, together with South Vietnamese military units, had engaged in covert warfare and electronic surveillance, which had included a raid along the North Vietnamese coast in late July. The North Vietnamese patrol boat "attack" of August 2 probably was undertaken as retaliation against ships that the North Vietnamese associated (incorrectly but not unreasonably) with the raids of a few days earlier. The *Maddox*'s "routine patrol" had, in fact, been to conduct electronic surveillance of North Vietnamese military installations. Last, the Johnson administration never acknowledged the uncertainty of the August 4 "attack." Even Johnson privately admitted a few days later his own doubts about the events of August 4; he told an adviser: "Hell, those dumb, stupid sailors were just shooting at flying fish."

To Johnson, the lack of candor was justified by the opportunity to assert U.S. power in a way that would send a warning to North Vietnam and would reassure South Vietnam of American support. Besides those "messages" to North and South Vietnam, Johnson's action served a third purpose: to silence criticism of his Vietnam policy during the 1964 presidential campaign. The Republican presidential nominee, Senator Barry Goldwater of Arizona, repeatedly charged that Johnson was failing to meet the communist challenge in Vietnam. Through the air raid and resolution, Johnson seemed to be exercising strength tempered by restraint. The United States would fulfill its commitments, Johnson was saying, but would not go to war. Democrats capitalized on Goldwater's belligerent rhetoric to portray him as an irresponsible, trigger-happy candidate who would plunge the country into war in Vietnam. In the ensuing campaign, Johnson was thus able to stand as the candidate of "peace" and assure audiences that he had no intention of sending "American boys nine or ten thousand miles away from home to do what Asian boys ought to be doing for themselves." On November 3, Johnson won the presidential election in a landslide.

Johnson's assurances to the public notwithstanding, he privately anticipated the likelihood of greater U.S. military involvement. Reports from Saigon indicated that the Viet Cong were intensifying their guerrilla warfare against a South Vietnamese government whose leadership was increasingly fragmented. While continuing attacks against the South Vietnamese government, the Viet Cong begun targeting assaults against the growing American presence. On Saturday, October 31— three days before the presidential election—the Viet Cong attacked the U.S. air base at Bien-hoa, leaving four Americans dead and thirty wounded. A few weeks later, on December 24, the Viet Cong bombed the Brinks Hotel in Saigon, which housed U.S. military personnel, leaving two Americans dead and fifty injured. The National Security Council (NSC) Working Group on Vietnam, which Johnson had appointed to review policy options, proposed "a slow, controlled squeeze on North Vietnam" through a systematic, escalating bombing campaign. Rusk, Bundy, and McNamara told Johnson that they favored planning for such a bombing campaign.

While concurring with that recommendation, Johnson doubted whether warfare against North Vietnam would remedy the chronic political instability in South Vietnam. In a rambling discussion with advisers, Johnson lamented that there was "no point hitting North if South not together. . . . Why not say 'This is it!' Not send Johnson City boys out to die if they are acting as they are. . . . Day of reckoning is coming. Want to be sure we've done everything we can. Got to be some things still to do. What? We could have kept Diem."

Determined to hold a disintegrating South Vietnam and skeptical of a bombing campaign, Johnson soon concluded that the introduction of U.S. ground troops into South Vietnam was the only way to combat the Viet Cong. In essence, if the South Vietnamese government and army could not bring political stability, the Americans would have to do the job. In a pointed December 30 message to Taylor, an impatient Johnson demanded a broadening of strategic planning:

> Every time I get a military recommendation it seems to me that it calls for large-scale bombing. I have never felt that this war will be won from the air, and it seems to me that what is much more needed and would be more effective is a larger and stronger use of Rangers and Special Forces and Marines, or other appropriate military strength on the ground and on the scene. I am ready to look with great favor on the kind of increased American effort, directed at the guerrillas and aimed to stiffen the aggressiveness of

Vietnamese military units up and down the line. Any recommendation that you or General Westmoreland make in this sense will have immediate attention from me, although I know that it may involve the acceptance of larger American sacrifice. We have been building our strength to fight this kind of war ever since 1961, and I myself am ready to substantially increase the number of Americans in Vietnam if it is necessary to provide this kind of fighting force against the Viet Cong.

Johnson's anticipation of a ground war astonished his advisers. McNamara, in his memoir, recalls that "this suggestion for large-scale deployment of U.S. ground forces came from out of the blue." It troubled Taylor, who immediately warned Johnson of the enormity of the task that he was proposing. The growing strength of the Viet Cong (estimated at 100,000)—coupled with their logistical support from North Vietnam and their capacity to exploit the instability in the south—made it a formidable foe. "I do not recall in history," Taylor advised, "a successful anti-guerrilla campaign with less than a 10 to 1 numerical superiority over the guerrillas and without the elimination of assistance from outside the country." To Taylor, the appropriate course was to launch air warfare against North Vietnam as a means of pressuring Hanoi to end its support of the southern insurgency. Johnson concurred that "we are going to have reprisals [because they] may help to give [South Vietnam] more stability," but he doubted whether bombing would be sufficient.

The political chaos in South Vietnam—what Taylor described on January 6, 1965, as a "seriously deteriorating situation [marked by] chronic factionalism, civilian-military suspicion and distrust, absence of national spirit and motivation"—threatened the very survival of the Saigon government. On January 9, the military government, which had been in power for less than four months, yielded authority to civilian leadership under Premier Troung Van Huong. That government lasted just eighteen days; on January 27 Gen. Nguyen Khanh again seized power in a bloodless coup. It was the third time in a year of Saigon's confusing coups and countercoups that General Khanh had taken power. American officials feared that Khanh, together with Buddhist leaders, who had supported his return, would pursue negotiations with the National Liberation Front.

To Johnson and other officials, the unraveling of the South Vietnamese government made an American military role imperative. Johnson seized upon Khanh's return, telling his advisers that "Khanh was our boy" and "stable government or no stable government, we'll do what we ought to do. I'm prepared to do that." McNamara and Bundy agreed. "Our current policy can lead only to disastrous defeat," they wrote to Johnson, "wait[ing] and hop[ing] for a stable government . . . [an] essentially passive role which can only lead to eventual defeat and an invitation to get out in humiliating circumstances." Johnson cabled Taylor on January 27: "I am determined to make it clear to all the world that the U.S. will spare no effort and no sacrifice in doing its full part to turn back the communists in Vietnam."

Within a few days, Johnson was fulfilling that promise. In the early morning hours of February 7, the Viet Cong dynamited the American enlisted men's barracks at the South Vietnamese military base at Pleiku, in the central highlands region, and simultaneously bombarded a nearby U.S. air base. McGeorge Bundy, whom Johnson had sent to South Vietnam to review the situation, had already concluded that air attacks had to be launched soon and now cabled to Washington that the Pleiku attack "produced a practicable point of departure" for reprisals against North Vietnam. Bundy, who normally was cautious in his advice, was now unequivocal: "Without new U.S. action defeat seems inevitable. . . . There is still time to turn it around, but not much."

Johnson did not hesitate. The Pleiku attack not only provided the pretext for launching reprisals that Johnson had already accepted as inevitable, but the very nature of the assault and the heavy losses (eight Americans killed, one hundred wounded, in addition to the destruction of ten aircraft) deeply angered Johnson. "We have kept our gun over the mantel and our shells in the cupboard for a long time now," Johnson told the NSC, "and what was the result? They are killing our boys while they sleep in the night." Johnson's determination silenced everyone at the meeting except Senator Mansfield, who challenged the president to consider alternatives. Mansfield renewed his call for withdrawal, telling Johnson: "I would negotiate. I would not hit back. I would get into negotiations." The president curtly dismissed such suggestions, saying "I just don't think you can stand still and take this kind of thing. You just can't do it!" Afterward, in a public statement, Johnson underlined his determination: "We have no choice now but to clear the decks and make absolutely clear our continued determination to back South Vietnam in its fight to maintain its independence."

Within ten hours of the Viet Cong attack, the United States launched

bombing raids against military targets in North Vietnam, the first attacks since the Gulf of Tonkin incident six months earlier. In his memoir,
Johnson reflected on his hope that this step might be decisive: "I
thought that perhaps a sudden and effective air strike would convince
the leaders in Hanoi that we were serious in our purpose and also that
the North could not count on continued immunity if they persisted in
the south." He knew that was unlikely.

This time the bombing would not be a brief, retaliatory measure,
but rather the beginning of sustained warfare. Bundy, having rushed
home from Saigon, immediately pressed Johnson to approve "graduated and continuing reprisal" against North Vietnam. To Bundy, credibility was on the line; in the key passage of an eight-page report, he
argued: "There is only one grave weakness in our posture in Vietnam
which is in our power to fix—and that is the widespread belief that we
do not have the will and force and patience and determination to take
the necessary action and stay the course." With the NSC endorsing Bundy's proposal, Johnson authorized the "graduated and continuing"
bombing campaign.

While Johnson's decision reflected the consensus of his advisers,
there were notable dissenters. Senator Mansfield renewed his call for
caution, and he was joined by a new voice, that of Vice President Hubert Humphrey. Having been rebuffed by Johnson at the NSC meeting,
Mansfield wrote to Johnson, warning him that the bombing campaign
would not work and that America would be drawn into an indecisive
land war.

Meanwhile, Humphrey had been in office less than a month when
he wrote to Johnson on February 15 urging reconsideration of the commitment in Vietnam. Humphrey foresaw a war that the American public would not support. Humphrey—whose work as a congressman and
senator before being tapped by Johnson as his running mate in 1964 had
made him a preeminent spokesman for American liberalism—observed
that wars had to be "politically understandable. . . . There has to be a
cogent, convincing case if we are to enjoy sustained public support. In
World Wars I and II, we had this. In Korea, we were moving under
United Nations auspices to defend South Korea against dramatic,
across-the-border conventional aggression." Vietnam, however, was a
different case. "The arguments in fact are probably too complicated (or
too weak) to be politically useful or effective." The daily reports of political turmoil in Saigon left Americans unable "to understand why we

run grave risks to support a country which is totally unable to put its own house in order." Humphrey concluded that "it is always hard to cut losses," but 1965 was the time to do so in Vietnam "at minimum political risk . . . without being preoccupied with the political repercussions of the Republican right." Military escalation risked the loss of liberal support, which was vital to the realization of the Great Society. "We are now creating the impression," Humphrey maintained, "that we are the prisoner of events in Vietnam," and he urged that Johnson turn his political talents toward reaching a peaceful settlement.

Humphrey's warning had no effect, other than to reduce his influence with Johnson. Offsetting the cautionary advice of Mansfield and Humphrey, former president Dwight D. Eisenhower visited the White House on February 17 and told Johnson that the time had come to begin a bombing "campaign of pressure" against North Vietnam and, if necessary, to send combat troops to prevent South Vietnam's collapse. Shortly after listening to Eisenhower, Johnson set February 20 as the date for launching the bombing campaign.

Poor weather and renewed political chaos in Saigon—the Khanh government was toppled and was replaced by still another regime, this one headed by a civilian, Dr. Phan Huy Quat—forced a delay in the bombing. During the pause, Under Secretary of State George Ball added his dissent. He managed to bring to Johnson's attention his sixty-seven-page analysis of the situation, which recommended working toward "a political settlement without direct U.S. military involvement under conditions that would be designed hopefully to: a) check or to at least delay the extension of communist power into South Viet Nam; b) provide the maximum protection for Thailand, Malaysia, and South Asia; c) minimize the political damage resulting to U.S. prestige." Like Mansfield and Humphrey, Ball predicted that the bombing would fail and that Americans would become involved in a lengthy, indecisive land war ("once on the tiger's back, we cannot be sure of picking the place to dismount"). Last, Ball turned the "credibility" argument on its head, warning that allies already saw the United States engaging "in a fruitless struggle in Vietnam" and that military escalation would lead to a "general loss of confidence in American judgment."

Ball's criticism prompted Johnson to summon him, McNamara, and Rusk to the White House. Meeting on February 26, McNamara and Rusk dismissed Ball's concerns. McNamara presented an array of statistical data—later described by Ball as "a pyrotechnic display of facts

and statistics"—to show that the situation was improving. Rusk foresaw danger in not moving ahead militarily. That ended consideration
of Ball's recommendations; Ball reflected in his memoir that "my hope
to force a systematic reexamination of our total situation had mani-
festly failed."

So the bombing campaign—Operation ROLLING THUNDER—went
forward, bringing sustained U.S. military power directly into the Vietnam conflict. It began on March 2, 1965, when more than one hundred
U.S. war planes from carriers in the South China Sea and air bases in
South Vietnam struck North Vietnam. Operation ROLLING THUNDER
was destined to last for more than three years.

ROLLING THUNDER quickly prompted the dispatch of the first U.S.
combat troops. Westmoreland requested that a military unit be sent to
protect the U.S. air base at DaNang, which was to be one of the launching points for air raids. Johnson quickly approved, but with the proviso
that their role was to be defensive; the JCS ordered that the thirty-five
hundred marines "will not, repeat will not, engage in day to day actions
against the Viet Cong." Yet their arrival on March 8, 1965, brought
American combat troops, however limited in number and mission, to
Vietnam.

The imposition of American power did not halt the deterioration of
South Vietnam. Hanoi calculated that the political instability in Saigon
provided an opportunity to defeat the South Vietnamese army quickly.
The North Vietnamese increased the movement of men and supplies
across the demilitarized zone and down the Ho Chi Minh Trail. This
brought the overall North Vietnamese–Viet Cong strength in the south
to about 150,000 and solidified control of most of the countryside. The
South Vietnamese army lacked the resources, training, and determination to resist this mounting pressure. It was evident that only increasing
U.S. military intervention offered any possibility of preventing the collapse of South Vietnam.

In this situation, Johnson was not a reluctant warrior. Indeed, he
was at the center of the movement toward Americanization of the war.
As the army chief of staff, Gen. Harold Johnson, prepared to leave in
early March for a review of the situation in Vietnam, the president complained: "You're not giving me any ideas and any solutions for this
damn little pissant country. Now I don't need ten generals to come in
here ten times and tell me to bomb. I want some solutions. I want some
answers. You get things bubbling, General." When General Johnson re-

turned on March 14, he predictably proposed a vastly expanded military role, projecting a five-year war that would ultimately require 500,000 U.S. troops. The president pressed the JCS to propose measures that would "kill more Viet Cong." Not surprisingly, the JCS recommended sending more troops and permitting them to undertake offensive operations. With the kinds of recommendations before him that he had been seeking, Johnson authorized an increase of twenty thousand marines and an offensive combat role in patrol areas within fifty miles of their bases.

Always sensitive to political undercurrents, Johnson tempered his belligerency with a bold gesture for peace. In an address at Johns Hopkins University on April 7, Johnson followed a strongly worded statement of American determination to assure the independence of South Vietnam with the dramatic proposal of a gigantic program of economic development that would benefit both North and South Vietnam. He pledged a billion-dollar U.S. investment toward a multilateral Mekong River Project, modeled on the Tennessee Valley Authority, which would improve the lives of one hundred million people in Southeast Asia. He invited the participation of the Soviet Union and North Vietnam "as soon as peaceful cooperation is possible." The project depended on North Vietnam agreeing to "unconditional discussions." This offer blended the domestic and international pressures for negotiations in Vietnam with Johnson's faith in the capacity of governments to improve the lives of people. It also reflected Johnson's confidence in political compromise. He believed that the North Vietnamese would be won over; after the speech, he told an adviser, "old Ho can't turn that down."

Johnson's proposal won wide praise. Editorials in the American press compared the Mekong Valley proposal to the Marshall Plan, which had helped to rebuild Western Europe after World War II. Leaders in many European and Asian countries welcomed the prospects of reversing the drift to war and benefiting Southeast Asian peoples in the process.

Yet, contrary to Johnson's expectations, "old Ho" did turn him down. North Vietnam's response confounded Johnson, who seemed unable to understand North Vietnam's basic differences with the United States. Dismissing the proposal as a "bribe," Hanoi countered with a Four Point formula for peace, which included the provision that the "internal affairs of South Vietnam be settled by themselves in accordance with the program of the National Liberation Front." That remained unacceptable to American officials, who viewed any NLF participation in a settlement as inevitably resulting in communist control.

So the momentum toward war resumed, and Johnson pressed more forthrightly for a military plan to hold South Vietnam. As intelligence reported an increase in North Vietnamese infiltration and communist forces continued to inflict heavy casualties on the South Vietnamese, Johnson dispatched McNamara and Bundy to Honolulu to meet on April 20 with Taylor and Westmoreland, who were ordered in from Saigon, and with Admiral U. S. Grant Sharp, commander in chief in the Pacific. They readily agreed that, with South Vietnam on the verge of collapse, the United States should commit another fifty thousand troops (bringing the total committed to eighty-two thousand). These troops would be necessary "to demonstrate Viet Cong failure in the South"—which would take perhaps a year or two to achieve. Combined with the "pain" that bombing was inflicting on North Vietnam, the United States would "break the will of the North Vietnamese by denying them victory." Johnson immediately approved the recommendation. As was his pattern through this period of escalation, Johnson downplayed the significance of the troop increase, rejecting McNamara's suggestion that he inform congressional leaders of the planned deployments.

Paralleling the troop increase, Johnson authorized the further expansion of the American combat role. He approved Westmoreland's request that American forces be permitted to assist South Vietnamese units that were in serious trouble. Soon Johnson took the inevitable next step, authorizing combat "independently of or in conjunction with" the South Vietnamese. So, within four months of the introduction of combat units, their numbers had increased from thirty-five hundred to eighty-two thousand and their mission had grown from defending U.S. bases to supporting the South Vietnamese and now to fighting independently. As these measures were being implemented, it was clearly evident that they could not prevent the imminent collapse of South Vietnam. The Viet Cong and North Vietnamese continually battered demoralized South Vietnamese forces, which suffered heavy casualties and desertions.

Johnson now confronted directly what he had long anticipated: that the survival of South Vietnam required a large-scale American military intervention. On June 7, Westmoreland requested another 41,000 troops immediately, to be followed by an additional 52,000, thus increasing the total commitment to 175,000 men. The Joint Chiefs of Staff urged prompt implementation. This escalation meant that the United States would assume the major combat role, in effect Americanizing the war. McNamara recalled that, "of the thousands of cables I received during my seven years as Secretary of Defense, this one disturbed me most. We were forced to make a decision. We could no longer postpone a choice about which path to take. The issue would hang over all of us like a menacing cloud for the next seven weeks."

As Johnson considered Westmoreland's request, South Vietnam went through still another political convulsion. On June 12 the government headed by the indecisive Prime Minister Quat yielded power to the military, this time in the name of a National Leadership Council headed by Air Marshall Nguyen Cao Ky and Gen. Nguyen Van Thieu. The new leaders told Taylor that only a substantial U.S. military commitment could save their country from communist takeover.

The stark situation in Vietnam and the magnitude of Westmoreland's request troubled Johnson but did not alter his fundamental assumptions. On June 21, he confided to McNamara: "I'm very depressed . . . because I see no program from either Defense or State that gives me much hope of doing anything except just praying and grasping to hold on during [the] monsoon [season] and hope they'll quit. And I don't believe they're ever goin' to quit. And I don't see . . . that we have any . . . plan for victory militarily or diplomatically." Withdrawal, however, remained an unacceptable alternative, for in the end Johnson saw the problems in Vietnam within the context of American commitment and credibility. He continued, "With our treaty like it is and with what all we've said . . . it would just lose us face in the world and I just shudder to think what all of 'em would say."

Several colleagues quietly tried to change Johnson's mind. Senator Russell was in frequent contact with the president, telling him that Vietnam lacked political, economic, or strategic value and that the United States ought not engage its resources there. Rather, Johnson should use the political chaos in Saigon as the basis for disengagement. Senator Fulbright, after guiding the Tonkin Gulf resolution through the Senate, had become critical of the growing military commitment, and he urged that Johnson work toward a negotiated settlement; this, he conceded, would result in a communist Vietnam, but that would not necessarily mean a government under Soviet or Chinese domination. Senator Mansfield reiterated his reservations, writing to Johnson about the bleak situation: "There is not a government to speak of in Saigon. . . . We are simply acting to prevent a collapse of the Vietnamese military forces which we pay for and supply in any event. . . . There are no significant American interests which dictate [a] . . . massive unilateral American military effort."

Finally, Under Secretary Ball put the case against escalation to Johnson in similar terms: "We are drifting to a major war—that nobody wants" on behalf of a country "with an army and no government." Ball foresaw that direct U.S. warfare against the Viet Cong would lead to an open-ended escalation. He challenged the assumption that "credibility" required "saving" South Vietnam. Warfare on behalf of "a tottering government that lacks adequate indigenous support" would undermine American stature. Reminding Johnson that "any prudent commander carefully selects the terrain on which to stand and fight" and warning that "even if we were to commit five hundred thousand men to South Vietnam we would still lose," Ball concluded that it was time to "cut our losses in Vietnam."

Ball's challenge was again undercut by Bundy, who placed before Johnson both Ball's recommendations and the written responses of McNamara and Rusk. McNamara challenged Ball's gloomy predictions and foresaw that the commitment of U.S. forces, together with a "worldwide diplomatic campaign to pressure Hanoi to give up its goal of taking South Vietnam," would be supported by the American public and "bring about a favorable solution to the Vietnam problem." For his part, Rusk said that there could be "no serious debate" over America's commitment to South Vietnam. Preserving "credibility" was nothing less than upholding global order: "The integrity of the U.S. commitment is the principal pillar of peace throughout the world. If that commitment becomes unreliable, the communist world would draw conclusions that would lead to our ruin and almost certainly to a catastrophic war." As he forwarded these views, Bundy advised Johnson "to listen hard to George Ball and then reject his proposal."

Reinforcing the advice of McNamara, Rusk, and Bundy, the nation's foreign policy elite reassured Johnson that Vietnam was a crucial test of American resolve. Eisenhower again urged going forward militarily, telling Johnson "you have to go all out." The President's Special Advisory Group—the so-called Wise Men, a group of foreign policy elder statesmen who had served in high-level positions in previous administrations—were summoned to Washington for a briefing on the Vietnam situation. The Wise Men reached an unequivocal conclusion that in "view of the grave stakes . . . there should be no question of making whatever combat force increases were required."

Shortly after receiving their advice, Johnson hinted publicly of momentous decisions in the making. In a July 9 press conference, he stated that "we expect that it will get worse before it gets better. . . . Our manpower needs there are increasing, and will continue to do so. There are some seventy-five thousand that will be there very shortly. There will be others that will be required. . . . Whatever is required I am sure will be supplied." Four days later Johnson again met with the press to announce that McNamara was heading a mission to South Vietnam and that he would "give careful consideration to their recommendations. . . . And we will do what is necessary. . . . It is quite possible that new and serious decisions will be required in the near future."

McNamara's mission wasted no time in pressing the case for escalation. The trip to Saigon convinced McNamara that the Westmoreland-JCS request—now formulated as 175,000 troops by the end of 1965 and and another 100,000 in 1966—offered the only hope for South Vietnam's survival. Returning to Washington, McNamara reported that the North Vietnamese and Viet Cong were poised to "dismember the nation and to maul the army, [showing] . . . no signs of settling for less than a complete takeover." He duly presented Johnson with three alternatives, but as was typical in his framing of recommendations, McNamara defined the options so that only one was acceptable. The wording of the first option—"cut our losses and withdraw under the best circumstances that can be arranged—almost certainly conditions humiliating the U.S. and very dangerous to our future effectiveness on the world scene"— precluded its consideration. The second—maintain present troop levels, "playing for the breaks—a course of action which, because our position would grow weaker, almost certainly would confront us later with a choice between withdrawal and emergency expansion of forces, perhaps too late to do any good"—was no better. So that left the third option, which McNamara presented and defended at length: "expand promptly and substantially the U.S. military pressure . . . while launching a vigorous effort on the political side." The "military pressure" meant fulfilling the Westmoreland-JCS request.

On the brink of taking the nation to war, Johnson moved deliberately. "I wanted to go over this proposal with great care," he recalled in his memoir. "I realized what a major undertaking it would be." He ordered a series of meetings to consider his options. Intended to reach a critical decision within the framework of a rapidly deteriorating situation overseas, the urgency of the meetings that began on Wednesday, July 21, resembled those conducted by Truman over the Korean crisis during the last week of June 1950. Conducted in considerable secrecy, the round of meetings constituted the fullest debate within the Johnson administration on whether the country should go to war.

While Johnson occasionally agonized in these meetings over the magnitude of the decision, his earlier orders and comments betrayed his predilection toward accepting the military solution. He posed basic questions, but he did not insist that they be fully addressed. The nature of the decision-making process came into focus during a meeting with several advisers on the morning of July 21.

Johnson, in a rambling discourse, prodded them with questions and urged that they "consider carefully all our options." He immediately, however, ruled out conciliation: "Negotiations, the pause, all the other approaches have all been explored. It makes us look weak—with cup in hand. We have tried." As McNamara and others supported the troop request, Johnson stated that "our mission should be as limited as we dare make it." He asked, "Is anyone of the opinion we should not do what the memo says—If so, I'd like to hear from them now, in detail." Ball spoke out. Describing escalation as a "perilous voyage . . . very dangerous," he expressed "great apprehension that we can win under these circumstances." Johnson responded: "But is there another course in the national interest that is better than the McNamara course? We know it's dangerous and perilous, but can it be avoided?" Ball did not retreat: "If we get bogged down, our cost might be substantially greater. The pressures to create a larger war would be irresistible." Johnson came back, asking "what other road I can go?" Ball again did not back down from the implications of his proposal: "Take our losses, let [the South Vietnamese] government fall apart, negotiate, discuss, knowing full well there will be a probable take-over by the communists." When two other officials (Henry Cabot Lodge, former ambassador to South Vietnam, and Carl Rowan, director of the U.S. Information Agency) lent some support to Ball by underscoring the weakness of the Saigon government, Johnson requested that Ball state his views more fully after the group recessed for lunch.

As the morning session concluded, Johnson posed tough questions for McNamara and Wheeler: "What will happen if we put 100,000 more men and then two, three years later you tell me you need 500,000 more? How would you expect me to respond to that? . . . And what makes you think that if we put in 100,000 men, Ho Chi Minh won't put in another 100,000?" Wheeler turned that question to the advantage of those seeking escalation: "That means greater bodies of men, which will allow us to cream them." Johnson pushed again: "But what are the chances of more North Vietnamese soldiers coming in?" Again Wheeler discounted the problem: "About a fifty-fifty chance. The North would be foolhardy to put one-quarter of their forces in [South Vietnam]. It would expose them too greatly in the North."

At the afternoon session, Ball set forth his case against intervention: "We cannot win, Mr. President. This war will be long and protracted. The most we can hope for is a messy conclusion. There remains a great danger of intrusion by the Chinese. But the biggest problem is the problem of a long war." Ball appealed directly to Johnson: "Every great captain in history is not afraid to make a tactical withdrawal if conditions are unfavorable to him. [In Vietnam] the enemy cannot be seen. . . . He is indigenous to the country. I truly have serious doubt that an army of westerners can successfully fight orientals in an Asian jungle." Johnson seemed to be impressed; he picked up on Ball's point: "Can Westerners . . . successfully fight Orientals in jungle rice-paddies? I want McNamara and General Wheeler to seriously ponder this question."

As Ball continued his argument for disengagement, Johnson countered: "Wouldn't all these countries say that Uncle Sam was a paper tiger? Wouldn't we lose credibility breaking the word of three presidents?" Ball shot back that the "worse blow would be that the mightiest power in the world is unable to defeat guerrillas." As Johnson pressed the credibility issue further, Ball said that the weakness of the Saigon government rendered the issue meaningless: "If we were helping a country with a stable viable government, it would be a vastly different story."

Then Johnson summed up his concerns: "There are two basic troublings with me. First, that westerners can even win a war in Asia. Second, I don't see how you can fight a war under direction of other people whose government changes every month." At the president's urging, Ball restated his position that the options were "distasteful" but also clear. Americanization would lead to a "long, protracted war costly, very costly, with North Vietnam digging in for the long term. This is their life and driving force." The alternative of withdrawal meant "short-term losses . . . [which means] we come out ahead of the McNamara plan."

Ball's plea for withdrawal won no converts. The other principal policymakers dismissed his arguments. To Bundy, it was "disastrous." To Rusk, credibility demanded undertaking whatever challenges the United States faced: "If the Communist world finds out we will not pursue our commitment to the end, I don't know where they will stay their hand." He went on to dismiss Ball's concerns about escalation leading to substantial casualties: "I don't see great casualties unless the Chinese come in." To McNamara, Ball understated the cost of withdrawal and overstated that of escalation. To Wheeler, the United States could prevail militarily. Johnson was impressed by Rusk's credibility argument; in his memoir, he wrote that Ball "had not produced a sufficiently convincing case of a viable alternative."

Indeed, when he met with McNamara and military leaders the next day, July 22, Johnson was contemptuous of negotiations as "bugging out." Since continuing the present course amounted to "los[ing] slowly," the only reasonable option was meeting Westmoreland's request, adding 100,000 men while "recognizing that may not be enough—and adding more next year." To achieve American objectives, McNamara predicted that it would take a total of 300,000 men, but Marine Corps Commandant Gen. Wallace Greene projected that it would require five years and half a million men. Johnson was concerned about China's reaction and the lack of international support for the United States: "I think [the Chinese] are going to put their stack in. Is this the best place to do this? We don't have the allies we had in Korea." Military advisers could only acknowledge that China's intervention would mean "another ball game," but McNamara and the military leaders contended that the stakes in Vietnam were worth such risks. McNamara fell back on the domino theory, foreseeing that an American withdrawal would lead, within a few years, to communist domination of Laos, Cambodia, Thailand, Burma, and Malaya, with a "ripple effect" that would be felt throughout Asia and as far away as Greece and Turkey, which would change from American allies to neutral nations.

After further discussions with Rusk, McNamara, and other civilian leaders later on July 22, Johnson described the alternatives tersely: "Sit and lose slowly, get out, put in what needs to be done." While the phrasing clearly pointed toward the third option, he linked resolve with restraint. Military escalation had to be accompanied by evidence of determination to avoid a larger war and to deal reasonably with the adversary. Johnson chided the State Department to be more energetic in proposing diplomatic measures. "We have to keep peace proposals going," Johnson said. "It's like a prize fight. Our right is our military power, but our left must be our peace proposals. Every time you move troops forward, you move diplomats forward. I want this done." Johnson's call to "move diplomats forward" reflected his apprehension of repeating Truman's mistake of provoking China's intervention and reflected continuing pressure from critics of escalation. During this intense period, Clark Clifford (a prominent Washington lawyer and confidante to Democratic presidents), former ambassador to India John Kenneth Galbraith, and again Senator Mansfield all told Johnson that military escalation in Vietnam would be a mistake.

Johnson's agonizing concluded when he invited McNamara, Clifford, and a few other advisers to accompany him to the Camp David presidential retreat in the Maryland foothills on Sunday, July 25. That afternoon he listened as McNamara and Clifford reiterated familiar arguments for and against escalation. Clifford challenged the credibility argument, saying that "a failure to engage in an all-out war will not lower our international prestige. This is not the last inning in the struggle against communism. We must pick those spots where the stakes are highest for us and we have the greatest ability to prevail." Clifford also questioned whether the United States could win militarily: "I do not believe that we can win in South Vietnam. I hate this war. If we send in 100,000 more men, the North Vietnamese will match us. If the North Vietnamese run out of men, the Chinese will send in 'volunteers.' Russia and China don't intend for us to win the war. If we 'won,' we would face a long occupation with constant trouble." He foresaw impending disaster: "If we don't win after a big buildup, it will be a huge catastrophe. We could lose more than 50,000 men in Vietnam. It will ruin us. Five years, 50,000 men killed, hundreds of billions of dollars—it is just not for us." Closing his remarks, Clifford advised quiet pursuit of "an honorable way out."

Johnson then engaged in solitary reflection when, it seems, he finally resolved to go forward with escalation. He drove alone around the Camp David grounds and then walked along footpaths. According to his memoir, Johnson feared, above all, the domestic consequences of losing Vietnam. If South Vietnam collapsed, he foresaw a debate over "who lost Vietnam" in which he would be held responsible. He did not want the war to shatter his dream of the Great Society, but he knew that if Vietnam became a subject of national debate, "that day would be the beginning of the end of the Great Society." So there was no choice but to escalate, but to do so in a limited way that would "meet commitments," and then to "get out."

Returning to Washington, Johnson the next day told the NSC of his decision and of his determination "to play our decisions low key." Toward that end, he would not mobilize the reserves or seek a declaration of war. Two meetings—first with the NSC, then with congressional leaders—were called for the evening of Tuesday, July 27. Their purpose was to sanction the president's decision. Before both groups, Johnson reviewed his options in the pattern characteristic of the shaping of Vietnam policy—a presentation that led to only one conclusion. This time there were five options, the first four of which were presented in terms that precluded their consideration: (1) use the air force to annihilate the enemy, which Johnson said the public did not support; (2) withdraw completely, which the public also opposed and which ran counter to commitments by Eisenhower and Kennedy; (3) continue at present levels, but "you wouldn't want your boy out there . . . crying for help and not get[ting] it"; (4) go all-out to war by calling up the reserves, declaring a state of emergency, and taking other provocative measures that would force North Vietnam to seek help from the Soviet Union and China. That left only the fifth option: giving the "commanders the men they need out of forces in this country." When Johnson asked the NSC whether anyone disagreed, predictably no one did.

Johnson then met with congressional leaders. Conspicuously not included were several senators, including Fulbright, who had become critical of involvement in Vietnam; the only known critic present was Mansfield, who had thus far confined his thoughts to private communications with the president. Before his hawkish audience, Johnson reiterated his five options. Even among those supportive of his decision, there were misgivings. Republican Congressmen Gerald Ford of Michigan and Leslie Arends of Illinois asked why Congress was not being involved and how many troops would be required. Republican Senator Everett Dirksen of Illinois advised that Johnson "tell the country we are engaged in very serious business" and warned against withholding information. An impatient Johnson tried to deflect the questions. Then, when he asked if there were further comments, Mansfield—to the astonishment of his colleagues—openly challenged Johnson's decision. Reminding the group that the United States had only pledged "to *assist* South Vietnam" and that since Diem's assassination there "had been no government of legitimacy," Mansfield stated that "we owe this govern- ment nothing." He closed with a warning that "we are going deeper into war. Even total victory would be vastly costly. [Our] best hope for salvation is a quick stalemate and negotiations. We cannot expect our people to support a war for 3–5 years. We are about [to embark upon] an anti-communist crusade. Escalation begets escalation." Johnson tersely responded: "Well, Mike, what would *you* do?" Mansfield did not reply. The tense session ended with the Speaker of the House, John McCormack (D.-Mass.), assuring Johnson of the support of all true Americans.

Johnson, however, realized that the support at the meeting was mis- leading. If he needed a reminder, Mansfield sent him a report on a meeting that Mansfield had arranged earlier that day with five promi- nent senators who had not been invited to the White House—Fulbright, Russell, Cooper, George Aiken (R.-Vt.), and John Sparkman (D.-Ala.)— who shared the conviction that Johnson was making a tragic mistake. A list of their concerns ended with their collective crisp advice: "We are deeply enmeshed in a place where we ought not to be. . . . The situation is rapidly getting out of control, and . . . every effort should be made to extricate ourselves."

Johnson had already dismissed the voices of restraint, and all that remained was to tell the American public of his decision. He did so in a deliberately low-keyed manner. Rather than addressing Congress or delivering a national television address, he chose a midday press con- ference as his format. At 12:30 P.M. on Wednesday, July 28, Johnson read a carefully crafted and forceful statement, which described Vietnam as "a different kind of war" but one of vital importance:

> It is really war. It is guided by North Vietnam and is spurred by Communist China. Its goal is to conquer the South, to defeat American power, and to expand the Asiatic domination of communism. There are great stakes in the balance. . . . [If the United States was] driven from the field in Vietnam, then no nation can ever again have the same confidence in America's promise, or in American protection. . . . We did not choose to be the guardians at the gate, but there is no one else. Nor would surrender in Vietnam bring peace, because we learned from Hitler that success only feeds the appetite of ag-

gression. The battle would be renewed in one country and then another country, bringing with it perhaps even larger and crueler conflict, as we have learned from the lessons of history. . . . The solemn pledges [of three presidents] have committed themselves and have promised to help defend this small and valiant nation.

The United States still wanted to avoid a larger war, and toward that end Arthur Goldberg, the ambassador to the United Nations, was delivering a message to the U.N. secretary-general affirming America's interest in a peaceful settlement.

Finally, Johnson announced the expanded military commitment that had been at the heart of the previous week's discussions: "I have asked the Commanding General, General Westmoreland, what more he needs to meet this mounting aggression. He has told me. We will meet his needs. . . . I have today ordered to Vietnam . . . forces which will raise our fighting strength from 75,000 to 125,000 men almost immediately. . . . Additional forces will be needed later, and they will be sent as requested." Adding a note that reflected the agony behind his decision and the personal sacrifices it entailed, he said, "I do not find it easy to send the flower of our youth, the finest young men, into battle. . . . I think I know too much [how] their mothers weep and how their families sorrow." When a reporter inquired whether the additional troops meant any change in U.S. policy, Johnson replied that "it does not imply any change in policy whatever."

Johnson's combination of resolve and restraint won wide praise on the editorial pages of the nation's leading newspapers. "Strength and restraint, determination and discipline," according to a *Baltimore Sun* editorial, "are needed in almost equal amounts." A *New York Times* editorial said that the commitment had to "be held down to the absolute minimum necessary to prove to Hanoi and Peking that military aggression is not worthwhile and never will be." On the other side, a few columnists, most prominently the renowned Walter Lippmann, and a handful of newspaper editorials warned that the country was on the road to a major war on behalf of an unworthy government. Opinion polls showed that substantial majorities of the American public supported Johnson's handling of the Vietnam problem and accepted the proposition that the loss of South Vietnam would lead to communist domination of Southeast Asia.

FROM THE OUTSET of his presidency, Lyndon Johnson believed in, and pressed for, military measures as the principal way to address the intractable problem of Vietnam. While gradually increasing the U.S. military role to a point in July 1965 that far exceeded any expectations of a year and a half earlier, Johnson recognized the perils of escalation. He posed the fundamental questions: Why send Americans to fight for those who are not united against the enemy? Would not North Vietnam match every step of escalation? If the United States added 100,000 men, would North Vietnam not do the same? Could Westerners prevail against Orientals in the jungles and rice paddies? Did he have sufficient constitutional justification for intervention? Despite all the meetings and the countless cables and memos, those tough questions—all demanding of careful consideration—were never fully addressed. Decision making was more time-consuming than it was thorough.

To the extent that there was an internal debate, it was about the fundamental issue of whether U.S. security necessitated holding South Vietnam. The critics (Ball, Mansfield, Russell, Fulbright, and Humphrey, among others) were essentially outsiders who were always trying to be heard amid the insiders (principally Rusk, McNamara, and Bundy), who had more frequent and routine contact with Johnson. The critics' task was made more formidable because they were challenging Johnson's assumption that the outcome of the Vietnam struggle was central to the fabric of international order. To him, it was logical: American credibility sustained respect among friends and foes; he inherited a commitment from Eisenhower and Kennedy; therefore, the United States had no choice but to assure South Vietnam's survival. If the United States failed, small countries would lose heart and would turn from the West and toward the Sino-Soviet bloc.

Such thinking paralleled the strategic assumptions that had driven Truman to intervene in Korea, but there was a significant difference between the two administrations in how they considered the crises. In 1950, no advisers or influential members of Congress questioned the strategic necessity of going to war. While Truman had unanimity behind his decision for war, Johnson had only a consensus. The critics tried repeatedly to get Johnson to reconsider the prevailing view of American strategic interests. They did not question the importance of American credibility and the prevention of Sino-Soviet domination of Southeast Asia, but they did question whether South Vietnam was vital to the realization of those objectives. The United States, they stressed, ought not tie its prestige and resources to support of the weak, divided, and unpopular South Vietnamese government.

Ten years of American economic and military assistance had failed to build a viable and representative government in Saigon. Its chronic instability and lack of purpose made it demonstrably incapable of resisting the increasing military pressure of the Viet Cong and North Vietnam. The United States had made no commitment to assure South Vietnam's survival, the critics argued, but only to assist it. Abandoning an untenable position would enhance American credibility. Committing more resources would not. Hence, the United States should seek a graceful exit from South Vietnam, which, the critics acknowledged, would lead to eventual communist domination. That would not necessarily have ramifications beyond Vietnam. Neither did it necessarily mean a Vietnam closely tied to one or both of the major communist powers. While the critics operated at a disadvantage in terms of access to Johnson, he knew their views and ultimately disregarded them as misguided.

Unwilling to reconsider the assumptions of established policy and facing the deterioration of South Vietnam, Johnson believed that military intervention offered the only possible means of saving an ally. Johnson knew that South Vietnam was a "mess." The very weakness of the Saigon government, which the critics saw as justifying withdrawal, became to Johnson and his closest advisers the most compelling reason to move toward military intervention. Also, to Johnson and other critics of the Kennedy administration's complicity in the overthrow of the Diem government, the United States had contributed to the instability in Saigon by removing the one leader who, they believed, had the best chance of rallying the South Vietnamese. Moreover, the uncompromising belligerency of the North Vietnamese, Johnson believed, left no choice: they were increasing their military involvement in the South; they had spurned his offer of regional development in the Johns Hopkins address; they demanded the political dominance of the National Liberation Front in South Vietnam.

In this situation, Johnson saw himself responding to the kind of challenge that the cold war had imposed on the United States. In his mind, the North Vietnamese were as guilty of aggression as the North Koreans had been in 1950. Unlike Truman, however, whose condemnation of North Korea had won wide support among America's allies as well as many newly independent countries, Johnson found that most of the international community, including European allies and much of the now vastly larger Afro-Asian bloc of nations, were indifferent to American claims of North Vietnamese aggression and skeptical about whether South Vietnam could or should be "saved." So, although Truman had been able to gain U.N. sanction for American objectives and had waged war under its aegis, Johnson acted in isolation, gaining negligible international support that was limited to a few allies. There was never a chance that this war could have been waged under the aegis of the United Nations. In fact, only South Korea was anxious to send troops to Vietnam. Among SEATO members, only Australia had made a troop commitment (a modest thirteen hundred men) by 1965. The Philippines and Thailand—the two Southeast Asian members of SEATO—both provided bases that were used by U.S. forces in Vietnam, but in 1965 neither made a troop commitment. (The Philippines sent a medical team.) The other SEATO members—Britain, France, New Zealand, and Pakistan—offered no support.

The movement toward Americanization of the war, moreover, was accompanied by remarkable inattention to how U.S. military resources could achieve the objectives of defeating the southern insurgency and restraining North Vietnam. A JCS report of July 1965 spoke vaguely of success "if such is our will—and if that will is manifested in strategy and tactical operations." At the same time, it cautioned that projections had to remain "tentative" for many reasons, including the South Vietnamese army's lack of experience in the kinds of operations that it would be called upon to perform. More importantly, military officers disagreed among themselves on the kind of warfare they would be encountering. In particular, many assumed that North Vietnam's introduction of more ground troops meant that it was now moving from guerrilla to conventional, large-unit warfare.

In one of the several points of self-criticism in his memoir, McNamara finds the shallowness of strategic planning an especially serious shortcoming.

> Looking back, I clearly erred by not forcing—then or later—in either Saigon or Washington—a knock-down, drag-out debate over the loose assumptions, unasked questions, and thin analyses underlying our military strategy in Vietnam. I had spent twenty years as a manager identifying problems and forcing organizations—often against their will—to think deeply and

realistically about alternative courses of action and their consequences. I doubt I will ever fully understand why I did not do so here.

Just as he ignored the skeptics of Vietnam's strategic importance and the question of whether military operations could achieve political objectives, Johnson also skirted the question of domestic support. Was the war's purpose explainable to the public and Congress? Did he have constitutional authority to wage a wider war? Much of the time Johnson acted as though these questions had been resolved by congressional approval of the Gulf of Tonkin resolution, which gave him a degree of constitutional legitimacy that Truman had lacked in waging war in Korea. At the same time, however, Johnson refused to confront Congress and the public with the full ramifications of the steps he was taking in the name of that authorization. He repeatedly presented the steps of greater involvement as a continuation of existing policy. To keep the Americanization of the war low keyed, he rejected the JCS request to activate the military reserves—a step that would have both provided additional forces for Vietnam and broadened markedly the national commitment to the war. General Wheeler later reflected on the position of the military leadership: "We felt it would be desirable to have a reserve call-up in order to make sure the people of the U.S. knew that we were in a war and not engaged in some two-penny military adventure. Because we didn't think it was going to prove to be a two-penny military adventure by any manner or means."

Behind Johnson's low-keyed approach to intervention were domestic and international concerns. He feared that focusing on Vietnam would draw attention from the Great Society program. Also, he was determined to avoid actions and rhetoric that the major communist powers would see as threatening.

Yet Johnson's calculation that the public and Congress could be ignored troubled his supporters as well as his critics. Among the former, McNamara advised him that circumstances by the summer of 1965 had changed significantly since the Gulf of Tonkin incident a year earlier and that additional congressional authorization ought to be gained before the commitment of American combat forces. At times, Johnson said that the language of the resolution was so open-ended as to permit any level of involvement being planned in 1965. In a conversation with McNamara on July 14, 1965, however, Johnson candidly acknowledged that, at the time of the Gulf of Tonkin resolution, "we had no intention of committing this many ground troops" and asked, "Do we want to be out on a limb by ourselves?" McNamara urged him to request congressional support of both his military buildup and the pursuit of negotiations. Johnson seemed to agree, but never took that step and so ended "out on a limb."

To critics, notably Vice President Humphrey, Johnson's mistake was more fundamental. Sustained public support was *not* Johnson's for the asking. Indeed, he was embarking on a precarious course where the public would not follow. Unlike the two world wars and Korea, Humphrey warned, the conflict in Vietnam could not be explained to Americans. The issues were not clear-cut. North Vietnam's shadowy movement of men and supplies through the mountainous jungle footpaths of the Ho Chi Minh Trail was a far cry from armies crossing international frontiers. Johnson himself seemed to recognize that public opinion polls showing support for his Vietnam policy in 1965 did not mean that it would continue once troops were committed and casualties mounted, but that realization neither restrained him nor led him to be more candid with the public and Congress.

So Johnson pursued his inconsistent course—taking the nation slowly but decisively into a ground war but failing in important ways: to mobilize the nation's resources by calling up reserves and taking the public fully into his confidence; to seek explicit congressional authorization for the measures being taken in 1965; to consider the reasons for and the ramifications of allied indifference toward the American effort in Vietnam; to confront the difficulty of explaining this "different kind of war" to the public and of sustaining support, especially if the war dragged on; and, most basically, to acknowledge fully the immense military challenge facing the United States. Another president, less inclined toward a military solution and prepared to force serious debate on issues, might have reached a different decision on Vietnam. If not, at least the decision to intervene would have been the result of more systematic consideration.

In Johnson's mind, his decisions were part of an intricate pattern designed to fulfill domestic and international objectives. By the summer of 1965, he was achieving his dream of leading the nation toward the Great Society. Congress, having passed the monumental Civil Rights Act of 1964, now was enacting the Voting Rights Act and the programs of the War on Poverty. The war in Vietnam could not be allowed to disrupt support for the Great Society, which meant that intervention had to be downplayed. At the same time, however, failure to hold South Vietnam would not only have the dangerous international implications that Johnson so frequently addressed publicly but also lead to recriminations at home. He would be subjected to conservative vilification for "losing" Vietnam. So South Vietnam had to be held, but at the minimum military commitment and with the least possible domestic and international disruptions. Johnson desperately needed a quick resolution of the Vietnam conflict, which meant getting the North Vietnamese and Viet Cong to accept the division of the country and the legitimacy of the fragile South Vietnamese government. No military or civilian adviser ever suggested that that objective could be easily attained. Johnson recognized all of the risks in Americanizing the war, but he gambled that the demonstration of power and resolve would force North Vietnam and the Viet Cong from the battlefield. It was a perilous way to take a nation to war.

The Strategy of Wishful Thinking

LYNDON JOHNSON was an energetic commander in chief at the center of strategic, political, and diplomatic action. Three priorities guided his leadership: that the commitment to South Vietnam having been made, that country's survival was vital to America's global credibility; that the warfare in Vietnam had to be restricted, lest it touch off a war with the major communist powers; that the commitment of manpower and resources to Vietnam could not divert attention and energies from the Great Society reform program.

In waging war, Johnson drew upon the "lessons" of Truman's experience in Korea. Johnson was determined that the limited U.S. objective in Vietnam would be clear from the outset and that military operations would not threaten the Chinese People's Republic or the Soviet Union. He was obsessed by the fear of provoking a wider war, as Truman had done in Korea. Johnson's guiding dictum was simple: "We shall do what is necessary, but only what is necessary," by which he meant that the only U.S. objective was to force North Vietnam's abandonment of its "aggression," which did not necessitate extending ground warfare beyond South Vietnam. The war was thus to be limited in scope and purpose, and "victory" would mean a settlement comparable to the Korean truce that had left that country divided.

To Johnson and his principal advisers, that limited objective seemed attainable through the measured use of U.S. military power on two levels: (1) the bombing of North Vietnam and (2) undertaking large-scale air and ground operations, in conjunction with South Vietnamese forces, against the North Vietnamese–Viet Cong in South Vietnam. Once U.S. determination and power were fully demonstrated, it was reasoned, the North Vietnamese would come to realize—just as the North Koreans and Chinese had fifteen years earlier—the necessity to curtail their ambitions and accept the division of Vietnam. Deprived of support from the north, the southern insurgency would "wither on the vine." The Americanization of the war, it was further assumed, would enhance the morale of the South Vietnamese people, would strengthen the resolve and capabilities of their army, and would bring political stability in Saigon. Together, Americans and South Vietnamese would

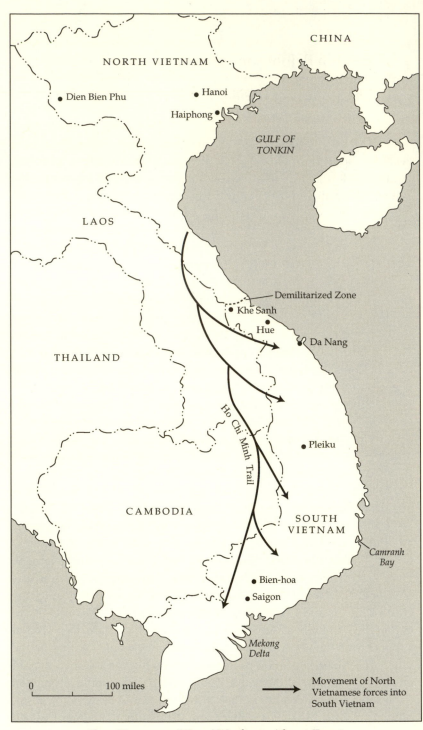

THE VIETNAM WAR: Warfare without Fronts

"pacify" the countryside by extending the authority of the Saigon government and undermining the position of the Viet Cong.

The essential element in this strategy was to intimidate North Vietnam. On the surface, this seemed simple enough. North Vietnam, which Johnson often dismissed as "that raggedy-ass little fourth-rate country," could not challenge a superpower with the world's most sophisticated weaponry and the capacity to unleash a massive array of firepower. Rather than launching all-out warfare, the United States would combine firmness with restraint, which would convince Hanoi of its "reasonableness." Consistent with prevailing theories of crisis management, the United States would prevail by using its power in measured steps, with each increment adding to the pressure on North Vietnam until, at some point, the "pain" would become unacceptable and it would accept the futility of continuing the struggle.

Waging such a war required astute leadership on strategic, political, and diplomatic levels. Strategically, Johnson and Secretary of Defense Robert McNamara were determined to employ military power in measured ways that would increase pressure on the communists while keeping the war limited to Vietnam. This necessitated restrictions on military operations. Johnson refused to extend the war into neighboring Laos and Cambodia, which the communist forces used as supply lines (the Ho Chi Minh Trail running through both countries) and as sanctuaries from the fighting in South Vietnam. He also authorized targets and otherwise monitored the bombing of North Vietnam, Operation ROLLING THUNDER. Politically, Johnson worked to assure the essential bases of support in the United States and in South Vietnam, tirelessly explaining his objectives to the American public and pressing the leadership in Saigon to undertake reforms that would enhance its legitimacy and support. Diplomatically, Johnson took initiatives and pursued opportunities to bring about negotiations with North Vietnam.

As he immersed himself in the war, Johnson followed the style of policymaking that had contributed to his political success. Faced with conflicting advice, he characteristically compromised and deferred decisions. "Johnson's career," his biographer Doris Kearns Goodwin writes, "was marked by continuing effort to avoid confrontation and choice, to prevent passionate and emotional divisions over issues." Waging war, however, was a different proposition than the give-and-take of domestic politics, which placed a premium on accommodation. In the end, Johnson's compromising as a wartime leader helped to provoke the very "passionate and emotional divisions" he so assiduously wanted to avoid.

Johnson was also an impatient leader. He was accustomed to having his way, sometimes through his skill in working at the art of compromise and at other times through a domineering personality that could bend others to his will. An inveterate manipulator, Johnson worked tirelessly on the issues at hand and pressed for solutions. Like his commitment to accommodation, this compulsive style ill-served Johnson as commander in chief. He went from one high-profile initiative to another. From the summer of 1965 until the fall of 1968, he emphasized, at various times, military solutions, diplomatic initiatives, pacification, South Vietnam's political development, international support, and domestic resolve. A president in wartime must play several roles, to be sure, but Johnson's compulsive style showed little attention to the complexity and interrelationship of issues, undermined relations with his military leaders, alienated and confused advisers, and, in the end, lessened confidence in his leadership.

As the war was Americanized, Johnson confronted disagreement between advocates of military escalation and diplomatic initiatives. Gen. William Westmoreland, commander of the U.S. Military Assistance Command, Vietnam, and the Joint Chiefs of Staff (JCS) consistently requested the commitment of more manpower and the elimination of restrictions on military operations. Gen. Earl Wheeler, chairman of the JCS, Admiral U. S. Grant Sharp, commander in chief Pacific, and Westmoreland argued that the attainment of U.S. objectives required the capacity to hit the enemy fully and decisively. From other officials, most prominently McNamara, came calls to limit operations and pursue initiatives that promised a peaceful settlement. Secretary of State Dean Rusk and National Security Adviser McGeorge Bundy were generally skeptical about the prospects for negotiations and wanted to maximize military pressures on North Vietnam but without expanding the war.

The earliest direct battle between U.S. and North Vietnamese forces, waged in the Ia Drang Valley in central South Vietnam in the fall of 1965, shaped the thinking of leaders. In a battle that lasted intermittently over several days before the North Vietnamese broke off the engagement, the United States inflicted heavy casualties while absorbing relatively light losses (those killed being estimated at thirteen hundred North Vietnamese and two hundred Americans). This confrontation taught conflicting "lessons" to different officials. To Westmoreland and the JCS, it confirmed that a strategy of "search and destroy" would enable the United States to win this war without fronts. "Search and destroy" exploited American advantages in mobility and firepower by moving U.S. forces quickly to engage the enemy and to inflict heavy casualties. Success would be measured not by territory captured but by the "body count"—in military parlance, "attriting the enemy."

The gaudy statistical "victory" of the Ia Drang battle suggested that the Americans, together with the South Vietnamese, could win a war of attrition. The army chief of staff, Gen. Harold Johnson, proclaimed after the battle that the "worst is behind us." To McNamara, on the other hand, the battle provided disturbing evidence that the initiative rested with the North Vietnamese. They had chosen the place to fight and the duration of the battle, a capacity that would enable them to limit the effectiveness of a search-and-destroy campaign. McNamara predicted that the North Vietnamese and Viet Cong "will hang on doggedly, effectively matching us man-for-man . . . and that, despite our efforts, we will be faced by early 1967 with stagnation on a higher level."

These differences shaped the continuing clash among Johnson's advisers. As the rate of infiltration of North Vietnamese regular troops and the number of Viet Cong increased, Westmoreland and the JCS urged that Johnson accelerate escalation, recommending an additional 200,000 troops in 1966. That would bring the total U.S. force to 410,000, far surpassing the earlier plan for 275,000 men by that date. Rushing to Saigon for hurried conversations with Westmoreland and Ambassador Henry Cabot Lodge (whom Johnson had persuaded to return to that position in August 1965), McNamara found that neither the South Vietnamese populace nor their army had been inspired by the large-scale U.S. intervention. He told the media that "it will be a long war." Disturbed by what he had found, McNamara on his return to Washington urged Johnson to undertake an initiative for peace—a pause in the bombing of North Vietnam—before implementing Westmoreland's request for more troops. The military leaders were aghast. They warned that North Vietnam would see a bombing pause as a sign of weakness that would enable them to increase the flow of men and supplies to the south.

Instinctively, Johnson sided with the military, but international and domestic pressures pushed him toward McNamara's position. Johnson was convinced that North Vietnam did not want peace: it had rejected his Johns Hopkins University speech offering a program of regional economic development and had not responded to earlier conciliatory gestures. He was, however, vulnerable to criticism that the United States was responsible for the lack of negotiations.

This criticism intensified when the journalist Eric Sevareid reported, in a November 1965 *Look* magazine article, that secret conversations had been conducted several months earlier between U.N. Secretary-General U Thant and the U.S. ambassador to the United Nations, Adlai Stevenson (who had since died). These conversations indicated that the State Department had rejected a North Vietnamese overture for bilateral negotiations. Privately, Johnson was contemptuous of this "mid-night brandy conversation between Stevenson and Sevareid that got us turning down a poor Vietnamese desire to make peace," but he could not ignore the point that the story had heightened an impression, both at home and overseas, of American intransigence.

In addition, Johnson was impressed by McNamara's blunt assessment of the military situation. In meetings at the White House in mid-December, he told the president that "a military solution to the problem is not certain—one out of three or one in two. Ultimately we must find . . . a diplomatic solution." Johnson asked, "Then, no matter what we do in the military field, there is no sure victory?" McNamara replied: "That's right. We have been too optimistic." So, to demonstrate his good will, Johnson announced a Christmas "ceremonial" cease-fire and bombing pause. When Rusk and Bundy reported indications that the Soviet Union might be prepared to play the role of an intermediary in negotiations, Johnson agreed to an indefinite extension of the bombing halt.

Never one to do things on a small scale, Johnson undertook a massive diplomatic offensive to demonstrate his commitment to a peaceful solution. He dispatched emissaries around the globe. Missions by Vice President Hubert Humphrey, Ambassador at Large Averell Harriman, U.N. Ambassador Arthur Goldberg, and Assistant Secretaries of State G. Mennen Williams and Thomas Mann delivered messages to 115 governments, assuring them of America's interest in negotiations without condition. Johnson sent personal appeals to heads of states. Rusk prepared a fourteen-point peace program and invited North Vietnam to participate in "negotiations without preconditions."* In his State of the

*Rusk's proposal contained little that was new. It indicated a willingness to discuss North Vietnam's Four Point program, which had been issued in response to Johnson's pro-

Union address on January 12, 1966, Johnson proclaimed that the United States had "made it clear—from Hanoi to New York—that there are no arbitrary limits to our search for peace. . . . We will meet at any conference table, we will discuss any proposals—four points or fourteen or forty—and we will consider the views of any group."

As the bombing pause continued and the diplomatic missions circled the globe, the JCS repeatedly pressed Johnson to resume ROLLING THUNDER. Johnson reluctantly approved McNamara's plea to continue the halt until the end of January, telling him, "I want to be patient and understanding and reasonable; on the other hand, I think you know my natural inclination." McNamara warned that bombing would lead to a "standoff at a higher level." The North Vietnamese–Viet Cong would "boost their own commitment to test U.S. capabilities and will to persevere at a higher level of conflict and casualties." He predicted that, within a year, American battlefield deaths would reach one thousand a month.

Despite those sober projections, Johnson prepared to resume ROLLING THUNDER and began by lining up political support at home. It was his for the asking. In a meeting with congressional leaders, Johnson predictably found only Democratic Senators Mike Mansfield of Montana and J. William Fulbright of Arkansas, the majority leader and chairman of the Foreign Relations Committee, respectively, and both known critics of the war, against the resumption of the bombing of North Vietnam. Reinforcing the support of most congressional leaders, Johnson summoned the Wise Men—the group of former national security officials on whom he occasionally called for advice—and that group also supported an end to the bombing pause.

Johnson's decision was facilitated by North Vietnam's repudiation of the peace offensive. Ho Chi Minh responded with a message, broadcast by radio from Hanoi, which accused the Americans of hypocrisy—

---

posals at Johns Hopkins University in April 1965. The program remained the basis of North Vietnam's conditions for negotiations throughout the war. It provided for (1) mutual recognition of the rights of the Vietnamese, including the right to live without foreign troops; (2) abstention from foreign military alliances of Vietnam's "two zones" pending reunification; (3) reunification as determined by the Vietnamese peoples in both "zones"; (4) settlement of internal affairs of the southern "zone" by the southern people "in accordance with the program of the National Liberation Front." Since the fourth provision in effect eliminated the existing South Vietnamese government and transferred power to the NLF, it was unacceptable to the United States. Rusk's new offer provided only that the NLF could be "represented" if North Vietnam halted its "aggression."

waging war with "extremely barbarous methods . . . napalm bombs, poison gases and toxic chemicals . . . [while] clamoring about their desire for peace." He reiterated the longstanding demand that the National Liberation Front (NLF) be recognized as the legitimate representative of the South Vietnamese. Talks would begin only when the United States ended "unconditionally and for good all bombing raids and other war acts against [North Vietnam]." U.S. officials gave prominence to Ho's statement as evidence of North Vietnam's intransigence. On January 30, Johnson announced an end to the bombing pause.

To Johnson, Ho's statement capped the futility of his month-long military restraint and diplomatic initiative and confirmed that the North Vietnamese did not want a peaceful settlement. All of the missions and messages of conciliation had yielded no breakthrough. Yet this massive diplomatic offensive was almost bound to fail, as Johnson must have anticipated. Successful negotiations typically require a quiet, deliberative process. By connecting the well-publicized American initiative to a bombing pause, Johnson essentially attempted to intimidate North Vietnam militarily and to put it on the defensive diplomatically. Chester Cooper, then a member of the National Security Council (NSC) staff, later reflected: "Where confidential and careful advance work was necessary, we proceeded with the subtlety of a Fourth of July parade. . . . The President was acting like a ringmaster of a three-ring circus, rather than the focal point of a carefully worked out exercise in diplomacy." Moreover, to many observers at home and overseas, the whirlwind of diplomatic activity emanating from Washington was a charade, intended to justify subsequent escalation. In a private letter, Johnson conceded as much: "Among the important effects of our total activity is surely a far greater understanding of the merits of our position, so that, as we move ahead with our reinforcement in the South and if and when we decide to resume bombing, we shall do so with greater support and understanding . . . and with some hope that worldwide support for our total position will be stronger than ever in the past."

Able to rationalize the resumption of ROLLING THUNDER and an increase in U.S. troops, Johnson changed his role to that of the determined warrior. As the worldwide diplomatic offensive ended with a whimper, Johnson called a high-level conference to chart the path for military and political progress. Just as Truman in 1950 had used the Wake Island conference to reassure himself and the American public that military objectives were being attained, Johnson assembled U.S. military leaders and South Vietnamese officials in Hawaii. The purpose, wrote one adviser, was to provide "a focal point for showing how bright the future for South Vietnam could be." Johnson also saw an opportunity to upstage the Senate Foreign Relations Committee, which had just announced plans to review his war policy. Accordingly, he summoned Westmoreland, Sharp, and, from South Vietnam, Prime Minister Nguyen Cao Ky and Chief of State Nguyen Van Thieu to meet in Honolulu in early February. Johnson—whose entourage included Rusk, McNamara, Bundy, and Wheeler—seemed more intense than usual during the Honolulu meetings. He pressed for assurance that the American effort was succeeding. He repeatedly asked Westmoreland how long the war would last and told him, "General, I have a lot riding on you." When Westmoreland assured Johnson that U.S. forces had prevented the defeat of South Vietnam and promised that an additional 200,000 men would enable him to take the offensive, Johnson foresaw the "nail[-ing] of the coonskin to the wall" by the end of the year.

Johnson also pressed the South Vietnamese leaders for a program to win the "other war"—the pacification of the rural areas where the Viet Cong thrived. He told Ky that he expected a new constitution, free elections, and social reform. To make his point, Johnson told Ky the story of two poker players. The betting ended, and the first player asked, "What do you have?" The second said, "Aces." The first asked, "How many aces?" And the second replied, "One aces." Johnson told Ky, "I hope we don't find out you had only one aces." No such doubts were permitted in public pronouncements. As the conference ended on February 8, Johnson and Ky issued the Declaration of Honolulu, which jointly pledged their governments to resist aggression, build a democracy, undertake social reform, and pursue "an unending quest for peace."

The well-publicized Honolulu conference only temporarily delayed the questioning about Vietnam policy that was sparked by the Senate Foreign Relations Committee under Fulbright's leadership. More than the testimony of any individual or the arguments for and against U.S. involvement, the hearings themselves were the story. The Senate Foreign Relations Committee, which had consistently supported presidents of both parties on major foreign policy issues throughout the cold war, was investigating the necessity and conduct of a war, just seven months after it had been Americanized. Coming in the midst of mounting antiwar protest at colleges and universities and more criticism of the war in much of the press, the Fulbright committee hearings underscored the extent to which the war was already dividing Americans.

Winning the war was the only way that Johnson saw to silence his critics. His militancy was reinforced by the counsel of Walt Whitman Rostow, whom he appointed on March 31 as special assistant to the president, replacing Bundy. A renowned economist who had been among the "action intellectuals" brought to Washington by President John F. Kennedy, Rostow had been chairman of the State Department's Policy Planning Council before moving to his post in the White House. Rostow quickly became Johnson's most hawkish adviser. As the commitment of U.S. ground forces escalated and the mounting North Vietnamese–Viet Cong casualties from the search-and-destroy campaign indicated "progress," Rostow supported the JCS recommendation to expand the bombing to include previously off-limits oil storage facilities in the Hanoi-Haiphong area. Johnson authorized the extension. Shown photographs of the destruction caused by the bombing raids, Johnson exclaimed that "them sons of bitches are finished now."

Such outward exuberance concealed Johnson's increasing melancholia as the evidence from Vietnam indicated minimal progress overall and, with the approach of the first anniversary of the war's Americanization, no sign that the enemy was cracking. The U.S. and South Vietnamese forces outnumbered the North Vietnamese–Viet Cong by a ratio of about three to one and the search-and-destroy missions were winning the battle of the "body count," but the communists showed a capacity to replace their losses and retained their strength in rural areas. They obviously planned for a long war, convinced that they could outlast the Americans. Disturbed by these developments, Johnson slipped into self-pity laced with paranoia. He frequently complained of the lack of answers to the problems that he faced. On one occasion, he lamented to confidantes that "people tell me what not to do, what I do wrong. I don't get any alternatives. What might I be asked next?" He told an assistant: "I can't trust anybody. What are you trying to do to me? Everybody is trying to cut me down, destroy me." He saw himself "trapped" by the "commitment" inherited from Eisenhower and Kennedy, a complaint that became increasingly shrill given Johnson's contempt for the slain president's brother, Robert Kennedy, now a senator from New York. Rostow tried to reassure Johnson by drawing parallels between his problems and those faced by President Abraham Lincoln during the dark days of the Civil War.

Johnson was not easily consoled. Accustomed to achieving political objectives through his domineering and manipulative style, he was frustrated by the ambiguity of the war and the limits of his power as commander in chief. Always in the back of his mind was how Truman had blundered into a larger war in Korea, and Johnson feared that the bombing of North Vietnam would provoke Chinese or Soviet intervention. As he often told advisers, he shuddered at the prospect of an American bomber with a pilot from Johnson City, Texas, dropping a bomb down the stack of a Russian ship in Haiphong Harbor. To the annoyance of military leaders, he insisted on personally approving bombing targets. Day and night, he compulsively searched for indications of progress, demanding the latest information on the bombing, ground warfare, and pacification.

For counsel on the war, Johnson relied principally on weekly meetings—the Tuesday Lunch—with his closest advisers. These sessions, which had begun in 1964, provided an opportunity for full and candid discussion of issues, with Vietnam soon becoming the overriding weekly concern. Rusk, McNamara, Rostow (replacing Bundy), and Press Secretary Bill Moyers were the regular participants, although occasionally others, including Vice President Humphrey, were also invited. (In 1967, the regular membership expanded to include Wheeler and CIA Director Richard Helms.) Johnson liked the Tuesday Lunch as a way of managing the war because it was an informal, off-the-record gathering with a small and intimate group of men who were loyal to him. He never had to worry about leaks to the media. Besides the Tuesday Lunch, Johnson met on occasion with the National Security Council (of which he was wary because the large membership increased the risk of leaks) and, as was his style, he also sought advice from friends outside the administration.

Adding to Johnson's frustration was mounting pressure at home and overseas to renew the search for a peaceful settlement. Contemptuous of North Vietnam for its intransigence in response to the Johns Hopkins offer and the January "diplomatic offensive," Johnson during the summer of 1966 encountered unwelcome initiatives. Canada, through retired diplomat Charles Ronning, tried to foster contacts between Washington and Hanoi. France's President Charles DeGaulle and India's

Prime Minister Indira Gandhi criticized U.S. policy and appealed for negotiations. In addition, British Prime Minister Harold Wilson disassociated his country from the intensified bombing against North Vietnam. With three of America's traditional allies and a prominent neutral country critical of U.S. warfare, Johnson named the seventy-four-year-old statesman W. Averell Harriman as his "ambassador for peace." Harriman's long diplomatic career was distinguished by his experience in dealing with communist governments, having served (among other positions) as ambassador to the Soviet Union, as Truman's special assistant during the Korean War, and as chief U.S. negotiator of the Geneva agreement on Laos in 1962. Given a mandate to explore all opportunities to end the war, Harriman undertook a diplomatic odyssey to meet with leaders of several Asian and European countries.

In the fall of 1966, the ever restless Johnson made another trip to the Pacific to reaffirm American resolve and to document progress since the Honolulu meeting in February. A conference of regional allies in Manila (October 23–25) provided the setting for a show of support of the U.S. effort in Vietnam and to solicit additional troop commitments. At Manila, Johnson met with the heads of the governments of South Vietnam, Australia, New Zealand, Thailand, South Korea, and the Philippines. General Westmoreland and Premier Ky were flown in to provide upbeat assessments. Westmoreland reported progress in all respects: the search-and-destroy campaign was inflicting heavy casualties; the pacification program was weakening the communist position in the rural areas; ROLLING THUNDER was forcing North Vietnam to pay a heavy price for the infiltration of men and supplies to the south; the spirit and fighting quality of the South Vietnamese had notably improved. Prompted by Johnson, Westmoreland urged that allies increase their support. He saw "light at the end of the tunnel" but warned that America and its allies had to be prepared for a long struggle because the communist strategy rested on the assumption that their greater "staying power" would enable them ultimately to prevail. Paralleling Westmoreland's military appraisal, Ky reported on the progress of the South Vietnamese government, foreseeing the imminent collapse of the Viet Cong. "[If] we can get to them the facts," he said, "the people will come back to us."

As he orchestrated the Manila conference, Johnson was aware that McNamara, among other officials, questioned the claims of progress by Westmoreland and Ky. Returning from a trip to South Vietnam earlier in October, McNamara had told Johnson that, despite its heavy losses in the ground war, the resilient enemy's strategy remained "keeping us busy and wait[ing] us out (a strategy of attriting our national will)." Moreover, ROLLING THUNDER had failed to slow the rate of infiltration, and "pacification" had not disturbed the infrastructure of the Viet Cong, who still prevailed through most of the rural areas. McNamara concluded that "the prognosis is bad that the war can be brought to a satisfactory conclusion within the next two years" and challenged the claims of Westmoreland and the JCS that more military power would bring victory. So McNamara again pressed for negotiations, emphasizing, as a first step, the importance of convincing North Vietnam that the United States really wanted a peaceful settlement.

While Johnson permitted no such skepticism to distract from the upbeat tone of the Manila conference, he blended this show of resolve with a diplomatic initiative. He took a cue from Soviet Foreign Minister Andrei Gromyko, who had suggested, during a visit to the White House earlier in October, that the United States should spell out the conditions for its total withdrawal from Vietnam. At Manila, Johnson prevailed upon the other leaders to support a statement (which was part of an elaborate set of documents emanating from the conference) pledging the complete withdrawal of all forces from South Vietnam "as the other side withdraws its forces to the North, ceases infiltration, and the level of violence thus subsides."

At the end of the Manila conference, Johnson decided to travel to Vietnam. Determined to assure America's fighting men of his personal support and that of their countrymen, he visited the U.S. base at Camranh Bay and told the troops: "I thank you, I salute you, may the good Lord look over you and keep you until you come home with the coonskin on the wall." It was an emotional experience for Johnson, who later wrote that "I have never been more moved by any group I have talked to, never in my life."

Buoyed by his Asian trip, Johnson soon learned of a possible diplomatic breakthrough. Code-named MARIGOLD, this secret initiative, which Harriman's mission helped to move along, seemed to provide a mutually satisfactory formula for starting negotiations through a Phase A/Phase B plan: the United States would cease the bombing unconditionally (Phase A) but on the basis of a previously arranged understanding that both sides would de-escalate (Phase B). This scheme addressed both sides' conditions for negotiations (i.e., North Vietnam's insistence on an unconditional end of ROLLING THUNDER and the U.S. insistence on mutual de-escalation). MARIGOLD, however, was inadvertently undermined when the United States resumed the bombing of Hanoi on December 2, after a delay of several weeks because of bad weather. To the North Vietnamese, the bombing showed American "bad faith," but in reality it reflected the difficulty of coordinating military and diplomatic operations. Military leaders, who authorized the renewed bombing of Hanoi (Johnson's approval being unnecessary, since he had given it prior to the delay), knew nothing of MARIGOLD. So North Vietnam used the resumption of ROLLING THUNDER as the pretext for closing the MARIGOLD discussions. Johnson was neither surprised nor disappointed, for he still doubted the genuineness of the North Vietnamese interest in negotiations.

Yet Johnson could not ignore the public pressure for a peaceful settlement. In mid-December, Harrison Salisbury of the *New York Times*, the first American journalist to be granted a visa by North Vietnam, visited Hanoi and wrote a series of articles detailing the devastation caused by American bombing. Salisbury's reports from Hanoi, accompanied by photographs, discredited the Pentagon's claims that the bombing was carried out with such accuracy that it avoided residential areas and took few civilian casualties.

Although terribly annoyed by Salisbury's criticism, Johnson took seriously Salisbury's report on a private interview with Premier Pham Van Dong, who seemed to suggest a compromise between the North Vietnamese and American conditions for negotiations that was similar to the Phase A/Phase B formula of MARIGOLD. In particular, Pham Van Dong, while holding to the standard North Vietnamese insistence on an unconditional end of bombing, added that such a step would be followed by North Vietnam "tak[ing] an appropriate stand." He later reiterated that, if the United States ceased "harm[ing] the North, we know what we should do."

Encouraged by this signal from Hanoi and by assurances from Soviet officials that the North Vietnamese would welcome an American initiative, the State Department undertook a renewed round of diplomatic activity, mostly secretive, that was code-named SUNFLOWER. Through its Moscow Embassy, the United States established contact with a North Vietnamese diplomat in the Soviet capital, but the latter soon broke off discussions. As the SUNFLOWER diplomatic channel was closing, the State Department was responding to another mission to

Hanoi in January 1967 by two private citizens—Harry Ashmore and William Baggs. Peace activists and journalists associated with the Center for the Study of Democratic Institutions in California, Ashmore and Baggs arrived in Hanoi as Salisbury was leaving, and they secured a meeting with Ho Chi Minh. Although reiterating the familiar insistence on an unconditional cessation of bombing, Ho seemed to offer some flexibility on North Vietnam's stipulation in its Four Point program that the NLF control the political program of South Vietnam. Johnson declined to meet with Ashmore and Baggs upon their return to the United States, but they did report to State Department officials, who drafted a letter from Ashmore and Baggs to Ho Chi Minh that called for evidence of reciprocal restraint if the United States halted the bombing. On January 29, a statement by North Vietnam's Foreign Minister Nguyen Duy Trinh demanded an unconditional bombing halt as the condition for negotiations, which the State Department interpreted as a rejection of the Ashmore-Baggs initiative.

Then, as the prospect for launching discussions through traditional means dimmed, Johnson dramatically appealed personally to Ho Chi Minh for cooperation in bringing the war to an end. Such an overture had been under consideration among Johnson's advisers for several weeks. It appealed to Johnson's wheeler-dealer instinct. Perhaps the two leaders could achieve the breakthrough that had eluded subordinates and intermediaries.

Transmitted through the North Vietnamese Embassy in Moscow on February 8, Johnson's message, however genuine an expression of Johnson's yearning for peace, restated demands that were known to be unacceptable to North Vietnam. Johnson appealed to Ho to recognize a mutual "heavy obligation to seek earnestly the path to peace" and the possibility that "our thoughts and yours, our attitudes and yours, have been distorted or misinterpreted." He suggested that the two of them plan for "direct talks between trusted representatives in a secure setting away from the glare of publicity." Then Johnson came to the contentious issue of conditions for negotiations and offered terms that were less conciliatory than the Phase A/Phase B approach. Johnson rejected the demand that the United States cease bombing permanently and unconditionally and tried to explain the American perspective: "There would inevitably be grave concern on our part whether your Government would make use of such action by us to improve your military position." Instead, Johnson offered the promise of ending both the bombing and the further augmentation of U.S. forces in South Vietnam "as soon as I am assured that infiltration into South Vietnam by land and sea has stopped." To show good faith, Johnson ordered a bombing halt as part of the Tet holiday truce.*

Ho Chi Minh's reply closed the door to negotiations and underscored a widening gulf between the Americans and North Vietnamese. Ho denounced the United States on several grounds: for "intervention" that had violated the Geneva agreements and prolonged the division of Vietnam; for "aggression" against the peoples of South Vietnam, which had transformed it "into an American colony and military base," and now against North Vietnam; for "war crimes and crises against peace and against humanity," which included bombing, chemical warfare, and destruction of villages. Most importantly, Ho refused to budge from the demand that negotiations had to be preceded by "unconditionally halting the bombing as well as other acts of war" against North Vietnam. "The Vietnamese people," he wrote, "will never yield to force nor agree to talks under the menace of bombs." The Johnson-Ho exchange underlined how far the two sides had moved away from the Phase A/Phase B formula, which had, however fleetingly, seemed to offer some promise of a breakthrough.

The spate of futile diplomatic initiatives having convinced him that Hanoi preferred to fight rather than negotiate, Johnson shifted his emphasis to winning the battle for the "hearts and minds" of the South Vietnamese people. He was determined to correct the badly coordinated program of pacification—the "other war"—that had failed to challenge the Viet Cong's strength in the rural areas. This had enabled the communists to control most of the warfare: the Viet Cong and North Vietnamese launched about 90 percent of the countless military engagements waged throughout South Vietnam; when confronted by U.S. firepower, they broke off the fighting and disappeared into jungle and countryside. The imperative of pacification was underscored in early 1967 when the U.S. and South Vietnamese forces undertook two large-scale search-and-destroy operations—CEDAR FALLS and JUNC-

---

*Simultaneously the last gasp of SUNFLOWER unfolded. British Prime Minister Harold Wilson played the role of intermediary, carrying the U.S. position on negotiations, which he understood to be a continuation of the Phase A/Phase B formula, to Soviet Premier Alexei Kosygin, with whom he was meeting in London. The initiative was poorly handled. The State Department had failed to inform Wilson that it was backing away from the Phase A/Phase B approach, and the Wilson initiative quickly unraveled.

TION CITY—against communist positions in the area west of Saigon near the Cambodian border. The offensives inflicted heavy casualties, bombarded bases, and captured supplies, leading one general to proclaim that the Americans and South Vietnamese had achieved "a turning point . . . a blow from which the communists in this area may never recover." He was wrong. Like the ongoing smaller-scale search-and-destroy warfare, Operations CEDAR FALLS and JUNCTION CITY underscored the enemy's resilience, for the communists limited their losses by cutting off the fighting and retreating from the area; then they returned after the Americans and South Vietnamese forces departed.

In the interest of reinforcing the sense of South Vietnamese American solidarity and spurring a renewed pacification effort, Johnson summoned high-ranking South Vietnamese and U.S. officials to Guam on March 20–21. (The U.S. air base on that small island launched many of the B-52 bombers that attacked North Vietnam.) Journeying to the Pacific for the third time in thirteen months, Johnson sought to integrate the pacification initiative with a large-scale regional development project. He revived the concept that he had proposed two years earlier in his Johns Hopkins University address. His entourage included David Lilienthal, the former director of the Tennessee Valley Authority, whom Johnson foresaw "working on a sort of TVA of the Mekong River. If we can get these things started, we'll really be getting someplace." To get this "other war" moving and to signal its importance, he planned a coordinated pacification program under the direction of a civilian who would be a deputy commander under Westmoreland. Johnson placed a trusted adviser, Robert Komer, in charge of this ambitious effort, officially called Civil Operations and Revolutionary Support.

At Guam, as at the Honolulu and Manila meetings, the mood was upbeat. Generals Ky and Thieu, having been criticized for slow progress in fulfilling promises made at Honolulu a year earlier, brought along the new South Vietnamese Constitution, which had recently been approved by a constituent assembly. They promised that elections would be held soon. In return, Johnson pledged that, once the war ended, the United States would assist in building a stable and prosperous society, centering on the Mekong regional development scheme. Westmoreland foresaw the ground war approaching the "cross-over" point, where enemy losses would exceed replacements.

Johnson was devastated, however, by Westmoreland's confidential projections. "As things now stand," Westmoreland told the president, "it may take ten years." Only a significant increase in U.S. forces would reduce the length of the war. Accordingly, Westmoreland requested more troops: a "minimum" of 80,000 (which would bring the total U.S. force to 550,000), a "maximum" of 200,000 (which would raise the total to 670,000).

As Johnson returned to Washington, Westmoreland's sober analysis provided the backdrop for a heated debate within his administration. Convinced that the failure of diplomacy justified escalation, the military leadership pressed for an enlarged war. Besides the additional troops, the JCS requested approval to carry the war into enemy sanctuaries in Laos and Cambodia and across the demilitarized zone into North Vietnam, to bomb and mine North Vietnam's ports, and to mobilize the nation's reserve forces. Wheeler and Westmoreland—whom Johnson had summoned back home to assure the public that, contrary to the arguments of protesters against the war, the U.S. effort was going well—met with Johnson at the White House on April 27. Johnson probed for answers: "Where does it all end? When we add divisions, can't the enemy add divisions? If so, where does it all end?" Westmoreland replied that, at the present level of 470,000 troops, "we would be setting up a meat grinder. We could do little more than hold our own . . . [and] the war could go on for five years." If the force was increased by 80,000, "the war could go on for three years." But if the U.S. force was increased by 200,000 men, "it could go on for two years." Without the additional troops, Wheeler foresaw a long war: "The momentum will die; in some areas the enemy will recapture the initiative. We won't lose the war, but it will be a longer one." Certainly not lost on Johnson was the approaching 1968 presidential election and his political interest in being able to demonstrate that the war was moving toward a successful conclusion.

In his public statements, capped by a message to a joint session of Congress, Westmoreland projected optimism, saying that only a lack of support at home could prevent America's ultimate victory. Great progress had been made, Westmoreland assured the members of Congress, in building a "shield of security" for South Vietnam. "In evaluating the enemy strategy it is evident to me that he believes our Achilles' heel is our resolve. . . . Backed at home by resolve, confidence, patience, determination, and continued support, we will prevail in Vietnam over the Communist aggressor."

As the public relations campaign masked the military leadership's analysis of the situation, several high-ranking officials in the Defense and State Departments were deeply troubled by the troop request. McNamara, Deputy Secretary of Defense Cyrus Vance, Assistant Secretary of Defense for International Security Affairs John McNaughton, and Under Secretary of State Nicholas Katzenbach doubted that adding troops and expanding the war would achieve victory but feared that it would increase the risk of war with the Soviet Union or China.

It was again McNamara who was at the center of the struggle to influence Johnson. In a lengthy May 19 memorandum, he warned Johnson that the JCS proposals would not necessarily bring victory but could lead to the "national disaster" of a larger war. Instead, escalation, which had acquired a self-perpetuating momentum, had to be scaled back, for it was not only failing to bring victory on the battlefield but also increasing the war's unpopularity at home. According to McNamara, "Most Americans do not know how we got where we are, and most, without knowing why, but taking advantage of hindsight, are convinced that we should not have gotten this deeply in. All want the war ended and expect their President to end it. Successfully. Or else." McNamara ruled out a "successful" conclusion. There was no acceptable way of winning: "The enemy has us 'stalemated' . . . [and] can and almost certainly will maintain the military 'stalemate' by matching our added deployments as necessary." Moreover, pacification was failing, a result of the chronic corruption and inefficiency of the South Vietnamese government. McNamara was blunt: "There is rot in the fabric. Our efforts to enliven the moribund political infrastructure have been matched by VC efforts. . . . The NLF continues to control [a] large part of South Vietnam, and there is little evidence that the [pacification] program is gaining any momentum."

So it was time, McNamara contended, to choose "among imperfect alternatives." With the present course leading to prolonged stalemate and the military's request entailing unacceptable risks, the wisest course was to limit escalation and to seek a way out through negotiations. McNamara suggested that Johnson should provide only 30,000 additional troops and set an ultimate limit of 570,000. Rather than expanding the bombing of North Vietnam, McNamara went on, Johnson should cut back ROLLING THUNDER to the area between the demilitarized zone and the twentieth parallel, a narrow area about 175 miles long, where bombing provided essential support for U.S. military operations in South Vietnam's northernmost provinces. Rather than mobilizing the reserves, Johnson should avoid that step, which would add to the mounting public disaffection with the war. Rather than anticipating an unattainable military victory, Johnson should be prepared to accept a negotiated settlement that might provide less than a stable, non-communist South Vietnam. In particular, McNamara said that the United States needed to think of a compromise "invoking, inter alia, a role in the South for members of the Viet Cong." McNamara cited regional developments to help justify his advocacy of reduced U.S. objectives and operations. The defeat of a communist coup in Indonesia and the turmoil within China arising from the Cultural Revolution worked to America's advantage and lessened Vietnam's strategic significance.

Finally, McNamara concluded that the war was damaging American credibility. "There may be a limit beyond which many Americans and much of the world will not permit the United States to go," he argued.

> The picture of the world's greatest superpower killing or injuring more than 1,000 noncombatants a month while trying to pound a tiny backward nation into submission on an issue whose merits are hotly disputed is not a pretty one. It could conceivably produce a costly distortion in the American national consciousness and in the world image of the United States—especially if we increase the damage to North Vietnam complete enough to be "successful."

To the military leadership, McNamara's "imperfect alternatives" spelled disaster. Any limits on military pressure would only encourage greater North Vietnamese resistance, the JCS responded, and limiting the bombing would "stir deep resentment at home, among our troops, and be regarded by the Communists as an aerial Dien Bien Phu." Failure to call up the reserves would weaken the overall U.S. military position, which might invite a North Korean assault on South Korea or a Chinese attack on Thailand.

No president ever confronted sharper differences over how to wage war, for at the heart of the disagreement in the spring of 1967 was the fundamental question of whether America's objectives were attainable. Johnson's attention was temporarily diverted in late May and early June by tensions in the Middle East and the ensuing Six-Day War, which threatened to involve the Soviet Union and the United States. As that situation came under control, Johnson returned to his preoccupation with Vietnam, but he avoided the full examination of strategy that was clearly called for. Regarding both the military and the McNamara proposals as too extreme, he compromised, but in ways that came closer to the McNamara alternative. He gave the military much less than it sought but not too much more than McNamara had suggested. He ultimately approved a modest increase of troops and a limited expansion of the bombing that did not include North Vietnam's ports. He refused to permit expansion of U.S. ground operations into North Vietnam, Laos, and Cambodia.

While taking these steps, which pleased neither side, Johnson undertook a series of initiatives that were intended to present the public image of a united and determined American government making progress in the war. He began by contriving to conceal the profound differences within his administration. Gathering McNamara, Wheeler, and Westmoreland for a joint news conference at the White House on July 13, 1967, Johnson announced disingenuously: "We have reached a meeting of minds. The troops that General Westmoreland needs and requests, as we feel it necessary, will be supplied." Then he asked each of the officials, who were seated uncomfortably on a sofa, for their agreement.

"Is that not true, General Westmoreland?"

"Yes, sir."

"General Wheeler?"

"Yes, sir."

"Secretary McNamara?"

"Yes, sir."

Westmoreland added that the military was making substantial progress and that reports of stalemate were "fiction." He compared critics of the war to parents who could not see the maturation of a child. All told, the episode at the White House was a charade that avoided the imperative to confront the disagreement between Westmoreland's "needs and requests" and what civilian authorities considered "necessary."

Johnson then dispatched a special mission to demonstrate the support for the war of the United States's Asian and Pacific allies. The mission was headed by the prominent Washington attorney, Clark Clifford, who was serving as chairman of the Foreign Intelligence Advisory Board, and by Gen. Maxwell Taylor, a presidential adviser who had previously served as chairman of the Joint Chiefs of Staff and ambassador to South Vietnam. Seeking greater troop commitments, Clifford and Taylor went to Thailand, Australia, New Zealand, the Philippines, and South Korea. Among those allies, only South Korea had sent a sizable contingent (forty-seven thousand men by 1967), while the others had provided token contributions.* The Clifford-Taylor mission managed to gain a pledge of additional troops only from Thailand, which promised to send the Queen's Cobras, a 2,000-man infantry unit.

Upon their return to Washington on August 6, Clifford and Taylor proclaimed that all the allied nations' leaders strongly supported the U.S. effort. Like the White House press conference a few weeks earlier, the Clifford-Taylor report ignored unpleasant realities: that much of the allied backing was rhetorical, that the war was unpopular among some allied peoples (notably in the Philippines), and, most importantly, that the troop commitment was modest. Yet Johnson seized upon the Thai contribution, together with a promise from Saigon to add 65,000 men to the South Vietnamese Army, to justify limiting the number of additional American troops to 50,000.

Through these measures, Johnson hoped to restore public confidence in his leadership. That was now an uphill battle. His was now a presidency under siege. The public's "approval" of his presidential performance plunged to 39 percent. Johnson's declining popularity resulted from not only the dissatisfaction over the lack of progress in the war but also a sense that the national fabric was unraveling. The summer of 1967 brought rioting to several large cities, and Johnson had to call on U.S. troops to restore order; the outgrowth of the persistence of poverty, especially among African Americans who were trapped within a world of urban decay, the riots triggered partisan finger pointing that left Johnson vulnerable and defensive. The ironies were inescapable: urban unrest unparalleled in American history occurring at a time when the Great Society had promised urban renewal and an end to poverty; U.S. troops simultaneously waging war in Vietnam and "pacifying" America's inner cities.

In Congress, both "hawks" and "doves" assailed Johnson's war policies. The Senate Armed Services Committee, headed by Democratic Senator John Stennis of Mississippi, held hearings on the conduct of the war that brought into the open the differences between the military and civilian leadership. The committee's hawkish members grilled McNamara on his refusal to follow the JCS recommendations. The

*By 1967, Allied support included, besides the South Koreans, the following troops: Australia, 6,618; Thailand, 244; New Zealand, 534; Philippines, 2,020. Only Thailand, which eventually sent some eleven thousand troops, increased its contribution beyond the 1967 levels.

Stennis committee issued a final report indicting the Johnson administration for failing to pursue a strategy that would lead to a decisive
victory. Meanwhile, Fulbright and his dovish colleagues on the Senate
Foreign Relations Committee conducted investigations into the legality
of the war, especially the murky circumstances surrounding the Gulf of
Tonkin incident, which Johnson had used to justify the congressional
resolution that he claimed gave him authority to wage war.

Still Johnson pushed ahead, convinced that, if he could demonstrate
progress in Vietnam, the nation's internal divisions would lessen. So he
seized upon an opportunity to celebrate South Vietnam's presidential
elections under the new constitution. The September 3 elections resulted in the victory of the military leadership of Nguyen Van Thieu
and Nguyen Cao Ky—who had been in power since 1965—as president
and vice president, respectively.* To lend credence to this "democratic
progress," Johnson sent twenty-two prominent Americans as observers.
They hailed the elections as fair and honest and, as one put it, "a moving
and profound example of the desire for self-determination." The election
reflected South Vietnamese popular sentiment within important limitations: no Communist or "neutral" candidates were permitted on the
ballot; the Thieu-Ky ticket enjoyed the support of the army, which dominated the government and society. The results were thus predictable,
but the Thieu-Ky ticket did not win the strong mandate that American
officials had expected. In a field of eleven presidential–vice presidential slates, most of which had no nationwide recognition, Thieu and Ky
received 35 percent of the total votes. To the dismay of the Americans,
the second-place presidential candidate, with 18 percent of the vote, was
Truong Dinh Dzu, who favored negotiations with North Vietnam and
the Viet Cong. Still, Johnson pointed to the fulfillment of the military
leadership's promise: South Vietnam had duly elected a president under
its new constitution.

Buoyed by the strengthening of the South Vietnamese government,
Johnson next extended a conciliatory gesture to Hanoi. Speaking at San
Antonio on September 29, he announced that "the United States is will-

---

*This marked a reversal in the power relationship between Thieu and Ky. In the regime
that had seized power in 1965, Ky had held the top position of prime minister. Ensuing
rivalry between the two men eventually prompted the South Vietnamese army leadership
to prevail upon Ky to accept the vice presidency in the new government. Thieu was regarded as more stable than the flamboyant Ky. Thieu's elevation was welcomed by U.S. officials.

ing to stop all aerial and naval bombardment of North Vietnam when this will lead promptly to productive discussions. We, of course, assume that while discussions proceed, North Vietnam would not take advantage of the bombing cessation or limitation." In his memoir, Johnson explained the reasoning behind the offer: "It relaxed somewhat the proposal we had made to Ho Chi Minh in February. We were not asking him to restrict his military actions before a bombing halt and once the bombing ended, we were not insisting that he immediately end his military effort, only that he did not increase it." Through the "reasonable" offer in what became known as the "San Antonio formula," Johnson hoped to hasten a new secret diplomatic channel to North Vietnam, code-named Operation PENNSYLVANIA. Growing out of contacts between two French academics and authorities in Hanoi, the scheme involved Henry Kissinger (later secretary of state under Presidents Richard Nixon and Gerald Ford), who worked as liaison between the Frenchmen and U.S. officials. Like earlier secret discussions, this initiative centered on the question of the conditions for negotiations. Besides extending the San Antonio formula, Johnson limited bombing of the Hanoi area (despite Wheeler's strenuous objections) as a signal of restraint.

When the North Vietnamese raised objections to Johnson's offer, the stress of the intractable problems at home and overseas increasingly showed in Johnson's demeanor. At a Tuesday Lunch in early October, he talked about the need to end the war quickly and asked what would be the effect if he did not seek reelection in 1968? The normally reticent Rusk immediately told Johnson that he could not quit: "You are the commander in chief and we are in a war. This would have a very serious effect on the country. . . . Hanoi would think they have got it made." Seeming to agree, Johnson continued to lament the dilemmas that he faced. At an October 23 meeting, a frustrated president sorted through the alternatives: The ground war was inconclusive, but military leaders had no imaginative solutions. ("It doesn't seem that we can win militarily. I asked the JCS [for] suggestions . . . but all of their proposals related to suggestions to take war outside Vietnam.") Neither was the diplomatic front working, as North Vietnam again failed to respond to his limitations on bombing. ("If we cannot get negotiations, why don't we hit all the military targets short of provoking Russia and China?") As Johnson ordered a resumption of bombing in the Hanoi area, McNamara reminded him of another alternative, to test Hanoi's willingness to negotiate by accepting its terms of an unconditional cessation of bombing. Johnson did not respond to what proved to be McNamara's last recommendation on Vietnam.

Having decided to resume bombing, Johnson reverted to his practice of seeking confirmation from those who were certain to give their approval. He again invited the Wise Men to the White House. Just as in previous meetings with substantially the same group (a few former Wise Men who had become critics of his conduct of the war were not invited this time, while some officials who had left his administration— notably Lodge, Ball, and Bundy—were included), Johnson controlled the agenda in ways that precluded a full appraisal of the situation and alternatives. The Wise Men were given optimistic briefings on the military and pacification efforts but were not made aware of McNamara's dissent or of other analyses that questioned the signs of progress. Led by Truman's secretary of state, Dean Acheson, who drew parallels between communist tactics in Korea and Vietnam, the Wise Men predictably concluded their deliberations by telling Johnson what he wanted to hear: the United States had to persevere in Vietnam.

Their advice helped to propel Johnson toward still another campaign to solidify popular support. At a press conference, he acknowledged mounting criticism of the war ("If I have done anything as president, it has been to insure that there are plenty of dissenters") but called for perseverance in a

> new kind of war for us. . . . Our American people, when we get into a contest of any kind—whether it is in a war, an election, a football game, or whatever it is—want it decided and decided quickly; get in and get out. . . . That is not the kind of war we are fighting in Vietnam. . . . We don't march out and have a big battle every day in a guerrilla war. . . . We are pleased with the results that we are getting. We are inflicting greater losses than we are taking.

Besides his own public assurances of progress, Johnson summoned home General Westmoreland and Ellsworth Bunker, who had replaced Lodge as ambassador to South Vietnam, for a series of speeches and interviews to certify that the war was going well. Bunker spoke of "steady progress . . . not only militarily, but in other ways as well: in the evolution of the constitutional process, in the pacification program. . . . There is every prospect that the progress will accelerate." In the most widely reported aspect of Johnson's public relations campaign, Westmoreland addressed the National Press Club and spoke of the war approaching its end: "Whereas in 1965 the enemy was winning, today he is losing. There are indications that the Viet Cong and even Hanoi know this. . . . It is significant that the enemy has not won a major battle in more than a year." The war had entered a new phase "when the end begins to come into view."

As Westmoreland and Bunker concluded their visit, McNamara, at Johnson's instigation, was preparing to leave office. On November 29, he announced his resignation as secretary of defense but, as he later wrote, "I do not know to this day whether I quit or was fired. Maybe it was both." Regardless of the circumstances, McNamara departed to become president of the World Bank, an assignment that interested him and had been engineered by Johnson. McNamara's by now well-known disagreements with the JCS had made him increasingly a political liability. Later, Johnson would tell colleagues that he feared the strains of the war had brought McNamara to a breaking point. He also confided to a biographer that he thought McNamara's resolve had weakened because of the influence of Robert Kennedy, whom Johnson distrusted. In his memoir, McNamara attributes the decision to his differences with Johnson: he believed the war could not be won, but Johnson had not yet reached that conclusion. Whatever the reasons, McNamara's departure and the appointment of the reputedly hawkish Clark Clifford as his successor were welcomed by the Pentagon and added to the image of Johnson's renewed toughness and resolve.

Just before Christmas, Johnson concluded the campaign to sell the war with a whirlwind four-day, 27,000-mile trip that took him to Australia, where he conferred with President Thieu, and then on to the Vatican, where he met with Pope Paul VI, whose assistance he sought in trying to encourage negotiations. In between, Johnson visited American troops at a base in Thailand and, for the second time, at Camranh Bay, in South Vietnam. There a combative Johnson proclaimed that the enemy had "met their masters in the field. . . . We're not going to yield. And we're not going to shimmy." In presenting a Distinguished Service Medal to Westmoreland, Johnson praised him for taking the war "from the valleys and depths and despondence to the cliffs and heights where we know now that the enemy can never win."

In the half-year since receiving conflicting recommendations from McNamara and the military leaders in May 1967, Johnson's leadership had reflected inconsistencies and ironies. Characteristically, his actions were a compromise, but one that came closer to McNamara's cautionary advice. Privately, it seems that Johnson accepted the thrust of the McNamara argument: that the war could not be won through any acceptable application of U.S. military power. Expanding the war, as the JCS recommended, substantially increased the prospects of Soviet or Chinese intervention. Yet to go as far toward meeting Hanoi's conditions for negotiation as McNamara recommended would have subjected Johnson to condemnation by the JCS and other hawks and would have risked the loss of the fundamental objective of South Vietnam's integrity. Unprepared to risk either the loss of South Vietnam or a larger war, Johnson had embraced imperfect alternatives.

More important than what he authorized during the last six months of 1967, however, was what he did not do. He increased the troop commitment by only one-fourth of the JCS request, declined to mobilize the reserves, and refused to permit the expansion of the ground war outside of South Vietnam. The expansion of the bombing of North Vietnam, while opposed by McNamara, fell short of the JCS plan. Over the objections of the JCS, he temporarily limited bombing to test the "San Antonio formula." In the end, however, it was a demoralized and shaken McNamara who was shuffled out of office just as Johnson was decorating and lavishly praising Westmoreland. This emphasized the irony that, after having embraced more dovish than hawkish alternatives, Johnson ended 1967 with a strident campaign proclaiming military victory. Having failed to meet the JCS request that promised, at best, victory by 1970, Johnson had to realize that claims of imminent victory were, at best, extravagant and, at worst, duplicitous. He risked, moreover, becoming trapped by his own desperate excesses. The end-of-the-year selling of the war's progress encouraged public expectations that, with the enemy on the "defensive," the war would soon end.

Then came the unexpected. Just as the promise of imminent victory in the Korean War had been shattered by Chinese intervention in late 1950, so was the projection of "light at the end of the tunnel in Vietnam" undermined by the Tet offensive that began in the last days of January 1968. Like Truman in the winter of 1950–51, Johnson in early 1968 grappled with the military and political implications of an unexpected manifestation of enemy strength. But unlike the Chinese attack in Korea, which triggered a painful retreat, the communist attack that began on January 30, 1968, during the Tet holiday truce, ended ambiguously, with the Americans and South Vietnamese able to claim "victory" in a tactical sense. Yet the strategic implications of the Tet offensive forced Johnson, like Truman after China's intervention in Korea, to undertake a fundamental reassessment of American capabilities.

During the first weeks of January 1968, U.S. intelligence detected a significant increase in the movement of North Vietnamese troops and supplies down the Ho Chi Minh Trail. American officials were thus anticipating a large-scale communist offensive, most likely directed against South Vietnam's northern provinces. That projection seemed to be confirmed when, on January 21, North Vietnamese forces attacked the U.S. base at Khe Sanh in the northwestern corner of South Vietnam. Johnson and Westmoreland immediately drew parallels between the assault on Khe Sanh and the communist siege of Dien Bien Phu in the same area in 1954, which had been the decisive battle of the French war in Indochina. Johnson became obsessed with the struggle for Khe Sanh, saying time and again, "I don't want any damn Dinbinphoo." He pressed the JCS for assurances that the post would be held. He ordered the construction, in the White House Situation Room, of a model of the battle site, which he frequently phoned or visited, even during the middle of his many sleepless nights, to be updated on developments.

Then, just when it seemed that the North Vietnamese had centered their resources on capturing Khe Sanh, they and the Viet Cong launched a series of nearly simultaneous attacks on more than a hundred cities and towns; the targets included Saigon and thirty-five provincial capitals. The communists had managed to smuggle some eighty thousand civilian-clothed soldiers and their weapons into the targeted sites. By bringing the war into the urban areas, which had largely been spared from the fighting, the North Vietnamese and Viet Cong wanted to demonstrate the vulnerability of South Vietnam. Their ultimate objective was to stimulate an uprising against the Saigon government.

The sheer dimension of the Tet offensive astounded the American public. Having been assured that the enemy was losing strength, Americans now confronted graphic television images of intense fighting in the cities, widespread confusion and destruction, and guerrillas even capturing part of the U.S. Embassy compound in Saigon. It made little difference that the American and South Vietnamese forces generally gained the upper hand within a few days (the one exception being the struggle for Hue, which lasted for a month). What mattered was the psychological effect: the enemy had demonstrated an impressive military capability, which give the lie to projections of an imminent victory.

Throughout the early days of the Tet crisis, Johnson and his advisers tried to make sense of a confusing situation. It was unclear whether Khe Sanh was the principal communist target or a diversionary move. There was concern that the Tet attacks on January 30–31 would be followed by a second wave of assaults on the cities and towns. The military leaders argued more strenuously than ever for expanding the war. While publicly proclaiming that the communists were suffering an enormous defeat as the Americans and South Vietnamese gained control, Westmoreland cabled a different picture:

> From a realistic point of view, we must accept the fact that the enemy has dealt a severe blow. He has brought the war to the towns and cities and has inflicted damage and casualties on the population. Homes have been destroyed, distribution of the necessities of life has been interrupted. Damage has been inflicted on the [lines of communication] and the economy has been decimated. Martial law has been invoked with stringent curfews in the cities. The people have felt directly the impact of the war.

Johnson fell into a familiar pattern of blending self-pity with numerous meetings at which he raised (but did not demand answers to) important questions and the dispatch of another special mission to Vietnam. At the annual presidential prayer breakfast, Johnson shared his agony: "The nights are very long. The winds are very chill. Our spirits grow weary and restive as the springtime of man seems farther and farther away." In a meeting where he faced difficult questions from normally supportive Democratic Party congressional leaders, Johnson lamented that "nothing is as dirty as to violate a truce during the holidays. But nobody says anything bad about Ho Chi Minh. They call me a murderer. But Ho has a great image. . . . We've got all we can of this 'what's wrong with our country?'" On another occasion, Johnson lashed out to his advisers: "Well, it looks as if all of you have counseled, advised, consulted, and then—as usual—placed the monkey on my back again."

Meeting with several officials on February 9, a desperate Johnson searched for direction. When Wheeler urged reinforcing Westmoreland's forces, Johnson could not control his fury: "All last week I asked two questions. The first was 'Did Westmoreland have what he needed?'

You answered yes. The second question was 'Can Westmoreland take care of the situation with [what] he has there now?' The answer was yes. Tell me what has happened to change the situation between then and now?" Wheeler, who had urged Westmoreland to request additional troops, responded that it was necessary to match an increase in North Vietnam's forces, which intelligence indicated had been significantly strengthened, especially in the area around Khe Sanh, where the fighting continued as that in the cities and towns abated. To buttress the case for more troops, the JCS also presented new estimates of heavy South Vietnamese army casualties during the Tet offensive.

Although plainly annoyed, Johnson sensed that he was trapped: if he did not meet the military's request, he would be blamed for any further reversals on the battlefield. He wondered whether he had the necessary support at home. Turning to Rusk, he asked whether the administration should "have more than the Gulf of Tonkin resolution going into this? Should we ask for a declaration of war? . . . What would be the impact internationally of a declaration of war?" Rusk doubted that Congress would approve a declaration and, if it did, such a step would be seen in Moscow and Beijing as provocative. It was up to incoming Defense Secretary Clark Clifford to point out the incongruity of the administration's response to the Tet offensive:

> There is a very strong contradiction in what we are saying and doing. . . . We have publicly told the American people that the communist offensive (a) was not a victory, (b) produced no uprising among the Vietnamese in support of the enemy, and (c) cost the enemy between 20,000 and 25,000 of his combat troops. Now our reaction to all of this is to say that the situation is more dangerous than it was before all of this. We are saying that we need more troops, that we need more ammunition and that we need to call up the reserves. I think we should give some very serious thought to how we explain on one hand the enemy did not take a victory and yet we are in need of many more troops and possibly an emergency call up.

Three days later, Johnson dispatched Wheeler to Vietnam to report on the situation and acted on Westmoreland's urgent appeal for reinforcements by authorizing a modest increase of 10,500 men. He told advisers: "Frankly, I am scared to death about Khe Sanh. . . . I have a mighty big stake in this. I am more unsure every day."

Wheeler's ensuing recommendations, which Johnson received at the end of February, touched off the administration's most intensive debate on the war since July 1965. Concerned about a weakening of the American global military position and still hoping for authorization of a more aggressive strategy in Vietnam, Wheeler used the Tet crisis and the continuing battle at Khe Sanh to request an additional 206,000 men. He portrayed a bleak situation; Tet had been a "very near thing," and while the enemy had suffered heavy losses, its resiliency left the countryside and cities of South Vietnam vulnerable to renewed attacks. Unless additional forces were sent, the "critical year" ahead could bring American losses.

Johnson and his civilian advisers received Wheeler's recommendation with incredulity. Even allowing for the military leadership's practice of asking for more than it expected to receive, this request was staggering. Johnson instructed Clifford to head a small group of officials from various agencies to conduct a systematic overview of the situation and to "give me the lesser of evils." The task force conducted a hurried but comprehensive review. For the new secretary of defense, the most revealing phase was an extended meeting with the JCS at which it became evident that the military leaders had no plan to achieve victory, even if the 206,000 additional troops were committed. Clifford was "appalled" by what he termed "the weakness of the military's case." On March 4, the task force gave Johnson the "lesser of the evils." Most importantly, it recommended a troop increase of only twenty-two thousand men (and that reserve forces should also be called up to meet overall strategic needs) and reexamination of the existing strategy. Clifford wasted no words, telling Johnson that Vietnam was a "sinkhole." The North Vietnamese would match any troop increase, Clifford warned, and that would lead to "more and more fighting with more and more casualties on the U.S. side and no end in sight."

As Clifford sounded surprisingly like his predecessor McNamara, Rusk, also unexpectedly, urged a halt to the bombing of North Vietnam in the interest of encouraging negotiations. He had opposed such gestures in the past but was now troubled by the influence of the Tet offensive on the American public and the seemingly endless unrest directed against the war. He had also been influenced by U.N. Secretary-General U Thant's entreaties to U.S. officials, in which he conveyed Hanoi's willingness to negotiate quickly if the bombing ended. Other officials with whom Johnson consulted—including Ambassadors Goldberg and Harriman, former National Security Adviser Bundy, and White House aide and speech writer Harry McPherson—were convinced that a bombing halt was essential to finding a way out of the war. On the other side, National Security Adviser Rostow, Ambassador Bunker, and Supreme Court Justice Abe Fortas (a longtime Johnson confidante) joined the JCS in telling Johnson to expand the bombing and to approve the troop request.

Besides strategic considerations, Johnson for the first time had to confront the effects of the war on the American economy. Having financed the enormous cost of the war largely through deficit spending, Johnson had helped to trigger the highest rate of inflation since the Korean War, rising interest rates, a sluggish economy, and the decline of America's balance of payments—all of which were eroding international confidence in U.S. leadership of the world's economy. Clifford told Johnson to weigh the impact of the troop increase on the nation's "economic stability," a point that Rusk picked up: "We have got to think of what this troop increase would mean in terms of increased taxes, the balance of payments picture, inflation, gold, and the general economic picture." For Johnson, further escalation meant accepting sacrifices that he had consistently rejected: calling up the reserves, tax increases, and paring back his domestic agenda.

A beleaguered Johnson was losing control not only of the war and the economy, but also of his own administration and party. On March 10, the lead story in the *New York Times* revealed the Westmoreland request for 206,000 troops, which touched off a new wave of public controversy and added to distrust of the administration's version of the war. If the war was being won and Tet had been a victory, many Americans wondered, why did Westmoreland need more troops? A Gallup poll revealed that half of the public believed that the United States had been wrong to become involved in Vietnam and only one-third believed the administration's claims of progress. From within his own party, pressures mounted on Johnson for an end to escalation. On March 12, the voters of New Hampshire cast their ballots in the year's first presidential primary. On the Democratic side, Johnson (who did no campaigning) was expected to prevail over the obscure Senator Eugene McCarthy of Minnesota, whose candidacy was based on his opposition to the war and advocacy of a negotiated settlement. In fact, Johnson won but only narrowly; the real story was the surprisingly strong support for McCarthy, an indication of the discontent with Johnson's conduct of the war. Four days later, on March 16, Senator Robert Kennedy, Johnson's bête noire, announced that he, too, would be a candidate for the

Democratic Party's presidential nomination, running principally on his criticism of Johnson's war policy.

Bitter over the erosion of support within his party and resentful of Kennedy's opportunism in entering the presidential race, Johnson instinctively fell back on belligerent rhetoric. In speeches on March 16 and 17, he struck a hawkish tone, telling one audience "we shall and we are going to win" and exhorting the other "to support our leaders, our government, our men, and our allies until aggression is stopped, wherever it has occurred." To his advisers, Johnson spoke of going all-out militarily: "Let's make it troops and war. Later we can revive and extend our peace initiatives."

Behind the bluster, however, Johnson realized the dire political and economic consequences of further escalation. On March 20, he told Clifford, "I've got to get me a peace proposal." The first public evidence of the reorientation of Vietnam policy came three days later, with Johnson's announcement of Westmoreland's "promotion" to become army chief of staff, which reflected Johnson's disenchantment, influenced by Clifford's analysis of the bankruptcy of the JCS strategy, with Westmoreland's war of attrition.

The unexpected counsel of the Wise Men added to the pressures. Former Secretary of State Acheson had already told Johnson earlier in March that he was getting poor advice from military leaders. Although disarmed by Acheson's skepticism, Johnson was not prepared for the advice that he received from the previously hawkish Wise Men as a group. After briefings with military, intelligence, and diplomatic officials, they met with Johnson on March 26, with Acheson assuming his familiar role as the group's spokesman. He told Johnson that he had changed his mind: the war could not be won. Most of the other Wise Men concurred that it was time to disengage. The consensus was that Johnson had to take the initiative of a bombing halt as a move toward negotiations. Johnson was stunned, but he could not ignore the significance of the Wise Men's disaffection. While he privately castigated them ("the Establishment bastards have bailed out on me"), in his memoir he reflected on their influence: "They were intelligent, experienced men . . . [and] if they had been so deeply influenced by the reports of the Tet Offensive, what must the average citizen in the country be thinking?"

Johnson accepted the inevitability of not just another conciliatory gesture to North Vietnam, but a concession that would meet its conditions for negotiations. The former national security adviser McGeorge

Bundy reminded Johnson of the diplomatic and political imperatives. "If we get tagged as mindless hawks, we can lose both the election and the war. . . . The only [act] that the whole world—and Kennedy and McCarthy too—will call serious is a bombing halt. I've been against them all up to now—but no longer. . . . A full halt in the bombing— one which ends only by the evident fault of Hanoi—seems to be the indispensable missing ingredient in our package for 1968." Johnson was thus responsive to suggestions from Clifford and McPherson that he take the occasion of a nationally televised address, scheduled for Sunday evening March 31, to change America's course in Vietnam. As his advisers worked on the speech, it underwent a fundamental change that was evident in the opening words. "Tonight, I want to speak to you about the war in Vietnam," was transformed into "Tonight, I want to speak to you about peace in Vietnam."

Johnson's speech from the Oval Office, watched by millions of Americans on television, changed the war and American politics. In the interest of prompt and serious talks about peace, Johnson announced that he was taking the "first step to de-escalate the conflict. We are reducing—substantially reducing—the present level of hostilities. And we are doing so unilaterally, and at once." He announced an end to the bombing of North Vietnam except for the area immediately north of the demilitarized zone, adding that "even this limited bombing of the North could come to an early end if our restraint is matched by restraint in Hanoi." The United States was prepared to enter into discussions with the North Vietnamese at any time and place. In closing, Johnson withdrew from the presidential race: "I have concluded that I should not permit the Presidency to become involved in the partisan divisions that are developing in this political year. . . . I do not believe that I should devote an hour or a day of time to any personal partisan causes or to any duties other than the awesome duties of this office—the Presidency of your country. Accordingly, I shall not seek, and I will not accept, the nomination of my party for another term as your President."

The American public welcomed Johnson's initiative to end the war but were stunned by his withdrawal from the presidential race. His political demise underlined how completely the war had destroyed the broad consensus that had given him a landslide victory in 1964 and had provided the backing for his Great Society. Within a month, three of the chief architects of American escalation had become casualties of the war: McNamara had left office on February 28, Westmoreland had been "kicked upstairs" on March 23, and now Johnson had become a "lame duck" president.

For the remaining ten months of his presidency, Johnson fulfilled his pledge to work for peace, but it was an elusive goal. In response to the unconditional bombing halt, which substantially met its condition for negotiations, North Vietnam indicated a willingness to talk, and discussions began in Paris in May. How to negotiate an end to the war divided Johnson's advisers just as sharply as had early aspects of the war. The dovish advisers, led by Clifford and Harriman, questioned the capacity of the South Vietnamese government to survive on its own and believed that the United States had to concentrate on other, more important international matters. They urged an early and conciliatory approach toward negotiations, which would lead to a face-saving exit from a hopeless cause. The hawkish advisers, still led by Rusk, Rostow, and Wheeler, argued that the conflict remained a test of American credibility, which necessitated continuation of military pressure on the enemy, support of South Vietnam, and a settlement assuring its survival.

As always, Johnson was frustrated by the stark alternatives. He refused to abandon the objective of a strong South Vietnam, and he renewed pressures on Saigon to intensify its military commitment. Distrustful of Hanoi, he privately yearned to unleash America's power against North Vietnam. Yet he recognized the war's continuing influence on an American society that, throughout the spring and summer of 1968, seemed to be coming apart.

The war protesters pushed for an early settlement. Within the Democratic Party, the antiwar candidates McCarthy and Kennedy drew strong support in their bids for the presidential nomination. At the other extreme, Alabama governor George Wallace, running as an independent for president, led an assault on the reforms of the Great Society and called for military victory. The assassination of Martin Luther King on April 4 touched off widespread disturbances and rioting in several cities. The assassination two months later of Robert Kennedy staggered the American public, which increasingly asked why America had become such a violent society. The antiwar protests and the police violence on the streets of Chicago during the Democratic Party convention in August further underlined the profound divisions generated by the war. Inside the convention hall, the delegates, controlled by Johnson loyalists, repudiated the sentiment of voters in the primaries, duly endorsed Johnson's Vietnam policy, and nominated Vice President Hubert

Humphrey for president. It was a moment described by one journalist as a "man of peace being nominated in the midst of violence." Meanwhile, the Republican Party nominated former Vice President Richard Nixon, who promised to bring law and order at home and to end the war through a "secret plan." And in Vietnam, the war went on with an intensity that made 1968 its bloodiest year, as both sides tried to gain military advantages that would strengthen their bargaining positions.

In Paris, the talks dragged on, with no movement on substantive issues. North Vietnam demanded an unconditional bombing halt of all of its territory, while the United States sought evidence of "restraint" before taking that step. (Doves and hawks within the Johnson administration differed over whether Hanoi was showing "restraint.") In a war fought basically over the political status of South Vietnam, negotiations were also delayed by the question of how that half of Vietnam should be represented in negotiations. North Vietnam contended that the NLF was the legitimate representative of South Vietnam and refused direct talks with the Saigon government, which, in turn, dismissed the legitimacy of the NLF.

Finally, in October, after weeks of procedural wrangling, Harriman crafted a compromise scheme on these issues: the United States would end the bombing completely with the expectation that North Vietnam would curtail military activities; four parties would be represented at the bargaining table as "two sides" (North Vietnam and the NLF; the United States and South Vietnam), thus obscuring the issue of who legitimately represented the South Vietnamese. General Thieu, however, feared that his government was being sold out by the Americans and believed that a Republican administration would give him stronger support (a view that Republican intermediaries inappropriately encouraged). He threatened to sabotage the negotiations. Johnson, desperate to get the peace process moving, warned Thieu not to interfere. Despite Saigon's opposition, Johnson on October 31 announced a complete end of the bombing of North Vietnam.

Progress toward a negotiated settlement still eluded Johnson during the remaining weeks of his presidency. The South Vietnamese government, which Johnson had saved from collapse by committing American resources and prestige in 1965, now distrusted his intent. Thieu reluctantly agreed to send representatives to Paris, but, encouraged by Nixon's election, they engaged in delaying tactics until the new administration took office in January 1969.

So, for the second time in sixteen years, a beleaguered Democratic president turned over an unfinished war to his Republican successor, whose election reflected in part the public's dissatisfaction with indecision on the battlefield. There was, however, an important difference. By the time that Truman passed the Korean War along to Eisenhower in 1953, the negotiations were well advanced and had only to resolve the prisoners-of-war issue; an armistice was signed six months after Truman left office. As Johnson passed the Vietnam War to Nixon, though, negotiations on substantive issues had yet to begin, and it was to take all of Nixon's first term to end U.S. involvement.

Drawing to some extent on Eisenhower's tactic of intimidation, which had helped to achieve the Korean armistice, Nixon, who had been Eisenhower's vice president, combined Vietnamization—the gradual withdrawal of U.S. troops and the major buildup of the South Vietnamese military—with the occasional unleashing of power in ways that Johnson had always vetoed. Nixon thus ordered the secret bombing of enemy supply lines in Cambodia in 1969, and a year later, in a highly controversial move, he authorized an American–South Vietnamese ground assault against communist positions in Cambodia. Nixon also moved to reduce tensions with the Soviet Union and the Chinese People's Republic, partly in the expectation that they would induce North Vietnam to end the war.

As the fighting continued in Vietnam, both sides suffered from exhaustion, which played to the advantage of whomever held the upper hand militarily. In the largest offensive since Tet, the North Vietnamese launched a major assault on South Vietnam's northern provinces in the spring of 1972—the Easter offensive—which led to weeks of bitter fighting and led Nixon to resume the bombing of North Vietnam, including the mining of Haiphong Harbor. The Easter offensive ended with the South Vietnamese army, with U.S. support, regaining cities seized by the North Vietnamese, but with deepening war weariness among the battered South Vietnamese people.

Meanwhile, in Paris, American–North Vietnamese negotiators finally reached agreement on ending the war. Toward the end of the 1972 presidential campaign, Henry Kissinger, the national security adviser who was the chief U.S. negotiator, announced that "peace was at hand." The South Vietnamese government tried to subvert a settlement that compromised its integrity. Those apprehensions in Saigon were well founded, but the outcome of the negotiations was, in many ways, inevitable. The United States could not gain at the bargaining table what it had failed to achieve on the battlefield. In the end, the United States imposed a settlement on its ally.

The agreement, signed in Paris in January 1973, ended the U.S. involvement on terms that were not significantly different from what Johnson might have been able to secure had he pursued negotiations more vigorously. Militarily, the agreement provided for the withdrawal of the few remaining U.S. forces, but not North Vietnamese troops, from South Vietnam. Politically, the settlement was a mishmash of complicated procedures that could not conceal the inability of the parties to resolve their fundamental differences over the status of South Vietnam. The legitimacy of the Thieu government was recognized, but so too was the People's Revolutionary Government (formerly the NLF). The agreement stipulated a cumbersome, and inherently unworkable, process to establish a unified South Vietnamese government and included references to eventual reunification of the entire country. The settlement reflected the fundamental reality that the Saigon government had never effectively controlled its own territory and represented its people. The flaws of the agreement and the dismay of the Thieu government notwithstanding, a cease-fire was proclaimed on January 21, 1973.

The day after the cease-fire, Lyndon Johnson died of a heart attack at his Texas ranch. The war that he had waged was over in one sense, but participants and observers recognized that the political status of South Vietnam would eventually be settled militarily by the Vietnamese themselves. Two years later, the North Vietnamese launched a major attack that overwhelmed a demoralized South Vietnamese army and brought about the reunification of Vietnam under communist leadership.

IT WAS THUS Johnson's fate to be the president who led the United States into the nation's only war that ultimately ended in defeat. Although Nixon, too, waged war in Vietnam, he was also simultaneously withdrawing forces and negotiating an end to American involvement. It was Johnson who made the decisions for war and who steadily escalated the bombing and troop commitment, so the conflict will be remembered as "Mr. Johnson's War."

The style that served Johnson so well as leader in other areas was ill-suited to his role as commander in chief. The restless energy that propelled him from one high-profile initiative to another produced hastily conceived and highly public policies in situations where careful consideration and time were often needed. The "peace offensive" of early 1966 and the Mekong development pacification emphasis at the Guam conference a year later are conspicuous examples of inherently flawed initiatives, both reflecting an insensitivity to the complicated issues at hand and the need for deliberative processes to bring about the desired ends. The pressures on the South Vietnamese government to undertake constitutional reforms and Johnson's ensuing proclamations of "progress" obscured the limitations of political change and the fundamental weaknesses of the Thieu-Ky regime. Seeing time working against him as domestic opposition to the war increased, Johnson became enmeshed in a downward cycle: the more he pressed for the elusive indicators of progress, the more he contributed to the popular disillusionment as stalemate on the battlefield continued.

The art of compromise, which Johnson had perfected in dealing with political issues at home, likewise failed him. He sought a "deal" with North Vietnam and blamed failure to negotiate on Ho Chi Minh. Yet Johnson, who as a Washington wheeler-dealer was sensitive to the interests and concerns of other political players, could not bring himself to understand the war from North Vietnam's perspective. He could not understand why North Vietnam saw the United States as an "aggressor" and why it saw Vietnam as temporarily divided and hence was unwilling to recognize the legitimacy of the South Vietnamese government. In waging war, Johnson's persistent compromising between "hawks" and "doves" satisfied neither, especially not the military leaders, who engaged in sniping and maneuvering against Johnson and McNamara and in endless complaints that Johnson's restraints deprived them of achieving victory. If Johnson did anything right in Vietnam, it was to limit U.S. warfare in the interest of avoiding a larger war. He was correct in recognizing that, had American warfare threatened the survival of North Vietnam, there is no reason to doubt that the Soviet Union or China would have intervened. In the end, Johnson's wartime leadership gave the United States an incoherent and contradictory set of military, diplomatic, and political strategies. Wishful thinking proved no substitute for systematic analysis and tough decisions.

To criticize Johnson's leadership does not mean that another president could have waged the war more successfully. Having decided to Americanize the war in July 1965, Johnson was trapped in a fundamentally unwinnable situation. As several advisers had warned him it would, Vietnam became a quagmire, draining resources and prestige into a hopeless cause. To be sure, Americanization prevented the collapse of the South Vietnamese government, but it could do little more than that. It could not create a sense of unity and purpose among the South Vietnamese people. It could not transform the Saigon government into a democracy responsive to the need for social and economic reform—an objective that was never a priority of South Vietnamese leaders and that, in any event, would have required years of pacification to attain. It could only marginally reduce the strength of the Viet Cong in the rural areas. It could disrupt but not end North Vietnam's capacity to wage war and to move personnel and supplies to the south. And it could not stop the Soviet Union and China from supplying North Vietnam with the weapons and technology to withstand the U.S. warfare. So the Americanization of the conflict, with the sacrifice of fifty-eight thousand lives, only delayed by a decade the collapse of South Vietnam and the country's unification under communist leadership. Another president might have waged war differently but probably not much more successfully. In the end, Johnson tacitly accepted, as did most of his country, the conclusion that no acceptable level of military power could achieve the American objective in Vietnam.

"This aggression will not stand"

GEORGE BUSH WAS AT THE WHITE HOUSE on the evening of Wednesday, August 1, 1990, when he learned of Iraq's invasion of Kuwait. Although American officials had been concerned about Iraqi threats against Kuwait, they were shocked by Iraq's aggression. It soon became evident that the Iraqis were meeting scant resistance, and reports indicated that they might be planning to attack Saudi Arabia next. Bush took the initiative in defining the international response to an act of aggression as blatant as that in Korea forty years earlier.

Like Truman in confronting the North Korean invasion and Johnson in responding to the crisis in Vietnam, Bush believed that the preservation of international order was at stake in the Persian Gulf. But whereas Truman and Johnson had acted within a cold war context, Bush was encountering the first post–cold war crisis. A series of unanticipated and quickly unfolding events during the previous two years had ended the cold war "not with a bang, but a whimper": democratic reform swept across eastern Europe, ending four decades of communist rule and Soviet domination of the region; Germans, divided since World War II, dismantled the Berlin Wall—long the symbol of Soviet-American confrontation—and reunified their country; nationalist groups within the Soviet Union demanded greater autonomy. Premier Mikhail Gorbachev desperately worked to reform a disintegrating economy and to hold the Soviet state together. With the Soviet Union no longer a threat, Americans felt less a sense of triumph than an uncertainty about the role of the United States in a less predictable and perhaps less stable world.

Unlike Truman and Johnson, Bush came to the presidency with considerable experience in foreign affairs. Sixty-six years old as the Gulf crisis unfolded, Bush came from a background of New England aristocratic privilege. He had been a senior at Phillips Andover Academy when the Japanese attack on Pearl Harbor had taken the United States into World War II. Two days after graduating, Bush enlisted in the navy and served as a pilot in the Pacific, winning a Distinguished Flying Cross for heroic action in which he nearly lost his life. After the war and his graduation from Yale University, Bush went to Texas, where he made a fortune in the oil business.

Bush then followed the example of his father, who had been a senator from Connecticut, by entering politics. After failing in a bid for a U.S. Senate seat in 1964, he was elected to the House of Representatives in 1966 from a Houston district, and, after two terms, he ran a second time for the Senate but again fell short. That defeat could have ended his political career, but, with the support of President Richard Nixon, Bush became a prominent national figure. Nixon named him ambassador to the United Nations, and Bush went on to serve as chief of the U.S. Liaison Office in the Chinese People's Republic (CPR) and as director of the Central Intelligence Agency (CIA). In 1980, he sought the Republican presidential nomination, but, after doing poorly in several presidential primaries, he withdrew in favor of the more popular Ronald Reagan. To the surprise of political pundits, Reagan subsequently offered him the vice presidential nomination. Saved again from political oblivion, Bush served eight years as Reagan's dutiful vice president while strengthening his following among rank-and-file Republicans. Bush sought and easily gained the 1988 Republican presidential nomination.

That accomplishment transformed Bush, or at least the popular image of him. During his long pursuit of the presidency, Bush had suffered from a reputation for being deferential and indecisive, and political opponents, pundits, and cartoonists portrayed him as a "wimp." During the 1988 presidential campaign, Bush took the offensive in a calculated and ultimately successful effort to change that perception. In a masterful acceptance speech at the Republican National Convention, Bush presented himself to the American electorate as a forceful leader. During the ensuing weeks, he waged an aggressive and, in some ways, mean-spirited campaign against his Democratic opponent, Governor Michael Dukakis of Massachusetts, and won the presidency in a landslide.

During his first year in the presidency, Bush asserted his leadership in foreign policy when he authorized an invasion of Panama to overthrow the despotic, defiant, drug-dealing Gen. Manuel Noriega. Justifying this use of force—labeled Operation JUST CAUSE—in the name of restoring Panamanian democracy and bringing Noriega to trial, Bush won wide popular support for this action, which ended quickly with few American casualties.

In formulating foreign policy, Bush relied on frequent meetings of the National Security Council (NSC) and informal consultation with trusted advisers. Closest to the president were National Security Adviser Brent Scowcroft, Secretary of Defense Richard Cheney, and Secretary of State James Baker. As the assistant to the president for National Security Affairs, the self-effacing and meticulous Scowcroft, a retired air force general who was sometimes referred to as "Mr. Bush's Shadow," returned to the position that he had held under President Gerald Ford (when Bush had been CIA director and Cheney had been the White House chief of staff). Another longtime Bush associate was the low-keyed and pragmatic Cheney, who had left a seat in the House of Representatives (where he had held the second highest Republican leadership position) to became secretary of defense after the Senate had declined to confirm Bush's first nominee for the position. Baker, a fellow Texan and longtime friend of Bush's, lacked substantial foreign policy experience when Bush named him secretary of state. He had served as Reagan's White House chief of staff and secretary of the treasury, but as secretary of state he demonstrated something of a flair for diplomacy and thrived on its practice.

Bush's inner circle included four other advisers, who—together with Bush, Scowcroft, Cheney, and Baker—were commonly referred to as the Big Eight. They included Dan Quayle, vice president; Gen. Colin Powell, chairman of the Joint Chiefs of Staff (JCS); Robert Gates, deputy national security adviser; and John Sununu, White House chief of staff. At times, William Webster, director of the Central Intelligence Agency, also was part of the inner circle. Quayle had been a relatively unknown senator from Indiana when Bush selected him as his running mate in 1988. Despite a widespread popular impression that he lacked much substance, Quayle worked diligently as vice president and became a valued counselor to the president. Powell, a respected career army officer and veteran of the Vietnam War, had served as Reagan's last national security adviser and had briefly returned to regular army duty before Cheney named him to the nation's top military position. Sununu, the former governor of New Hampshire, worked closely with Bush on all important issues. Gates, as Scowcroft's deputy, formed a link between Bush's closest advisers and an ongoing "crisis management team" representing several agencies (the so-called Deputies Committee) that he chaired.

American leaders did not anticipate a crisis with Iraq. In fact, for the previous decade, a central aspect of Middle Eastern policy had been to cultivate closer ties with Iraq on the basis of a shared interest in limiting Iran's influence. The Iranian revolution of 1978, led by Ayatollah Khoemeni, had proclaimed a radical Islamic fundamentalism and a strident anti-Westernism that threatened moderate Arab governments as well as Western interests in the region. The United States had been humiliated by the revolution's overthrow of the pro-American government headed by the shah of Iran and by the ensuing "hostage crisis" engineered by revolutionaries who seized the U.S. Embassy in Teheran in November 1979 and then held over fifty Americans for 444 days.

During that crisis, Iraq, under the leadership of Saddam Hussein, attacked Iran. While longstanding territorial disputes provided a pretext for war, Saddam's overriding objective was to establish himself as the leader of the moderate Arab peoples. His expectations of a quick victory, however, were confounded as Iranians fought effectively, leading to a prolonged and costly war. After more than seven years of fighting, Iraq regained the initiative, thanks in large part to substantial supplies and sophisticated weaponry from several countries, including the Soviet Union, its longtime benefactor, and the United States. This support enabled Iraq to build a powerful military machine—the world's fourth largest army—which inflicted heavy losses on the Iranians during an offensive in early 1988, before both sides finally accepted a United Nations–sponsored cease-fire.

Saddam Hussein's image as a moderate leader made him appealing to governments in the West as well as in the Middle East. Underlying the American support, which began on a large scale during the Reagan administration, was the assumption that Iraq could be cultivated as a stabilizing force in a long-troubled region. Accordingly, the U.S. government provided billions of dollars in food credit loans to Iraq, so that, by the end of the 1980s, Iraq was among the leading importers of American wheat and rice. In addition, the United States removed Iraq from its list of governments that supported international terrorism and paid scant attention to the regime's widespread human rights abuses.

Although emerging from the war against Iran with enhanced status in the Arab world, Saddam Hussein was disappointed by what he considered to be the insufficient appreciation of Saudi Arabia, Kuwait, and the United Arab Emirates (UAE) for Iraq's sacrifice in restraining Iranian expansionism. He contended that those oil-rich states should provide reconstruction assistance and should cancel loans to Iraq that had financed the war with Iran.

Iraq had indeed paid an enormous price for Saddam Hussein's pursuit of Arab leadership. The war left Iraq with a foreign debt of $80 billion and with reconstruction costs estimated at $230 billion. At the same time, Saddam continued building his military strength, including plans for the development of nuclear, chemical, and biological weapons of mass destruction. Iraq was dependent on imports that cost $17 billion annually ($5 billion of which was going to the purchase of military hardware and technology) and had annual debt payments of $5 billion. Oil imports brought in $7 billion annually, but that fell far short of addressing the country's financial problems. This financial crunch prompted Saddam's campaign with the members of the Organization of Petroleum Exporting Countries (OPEC) to adhere to quotas on production and to double the price of oil.

After becoming president, Bush reaffirmed the policy of cultivating cooperation with Iraq. National Security Directive 26 of October 1989 anticipated that a scheme of "economic and political incentives for Iraq . . . [would] moderate its behavior and . . . increase our influence with Iraq." This policy disturbed some members of Congress, who said that the United States should be imposing sanctions against a cruel dictator who had a well-documented record of suppressing his political opponents and the Kurdish minority, but supporters of the Bush administration's policy argued that criticism and punishment would foster Iraqi resentment and extremism. When John Kelly, assistant secretary of state for Near Eastern affairs, visited Baghdad on February 12, 1990, he assured Saddam of his importance to America as "a force for moderation in the region and that the United States wanted to broaden her relations with Iraq."

That objective was tested in early 1990 as Saddam Hussein embarked on a militant campaign seeking to address his economic concerns and to reassert leadership of the Arab peoples. The end of the cold war, he believed, was disastrous to the Arabs, for they would no longer be able to use military and economic aid from the Soviet Union to counter Israeli and American strength. In rhetorical outbursts, Saddam Hussein claimed that Arabs faced a "Zionist-American" plot, which made his leadership of the Arab peoples more imperative than ever. He denounced "America's flagrant interference in the internal affairs of Iraq" when an Arabic language broadcast by the U.S. government's Voice of America mentioned Iraq, among others, as a state where "secret police are still widely present." U.S. Ambassador April Glaspie quickly apologized, assuring Saddam that "it is absolutely not United States policy to question the legitimacy of the government of Iraq nor to interfere in any way in the domestic concerns of the Iraqi people and government."

Saddam Hussein was not mollified. At a meeting of the Arab Co-operation Council in late February, he indulged in an anti-American tirade, warning that the end of the cold war made the "imperialist" United States a threat to the Middle East. "With its known capitalist approach and its imperialist policy," he said, "[the United States] will continue to depart from the restrictions that govern the rest of the world." Israel would embark on "new stupidities as a result of direct or tacit U.S. encouragement. . . . If the Gulf people, along with all Arabs, are not careful, the Arab Gulf region will be governed by the United States." At the same meeting, Saddam bluntly demanded a moratorium on wartime loans and an additional $30 billion grant: "Let the Gulf regimes know that if they do not give this money, I will know how to get it." The threat was accompanied by Iraqi military maneuvers near the Kuwaiti border. Saddam repeatedly threatened Israel, warning in an April 2 speech of devastating chemical warfare should Israel attack Iraq's non-conventional arms facilities: "We will make fire eat half of Israel if it tries to do anything against Iraq."

Saddam Hussein's threats triggered an angry American response tempered by the commitment to cultivate him as a moderate leader. President Bush stated angrily that "this is no time to be talking about chemical or biological weapons. This is no time to be escalating tensions in the Middle East." The State Department denounced Saddam's "inflammatory, outrageous, and irresponsible" rhetoric. Yet the Bush administration discounted the seriousness of Saddam's threats and ruled out suggestions of economic pressures against Iraq. Ten days after Saddam's tirade against Israel, a delegation of senators, headed by Minority Leader Robert Dole (R.-Kans.), visited him in Baghdad. Bringing a letter from Bush that called upon Saddam Hussein to work for peace in the Middle East, they expressed the U.S. concern about Iraq's quest for chemical and nuclear weapons. Saddam Hussein responded that the weapons were needed for defense against Israel but spoke mostly of his interest in peace. The senators assured him of continued American support and of their opposition to any economic pressures on Iraq. Senator Alan Simpson (R.-Wyo.) blamed a "haughty and pampered" media as the source of any Iraqi problems with the United States. Meanwhile, in Washington, Assistant Secretary Kelly told the Senate Foreign Relations Committee that, while some recent Iraqi actions had caused concern, the Bush administration's "engagement" of Iraq remained the correct policy.

American assurances, however, did not lead to any moderation of Saddam Hussein's rhetoric. He soon condemned Kuwait and the UAE for their overproduction of oil, telling a meeting of the Arab League of Iraq's plight: "For every single dollar drop in the price of a barrel of oil our loss amounts to $1 billion a year. . . . This is in fact a kind of war against Iraq. . . . One day the reckoning will come."*

In mid-July Saddam Hussein suddenly intensified the pressure on Kuwait. He dispatched some thirty-five thousand Iraqi troops, headed by the elite Republican Guard, to positions along the border. In a strongly worded statement to the members of the Arab League, he charged that Kuwait-UAE violation of oil quotas had cost Iraq $89 billion since 1981 and that Kuwait had "stolen" $2.4 billion of oil from the southern part of Iraq's Rumalia oil field. He demanded that oil prices be increased, that Kuwait pay $2.4 billion for the "stolen" oil, and that war loans be canceled. The next day he delivered a speech tying the actions of Kuwait and the UAE to the "conspiracy of world imperialism and Zionism." He warned that, "if words fail to afford us protection, then we will have no choice but to resort to effective action to put things right and ensure the restitution of our rights."

The United States now reacted with a combination of diplomacy and military resolve. It encouraged Kuwait-Iraq negotiations. The State Department summoned the Iraqi ambassador in Washington and told him that the United States supported the sovereignty of states in the Persian Gulf and insisted on the peaceful settlement of disputes. Kuwait took the initiative; while rejecting Iraq's demands, it proposed mediation through the Arab League, which called upon Egyptian President Hosni Mubarak to meet with leaders of both countries. Going first to Baghdad on July 24, Mubarak found Saddam Hussein prepared to negotiate but not to disavow military action: "As long as discussions last between Iraq and Kuwait, I won't use force. I won't intervene with

---

*The Arab League was established in 1945 as a consultative body of Arab states. The original members were Egypt, Jordan, Iraq, Lebanon, North Yemen, Saudi Arabia, and Syria. By 1990, the league's membership had increased threefold, and its twenty-two members included other Arab nations in the Middle East and northern and western Africa, as well as the Palestine Liberation Organization.

force before I have exhausted all the possibilities for negotiations." He agreed to Mubarak's suggestion that Iraqi and Kuwaiti diplomats meet face to face in the Saudi Arabian city of Jiddah. Mubarak cabled Bush that Saddam was "receptive and responsive" and predicted that an "accommodation can be worked out without delay." After consultations with the Kuwaitis, Mubarak arranged for a meeting on July 31 in Jiddah. Convinced that his mission had eased the crisis, Mubarak stated publicly that Iraq "had no intention of attacking Kuwait."

At the same time, the United States exerted military pressure on Saddam Hussein. When the UAE requested two KC-135 aircraft, the Defense Department proposed a joint naval exercise with the UAE as a "cover" for moving the aircraft into the Persian Gulf. Overruling the objections of the State Department, which feared that any military pressure would alienate Arab leaders, Bush approved the Defense Department plan. This operation, announced on July 24, was justified in terms of "supporting the individual and collective self-defense of our friends in the Gulf" and defending the "principle of freedom of navigation and [ensuring] the free flow of oil through the Strait of Hormuz." This show of strength was accompanied by a U.S. warning that "Iraq and others know that there is no place for coercion and intimidation in a civilized world" and that the United States would support "our friends in the Gulf with whom we have deep and longstanding ties." As the State Department had feared, several Arab leaders were concerned that the U.S. maneuvers undermined their ability to resolve the crisis.

For his part, Saddam Hussein reacted by summoning Ambassador Glaspie to the Presidential Palace on July 25. His performance combined bluster with conciliation. Charging that the United States was supporting Kuwait's economic warfare against Iraq, he threatened terrorist retaliation: "Do not push us. . . . If you use pressure, we will deploy pressure and force. We cannot come all the way to the United States, but individual Arabs may reach you." Glaspie responded that there was no American hostility toward Iraq and, indeed, that she had instructions from Bush to seek better relations with Iraq. "President Bush is an intelligent man," she went on. "He is not going to declare an economic war against Iraq." Instead, Glaspie assured Saddam that the United States recognized his need for funds and indicated that other Arabs should support his objective of assuring compliance with the oil quotas established by OPEC. Last, she added that the United States did not have an "opinion on inter-Arab disputes like your border dispute with Kuwait," but it "could never excuse settlement of disputes by any but peaceful means."

Interrupting his conversation with Glaspie, Saddam Hussein excused himself to take a phone call from Mubarak and, upon his return, became more compromising. He said that Iraq and Kuwait would negotiate in Saudi Arabia the following week. The Kuwaitis, he said, were "scared," but "we are not going to do anything until we meet with them." He added cryptically that, "when we meet and when we see there is hope, then nothing will happen. But if we are unable to find a solution, then it will be natural that Iraq will not accept death, even though wisdom is above everything."

A relieved Glaspie interpreted her conversation to mean, as she reported to Washington, that "his emphasis that he wants a peaceful settlement is surely sincere." The military maneuvers "have fully caught his attention, and that is good. I believe that we would be well-advised to ease off on public criticism of Iraq until we see how the negotiations develop." On the same day as the Saddam-Glaspie meeting, OPEC ministers reached new agreements on oil prices, which Iraq announced were satisfactory, and Kuwait and the UAE promised to follow the new prices and quotas. So, by the last few days of July, it seemed likely that Saddam would return to his customary "moderate" leadership. Bush sent a conciliatory response to the Iraqi leader, praising his agreement to negotiate with Kuwait and adding that "we still have fundamental concerns about certain Iraqi policies and activities, and we will continue to raise these concerns with you in a spirit of friendship and candor."

The expectations of compromise quickly gave way to the reality of war. The meeting at Jiddah ended after one day, as the Iraqi delegation demanded financial and territorial concessions from Kuwait and then abruptly departed. Saddam Hussein met secretly the next evening with his Revolutionary Command Council and recommended the invasion and annexation of Kuwait. That objective went far beyond the immediate issues that Saddam had been pressing and reflected long-held Iraqi strategic and historical concerns. To Iraqis, Kuwait's very existence presented a threat; it was seen as always being able to gain the support of major powers to counter Iraq's territorial and economic grievances. More fundamentally, the Iraqi version of the region's history taught that Kuwait was a part of Iraq and thus had no legitimacy as an independent nation. Annexation would thus remedy what Iraqis believed to be a strategic threat and a historical "wrong."*

Iraq's invasion shattered the image of Saddam Hussein's moderation and triggered indignation throughout much of the world. This was a classic example, immediately reminiscent of the aggression of the 1930s, of the strong attacking the weak. Iraq is more than twenty times larger and ten times more populous than its tiny neighbor, which is about the size of the state of Connecticut and has a population of about two million. The outnumbered Kuwaiti forces offered only slight resistance to the advancing Iraqis, but, contrary to Saddam's expectations, the Kuwaitis did not welcome the Iraqis as liberators. Internationally, Saddam found neither the support of fellow Arabs nor the acquiescence of the major powers that he had foreseen; instead, the invasion met with almost universal condemnation.

FROM THE BEGINNING of the crisis, Bush assumed that the United States needed to provide international leadership. Like Truman in a similar situation forty years earlier, Bush immediately saw the issue as a test of both American resolve and the United Nations. In his memoir, Bush recounts his thinking at the start of the invasion. It is remarkably similar to Truman's reflections on the first day of the Korean crisis.

> I was keenly aware that this would be the first post–Cold War test of the Security Council in crisis. I knew what had happened in the 1930s when a weak and leaderless League of Nations had failed to stand up to Japanese, Italian, and German aggression. The result was to encourage the ambitions of those regimes. The U.N. had been set up to correct the failings of the League, but the Cold War caused stalemate in the Security Council. Now, however, our improving relations with Moscow and our satisfactory ones with China offered the possibility that we could get their cooperation in forging international unity to oppose Iraq.

*The Iraqi claim to Kuwait was based on an interpretation of history dating to the time when the area comprising the modern states of Iraq and Kuwait had been part of the Ottoman Empire. Kuwait had been a district in Basra Province, which together with two other Ottoman provinces had been reconstituted as the nation of Iraq in 1932. By that time, however, Kuwait had become an "independent sheikdom under British protection." When Britain withdrew in 1961, Kuwait emerged as a fully sovereign state, recognized as such by the members of the Arab League and most other nations. Iraq, however, had never accepted the "loss" of Kuwait. If not questioning the legitimacy of Kuwait, it periodically challenged the legality of the existing border as well as Kuwait's control of the islands of Warba and Bubiyan.

Bush instructed Ambassador Thomas Pickering to draft a resolution for the U.N. Security Council, which was summoned into an emergency session at 2 o'clock in the morning of August 2. Resolution 660 condemned the Iraqi invasion, demanded Iraq's immediate and unconditional withdrawal, and called for Iraq and Kuwait to begin immediate negotiations of their differences. As Bush had hoped, the Security Council vote underlined the international opposition to Iraq's action. Voting at 6:00 A.M., all five permanent members were joined by nine of the ten nonpermanent members in support of Resolution 660. (One member, Yemen, abstained.)*

Gratified by this U.N. stance, Bush met at eight that morning with his National Security Council to review the situation. Like the early Blair House meetings, in which Truman had attempted to come to terms with the Korean crisis, this NSC session was conducted in the midst of fast-moving developments and without the benefit of any plan for the contingency at hand. Unlike Truman, whose advisers all agreed that the North Korean invasion could not be tolerated, Bush found his advisers uncertain whether the United States could or should reverse Iraqi aggression.

While details were unclear, it was evident that Saddam Hussein had sent a 100,000-man force into Kuwait and that, with its takeover, he would control 10 percent of the world's oil production. Although the Arab League had condemned the Iraqi attack, the resolve of the Arab states was problematic; left to their own, they would probably accommodate Saddam. America's military capacity was limited. Gen. Norman Schwarzkopf, commander in chief of the Central Command (which was responsible for the Middle East), saw two possibilities: retaliatory air strikes from carriers in the Persian Gulf or the movement of a large army to the region. Neither Schwarzkopf nor General Powell supported the first option, since it would have negligible effect; in Powell's phrase, a "pinprick at something has no relevance." With respect to ground warfare, the Central Command's Plan 1102-90 dealt only with the contingency of defending Saudi Arabia, and that would necessitate the movement of 200,000 U.S. troops to the region. Military planning had not addressed the contingency of an invasion of Kuwait. Reflecting the

---

*The membership of the U.N. Security Council in 1990 included, in addition to the five permanent members with veto power, the following nonpermanent members, elected by the General Assembly for two-year terms: Canada, Colombia, Cuba, Ethiopia, Finland, Ivory Coast, Malaysia, Rumania, Yemen, and Zaire.

limited precrisis thinking, Powell suggested that the United States should "draw the line in the sand"—which meant accepting the takeover of Kuwait while preparing to defend Saudi Arabia. The meeting ended inconclusively.

Bush then departed for Aspen, Colorado, where he was to deliver an address to the Aspen Institute and to meet with British Prime Minister Margaret Thatcher. En route, Bush agreed to Scowcroft's suggestions that the speech, which was to focus on America's security needs in the post–cold war world, be revised to include an expression of outrage over the Iraqi invasion and determination to meet this challenge. Thus, in his address, Bush spoke of the "brutal aggression launched last night against Kuwait," which meant that "the world remains a dangerous place with serious threats to important U.S. interests" and that the United States needed "resources for supporting the legitimate self-defense needs of our friends and of our allies. This will be an enduring commitment. . . . Let no one, friend or foe, question this commitment." In private meetings, Thatcher fully shared Bush's outrage and reinforced his determination. As Bush said during a brief talk with reporters afterward, "We're not ruling any options in. And we're not ruling any options out."

Besides his conversation with Thatcher, Bush talked by phone with Egypt's President Mubarak, Jordan's King Hussein, and Saudi Arabia's King Fahd. As U.S. officials had anticipated, these leaders did not share the Anglo-American indignation over Iraq's aggression. Mubarak and King Hussein urged caution while they pursued an "Arab solution" to the crisis; both planned to speak with Saddam Hussein and anticipated his imminent withdrawal from Kuwait. King Fahd likewise supported an Arab summit to deal with the situation, leaving Bush apprehensive that he would accept the takeover of Kuwait in return for Iraqi guarantees of Saudi Arabia's integrity. Disappointed by the tepid Middle Eastern response, Bush directed Secretary of State Baker, who was in the Soviet Union when the crisis erupted, to seek Soviet support for an arms embargo against Iraq. As the leading supplier of arms to Iraq, the Soviet Union was key to an effective boycott. Although both Premier Gorbachev and Foreign Minister Eduard Shevardnadze deplored the Iraqi attack and wanted to continue cooperation with the West, the Soviet Union had enjoyed close ties with Iraq and had some eight thousand of its citizens working in Iraq. At length, Baker prevailed, and Shevardnadze agreed to a statement, issued on August 3, in which the two erstwhile cold war rivals called "upon the rest of the international community to join us in an international cut off of all arms supplies to Iraq."

Meanwhile, in Washington, Bush, Scowcroft, and Cheney forced consideration of the projection of military power into the region. Military leaders were reticent. In a meeting with Cheney, Powell predicted that "Iraq will withdraw, but Saddam Hussein will put his puppet in. Everyone in the Arab world will be happy. . . . I don't see the senior leadership taking us into armed conflict for the events of the last twenty-four hours." The United States should concentrate on the defense of Saudi Arabia, he argued, not the liberation of Kuwait, the priority should be "communicat[ing] to Saddam Hussein that Saudi Arabia is the line." Convinced that such acquiescence in aggression would be a mistake, Bush and Scowcroft had been disturbed by the hand-wringing at the August 2 NSC meeting which, as Scowcroft writes, revealed "a huge gap between those who saw what was happening as the major crisis of our time and those treated it as the crisis *de jour*." Hence, before the NSC next met on August 3, Bush agreed to a strategy whereby Scowcroft, Cheney, and Under Secretary of State Lawrence Eagleburger would take the initiative by presenting the case that Iraq was poised to dominate the Middle East, which would threaten the economic interests of the West, the survival of Israel, and the hope for a post–cold war international order.

Scowcroft's opening statement set the tone for the decisive NSC meeting. He was blunt. Noting his dismay that some officials had suggested that "we might have to acquiesce in an accommodation," he stated that "my personal judgment is that the stakes in this for the United States are such that to accommodate Iraq should not be a policy option." Eagleburger spoke of "this [as] the first test of the postwar system." Cheney warned that "Saddam has done what he has to do to dominate OPEC, the Gulf, and the Arab world. . . . The problem will get worse, not better." While Powell remained skeptical of the feasibility of the military option beyond the defense of Saudi Arabia, the consensus was that sought by Bush: U.S. power had to be exerted through the imposition of economic sanctions and the movement of forces to Saudi Arabia.

Before that deployment could take place, Saudi Arabia, of course, had to give its approval. The Saudis recognized their vulnerability (the CIA, they knew, predicted that the Iraqi army could overrun their country in three days), but King Fahd seemed to be more irritated with, than threatened by, Saddam Hussein. Moreover, the Saudis doubted American resolve and commitment to their defense. After the NSC adjourned, Scowcroft met with Saudi Arabia's ambassador, Prince Bandar Ibn Sultan, who, as the nephew of King Fahd and son of the Saudi minister of defense, had much influence within the Saudi government. Scowcroft pledged that, if U.S. troops went to Saudi Arabia, their mission would be to defend the country. Scowcroft even arranged for Prince Bandar to see the details of the planned troop deployment, the dimensions of which impressed the ambassador, who agreed that the United States should send officials to brief the king on the proposed troop deployment.

When Bush convened the NSC on August 4 at Camp David, where he spent the first weekend of the crisis, the military option dominated the agenda. Pending Saudi Arabia's approval, Powell and Schwarzkopf outlined plans to dispatch a sufficiently large ground force—"to show the flag"—to deter Iraq from attacking. Military and civilian advisers, however, disagreed over whether the United States had the military capability, as well as sufficient domestic and international support, to liberate Kuwait. Bush remained concerned that the Saudis "might bug out" and foresaw "a problem if Saddam does not invade Saudi Arabia but holds on to Kuwait." Powell said that the United States should be ready to "do more than simply show the flag," which led a member of the NSC staff to envision "something along the lines of the Korean War model of a U.S.-led multinational force."

With military planning at the NSC meeting still tentative, Bush afterward phoned King Fahd, who seemed emboldened by the U.S. assurances of his country's defense. King Fahd said that the "only solution must involve the return of the Emir to Kuwait" and agreed that American and Saudi officials needed to discuss various military options. To dispel any doubts about U.S. resolve, Bush told the king that "the security of Saudi Arabia is vital—basically fundamental—to U.S. interests and really to the interests of the Western world. And I am determined that Saddam will not get away with this infamy. When we work out a plan, once we are there, we will stay until we are asked to leave. You have my solemn word on this."

With Saudi and American objectives converging, Bush publicly affirmed his resolve in words that struck some observers as a virtual declaration of war. When he returned to the White House on the afternoon of Sunday, August 5, he denounced Iraq's "brutal, naked aggression" and said an Iraqi-installed "puppet" government would "not be acceptable." Responding to questions, Bush concluded with an unequivocal commitment: "I view seriously our determination to reverse this awful aggression. . . . There are an awful lot of countries that are in total accord with what I've just said. . . . We will be working with them all for collective action. This will not stand. This will not stand, this aggression against Kuwait."

As Bush spoke, Cheney, accompanied by Schwarzkopf and Robert Gates, the deputy national security adviser, undertook their mission to Saudi Arabia. Meeting the next evening with King Fahd and his advisers, the Americans shared intelligence reports that Saddam Hussein had moved some seventy thousand troops to positions along the border and had missiles pointed toward Saudi Arabia. Cheney assured the Saudis that the United States would send a force large enough to defeat the Iraqis. King Fahd, after a brief discussion with his advisers, agreed to the deployment of U.S. forces. The Saudi Arabian approval was a major breakthrough, and the Central Command quickly began the first troop movements.

While planning for the use of U.S. military power, Bush simultaneously built international support for the imposition of economic sanctions against Iraq. He remained in frequent telephone contact with other leaders. Prime Minister Thatcher, French President François Mitterand, German Chancellor Helmut Kohl, Canadian Prime Minister Brian Mulroney, Japanese Prime Minister Toshiki Kaifu, and Turkish President Turgut Ozal agreed on the necessity of collective pressure.

With Bush and other U.S. officials having lined up support, the U.N. Security Council on August 6 imposed sanctions. Resolution 661 called for the termination of all trade with Iraq except to provide medical supplies and, "in humanitarian circumstances, foodstuffs." Despite misgivings, the Soviet Union and the Chinese People's Republic supported Resolution 661, as did all other Security Council members except Cuba and Yemen, both of which abstained. In Washington the next day, Bush, with Prime Minister Thatcher and North Atlantic Treaty Organization (NATO) Secretary-General Manfred Woerner at his side, strongly endorsed the embargo. The United Nations' imposition of sanctions was a major diplomatic accomplishment, which underscored Saddam Hussein's international isolation.

Speaking on national television on August 8, Bush announced the deployment of U.S. forces to Saudi Arabia: "The mission of our troops is wholly defensive. Hopefully, they will not be needed long. They will not initiate hostilities, but they will defend themselves, the kingdom of Saudi Arabia, and other friends in the Persian Gulf." Although the military deployment was defensive, Bush affirmed that the overriding American objective was the "immediate, complete, unconditional withdrawal of Iraqi forces from Kuwait and the restoration of the Kuwaiti government."

With that announcement, Bush concluded a hectic week of decisions that established the political, military, and economic bases of international opposition to Iraq. Five assumptions guided the development of U.S. policy. First, the Iraqi invasion challenged the fabric of international stability, what Bush a month later would describe as "the new world order." He stated that "this is not an American problem or a European problem or a Middle East problem. It is the world's problem." Like other presidents who had faced crises since World War II, Bush was guided by the "lessons of the 1930s," when democracies had tolerated aggression by Germany, Japan, and Italy only to have to fight the aggressors later. Bush told Americans in his August 8 speech that, "if history teaches us anything, it is that we must resist aggression or it will destroy our freedom."

Second, Iraq's aggression posed an economic threat to the United States, western Europe, Japan, and other countries dependent upon imports of Middle Eastern oil. As Bush put it, "The stakes are high. Iraq is already a rich and powerful country that possesses the world's second largest resources of oil and over a million men under arms. It's the fourth largest military in the world. Our country now imports nearly half the oil it consumes. Much of the world is even more dependent upon imported oil and is even more vulnerable to Iraqi threats." Bush linked his determination to reverse aggression to historical American interests in this critical region: "My administration, as has been the case of every president from President Roosevelt to President Reagan, is committed to the security of the Persian Gulf."

Third, if the United States failed to provide leadership, Saddam Hussein would almost certainly get away with the takeover of Kuwait. Left to themselves, the Arab states would probably have compromised Kuwaiti integrity. Scowcroft has reflected on the uneasiness of dealing with Iraq's neighbors during the first days of the crisis: "I was wary of an 'Arab solution,' fearing that it might end up in compromise with Saddam. It was a real dilemma. If we refused to give time for a possible Arab settlement, we could alienate our best friends when we needed them badly. But if we acquiesced, and the Arabs came out with a compromise, how could we reject it?" By the time that Bush spoke on August 8, the strong stand of the United States and Saddam Hussein's defiance of U.N. Security Council resolutions had defused the "Arab solution."

Fourth, the invasion provided a critical test for the United Nations as a vehicle for upholding order in the post–cold war world. The international organization, freed from the impasse resulting from the cold war, could finally achieve the peacekeeping role that its founders had envisioned in 1945. The crisis demonstrated that, for the first time, all five permanent members of the Security Council could work together in resisting an aggressor.

Fifth, the U.S. objective had to be the unconditional withdrawal of Iraqi forces and the restoration of the legitimate Kuwaiti government. Any compromise would undermine the principles that guided U.S. thinking. Saddam Hussein, it was recognized, might try to enhance his stature among Arab peoples by linking a withdrawal from Kuwait with a resolution of the Palestinian issue, but the United States consistently opposed any suggestions of a "deal," for that would essentially "reward" aggression.

Bush and his advisers recognized, however, that holding the coalition together would be a considerable challenge. While all the major powers shared disdain for Saddam Hussein's behavior and had come together on the early U.N. Security Council resolutions, the appropriate level of response continually divided them. Not all were fully committed to unconditional Iraqi withdrawal.

Great Britain was adamant in pressing for a strong stand on behalf of the principle of resisting aggression. France and the Soviet Union, both of which had close ties with Iraq and had been principal suppliers of its arms, were more reluctant partners. France, under Mitterand, combined support for the coalition with efforts to pursue an independent, conciliatory role. The joint Shevardnadze-Baker statement assured the Soviet Union's initial support, but U.S. leaders recognized that it would be difficult to gain Moscow's backing for more coercive measures. Within the Soviet government, Gorbachev's and Shevardnadze's cooperation with the United States was tempered by an Arabist group that sought to exploit the tie to Iraq as a means of fostering a settlement and reestablishing Soviet prestige in the Middle East.

The Chinese People's Republic, the other permanent member of the Security Council, likewise had to be cautiously cultivated. Fancying itself as a champion of peoples of the developing world, Beijing was anxious not to be seen as an accomplice in anything resembling Western hegemony in the Middle East; at the same time, however, it needed Western markets and technology and could hardly allow Saddam Hussein to interfere with Sino-American rapprochement. Moreover, Bush's studied indifference to the Chinese government's crackdown on democratic forces in the Tiananmen Square incident in 1989—for which he had been widely criticized at home—gave him some leverage in seeking China's support. Although not members of the Security Council, Germany and Japan were also critical to the maintenance of international pressure on Saddam Hussein. With vital economic interests in the Middle East, both could be counted on to provide diplomatic and financial support for the American position.

From the outset of the crisis, Saddam Hussein's behavior helped to solidify the coalition. The same day that Bush announced the troop deployment, Saddam tried to present the world with a *fait accompli* when his government announced the "comprehensive and eternal merger" of Kuwait with Iraq. The international reaction was immediate and unequivocal. In New York, the U.N. Security Council passed Resolution 662, which declared the annexation "null and void" and called on all nations not to recognize the merger. This resolution passed unanimously. In Cairo the next day, the Arab League adopted a resolution condemning the invasion and annexation of Kuwait and providing for the dispatch of Arab troops to join the American force being assembled in Saudi Arabia. The majority of league members refused to be intimidated by a defiant Iraqi delegation and took the historic step of sending troops to join with a Western army for a possible conflict against a fellow Arab state.* The first Egyptian troops shortly began arriving in Saudi Arabia. Undeterred, Saddam Hussein attempted to appeal to Arab sentiment by linking his cause to the Palestinian issue. He pro-

---

*Twelve of the twenty-one members of the Arab League (including Egypt, Lebanon, and Syria) supported the resolution. Only the Palestine Liberation Organization and Libya supported Iraq. Two nations, including Yemen, abstained, while Jordan was among three nations that expressed "reservations."

posed the withdrawal of Israel from the "occupied territories" in return for discussion on the Kuwait situation, "with recognition of Iraq's historic claims," but the Arab League refused to listen.

Saddam Hussein next resorted to blackmail. He ordered the closing of the borders of Iraq and Kuwait, which resulted in the detention of more than one million Asian and Arab guest workers (foreigners constituted about 80 percent of the work force of Kuwait) and some thirteen thousand Westerners. In an obvious effort to curry the favor of the developing world, Saddam Hussein granted exit visas to residents of Arab, Asian, and African nations but not to Western nationals. On August 16, he ordered the twenty-five hundred Americans and four thousand Britons in Kuwait to report to hotels in Kuwait City; they and other Westerners were now referred to as "restrictees." Within a few days, about eighty American and British citizens were taken from the hotels and moved to Iraqi defense installations. Saddam repeatedly threatened to turn Kuwait into a "graveyard" in the event of warfare. In a message to Bush, he warned that "you are going to receive some American bodies in bags."

Saddam Hussein's manipulation of innocent people outraged Americans and Europeans and backfired in the developing world. The release of non-Western residents caused a flow of refugees into neighboring countries, which lacked resources to accommodate them. The native countries of the refugees resented the loss of money that their nationals had sent home from their well-paying jobs in Kuwait. Again, the international reaction to Saddam Hussein's action was quick and unequivocal. On August 18, the U.N. Security Council passed—in another unanimous vote—Resolution 664, expressing concern over the treatment of foreign nationals and calling upon Iraq to abide by international law. The next day Saddam Hussein promised the release of "foreign guests" if the West pulled its forces out of the Gulf region.

Saddam Hussein's treatment of his "guests" deeply angered Bush. In a strongly worded speech at the convention of the Veterans of Foreign Wars in Baltimore on August 20, an indignant president said that Americans might be called upon to "make personal sacrifices . . . to protect our world from fundamental evil. . . . We have been reluctant to use the word 'hostage.' But when Saddam Hussein offers to trade the freedom of those citizens of the many nations he holds against their will in return for concessions, there can be little doubt that, whatever these people are called, they are in fact hostages." Although Bush regarded Saddam Hussein's holding of hostages as further evidence of his depravity, which added to Bush's resolve, he was determined not to allow the treatment of hostages to obscure the basic issue of Iraqi aggression. He also wanted to avoid becoming personally obsessed with the hostages, as had President Jimmy Carter during the Iranian crisis, to the detriment of his presidency.

Bush moved to tighten the economic pressure on Iraq. The vast majority of nations voluntarily halted trade with Iraq, but Jordan—which was dependent upon Iraqi oil and was fearful of retaliation if it enforced the embargo—continued trade across its frontier with Iraq, and some goods bound for Iraq moved through the Jordanian port of Aqaba. Bush wanted to use the U.S. Navy to halt shipments bound for Iraq, but his authority was unclear. While he claimed publicly on August 11 that he could act under U.N. Charter Article 51, which affirms "the inherent right of individual or collective self-defense," Bush recognized that unilateral enforcement would divide the international coalition. France and the Soviet Union insisted that implementation of a blockade required the approval of the U.N. Security Council. When the emir of Kuwait, at Secretary of State Baker's prodding, requested enforcement of the blockade, Baker asserted that "we now have the ability, the legal basis, for interdicting . . . shipments."

Still Bush moved cautiously. Meeting on August 22 with advisers at his summer home in Kennebunkport, Maine, where he spent much of the last three weeks of August, Bush found wide agreement that the United States needed to enforce the embargo, both to tighten the economic pressure and to uphold American credibility. For once, Bush rejected the advice of Scowcroft and Thatcher, whom he telephoned in London; they argued that Article 51 gave him sufficient authority. Bush instead concurred with those advisers who contended that preserving the coalition necessitated U.N. Security Council authorization. Informed of this decision, a distressed Thatcher said "all right, George, all right. But this is not the time to go wobbly."

Among the several measures that the United States brought before the U.N. Security Council during the first month of the crisis, that authorizing the enforcement of sanctions was the most controversial. Resolution 665 took the United Nations beyond diplomatic and economic pressure to the use of force. It authorized the U.S. Navy, and those of other nations whose governments chose to enforce the embargo, to stop and warn ships suspected of taking embargoed materials to Iraq and, if inspection were denied, to open fire and disable the ship. Support of the Soviets was critical. Bush and Baker phoned Gorbachev and Shevard-nadze, respectively, and urged solidarity as a critical test of Soviet-American cooperation. Yet Bush and Baker also made clear that, if nec-essary, the United States would enforce the embargo on its own. Before committing his government, Gorbachev wrote a stern warning to Sad-dam Hussein, only to receive a defiant response from Baghdad. That was enough to bring the Soviets in line, with the result that, on August 25, the U.N. Security Council passed Resolution 665 by a vote of thir-teen to zero. Cuba and Yemen abstained. The resolution called upon members to "use such measures commensurate to the specific circum-stances . . . to halt all inward and outward maritime shipping to inspect and verify their cargoes and destinations and to ensure strict imple-mentation of the provisions . . . [of] resolution 661." Within the next week, the U.S. Navy began enforcing the embargo in the Arabian and Red Seas by stopping and boarding Iraqi ships and other vessels headed to Iraq.

Over the next several weeks, as anxious leaders and peoples waited for Iraq's response to sanctions, Bush contemplated the possibility that military force would be required to liberate Kuwait. He received CIA reports suggesting that the sanctions would have a marginal effect and that the Iraqi leader would continue his defiance. Sanctions, the CIA projected, would not force Saddam Hussein out of Kuwait in the "short or medium term" and would do the greatest harm to the Iraqi masses, not to the country's leadership or armed forces. Satellite photos re-vealed that Iraq had increased the size of its force in Kuwait and vicin-ity to 430,000 men and was building an elaborate line of defense along the border with Saudi Arabia and on the coast of Kuwait.

In addition, the CIA completed a psychological profile of Saddam, which concluded that he probably would not succumb to pressure; when cornered, he habitually fought without concern for the death and suffering that his actions might bring. To Bush, Saddam Hussein's con-tinuing brutality underscored his defiance of international opinion. Re-ports of Iraqi atrocities against the Kuwaitis profoundly affected Bush. The emir of Kuwait visited the White House in September and re-counted the killing of innocent Kuwaitis. To Bush, these incidents added to the urgency of reversing aggression. He wrote in his diary on September 12: "The problem is, unless something happens soon, there may not be a Kuwait." As he later recalled, "I began to move from viewing Saddam's aggression exclusively as a dangerous strategic threat and an injustice to its reversal as a moral crusade."

If force would be required, Bush recognized the need for international and domestic support. The initial signs were not encouraging. The Soviet Union remained essential to an effective coalition, but when Bush met with Gorbachev on September 9 in Helsinki, the Soviet leader contended that Saddam Hussein had been effectively contained; he then presented plans for a face-saving retreat from Kuwait that would be tied to a general Middle East peace conference. When Bush refused to consider the linkage of Iraqi aggression with other Middle Eastern issues, Gorbachev backed away and agreed to a joint statement that essentially reaffirmed the joint Soviet-American interests in Iraq's withdrawal from Kuwait. Still, the discussions with Gorbachev revealed that the Soviets were far from considering a military solution.

Similarly, when Bush met with Republican and Democratic congressional leaders a few days later, he found a strong bipartisan consensus that sanctions had to be given an adequate trial. In early October, both the House of Representatives and the Senate passed resolutions supporting Bush's action in the Persian Gulf and calling for continuing efforts to reach a diplomatic solution. By that time, Bush was contemplating the necessity of an open-ended congressional resolution. His model was Lyndon Johnson, and his memory was that Johnson had gained overwhelming congressional backing for his objectives in Vietnam. This was ironic, in that the Gulf of Tonkin resolution had become widely seen as an example of presidential manipulation of Congress and as a dubious authorization for the Americanization of the war. Indeed, it symbolized much of the ongoing congressional resentment of presidential prerogatives in war making. In any event, Bush requested that White House Counsel Boyden Gray review the Tonkin Gulf resolution. Gray's report distorted the historical record, making it appear that Johnson had encouraged careful congressional consideration and ignoring his pressure to rush the resolution through Congress. Unmindful of the historical inaccuracies, Bush had the "lesson" he wanted: "[Johnson's] effort made a big impression on me, and I began to think about seeking a similar congressional vote of support."

Despite the lack of international and domestic support for moving beyond sanctions, Bush in early October pressed military leaders for offensive plans. He found the military equally unenthusiastic. It would take another two months before the defensive force was in place, Powell and Schwarzkopf reported, and even longer to determine whether sanctions would work. In an interview, an outspoken Schwarzkopf dismissed the military option as premature: "Now we are starting to see evidence that the sanctions are pinching. So why should we say 'Okay, gave 'em two months, didn't work. Let's get on with it and kill a whole bunch of people?' That's crazy." Rather than return to Washington to participate in discussions on an offensive contingency phase, Schwarzkopf pleaded that he was needed more in Saudi Arabia and sent his chief of staff, Gen. Robert Johnston, in his place.

Meeting with Bush and other high-level officials at the White House on October 11, Johnston and the other members of the Central Command team presented an offensive plan that disappointed both Bush and Scowcroft, who described it as "unenthusiastic, delivered by people who didn't want to do the job." It called for an intensive bombing campaign first against Iraq's military facilities and infrastructure and then against Iraq's ground forces in Kuwait. If necessary, U.N. ground forces would attack the Iraqi army in Kuwait. Scowcroft challenged the Central Command's ground war plan for a one-corps attack on Iraqi forces at Iraq's point of strength in Kuwait and urged instead a flanking operation that would bring U.N. forces in a large, enveloping operation from the west. The meeting ended with no doubt of either Bush's anticipation that the military option would be required or the inadequacy of the planning for a ground war. Powell and Schwarzkopf, who had been humiliated by the dismissal of his command's ground war plan, were instructed to present a modified plan based on Scowcroft's dual-offensive scheme.

As U.S. officials planned for the contingency of war, the enforcement of the embargo and the plight of the hostages touched off some diplomatic initiatives. From Bush's perspective, discussions between Saddam Hussein and officials of other countries or private citizens risked a compromise that the United States would find unacceptable. The Iraqi leader, however, remained his own worst enemy. Especially graphic to Westerners was Saddam's appearance on Iraqi television with British hostages. With characteristic clumsiness, Saddam patted on the head an obviously ill-at-ease seven-year-old boy and told the hostages that their detention served the interest of peace. Hurried missions to Baghdad by several emissaries, including the Rev. Jesse Jackson and former United Nations Secretary-General Kurt Waldheim, resulted in Iraq's release of a few sick and elderly hostages, but no resolution of the overall detention of foreign nationals.

On the status of Kuwait, Saddam Hussein ignored various diplomatic initiatives. Jordan's King Hussein, U.N. Secretary-General Javier Perez de Cuellar, French President Mitterand, and Soviet President Gorbachev each offered incentives for Iraq's withdrawal. King Hussein tried to play on his cooperation with Iraq to press Saddam Hussein into negotiations, but to no avail. Perez de Cuellar journeyed to the region and proposed that the United Nations establish a peacekeeping force to monitor Iraq's withdrawal from Kuwait, which was to be followed by United Nations–supervised negotiations between Iraq and Kuwait; again, Iraq refused to consider any withdrawal.

Then Mitterand, without consulting the United States, got into the act; in a September 24 speech to the U.N. General Assembly, he proposed seeking the "logic of peace" rather than the prevailing "logic of war." Mitterand insisted on unconditional withdrawal from Kuwait, but then he seemed to offer what U.S. officials saw as "reward" for aggression by saying that resolution of the Kuwaiti crisis should be followed by negotiations on all regional issues, including the Palestinian question. Saddam Hussein, who considered France the weak link in the coalition against him, did not respond directly to Mitterand's overture, but he did release several French hostages.

U.S. officials were most troubled by the Soviet Union's initiative. In early October, Gorbachev sent to Baghdad Yevgeny Primakov, a member of his council and a Middle East specialist who had known Saddam Hussein for many years. Primakov's ensuing conversations with Saddam led to speculation that the Iraqi leader was prepared to compromise, but this was dashed when the Iraqi News Agency proclaimed that "Kuwait was and will continue to be Iraqi land forever." Gorbachev wanted to have Primakov brief Bush, who resented the Soviet mission but had no choice but to receive Primakov. Bush said that he would listen to any "positive signal" from Baghdad. Primakov duly returned to Iraq, where he met again on October 28 with Saddam, who reiterated his refusal to withdraw and his demand to connect the Kuwait and Palestinian issues. On the surface, however, Soviet and Iraqi leaders talked optimistically; Saddam Hussein described the Primakov conversations as "profound and very useful," while Primakov said the issues could be resolved peacefully. As the Primakov mission ended ambiguously, Gorbachev journeyed to Paris where, after discussions, he and Mitterand issued a joint statement that American officials found reassuring. The Soviet and French leaders called for Iraq's release of all hostages and withdrawal from Kuwait. Gorbachev added that "President Hussein should not base his calculations around the idea of dividing us, of creating a split among [us]. . . . If he thinks like this, he is very wrong."

While the various diplomatic initiatives floundered, Bush, like much of the American public, remained deeply disturbed by the treatment of hostages. His advisers differed on whether the issue should be stressed as a justification for tightening pressure on Saddam Hussein. Baker believed that it would unite Americans and would also solidify international support, since almost all nations had citizens being detained in Iraq, but Scowcroft feared that emphasizing the hostage issue would divert attention from the overriding concern of aggression. Increasingly, Bush saw the two concerns as interrelated evidence of Saddam Hussein's immorality. In public comments, he compared the Iraqi leader to Hitler, which led some observers to fear that Bush's emotion was clouding his judgment.

The depth of Bush's feeling was especially evident when he met with fifteen congressional leaders at the White House on October 30. In an emotional statement, he recounted stories of the mistreatment of hostages, which he related to a history of World War II that he was reading and that had served to remind him of the futility of appeasing dictators. The congressional leaders were primarily concerned with reports that Bush was planning a troop increase; the speaker of the House, Representative Thomas Foley (D.-Wash.), submitted an "expression of concern" signed by eighty-one Democratic members of Congress; the document opposed any offensive military action and insisted that war, if ultimately necessary, could be waged only with congressional authorization. Bush said that consideration of augmenting the U.N. force was justified on the grounds that sanctions seemed to be having little effect and that Iraq had increased the size of its army in and around Kuwait. The Senate Majority Leader, George Mitchell (D.-Maine), as well as Foley and other leaders from both parties, cautioned Bush to move slowly or risk the loss of congressional and public backing. They urged that sanctions be given more time—as one said, "the case has not been made that sanctions have failed"—and that Congress be fully involved in any decision for military action. "Unless there is gross provocation," Foley warned, "you won't have public support." Moreover, Bush's version of events in Kuwait was challenged by both Mitchell and Senator William Cohen (R.-Maine), vice chairman of the Senate Intelligence Committee, who questioned whether there was credible evidence of worsening treatment of the hostages. The unproductive meeting underlined the beginning of a serious divergence between the White House and Congress over the means of projecting U.S. power and the war-making authority of the president.

The reticence of the congressional leaders, while disturbing, did not restrain Bush. As he met with Baker, Cheney, Scowcroft, and Powell later that day, Bush stated the alternatives:

> The time has come to determine whether we continue to place most of our eggs in the sanctions basket, which would take a good deal more time as things now stand but would possibly avoid the risks and costs of war, or whether we raise the pressure on Saddam by pressing ahead on both the military and diplomatic tracks. I realize that if we do give Saddam some kind of deadline, we are in effect committing ourselves to war. I also realize that by making such a threat and by preparing for it, we may also increase the odds that Saddam agrees to a peaceful solution. Indeed it may be necessary to push things to the brink of war if we are to convince Saddam to compromise.

With the 250,000-person force required to defend Saudi Arabia now in place, the issue was whether to move to offensive capability through the deployment of an additional 200,000 soldiers. While Bush's inner circle agreed with his assessment of the military and diplomatic benefits of the troop increase, they recognized that international and congressional support was problematic. U.N. Security Council authorization of the use of force and establishment of a deadline for Iraqi withdrawal seemed essential, but Baker doubted whether the French and Soviets would support the offensive option. He was nonetheless assigned the task of gaining Saudi Arabia's approval to station more troops on its soil and then of lining up support for a U.N. Security Council resolution.

The public announcement of the decision to double the size of the military deployment, however, was not made until November 9. The delay resulted in part from the necessity of gaining Saudi approval, which Baker secured during a hurried visit to meet King Fahd. Also, with congressional elections on November 8, an announcement before that date would have interjected the Persian Gulf policy into the campaign. Relations with congressional leaders were further strained by the White House's delay in informing them of Bush's decision until shortly before it was announced. The troop increase, Bush stated, gave the United Nations an "offensive military option"—a step necessitated by Saddam Hussein's defiance of U.N. resolutions. Bush again took the occasion to define the issues as reaching beyond the region: "Iraq's aggression is not just a challenge to the security of Kuwait and other Gulf nations, but to the better world that we all have hoped to build in the wake of the Cold War."

This escalation of the U.S. military presence triggered vigorous criticism in Congress and much of the nation's press. The congressional assertion of its war-making prerogatives had been strong ever since the Vietnam War; in 1973, Congress had passed the War Powers Resolution, which set forth procedures intended "to ensure the collective judgment" of Congress and the president before committing U.S. forces to hostilities. Basically, the resolution sought to impose limits on a president's power to use the commander-in-chief clause to wage an undeclared war. Senator Mitchell, the majority leader, issued an ultimatum: "The President must come to Congress and ask for a declaration. If he does not get it, then there is no legal authority for the United States to go to war." Fifty-three Democrats in the House of Representatives and one in the Senate, led by Representative Ron Dellums of California, filed an injunction in federal court to prohibit Bush from using force without explicit congressional approval.* Bush's fellow Republicans were in disarray. Senator Dole, the minority leader, and another influential Republican, Senator Richard Lugar of Indiana, called for a special session of Congress to debate the Persian Gulf crisis, but Bush feared that such a debate would play into Saddam Hussein's hands, giving the appearance of disunity undermining American resolve.

Bush tried to reach some understanding with Congress when he met again with its leaders on November 14. Bush defended his decision and promised continuing consultation with Congress, but Democrats and some Republicans questioned the timing of the troop buildup and reiterated that war could be waged only with the approval of Congress. Bush managed to gain agreement to delay any debate until the newly

*In December, Judge Harold H. Greene, although agreeing that Congress alone had the authority to declare war, ruled against the plaintiffs on the grounds that, since Congress had not yet taken a stand on war or peace, no court could rule on the issue.

elected Congress convened in January, but he left the meeting convinced that the odds were against any congressional authorization for war.

International support for U.S. policy would enhance the prospects for congressional and popular backing. Bush relied principally on Baker to line up support of the governments represented on the U.N. Security Council. During the first three weeks of November, Baker undertook a diplomatic odyssey, carrying with him a draft Security Council resolution authorizing "all necessary means, including the use of force" to assure implementation of the Security Council resolutions. Bush gave Baker considerable latitude to offer concessions and other inducements to win support. Both men recognized that the Soviet Union might object to the "use of force" clause and were prepared to modify it if necessary to gain Soviet support; the authorization of "all necessary means" implicitly included force, in any event. They also recognized that Security Council procedures necessitated moving quickly. Each month a different member presided over the council; during November, the United States held the presidency, but in December it would rotate to Yemen, which was certain to oppose the resolution. Since the presidency brought with it certain prerogatives regarding the agenda and procedures, it behooved the United States to have the resolution considered before the end of November. Last, because of the importance of the resolution and the time factor, Bush and Baker decided that Baker should meet only with heads of state or foreign ministers, not with ambassadors at the United Nations. "It was simply too momentous a decision," Baker remembers, "to be handled at anything less than the highest levels."

After securing Saudi approval of the troop increase, Baker journeyed to Cairo, where he met with Quin Qichen, the foreign minister of the Chinese People's Republic. In return for supporting the Security Council resolution, Quin wanted the promise of a visit to China by Bush or Baker. Baker, however, demurred; such a visit would trigger substantial domestic criticism, since it would imply endorsement of the regime responsible for the repression at Tiananmen Square. Baker made clear that a Chinese veto in the Security Council would harm its relations with the United States; he told Quin that "we don't hold it against our friends that they are not joining us . . . but we do ask that they do not stand in our way." Quin seemed to understand, and Baker cabled

Bush that China would support or, at the worst, abstain when the U.N. Security Council considered the U.S. resolution.

As expected, the most extended discussions were with the Soviet leaders. Journeying to Moscow on November 7, Baker met with Foreign Minister Shevardnadze, who eventually came to accept the logic of threatening the use of force. Shevardnadze, however, was skeptical of the prospects for quick military success (the Soviet humiliation in Afghanistan being fresh in his memory), which led Baker to take the extraordinary step of sharing the details of military planning. Shevardnadze was won over. His only question was whether the Iraqi Scud missiles (which the Soviets had provided to Iraq) posed a threat, but the U.S. military representative accompanying Baker said that they were so inaccurate as not to cause the Americans worry.

Shevardnadze then called Gorbachev, and together he and Baker went to Gorbachev's dachau. The Soviet president said he was determined to work with the United States but was reluctant to support the resolution, for it asked the Soviet Union to approve the use of American force against a longtime ally. He proposed two resolutions: the first authorizing the use of force, but only after a six-week period to explore peaceful solutions, and the second ordering an actual start of hostilities. Baker rejected that alternative as too cumbersome and proposed instead that the U.S. resolution be modified to provide a negotiating interlude. Gorbachev remained noncommittal but promised to reach a decision before he was scheduled to meet with Bush in Paris eleven days later, when both would be attending the Council on Security and Cooperation in Europe. After thirteen hours of give-and-take with Shevardnadze and Gorbachev, an exhausted but confident Baker cabled Bush that the Soviet interest in ongoing cooperation would probably lead to support of the U.S. resolution.

The discussions with Chinese and Soviet officials having gone as well as could be expected, Baker next went to London and Paris to meet with the leaders of the two other permanent members of the U.N. Security Council. British support had always been certain, but as always, the French were more problematic. After lengthy discussions with Baker, Mitterand eventually gave his approval. While cynical about sending French troops to salvage the authoritarian regime of Kuwait, Mitterand was utterly disdainful of Saddam Hussein and agreed that he had to be contained. Baker moved on to meet with the nonpermanent members of the Security Council. He conferred with the foreign ministers of Ivory Coast, Ethiopia, and Zaire in Geneva and with the foreign minister of Rumania in Paris. He later journeyed to Yemen and Colombia for meetings with the heads of those states and to Los Angeles, where he met the foreign minister of Malaysia. Given the magnitude of the resolution, Baker's discussions with these leaders were usually intensive, but in the end all except Yemen agreed that Saddam Hussein's contempt for the United Nations justified the threat of force to liberate Kuwait. So, by November 25, Baker had met with high-level officials of all members of the Security Council except Cuba and was certain of the support of all except the Soviet Union, China, Cuba, and Yemen. Yemen, it was assumed, would oppose the resolution. China had promised that it would not exercise its veto power.

Soviet support still seemed probable, but given the two decades of close ties between the Soviet Union and Iraq and the sharp differences within the Soviet government, Gorbachev's hesitation was understandable. Despite Gorbachev's assurances of a decision by the time of the meeting in Paris on November 18–19, the continued debate within the Soviet government precluded the support that Bush sought when the two leaders met. The Americans accommodated the Soviets by agreeing to modify the resolution to eliminate reference to the "use of force" and to insert a deadline date to allow for negotiations. Shevardnadze told Baker that, while the Soviet Union would vote for the resolution, it could not commit itself openly, since it wanted to make one more effort to deal with Saddam Hussein diplomatically. A few days later Gorbachev warned Iraq of the Soviet intention to stand with the United States unless there was some sign of compromise, but the threat had no apparent effect on Saddam Hussein, thus assuring at last Soviet support for the resolution.

Determined to force a showdown in the U.N. Security Council while the United States still presided over its sessions, Bush and Baker worked for a vote on November 29. Shevardnadze delivered on his promise of Soviet support. The day before the vote, he and Baker agreed on the final language of the resolution, setting January 15, 1991, as the deadline date for Iraq's compliance with the demand to withdraw from Kuwait or face the use of force. Having lobbied all other members of the Security Council, Baker made what he correctly anticipated would be a futile bid for the support of Cuba (his meeting with Cuba's foreign minister being the first such high-level meeting of a U.S. and Cuban official in thirty years). He also made a final but ultimately frustrating effort to gain an affirmative vote from China. When informed that Yemen, as expected, would vote against the resolution, Baker told aides it would be a costly vote. (Yemen had hitherto been the recipient of $70 million of American economic assistance per year.)

With Baker presiding, the U.N. Security Council convened on the afternoon of Thursday, November 29, for one of the most important votes in its history. All but two member nations were represented at the foreign secretary level—a testimony to the significance of the issue before the council. In his introductory comments, Baker drew from history to justify the threat of force. Quoting the unheeded appeal of Ethiopian Emperor Haile Sellasie to the League of Nations when his country was being overrun by Italy in 1936 (Ethiopia was among the members of the Security Council in 1990), Baker said that "history now has given us another chance. . . . We must not let the United Nations go the way of the League of Nations. We must fulfill our common vision of a peaceful and just post–Cold War world. But if we [are] to do so, we must meet the threat to international peace created by Saddam Hussein's aggression."

The meeting lasted barely two hours and, after several delegates (including the representative of Iraq, which had been invited to the session) spoke, the vote on Resolution 678 followed the expected pattern: twelve voted in favor, Cuba and Yemen opposed it, and China abstained. The resolution allowed "one final opportunity, as a pause of goodwill," for Iraq to withdraw from Kuwait by January 15, 1991; if it did not, U.N. members were authorized "to use all necessary means . . . to restore international peace and security in the region."

Having gained international authority for the use of force, Bush had to confront the growing domestic criticism of his policy. The public and Congress had generally backed the initial buildup of U.S. forces, but the movement to an offensive capability troubled many Americans. In November, public opinion polls showed that popular approval of Bush's handling of the crisis, which had stood at 80 percent in August, had dropped to 54 percent and, more importantly, that Americans were evenly divided over whether doubling the number of troops was necessary. When asked whether they favored using force to drive the Iraqis out of Kuwait if the Iraqis did not withdraw by January 15, Americans were reluctant: only 37 percent favored war under such a circumstance, while 51 percent opposed it. And by a margin of 61 percent to 28 percent, Americans favored keeping a defensive force in place rather than initiating a war to drive the Iraqis out of Kuwait.

Several prominent former officials charged that Bush was rushing to war. The principal forum was hearings conducted by the Senate and House Armed Services Committees. Former Secretary of Defense James Schlesinger stressed that "severe punishment has already been meted out" and warned of warfare in the "fragile, inflammable, and unpredictable" Middle East and of the United States ending up "obliged to involve itself in the reconstruction of the region in the aftermath of a shattering war." Those concerns were echoed by the former head of the National Security Agency William Odom and former Secretary of the Navy James Webb, who said that Bush should reinstitute the draft and get a congressional declaration of war before going any further. The most widely publicized and politically damaging testimony came from Admiral William J. Crowe, former chairman of the Joint Chiefs of Staff, who said that the United States should wait at least another year to determine whether sanctions would prove effective: "We should give sanctions a fair chance before we discard them. . . . The trade-off of avoiding war with its attendant sacrifices and uncertainties would, in my view, be more than worth it." Former Under Secretary of State George Ball, who was renowned for his efforts to restrain Lyndon Johnson from taking the country to war in Vietnam, wrote that Bush should make fuller use of the United Nations peacekeeping ability before plunging into war. Among the former officials called by the committee, only former Secretary of State Henry Kissinger supported Bush's policy. Before the committee as well as in several articles and interviews, Kissinger argued that the risks and sacrifice of warfare were necessary to punish Saddam Hussein for his aggression and to preserve international order.

With U.N. Security Council Resolution 678 allowing forty-seven days for a peaceful settlement and with the American public and Congress hesitant to accept the military measures that the resolution authorized, Bush was compelled to reassure the international community and his domestic constituency that he would go—as he stated on November 30—"an extra mile for peace." He proposed direct United States–Iraqi talks by having Baker meet with Saddam Hussein in Baghdad while Tariq Aziz would come to Washington. Besides providing evidence of the "extra mile," Bush saw bilateral discussions as the most forceful means of communicating to the Iraqis the international community's commitment to liberate Kuwait.

As he proposed the exchange, Bush reiterated his rejection of compromise: "I am not suggesting discussions that will result in anything less than Iraq's complete withdrawal from Kuwait, the restoration of Kuwait's legitimate government, and freedom for all hostages." If Iraq did not comply by January 15, Bush said the United Nations would resort to force, and he did not mince his words: "This will not be another Vietnam. This will not be a protracted, drawn-out war. . . . If one American soldier has to go into battle, that soldier will have enough force behind him to win and then get out." After he finished his prepared remarks, Bush received questions from the media. One journalist asked whether he would risk the lives of his own grandchildren over the issues in the Persian Gulf. Bush repeated that U.S. vital interests were at stake and added that he would "do [his] level best to bring those kids home without one single shot fired in anger," but if war came, "there will be no murky ending."

As some of his advisers had feared, it was Bush's conciliatory gesture, not his tough words, that attracted the greatest attention. Scowcroft in particular had opposed the offer of discussions, predicting that it would be seen by Saddam Hussein and other Arab leaders as a sign of irresolution, which would undermine the coalition's unity within days of the impressive U.N. Security Council passage of Resolution 678.

Iraq's response to Bush's offer underlined the soundness of those concerns. The Baghdad media proclaimed Bush's move a "submission to Iraq's demand . . . to open a serious negotiation on the region's issues." Saddam Hussein, described by one correspondent as believing that he "had the Americans on the run," took to Baghdad television on December 2 to say that there was a 50-50 chance of a settlement, provided that Bush was acting in good faith; if not, the Iraqi president warned, "in that case we are closer to war." Saddam was further encouraged when the Foreign Ministers of the European Economic Community (EEC) on December 5 invited Tariq Aziz to confer with them. Trying to exploit the situation, Saddam, after referring to the growth of antiwar sentiment in America and the EEC interest in negotiations, promised the unconditional release of the remaining hostages. Four days later the U.S. Embassy chartered an airplane, which took 325 hostages from Baghdad, and many more hostages soon followed. Relieved by the release, Bush remarked that now he had "one less worry."

Meanwhile, America's partners in the Arab world were plainly annoyed with Bush for what they saw as a peremptory and ill-considered initiative. Saudi Arabia's ambassador told Scowcroft that, "to you, sending Baker is good will; to Saddam Hussein, it suggests you're chicken" and predicted that Saddam Hussein would wait until the last minute before receiving Baker. Saudi Arabia, Egypt, and Syria quickly moved to disabuse Saddam Hussein of any weakening of their resolve; their foreign ministers issued a joint warning on December 3 that he had better take advantage of the "last chance for avoiding war."

Bush saw Saddam Hussein's misreading of his resolve and the anxiety of the friendly Arab states as the price that had to be paid to reassure the American public and Congress. On the evening of his overture to Iraq, Bush met with congressional leaders and said that he would work with them, but added his conviction that constitutionally he did not need congressional approval before going to war. Congressmen of both parties resented such claims, and most also held that sanctions ought to be tested for a longer period and doubted whether a war could be brief and decisive.

After the meeting Bush confided to advisers that he still doubted whether he could get enough votes in Congress for a resolution authorizing the use of force, but he believed that the public and Congress would come eventually to support his policy. The CIA, he learned, would soon report to Congress on the limited effect of sanctions on Iraq's military capability, and that would be important in justifying the resort to force. He was also encouraged by the support of a newly established bipartisan Committee for Peace and Security in the Gulf, which was spearheaded by the prominent Democratic Congressman Steven Solarz of New York.

Bush's greatest ally in building domestic support proved to be Saddam Hussein, who was as uncompromising and insensitive as ever. Evidently believing that time was working in favor of his long-held dream of being able to link the Kuwait issue to a comprehensive Middle Eastern settlement, he haggled over the terms of direct talks with U.S. officials. At one point, Aziz's visit to Washington was tentatively set for December 17, but that fell through when Iraq failed to reciprocate by indicating when Baker could visit Baghdad. On December 15, Saddam

Hussein virtually ruled out negotiations: "We will not go to the United States to receive orders. If the U.S. President George Bush insists on repeating the U.N. resolutions, there will be no reason for us to go." The next day he stated that the Kuwait question could not be discussed until the Palestinian issue had been completely settled. He even repudiated initiatives by fellow Arabs. In particular, Algeria undertook a mediating effort (supported by Jordan, Iran, and Oman), and its president, Chadli Benjedid, went to Baghdad and proposed simultaneous Iraqi and U.N. withdrawals from Kuwait and Saudi Arabia. The Iraqis were not interested; Benjedid was told that "Kuwait is Iraq—past, present, and future—and not an inch of it will be given up."

While Bush and his advisers continued to hope that such statements might be mostly bluster and that, in the end, Saddam Hussein would avoid war, they had to prepare for the military option. Privately, Bush, according to close associates, seemed resigned to the inevitability of war. The public comments of American commanders in the field, however, caused him concern. Schwarzkopf stated that a war could last as long as six months; he foresaw Iraq putting up a "tough fight." His deputy, Lt. Gen. A. H. Waller, told reporters that the military coalition would not be in place to fight by January 15 and said that February 1 was a more realistic deadline. Returning from a mission to Saudi Arabia on December 24, Cheney and Powell reassured Bush that, on the contrary, the offensive could be launched when the deadline expired on January 15.

On New Year's Day 1991, Bush met with Scowcroft, Cheney, Powell, and Gates at the White House. They read of still another defiant statement from Saddam Hussein, who had visited his troops in Kuwait the day before and boasted that "the U.S.-dominated buildup has failed to force Iraq to blink . . . [and] Iraq is growing more and more resolved not to cede any of its rights." Such intransigence notwithstanding, Bush believed that he had to make still another effort to bring American and Iraqi diplomats together. As he and his advisers saw the situation, this was the only way of making certain that Saddam realized the strength and determination of the U.N. coalition. Moreover, another U.S. initiative would enable Washington to control diplomacy with Baghdad; this was of concern, since the EEC was scheduled to meet on January 4 to consider a last-minute gesture to Iraq, and France continued to hint of a deal linking Iraq's withdrawal with Israel's from the West Bank. Finally, when Congress reconvened on January 3, it would focus on the issues of whether sanctions should be tested beyond January 15 and whether Bush needed to seek a resolution of war before implementing U.N. Resolution 678.

On the morning of January 3, Bush proposed direct discussions between Baker and Aziz sometime from January 7 to 9, but the terms were stark: "No negotiations, no compromises, no attempts at face saving, no rewards for aggression." Within a few hours, Iraq proposed—and the United States accepted—a meeting between Baker and Aziz in Geneva on January 9.

Bush saw Baker's mission to Geneva as the last opportunity to communicate his resolve to Saddam Hussein while establishing that he had gone the "extra mile" to avoid war. Concerned that Aziz would not tell Saddam the unpleasant truth about Iraq's precarious position, Bush decided to have Baker carry a personal letter to the Iraqi leader. The letter was blunt:

> Mr. President: We stand today at the brink of war between Iraq and the world. This is a war that began with your invasion of Kuwait, this is a war that can be ended only by Iraq's full and unconditional compliance with Security Council Resolution 678. There can be no reward for aggression. Nor will there be any negotiation. Principle cannot be compromised. However by its full compliance, Iraq will gain the opportunity to rejoin the international community. . . . Mr. President, U.N. Security Council Resolution 678 establishes the period before January 15 of this year as a pause of good will so that this crisis may end without further violence. Whether this pause is used as intended, or merely becomes a prelude to further violence is in your hands, and yours alone. I hope you weigh your choice carefully and choose wisely for much will depend on it.

Baker departed from Washington on January 6 for consultations with British and French leaders before the Geneva meeting. In London, Britain's new Foreign Minister Douglas Hurd reassured Baker of Britain's continued support of U.S. policy. In Paris, President Mitterand, who had been offended by Aziz's rejection of an invitation to meet with the EEC foreign ministers and his statement that Iraq "resent[ed] the submissive policies pursued by certain European governments toward the aggressive and haughty American policies," was now firmly committed.

Meanwhile, back in Washington, Bush used the impending showdown to request congressional support of U.N. Security Council Resolution 678. In a carefully worded letter to congressional leaders on January 8, Bush chided Congress to act in the national interest. Saying that support would have been "constructive" for Baker's position in his meeting with Aziz and that he would have welcomed it earlier, Bush added that "there is still opportunity for Congress to act to strengthen the prospects for peace and to safeguard this country's vital interest." He then requested that the House of Representatives and Senate "adopt a resolution stating that Congress supports the use of all necessary means to implement U.N. Security Council Resolution 678." Bush emphasized, however, that the ultimate power was his and that he was inviting Congress to endorse whatever he decided: "I am determined to do whatever is necessary to protect America's security. I ask Congress to join with me in this task. I can think of no better way than for Congress to express its support for the President at this critical time."

Bush's decision to seek Congress's endorsement was a calculated risk, since many of its members questioned the necessity of resorting to force. Should Congress reject a war resolution (or pass some compromise measure), his position as leader of the U.N. coalition would be seriously weakened. On the other hand, failure to go to Congress risked alienating the public; an opinion poll in early January showed that 60 percent of Americans believed that Bush needed congressional authorization before taking military action. Bush thus showed a degree of respect for the constitutional process, which would enable him to lessen, if not entirely avert, charges of abusing presidential power, which had accompanied Truman's decision for war in Korea and had plagued Johnson's conduct of the Vietnam War. Waiting until the last minute to request approval would probably work to Bush's advantage, since fence-sitters in Congress would be inclined to support him lest they be held responsible for undermining national resolve at a time when 450,000 U.S. troops were poised to liberate Kuwait.

Meanwhile, the Baker-Aziz meeting in Geneva was a last opportunity to avert the movement toward war. Together with their small delegations, they gathered in the Salon des Nations at the Intercontinental Hotel on Wednesday, January 9. The atmosphere was icy. Asked to pose for a photograph before doors were closed, Baker agreed to shake hands with Aziz but refused to look him in the eye or to smile. Once the meeting began, Baker gave Aziz the Bush letter. It was in a sealed envelope with a copy on the outside. Aziz, with "hands trembling [and] sweating," read the copy, taking much time to do so, and then declined to accept the letter, saying "the tone is not appropriate for a head of state." Baker responded that "the letter is frank, but it is appropriate." When Aziz reiterated that he could not accept it, Baker came back: "You are taking onto your shoulders the responsibility of being the only official of your government to have seen this letter." Still Aziz refused. The session went on for nearly seven hours, with the Bush letter remaining on the table—a symbol of the American-Iraqi impasse.

The remainder of the meeting demonstrated its futility. Aziz was defiant, accusing the United States of "conspiring" against Iraq and the Palestinians. Baker reminded Aziz of the overwhelming power arrayed against Iraq, the certainty of war if there was no withdrawal from Kuwait, and the devastation awaiting Iraq in that event. Aziz asserted that Iraqis would endure hardships and outlast the Americans. After Baker made a final, futile effort to get Aziz to take Bush's letter, the meeting broke up.

After Baker had reported the impasse at Geneva, Bush publicly denounced this latest evidence that Iraq was "not interested in direct communication designed to settle the Persian Gulf situation" and warned that the "choice of peace or war [was] really Saddam Hussein's to make." Bush responded to a reporter who questioned whether this meant war: "I can't misrepresent this to the American people. I am discouraged. . . . There was no discussion [by Aziz] of withdrawal from Kuwait. . . . But this was a total stiff-arm . . . total rebuff."

As Congress was about to begin debate on a war resolution, Bush said that he wanted Congress's support but reiterated that he would act as he deemed necessary regardless of congressional action: "I don't think I need it. I have the authority to fully implement the United Nations resolutions. . . . I have tried to reach out to [congressional leaders] in various ways. I will continue to do it, because I want to see a solid front here as we stand up against this aggressor."

When congressional debate began on January 10, Bush benefited from the Iraqi intransigence, which convinced many Americans of the necessity for force. Public opinion polls conducted immediately after the Geneva meeting showed growing support for initiating war. Americans beforehand had been almost evenly divided between sanctions and force, but now there was a preference (50% to 36%) for the war option. Another poll showed that Americans, by a margin of 55 percent to 38 percent, favored war if Iraq did not withdraw from Kuwait by January 15. Underlying the hawkish trend in opinion was the belief of 60 percent of Americans that the United States had done all it could diplomatically to solve the crisis. Still, these polls showed that Bush's policy enjoyed majority, but far from overwhelming, support; about one-third of the public was still opposed to war, which made congressional authorization all the more important.

As time ran out in the Persian Gulf and with the American public inclined toward the military option, the two houses of Congress considered a war resolution. With virtually all members present and the galleries packed, the House of Representatives and Senate met for extended sessions that were covered live by television. The American public witnessed an historic debate that was widely praised for its high quality. The Republican leadership introduced resolutions in both houses that blended the president's request with an assertion of congressional prerogatives. Restating the record of Iraqi aggression and U.N. resolutions, it "authorized" the president to use U.S. forces pursuant to U.N. Security Council Resolution 678. Before doing so, however, the president was to inform Congress that all peaceful efforts at securing compliance with the U.N. resolutions had failed. In an affirmation of Congress's power, the resolution stipulated that its provisions derived "specific constitutional authorization" from the War Powers Resolution.*

With most of his critics being Democratic members of Congress and with that party holding a majority of seats in both houses, Bush's hope for passage of the war resolution depended on winning virtually all Republicans and picking up a sizable minority of Democrats. The House of Representatives, which traditionally had been more supportive of presidents on foreign policy issues than the Senate and included hawkish Democrats among its leaders, seemed certain to vote for the war resolution. The situation in the Senate was more problematic. From the outset of the crisis in August, several influential senators had criticized Bush's policy, and as an institution, the Senate historically, and especially since the Vietnam era, had been notably jealous of preserving its foreign policy prerogatives.

The congressional debate rarely questioned the objective of restoring Kuwait's sovereignty; rather, it focused on whether the use of force

---

*An alternate resolution, introduced by Democratic Party leaders, directed the president to continue diplomacy and economic sanctions and, if such measures failed, then to seek congressional authorization for the use of force. It was voted on but failed to gain a majority in either house.

was yet justified. Only a handful of speeches digressed into inaccurate irrelevancy like that of Democratic Congressman Romano Mazzoli of Kentucky, who charged that Bush had "deified" Kuwait into a "remarkably democratic, absolutely a pristine example of grassroots activity." Most critics of the Bush policy questioned the urgency of the military option and argued that sanctions should be given more time. In the House of Representatives, for instance, Jim McDermott (D.-Wash.) urged colleagues to "calm the rhetoric, slow the headlong rush to battle, give the sanctions time to work, pursue all diplomatic efforts, and talk this thing through fully and rationally before we take any action." He questioned whether "six hours of discussion is our best effort at peace." His colleague, Edward Markey (D.-Mass.), concurred that "it's time for Congress to force a pause in America's slide toward war." Another Democrat, James Shuer of New York, urged giving sanctions a full year to work: "A year's wait . . . [would be] a fraction of the cost of a month's wait, a month's cost, of a shooting war."

Bush's supporters in the House argued principally that time would work to Saddam Hussein's advantage and would enable him to develop his nuclear program. They pointed to the CIA report that sanctions were not working. "Time is something we cannot give this madman," argued California Republican Duncan Hunter—a view echoed by many others. "We must come to the harsh reality, rather than wishful thinking," Bud Shuster (R.-Penn.) added, "that . . . only force will remove Saddam Hussein." Republican Jim Leach of Iowa indulged in a gastronomical metaphor: "The message must unequivocally be delivered: the criminally carnivorous aggressor regime in Iraq must unconditionally disgorge Kuwait." Repeatedly members characterized the Iraqi leader as a latter-day Hitler and recalled the "lessons" of failing to halt aggression in the 1930s. One of Bush's most outspoken Democratic supporters, Ronald Coleman of Texas, recalled how appeasement "gives time for the dictators to grow stronger and bolder. . . . Now in our time we must not repeat that great mistake."

The debate in the House of Representatives did not approach the drama of that in the Senate, where the vote was certain to be close. While critics of Bush's policy reiterated the argument that he was rushing to war without allowing time for sanctions to be effective, they complained time and again of an abuse of presidential power and disregard for congressional authority to declare war. The Democrats contended that Congress should act only *after* Bush had exhausted other alternatives and had come to it requesting approval to wage war. They said that, if Congress passed the Republicans' war resolution, it would transfer the war-making decision to the president.

Mitchell, the majority leader, set the tone of the assault, criticizing Bush for failing to consult adequately with congressional leaders throughout the crisis and saying that the president should not be allowed to determine unilaterally whether the country went to war. Democrat Patrick Leahy of Vermont likewise contended that the president could not "initiate a war without the approval of Congress. . . . No one person should have such awesome power to send American men and women to war." Another leading Democratic Party critic, Patrick Moynihan of New York, dismissed the significance of Iraq's aggression; Bush had overreacted—"sending the largest set of armed forces since World War II . . . [when] a nasty little country invaded a littler but just as nasty country"—and passage of the resolution would mean "that the primacy of Congress on this issue under the constitution will have been denied."

Joseph Biden (D.-Del.) saw Bush manipulating Congress by waiting so long to request approval, but that delay did not excuse Congress from fulfilling its constitutional authority: "Failure by Congress to discharge our Constitutional role—to insist that the choice about the war be made by us and not by the President—would be a mistake of historic proportions." Armed with a letter signed by constitutional scholars, Ted Kennedy (D.-Mass.) warned that, "if we allow President Bush to start a war without prior Congressional approval, it will haunt us for years to come." The country should not go to war "just because President Bush set an unreal deadline." Massachusetts's other senator, Democrat John Kerry, a Vietnam War veteran, posed the question sharply: "Are we supposed to go to war simply because one man—the President—makes a series of unilateral decisions that puts [us] in a box—a box that makes war, to a greater degree, inevitable?"

While much of the opposition centered on charges of abuse of power, other critics stressed that sanctions had to be given more time; Democrat Bill Bradley of New Jersey charged that "the powerful tools of sanctions, multilateral action, and firm, patient pressure were abandoned before they were allowed to work." The fullest expression of this argument came from Sam Nunn (D.-Ga.) who, as chairman of the Senate Armed Services Committee, had earned wide respect as an authority on military affairs. He cogently observed that, when sanctions had been implemented in August, no one had expected that they would work within five months, and he asked why it was so "vital" to send Americans into combat before sanctions were fully tested.

These criticisms of what many Democrats considered presidential arrogance were answered only indirectly by Bush's supporters, who, like their colleagues in the House of Representatives, stressed the need for national unity in the face of Saddam Hussein's aggression. "Now is not the time for partisan politics," said Alfonse D'Amato of New York; rather, Americans should stand "behind our President and send a clear message to Saddam Hussein that our resolve is firm and that we speak with one voice." Don Nickles of Oklahoma stated that, "if this resolution fails, this will be a great victory for Saddam Hussein." Supporters also argued that its passage could help pressure Saddam to undertake a last-minute withdrawal from Kuwait. Orin Hatch of Utah said the resolution would "strengthen" Bush in the diplomatic arena by showing Saddam that Congress "back[ed] the President . . . [and] was willing to use force." Stephen Symms of Iowa added that congressional support of force would give Bush more leverage in dealing with Saddam and just might "achieve peace."

This argument helped to win over some Democratic senators. Charles Robb of Virginia, the son-in-law of Lyndon Johnson and a Vietnam War veteran, echoed a phrase from that conflict as he appealed to "give peace a chance by giving the President the authority he believes he needs to achieve it." The other most prominent Democratic Party supporter, who had also seen service in Vietnam albeit in a noncombat role, was Albert Gore of Tennessee. Behind the scenes, the Bush administration lobbied the "fence-sitters" and targeted in particular six Democratic senators from three states (Louisiana, Alabama, and Nevada). Assuming that each of them would find it easier to vote for the war resolution if their Democratic colleagues also did, the White House organized a pro-war letter-writing campaign from constituents to the six senators.

In the end, it was the closest vote on a war resolution in American history.* On January 12 both houses of Congress narrowly authorized the use of force. The House of Representatives approved the main reso-

---

*The support for the war resolution in 1991 was 58 percent in the House of Representatives and 52 percent in the Senate. Congress's declaration of war against England in 1812 had been almost as close. The vote in 1812 was 79 to 49 (62%) in the House of Representatives and 19 to 13 (59%) in the Senate.

lution, 250 to 183. As expected, the more dramatic vote was in the Senate, where the resolution carried by only 52 votes to 47. As the White House had calculated, a sufficient number of Democrats joined with virtually all Republicans to yield slender majorities. In the House of Representatives, 164 Republicans were joined by 86 Democrats to carry the resolution (only 3 Republicans voted with 179 Democrats in opposition). In the Senate, 10 Democrats (including all 6 of the "targeted" senators) broke ranks with the party's leadership and voted with 42 Republicans to give Bush his majority (2 Republicans and 45 Democrats were in the minority). However close the vote, all members of Congress as well as the public now saw the issue as closed. The constitutional process having been followed to the satisfaction of the vast majority of the public, no one questioned Bush's statement afterward that "we have now closed ranks behind a clear signal of our determination and our resolve . . . to Iraq that it cannot scorn the January 15th deadline."

BUSH'S LEADERSHIP during the Persian Gulf crisis blended boldness with caution. From the outset, he believed that Iraq's aggression could not be tolerated, and he never wavered from his determination that "this aggression will not stand." A less resolute U.S. position would probably have enabled Saddam Hussein to annex Kuwait. Within his own administration, Bush encountered the opposition of those, notably General Powell, who were prepared to accept an Iraqi takeover of Kuwait so long as the United States guaranteed the security of Saudi Arabia. Had his advice or the reticence of other advisers who questioned the political-strategic significance of the invasion been dominant in shaping U.S. policy, there would have been no reason to build an international coalition. The Arab states, left to their own devices, would almost certainly have accommodated Saddam Hussein's aggression.

During the early days of the crisis, Bush took a number of risks: that he could gain the support of the Soviet Union for the U.N. Security Council resolutions; that the Chinese People's Republic could be persuaded to at least acquiesce in the objectives of U.S. policy; that most of the Arab states would join outside powers in opposing Iraq's aggression; that Saudi Arabia would accept a U.N. military force that represented an unprecedented Western presence in a modern Islamic nation. Bush's extensive personal interaction with other leaders, coupled with Baker's painstaking efforts, especially with the Soviets, built the coalition. Diplomatic success, of course, ultimately depends on the message, more than the messenger. Bush's and Baker's efforts worked in large part because other states shared the fundamental abhorrence of aggression and were thus responsive to American leadership. Bush's success, of course, also owed much to his adversary's unrepentant belligerence. When cornered, Saddam Hussein, as U.S. intelligence had projected, instinctively became a fighter, and that played to Bush's advantage at home and overseas.

Throughout the crisis, Bush was determined not to lead where others would not follow. At every step he made certain of his international support. The spate of U.N. Security Council resolutions gave international legitimacy to his policy and helped to assure popular and congressional backing at home. Bush sought U.N. Security Council support even when some advisers thought it unnecessary or too risky, as was the case with the two most important projections of coalition power: Resolution 665 enforcing sanctions and Resolution 668 setting the deadline of January 15, 1991.

Bush's caution was also evident in his relationship with Congress. Like Truman and Johnson in similar situations, Bush claimed that, as commander in chief, he could unilaterally take the country to war. Unlike his predecessors, however, Bush confronted a Congress that was controlled by the opposition party and had strong reservations about the necessity for war. Bush could have handled Congress more effectively. He might have been more forthcoming about his plans to enlarge the U.S. force and move to an offensive capability, and certainly he deserved criticism for the manner in which leaders were ultimately informed of that decision and for delaying the announcement of the troop increase until after the congressional elections.

Still, throughout the crisis, Bush involved Congress about as fully as could be expected and certainly as much as other presidents had in comparable circumstances. "On over twenty occasions over the course of the crisis [Bush] met with or briefed Congress, its leadership, and bipartisan groups, not counting meetings with individuals." However frequent and open, presidential consultation with congressional leaders is inherently a difficult process. Presidents are jealous to maintain their prerogatives to determine policy, to direct diplomacy, and to employ economic or military pressure. What they seek is congressional approval without making it appear a requirement. On their side, members of Congress are reluctant to provide support if they doubt the wisdom of the president's course and out of fear of being drawn into decisions that could compromise congressional prerogatives. The interchanges between Bush and congressional leaders accomplished the objectives of the consultative process in that both parties presented their positions fully and, in most respects, candidly. Democratic charges during the debate on the war resolution of the "abuse" of presidential power had little substance; Bush used his constitutional authority to determine U.S. policy and project power during this crisis in ways that presidents had done historically and with considerable constitutional justification.

With the movement toward an offensive capability and U.N. Security Council approval of Resolution 678, Bush's political base at home became precarious. Much of the American public and Congress was opposed to, or at least skeptical of, the use of military force. To build domestic support, he took the risk that an offer to Baghdad of discussions would show a "good faith" effort to avoid war without weakening the U.N. coalition. This gesture bought him time and ultimately played to his enormous political advantage when Tariq Aziz "stiff-armed" Baker at Geneva. To assure a clear constitutional mandate, Bush took the risk that Congress would authorize implementation of U.N. Security Council Resolution 678. However indirect his language and however strong his insistence that authorization was unnecessary, Bush took a step that Truman had avoided and that Johnson made indirectly. He may have been driven more by domestic political considerations than by respect for the constitutional process, but still Bush put his leadership to the test of a congressional vote. Unlike Truman, who had no congressional backing as he waged war in Korea, and Johnson, who had a less explicit authorization for warfare in Vietnam, Bush could claim compliance with the constitutional process as he made the decision for war.

Ironically, the very success of his diplomacy also restricted Bush's options and ultimately made more likely that decision for war. The U.N. military presence in Saudi Arabia could not be expected to last for an extended period, and planning for war had to consider the impending hotter weather and Islamic holidays. Moreover, the diplomatic underpinning of the U.N. coalition was fragile, and the longer Saddam Hussein prolonged the crisis, the more difficult it would be for Bush to hold the diverse elements of the coalition together. While the Soviet Union and most of the European members of the coalition wanted to avoid any impression of rushing to war, the Middle Eastern partners feared that conciliatory gestures (even if accompanied by no equivocation on the demand for withdrawal from Kuwait) and delay showed a weakening of resolve. Of course, Saddam Hussein also drew similar conclusions. So, to Bush, an uncompromising stance against Saddam Hussein reflected not just his convictions but also a diplomatic imperative. The twin coercive measures taken in November—first, to move toward an offensive capability by doubling the size of U.S. forces and, second, to gain U.N. Security Council approval of the January 15 deadline for Iraqi withdrawal from Kuwait—constituted an ultimatum backed with power.

In the end, the decision for war was made in Baghdad, not Washington. It was Saddam Hussein whose aggression touched off the crisis. It was Saddam Hussein who was defiant at each step of the escalating diplomatic, economic, and military pressures that the United Nations put in place. As the January 15 deadline passed, it was Saddam Hussein who chose to accept the heavy casualties and devastation that the U.N. coalition had the power to inflict.

6   George H. W. Bush as Commander in Chief

The Imperatives of Coalition Warfare

ON THE EVENING OF JANUARY 16, 1991, George Bush authorized the launching of Operation DESERT STORM. Addressing the American public from the White House, Bush cast the war—just as Harry
Truman and Lyndon Johnson had done in similar situations—as essential to upholding international order. Aggression in the post–cold war
era was considered no less a threat to American security than it had
been when the Soviet Union or the Chinese People's Republic was seen
as benefiting from the advances of smaller communist countries.

The United States and its partners in 1991 were fighting for "a new
world order—a world where the rule of law, not the law of the jungle,
governs the conduct of nations. When we are successful—and we will
be—we have a real chance at this new world order, an order in which
a credible United Nations can use its peacekeeping role to fulfill the
promise and vision of the U.N.'s founders." After quoting Thomas
Paine's famed words from the American Revolution that "these are the
times that try men's souls," Bush foresaw that "out of the horror of combat will come the recognition that no nation can stand against a world
united, no nation will be permitted to brutally assault its neighbors."
The legacies of the Korean and Vietnam Wars were evident. Avoiding
Truman's mistake of ambiguous objectives, Bush made his objectives
both clear and limited: "Saddam Hussein's forces will leave Kuwait.
The legitimate government of Kuwait will be restored . . . [and] Iraq
will eventually comply with all relevant United Nations resolutions."
Speaking directly of the "lesson" drawn from the Vietnam War, he
promised that "this will not be another Vietnam . . . our troops will have
the best possible support in the entire world, and will not be asked to
fight with one hand tied behind their back."

Besides benefiting from the experiences of Truman and Johnson,
Bush took the country to war without the encumbrances that had undermined their leadership. He had the advantages of unambiguous
congressional authority to wage war, international support through
a series of U.N. Security Council resolutions, a U.N. military force in
place, an American military that was prepared to wage the kind of war

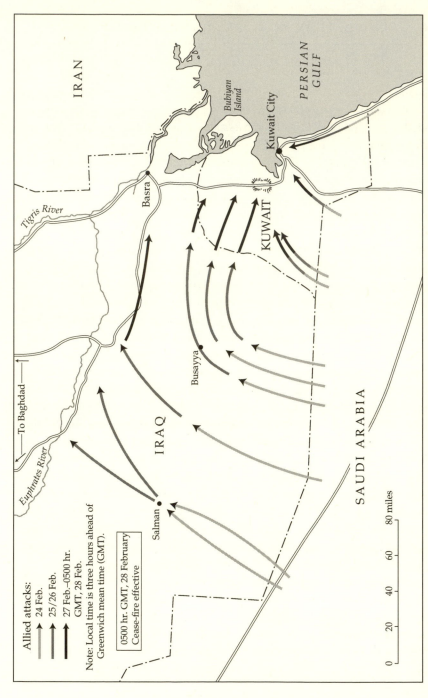

Allied attacks:
24 Feb.
25/26 Feb.
27 Feb.–0500 hr.
GMT, 28 Feb.

Note: Local time is three hours ahead of Greenwich mean time (GMT).

0500 hr. GMT, 28 February
Cease-fire effective

IRAN

Tigris River

To Baghdad

Euphrates River

Basra

Bubiyan Island

Kuwait City

PERSIAN GULF

KUWAIT

Busayya

IRAQ

Salman

SAUDI ARABIA

0   20   40   60   80 miles

THE PERSIAN GULF WAR: The Allied Ground Offensive

at hand, and an enemy that was inferior militarily and isolated inter-nationally.

Yet Bush was not assured of success. The situation was problematic in several ways: whether the American-led U.N. coalition could use its military superiority to force an Iraqi withdrawal from Kuwait without absorbing heavy casualties that would lessen support at home; whether Saddam Hussein's expected missile attacks on Israel would elevate him to heroic status among Arab peoples and undermine the Arab nations' participation in the U.N. coalition; whether Israel, if attacked, could be persuaded not to play into Saddam's hands by retaliating militar-ily; whether the Soviet Union's lukewarm support of DESERT STORM would lead to diplomatic initiatives that linked the Kuwaiti question to the Palestinian and other Arab-Israeli issues. To the Americans, "link-ing" constituted a reward for aggression and detracted from the essential task of liberating Kuwait. In sum, Bush's challenge was holding the U.N. coalition together until the U.N. objectives were achieved.

These problems demonstrated the fragility of the U.N. coalition, which was vital to the realization of U.S. objectives. Its importance was more political and financial than military. Building on the U.N. Security Council resolutions, the coalition gave international legitimacy to the American determination to reverse Iraqi aggression. It helped to shift the financing of DESERT STORM to the governments that stood to benefit the most from it; Saudi Arabia, Kuwait, Japan, Germany, and the United Arab Emirates underwrote most of the costs. Working with the armed forces of other nations complicated the planning by Gen. Norman Schwarzkopf, for many were not essential to the realization of military objectives. Altogether, thirty-five nations contributed to the military op-erations against Iraq, with twenty-four of them deploying troops. The American force was, by far, the largest, totaling 532,000; the other prin-cipal contributors were Saudi Arabia (110,000), the United Kingdom (42,000), Egypt (40,000), the United Arab Emirates (40,000), and France (20,000).* Eleven nations—all traditional allies of the United States—limited their support to planes or tanks; these token contributions re-

*Turkey deployed 120,000 troops along its border with Iraq, with the stipulation that they would be committed to combat only if attacked. Syria deployed 50,000 troops along its border with Iraq and stationed another 2,000 in the United Arab Emirates; it also pro-vided 19,000 troops for operations against Iraq. Kuwait contributed its 11,500-man army to the liberation of its homeland. Other nations deploying troops included Afghanistan, Argentina, Bahrain, Bangladesh, Canada, Czechoslovakia, Honduras, Hungary, Morocco, Niger, Oman, Pakistan, Poland, Qatar, and Senegal.

flected, in part, the divisions within many European countries over the necessity of DESERT STORM.*

As commander in chief, Bush deferred to the judgment of the military leadership on the implementation of strategy, but he was also determined to exercise ultimate control that would assure coordination with political objectives. For counsel, he relied most heavily, as always, on Brent Scowcroft, the retired air force officer who served as his national security adviser, as well as on Secretary of State James Baker, Secretary of Defense Richard Cheney, and Chairman of the Joint Chiefs of Staff Gen. Colin Powell. Powell, as a veteran of the Vietnam War, had long argued that the United States should wage war only under the circumstances at hand: military superiority, public support, and a clear objective. Powell was in constant contact with Schwarzkopf; consistent with American military tradition, he granted Schwarzkopf considerable latitude and deferred to his judgment on most aspects of military operations.

The imperative underlying Bush's diplomatic and military leadership reflected one of the central messages of Carl Von Clausewitz's classic study *On Strategy:* "The most far-reaching act of judgment that the statesman and commander have to make is to establish . . . the kind of war on which they are embarking; neither mistaking it for, or turning it into, something that is alien to its nature." In the Persian Gulf in 1991, that meant focusing on the objective of liberating Kuwait.

The clarity of that objective, however, brought attention to another challenge facing Bush: the American public generally saw the war as also leading to the overthrow of Saddam Hussein. Through his demonization of Saddam, including comparisons with Hitler, Bush had contributed to this sentiment, although the Iraqi leader's own actions were enough to convince Americans of his essential depravity. As the war began, a public opinion poll showed that only 12 percent of Americans thought it would be enough for Operation DESERT STORM to drive Iraq's troops out of Kuwait; 82 percent believed that the United States should "also see to it that Saddam Hussein is removed from power." If Saddam survived a battlefield defeat, Americans were bound to be disappointed. So Bush hoped that a U.N. coalition victory would embolden dissidents to establish a new regime in Baghdad.

Operation DESERT STORM began with the bombing campaign. The

*The nontroop contributors were Australia, Belgium, Denmark, Germany, Greece, Italy, Netherlands, New Zealand, Norway, Portugal, and Spain.

objectives of this first phase of the war were to incapacitate Iraq's command-and-control system, destroy its military supply facilities, cut its communications with Kuwait, and reduce its forces on the ground. After the bombing weakened Iraq's position, the U.N. coalition would begin its ground war. The air campaign went virtually as planned. American aircraft and missiles attacked with devastating accuracy. Iraq's air defense was ineffective, and its air force could not challenge the U.N. coalition's control of the skies; indeed, Saddam Hussein began sending aircraft to Iran to prevent further losses. Within the first two weeks, the U.N. coalition mounted nearly twenty-five thousand sorties against Iraq before shifting its emphasis to the bombing of Iraqi troops, particularly the Republican Guard, in southern Iraq. With CNN television coverage from Baghdad documenting the effectiveness of both laser-directed "smart" bombs and conventional bombing, some Americans expected that air power alone might bring victory.

Saddam Hussein retaliated, as he had threatened, by launching sporadic Scud missile attacks on Israel. These attacks began on January 18. The missiles were not very accurate, but they did cause considerable property damage and a few casualties. Saddam calculated that the missile assault would enhance his stature among Arab peoples and would provoke an Israeli military response, which would enable him to draw attention away from his aggression and to the Palestinian and other Arab-Israeli issues. Israel's instinct, of course, was to retaliate, and hawkish officials within Israel's government pressed Prime Minister Yitzhak Shamir to follow the country's historical policy of attacking terrorists. Bush pleaded with Shamir to exercise restraint in this instance. Under pressure from Washington and recognizing Israel's interest in isolating Iraq, Shamir did not retaliate. All told, Saddam Hussein found that his assault on Israel had negligible military or political effect.

Besides continually urging restraint on Israel in the face of further Scud attacks, Bush concentrated on delicate diplomatic issues resulting from the Soviet Union's unwelcome effort to play the role of peacemaker. Moscow's initiatives had to be handled within the complex fabric of Soviet-American relations. The Bush administration assumed that U.S. interests necessitated the continuation of Mikhail Gorbachev's reform leadership, which was facing increasing challenges. Simultaneous with the launching of Desert Storm, Gorbachev faced his own crisis in the Baltic states, where Lithuania's long-simmering drive for greater independence from Moscow erupted into a clash between Soviet troops and protesters. Conservatives within the Soviet foreign ministry and military leadership, who opposed Gorbachev's support of U.S. policy in the Persian Gulf, now pressed him to tighten control over the dissidents and to reassert an independent role in the Middle East. Bush and Secretary of State Baker wanted to be in a position to restrain Gorbachev in the Lithuanian crisis. They recognized that an open breach with him over the war in the Persian Gulf would not only weaken the U.N. coalition and embolden Saddam Hussein, but also play into the hands of Gorbachev's opponents and lessen Washington's ability to influence his policy in the Baltic. So Bush and Baker sought to conciliate Gorbachev without risking military operations. It was not an easy task.

Shortly after the beginning of the air war, Gorbachev suggested a bombing pause to allow him the opportunity to make a diplomatic approach to Saddam Hussein, an overture that Bush quietly deflected. Later, on January 26, the new Soviet Foreign Minister Alexander Bessmertnykh publicly criticized the bombing, seeing "the danger of the conflict going more in the direction of the destruction of Iraq, which was not in [the] spirit of the U.N. resolutions." These pressures led Baker, whose enthusiasm for Soviet-American collaboration sometimes clouded his judgment, into a diplomatic misstep. At the end of January, Bessmertnykh arrived in Washington to meet Baker, who was determined to continue the close relationship that he had enjoyed with Bessmertnykh's predecessor, Eduard Shevardnadze. At the conclusion of three days of meetings, Baker, without consulting Bush, agreed to a joint statement with Bessmertnykh, which (1) offered a cease-fire in return for Iraq's "unequivocal commitment" to withdraw from Kuwait and its compliance with all U.N. Security Council resolutions and (2) promised that afterward the United States and the Soviet Union would work toward an Arab-Israeli settlement and regional stability.

A "blind-sided" Scowcroft was angered when he learned of the statement from reporters, and it was he who told a stunned Bush of the secretary of state's inappropriate and unwelcome initiative. Not only did it (contrary to Baker's claims) provide "linkage" between Iraqi withdrawal and an Arab-Israeli settlement, but it offered an end to the war on Saddam Hussein's mere promise to withdraw from Kuwait. The statement fell short of Iraq's unconditional withdrawal and would have enabled Saddam to justify his invasion on the grounds that it had forced a resolution of the Arab-Israeli issue. Its release threatened to undermine the U.N. coalition, with the Arab partners and the Israelis especially feeling betrayed. So, to Baker's embarrassment, the White House quickly issued a "clarifying" statement that the Baker-Bessmertnykh communique did not change the U.S. position drawing a line between the resolution of the Persian Gulf War and the other issues in the region.

As the bombing campaign continued, Iraq again turned toward Moscow as an intermediary. Saddam Hussein clearly had an interest in bringing the war to an early end, for the longer the Iraqis absorbed the punishment being inflicted by the U.N. coalition's aerial assault, the more tenuous became his hold on power. Yet he was determined also to avoid abject acceptance of Bush's demands and sought a face-saving compromise before the ground war commenced. Gorbachev, whose international stature was being tarnished by the Baltic crisis and who remained under strong domestic pressure to reassert Soviet independence of the United States, saw an opportunity to restore his leadership. On February 9, the Soviet leader, claiming that the military operations were exceeding the U.N. mandate, announced that he would undertake a mediation effort. Two days later, he named Yevgeny Primakov, the leading Arabist in the Foreign Ministry, who was known for his closeness to Saddam Hussein, as his personal emissary to Baghdad. Primakov carried a proposal that called for Saddam to promise withdrawal from Kuwait under a specified timetable; in return, the Soviet Union would seek the U.N. coalition's acceptance of a cease-fire.

The Soviet leadership cautiously informed their American counterparts. Bessmertnykh told Baker by phone that Primakov's mission revealed "encouraging elements in Saddam's behavior" and that Saddam Hussein was sending Foreign Minister Tariq Aziz to Moscow for further discussions on ending the war. In a letter to Bush, Gorbachev was similarly optimistic and tried to extract a promise that the ground war would not begin so long as the Iraqi-Soviet meetings went on in Moscow. The Soviet initiatives disturbed Bush and his advisers, for the deal offered by Primakov fell short of Iraq's unconditional acceptance of the U.N. resolutions and the request to delay the ground war was unacceptable. After reading Gorbachev's letter, Bush dismissed it, with a curt "no way Jose."

Still, the Soviet initiative presented a problem, which became more dicey when Radio Baghdad announced on February 15 that Iraq was prepared "to deal with U.N. Security Council Resolution 660, with the aim of reaching an honorable and acceptable solution, including withdrawal from Kuwait." Saddam Hussein, however, quickly added conditions to withdrawal, including Israel's withdrawal from the "occupied territories" and the cancellation of all U.N. resolutions against Iraq. This enabled Bush to denounce the Iraqi statement as a "cruel hoax." He went on to call upon the "Iraqi military and Iraqi people to take matters into their own hands, to force Saddam Hussein the dictator to step aside."

Bush coupled the call for Saddam Hussein's overthrow with a promise to end his brutal aggression. Meeting with reporters, he spoke movingly of reports of the mistreatment of "innocents in Kuwait since that invasion in August" and foresaw "an end to that suffering very, very soon." He also reaffirmed the solidarity of the U.N. coalition by asserting, somewhat disingenuously, that the Soviet Union's role was "constructive. . . . I think they're trying very hard, and they're trying within the mandate of the United Nations resolutions." When asked whether he sought Saddam's overthrow, Bush stated that the goals had been set by the United Nations but reiterated words uttered earlier by British Prime Minister John Major: "I wouldn't weep if they put him aside."

Bush hoped that his harsh rhetoric directed at Saddam Hussein and his muted praise of the Soviets would discourage further efforts at mediation, but he soon faced another Gorbachev initiative. Taking advantage of Tariq Aziz's February 18 visit to Moscow, Gorbachev proposed a "four-point peace plan," which called for Iraq to withdraw unconditionally from Kuwait, with a cease-fire taking effect the day before the withdrawal began and the U.N. coalition agreeing not to fire upon retreating Iraqi forces. The Soviet leader still refused to abandon linkage. When Tariq Aziz asked about the Arab-Israeli issue, Gorbachev promised that the Soviet Union would insist that the United Nations deal "with the whole complex of Middle East issues and conflicts, including regional security." In a letter to Bush, Gorbachev argued that, while the Iraqis had not yet accepted his plan, there were signs of a "beginning of a shift in the understanding of realities by Hussein and his team," which should be considered in determining military actions in the next few days.

Gorbachev's incessant maneuvering disturbed Bush, who was determined not to squander the U.N. coalition's military advantage by indulging in prolonged cease-fire negotiations. Bush remained in close phone contact with other leaders. Most of the members of the U.N. coalition, especially the Arab states, agreed that the terms of a cease-fire should be nonnegotiable: Iraq had to withdraw its forces from Kuwait unconditionally. Moreover, the Gorbachev proposal did not stipulate Iraqi compliance with all of the U.N. Security Council resolutions and, of course, again held out the face-saving promise of a general Middle Eastern settlement. Bush thus dismissed the Gorbachev plan, saying publicly on the 19th that "it falls well short of what would be required." In a carefully phrased letter to Gorbachev, Bush expressed concern that the "incompleteness and ambiguities in your proposal may give heart to Saddam Hussein that he can somehow escape the consequences of his actions and obtain an unclear outcome, which he can exploit politically."

The fear of an "unclear outcome" profoundly troubled Bush, for he believed that DESERT STORM would be successful only if Iraq suffered a clear military defeat and was punished for its aggression. For that reason, he, Scowcroft, and Cheney hoped that the air war would not force Saddam Hussein to withdraw from Kuwait. They thus welcomed his continuing defiance despite substantial bombing-inflicted losses. Scowcroft writes that, "if Saddam withdrew with most of his armed forces intact, we hadn't really won."

At the same time, Bush recognized the reluctance of the American public and some military leaders to move to a ground war. Americans were buoyed by the televised evidence of the bombing campaign's success, which convinced many that it alone would achieve victory. The public remained concerned about the prospects of heavy casualties if ground forces were committed. As he had throughout the entire crisis, Powell remained a reluctant warrior, concerned about a lengthy war, substantial casualties, and deteriorating support at home. He felt obliged to caution Bush and Cheney. Somewhat patronizingly, he reminded them that there would be no more "antiseptic videos of a missile with a target in the cross hairs. . . . You can lose fifty to a hundred men in minutes. A battlefield is not a pretty sight. You'll see a kid's scorched torso hanging out of a tank turret while ammo cooking off inside has torn the rest of the crew apart. We have to brace ourselves for some ugly images." Whether Bush and Cheney needed what Powell later described as "the cold bath of reality" was questionable, but his concerns mirrored those of many Americans, who feared substantial American casualties. While determined to keep losses to a minimum, Bush, Scowcroft, and Cheney were convinced that the U.N. coalition could achieve a quick and decisive battlefield victory.

Bush was impatient to launch the ground campaign, but he had promised to move only when the military leadership gave its clearance. He wrote in his diary on February 18: "The meter is ticking. . . . I wish Powell and Cheney were ready to go right now. But they aren't, and I'm not going to push them even though these next few days are fraught with difficulty."

That "difficulty" continued to emanate from Moscow, where Gorbachev, undeterred by Bush's dismissal of his "four-point peace plan" and aware that the ground campaign was imminent, still maneuvered for a diplomatic solution. As Tariq Aziz left Moscow on February 21, he announced Iraq's support of a modified version of the Gorbachev proposal of a few days earlier. This new "eight-point peace plan" called for Iraq's commitment to a full and unconditional withdrawal in accord with U.N. Security Council Resolution 660, which was to be followed by a cease-fire and the lifting of all sanctions (when two-thirds of Iraqi forces had been withdrawn) and the nullifying of all U.N. resolutions (when the withdrawal was complete). On the same day that the Iraqi foreign minister was advancing what was intended to be a sign of conciliation, however, Saddam Hussein played into Bush's hands by delivering a defiant speech in Baghdad. The White House seized upon the Iraqi leader's tirade as "demonstrat[ing] his determination to maintain the aggression against Kuwait and the absence of compassion for his people and his country." The failure of the Soviet initiatives strained the U.S. relationship with Moscow. When informed by Bush of the terms of a cease-fire, Gorbachev charged that the Americans were more interested in a military solution than a political settlement—an observation that underlined the fundamental difference between the Soviet position, which sought a compromise to avoid the ground war (and to restore some of its influence), and the U.S. insistence on unconditional Iraqi withdrawal from Kuwait.

Bush and his advisers, however, realized that the United States had to take the initiative to prevent the frenzied Soviet-Iraqi diplomacy from compromising the U.N. resolutions. They feared that the Soviet Union would somehow get a proposal before the U.N. Security Council that would force delay of the ground war. Bush recalls that he kept thinking: "How do we stop Saddam from snatching victory from the jaws of a certain defeat?" When the military leadership indicated that the ground war could begin as early as February 22, Bush, after extensive discussion with advisers, concluded that the time had come to issue another ultimatum to Saddam Hussein.

This step required diplomatic-military coordination. The U.N. coalition showed strains. The Gorbachev peace initiatives had captured some support among Europeans, if not necessarily their governments, while the Arab partners wanted to press the military advantage. Within the U.S. command, tension developed between Powell and Schwarzkopf over the timing of the ground war. Powell, who thought that the field commander was overly cautious and who was sensitive to the diplomatic pressures on Bush, rejected Schwarzkopf's request for an additional two days of bombing, which would have delayed the offensive until February 24. So Powell's advice to Bush on the ultimatum was crisp: give Saddam Hussein twenty-four hours to begin the withdrawal from Kuwait.

As the deadline for compliance was being debated at the White House, reports reached Washington that the Iraqis were continuing to execute young Kuwaitis and had begun firing on Kuwait's oil wells, causing widespread destruction and fires. That helped to settle matters for Bush. He decided on the twenty-four-hour deadline and, together with Baker, gained the backing of the U.N. coalition partners.

On the morning of Friday, February 22, Bush issued the ultimatum. After denouncing Saddam Hussein's "scorched-earth policy" and failure to comply with the U.N. Security Council's "demand for immediate and unconditional withdrawal," Bush stated "with specificity just exactly what is required of Iraq if a ground war is to be avoided. . . . The coalition will give Saddam Hussein until noon Saturday to do what he must do: begin his immediate and unconditional withdrawal from Kuwait. We must hear publicly and authoritatively his acceptance of these terms." The ultimatum did not quiet the Soviets. In a series of phone conversations beginning on February 22 and continuing into the next day and even beyond the deadline, Gorbachev and Bessmertnykh pleaded with Bush and Baker to allow more time for them to find a diplomatic solution, contending that the Iraqis were going to accept the "eight-point peace plan." The Soviet leaders became more testy, warning of heavy casualties in the impending ground war and questioning the U.S. interest in avoiding further bloodshed. Bush firmly turned aside these last minute Soviet entreaties. British, French, Japanese, Turkish, and other leaders whom he consulted assured Bush of support for going ahead.

The long-awaited ground war was about to begin. Ten hours after the noon deadline had passed, Bush spoke to the American public from

the White House and announced that he had directed General
Schwarzkopf "to use all forces available including ground forces to eject
the Iraqi army from Kuwait." There was little doubt that the destruction
caused by the devastating bombing campaign and the U.N. coalition's
continuing control of the air and overwhelming technological superiority would bring ultimate victory, but Americans feared a long war and
heavy casualties. The U.N. coalition force outnumbered the Iraqi army
in the region, which was estimated at 540,000 (which later proved to be
an excessive figure). An invading force normally requires a five-to-one
numerical advantage to overcome a defensive unit as strong and well
fortified as the Iraqis reputedly were in Kuwait. Reportedly, the Pentagon anticipated that twelve thousand to sixteen thousand Americans
would be killed in the liberation of Kuwait.

America's anxieties dissipated as the U.N. coalition ground offensive swept to a quick and overwhelming victory. The two major operations went remarkably according to plan. First was the direct assault on
Iraq's military position in Kuwait. Striking along the Kuwaiti border,
American, British, Saudi, Egyptian, and Syrian forces easily broke
through Iraqi defenses. Saddam Hussein, it was discovered, had deployed his least-experienced troops, mostly young draftees, to defend
Kuwait, while the experienced elite units of the Republican Guard were
held in reserve. Badly demoralized Iraqi troops on the front line of defense surrendered in large numbers, some thirty thousand within the
first day. Meanwhile, coalition warships in the Persian Gulf bombarded
Iraqi coastal defenses in Kuwait, and other naval units engaged in diversionary movements that forced Iraq to maintain defensive positions
for protection against an amphibious landing.

The unexpectedly easy progress of the thrust into Kuwait led
Schwarzkopf to accelerate the launching of the second phase of the
ground operation—the "left hook" into Iraq. Some 200,000 French, British, and American forces invaded southern Iraq from the north and east
in a large, enveloping movement whose objective was to cut off Iraqi
military movement from Baghdad and to prevent the Republican
Guard, which was deployed inside Iraq just across the Kuwaiti border,
from reinforcing the front-line forces in Kuwait.

Saddam Hussein's objective became the survival of his regime. He
began to withdraw troops from Kuwait while using the Republican
Guard as a shield. On February 25, as he praised his "brave forces" for

standing up to the U.N. coalition army, he ordered their withdrawal. Radio Baghdad later announced that Iraqi forces would leave Kuwait "in an organized way to positions they held prior to 1 August 1990. . . . This is regarded as practical compliance with U.N. Resolution 660. Our armed forces, which have proven their ability to fight and stand fast, will confront any attempt to harm them while they are carrying out their orders." Saddam, however, had not ordered a surrender. He still had not committed himself to withdraw his forces by a specific time, had not renounced claims to Kuwait, and had not indicated compliance with all U.N. Security Council resolutions. A White House statement promised not to attack unarmed soldiers but warned that otherwise "the war goes on." In a message to the American public on the morning of February 26, an angry Bush denounced Saddam Hussein for trying to salvage his military power and continuing to defy the United Nations. "The coalition," Bush asserted, "will therefore continue the war with undiminished intensity."

On the battlefield, large numbers of Iraq's army of occupation continued to surrender, but most followed Saddam Hussein's order and fled toward Iraq. The retreat turned into a rout, as more than one thousand trucks (many of which were carrying loot from Kuwait) and tens of thousands of troops clogged the highway out of Kuwait City. The troops became an easy target for U.S. aircraft, whose relentless attacks made the escape route—the Basra Road—into a "highway of death." Meanwhile, to the west, the "left hook" encountered resistance from the Republican Guard, which was supported by a large force of armored vehicles. In a massive tank battle on the night of February 26–27, however, the coalition achieved a decisive victory and forced the Republican Guard into a full-scale retreat.

By Wednesday, February 27, the U.N. coalition's domination of the battlefield was complete. The assault on the retreating Iraqis on the Basra Road continued, with images of the slaughter reaching television audiences throughout the world. Intelligence reports confirmed that twenty-seven of Iraq's forty-two divisions in the war zone had been destroyed or otherwise rendered ineffective. Coalition forces, with Saudi and Kuwaiti units in the vanguard, liberated Kuwait City to the enthusiastic reception of survivors of the seven-month occupation.

Through his emissary at the United Nations, Saddam Hussein conceded defeat. Ambassador Abd al-Amir informed the Security Council that Iraq had withdrawn the last of its forces from Kuwait and was prepared to abide by all U.N. resolutions, which, he asserted, eliminated the justification for continuing sanctions.

In a televised press conference, a buoyant Schwarzkopf announced that the Iraqis were defeated and trapped by the U.N. coalition forces. The allies could have marched on to Baghdad, he asserted, but the capture of the Iraqi capital had never been the United Nations's purpose. His mission—"to make sure that the Republican Guard is rendered incapable of conducting the type of heinous act that they've conducted so often in the past"—had been accomplished. He boasted that "we almost completely destroyed the offensive capability of the Iraqi forces in the Kuwait theater of operations. The gate is closed. There is no way out of here." (He went on to modify this claim by explaining that, while civilians and their vehicles were still escaping, the "gate" was closed on Iraq's "military machine.") When a reporter asked whether a cease-fire might prevent the full realization of his objectives, Schwarzkopf proclaimed: "We've accomplished our mission, and when the decision-makers come to the decision that there should be a cease-fire, nobody will be happier than me."

At the White House on the afternoon of February 27, Bush considered the terms for ending the war. He had three concerns: first, that the carnage on the "highway of death" not continue needlessly and thus tarnish the reputation of the U.N. coalition internationally, especially among Arab peoples; second, that the timing of a cease-fire be acceptable to the military leadership; and third, that prisoners of war be exchanged quickly. Although all of the advisers on whom he had relied during the previous six months were present, Bush now looked principally to Powell. When Bush asked how much time the military needed, Powell replied that he and Schwarzkopf agreed that the coalition was at most twenty-four hours away from achieving its military objectives. Bush spoke of his concerns: "We do not want to lose anything now with charges of brutalization, but we are also very concerned with the issue of prisoners." The victory, he now recognized, would cripple Iraq but without completely destroying its military capability and with Saddam Hussein likely to be clinging to power. He compared the ambiguity of 1991 with the decisiveness of the conclusion of World War II: "The issue is how to find a clear end. This is not going to be like the battleship *Missouri*" (on which the Japanese had surrendered in 1945).

Still, the need to end the war was compelling. Bush reflected: "Why do I not feel elated? But we need to have an end. People want that. They are going to want to know we won and the kids can come home. We do not want to screw this up with a sloppy, muddled ending." Bush liked the suggestion of ending the ground war after one hundred hours of fighting; thus, the cease-fire was set for midnight Eastern Standard Time.

For all of his determination to coordinate his political objectives with the military leadership's priorities, Bush may have been ill-served by Schwarzkopf and Powell in the last hours of the war. Military commanders on the scene and CIA analysts regarded Schwarzkopf's press conference claims of a "closed gate" as premature. Another day or two of unrelenting warfare, they believed, would have enabled the U.N. coalition to inflict much greater damage on the fighting capacity of the Republican Guard and to complete the "closing of the gate." Planned operations, which were aborted by the cease-fire, could have achieved a far more decisive victory, forcing the surrender of large numbers of Iraqi soldiers and the capture of thousands of additional weapons. Iraq's military capacity thus could have been much more substantially reduced.

Powell, however, was sensitive to Bush's concern about the international consequences of the "highway of death" imagery and interest in avoiding unnecessary American casualties. Schwarzkopf, who was elated at the unexpectedly easy battlefield victory, was not prepared to challenge the pressures coming from Washington to end the war quickly. A few weeks later, however, he claimed otherwise. In a celebrated television interview, he stated that his "recommendation had been, you know, continue the march. I mean, we had them in a rout and we could have continued . . . to reap great destruction upon them." That unfortunate and inaccurate claim prompted an irate Powell to insist that a contrite Schwarzkopf join him in a corrective statement affirming that both of them had supported the ending of the war after one hundred hours and that "there was no contrary recommendation."

As the war ended, Bush accepted the limitations of the battlefield victory. Shortly after reaching the cease-fire decision, he received a cautionary message from Schwarzkopf warning, contrary to his celebrated public statement, that some Republican Guard units and tanks could slip through the "gate." While aware that he would face criticism for not continuing the war, the president stuck by his decision. In the end, Bush was determined—no matter how profound his animosity toward

Saddam Hussein and no matter how tempting the further annihilation of his army—not to exceed the U.N. mandate. Also, continuing the war after Schwarzkopf had publicly claimed victory within the context of the televised images of the slaughter of Iraqi forces would have seemed unjustified in the eyes of many peoples throughout the world. Bush has reflected that "we were concerned principally about two aspects of the situation. If we continued the fighting another day, until the ring was completely closed, would we be accused of a slaughter of Iraqis who were simply trying to escape, not fight? In addition, the coalition was agreed on driving the Iraqis from Kuwait, not on carrying the conflict into Iraq or destroying Iraqi forces."

In a televised address on the evening of February 27, Bush proclaimed victory and announced a cease-fire. "Seven months ago," he began, "America and the world drew a line in the sand. We declared that the aggression against Kuwait would not stand. And tonight, America and the world have kept their word." The U.N. coalition's imposition of a cease-fire was dependent upon Iraq's immediate release of all prisoners of war and other detainees, compliance with all relevant U.N. resolutions, and acceptance of responsibility for the costs of its aggression. After an exchange of several notes through which Iraq complied with these terms, a formal cease-fire agreement was signed on March 3 at the Iraqi town of Safwan near the Kuwait frontier.

Besides liberating Kuwait, the six weeks of U.N. coalition warfare had severely weakened Iraq's military capacity. About three-fourths of Iraq's tanks, armored personnel carriers, and artillery had been destroyed or captured. The number of Iraqi casualties, while a subject of some controversy, was unquestionably substantial. An early Pentagon claim of 100,000 Iraqi battlefield deaths has been dismissed as excessive; rather, it seems that, at most, Iraq lost about one-third of that total—which was still a substantial loss. Estimates of Iraqi soldiers killed during the air war range from 5,000 to 19,000 (the figure asserted by Baghdad) and of military deaths during the ground war range from 3,000 to 18,000. U.N. coalition casualties, on the other hand, were remarkably light: America's losses totaled 148 killed and 458 wounded in action, while its partners suffered 92 killed and 328 wounded.

The victory touched off a euphoria, reminiscent of the end of World War II, among the American public. Bush's popularity soared as public opinion polls indicated that an astounding 89 percent of Americans "approved" of his performance as president. Yellow ribbons, which had been adopted as the symbol of support for the troops in the Persian Gulf, and small American flags were everywhere, adorning clothing, trees, posts, front porches, cars, and store fronts throughout the country. Veterans of the war were welcomed home as heroes, as many celebrating Americans shouted, while proudly pointing index fingers upward, "We're Number One." This outpouring of popular sentiment reflected more than just patriotism stirred by victory. In some ways it was also an expression of relief that victory had come more easily than expected and with remarkably few casualties. Perhaps at its base was a sense of renewed confidence in the nation's international purpose and righteousness, which had been shattered by the Vietnam War. *New York Times* columnist Tom Wicker wrote that the "yellow fever" amounted to a "national rejuvenation [of] Americans' pride in their military strength and their national righteousness—missing since Vietnam— and much of their inherent belief in their fitness and ability to lead the world . . . [and] a resurgent sense that 'We're Number One,' and of right ought to be."

Bush's rhetoric played to such sentiments. He proclaimed on March 1 that "it's a proud day for America. And by God, we've kicked the Vietnam syndrome once and for all." Later that day, he spoke of the "noble and majestic . . . patriotism in this country now." Bush consistently cast the victory in terms of his vision of a "new world order." In a triumphant address before a joint session of Congress on March 6, he spoke of "a world where the United Nations, freed from cold war stalemate, is poised to fulfill the historic vision of its founders. A world in which freedom and respect for human rights find a home among all nations. The Gulf war put this new world to its first test. . . . And . . . we passed that test."

Bush's immediate concern was his determination that the decisiveness of the military campaign would yield a clear-cut political outcome. Saddam Hussein was clinging to power, but intelligence reports predicted that he would be overthrown within a year. While other Western members of the U.N. coalition shared Bush's abhorrence of any prospect of Saddam's reestablishing firm control in Baghdad, the United Arab Emirates and Saudi Arabia feared that his overthrow would bring a Shiite regime to power and, in the process, strengthen Iran's position in the region. Turkey and Iran were apprehensive that instability in Iraq would enhance the influence of the Kurds, which could spill over into their countries. So, to some members of the U.N. coalition and other countries, a weakened Iraq seemed the most stabilizing outcome.

Regardless of whether nations saw their interest in encouraging Saddam Hussein's overthrow or in weakening his position, they agreed that Iraq had to be punished and its military capabilities reduced. On April 2, the U.N. Security Council passed Resolution 687, which was unprecedented in the severity of the international organization's imposition of penalties upon a nation and the extent of its intervention in that nation's internal affairs. Iraq was obliged to accept an international commission's demarcation of its border with Kuwait, a demilitarized zone along that frontier, and the presence there of a U.N. peacekeeping force. Iraq was also required to return all property that had been taken during its occupation of Kuwait and to compensate all foreign nationals and companies for losses resulting from the occupation. In the most far-reaching penalties, Iraq was required to disclose full information on the development and production of its weapons of mass destruction—nuclear, chemical, and biological—and missile delivery systems and to cooperate with a United Nations Special Commission (UNSCOM) in their dismantling and destruction. Sanctions against everything except medical and health supplies remained in effect, as did the embargo on the export of oil. Compliance with the U.N. terms would determine the duration of the sanctions, which were to be reviewed every sixty days.

By the time that these draconian terms were being imposed, the victory already was beginning to seem shallow. Saddam Hussein not only survived the battlefield defeat, but also used the remnants of his armed forces to solidify his political position. Despite his nation's severe deprivations, he gave handsome salary increases to the Republican Guard and other security forces. Moreover, the Republican Guard had come out of the war stronger than U.S. intelligence had estimated; it still had seven hundred tanks and fourteen hundred armored personnel vehicles. So Saddam faced his internal opponents from a position of surprising strength.

Encouraged by Bush's call for Saddam Hussein's overthrow, the Shiite religious opponents of his regime and the Kurdish minority rebelled as the cease-fire took effect. The Shiite uprising gained control of Basra and several other southern cities, but, after two weeks, the Republican Guard reasserted Baghdad's authority. The Shiite groups expected support from U.S. forces in southern Iraq, Saudi Arabia, or their coreligionists in Iran. They were disappointed on all counts: Bush, refusing to become involved in Iraq's internal affairs, ordered American forces not to engage the Republican Guard; the Sunni leadership of Saudi Arabia, fearing a Shiite state on its frontier, avoided involvement; and the Shiites in Iran, distrusting the culturally different Iraqi Shiites, provided only limited assistance. Within a month after the cease-fire, as Americans were preparing to evacuate southern Iraq, their camps were being inundated by fleeing Shiites, who desperately sought food and medical care. By the end of March, some thirty thousand refugees were receiving U.S. help. Since the United Nations lacked facilities to protect the refugees, the allies airlifted over ten thousand Shiites to Saudi Arabia or Iran, while other Shiites scattered throughout the region.

Simultaneously with the Shiite rebellion, the Kurds living in northern Iraq captured control of a large area with the objective of establishing an autonomous state. The aspirations of the Kurds, who had a long history of resistance to Baghdad's authority, were shattered when Saddam Hussein, after crushing the Shiites, shifted Republican Guard units to the north. Their devastating attacks elicited considerable international sympathy, but little more, for the Kurds. The United States intervened only when Iraq violated the March 5 cease-fire agreement by using fixed-wing jet aircraft against the Kurds; U.S. fighter pilots shot down two Iraqi bombers. The Kurds pleaded with Bush to stop Iraqi use of helicopter gunships, but Schwarzkopf, who subsequently confessed to having been "snookered" by the Iraqi negotiators, had allowed Iraqi helicopters under the cease-fire because Iraqi commanders said they were necessary to rescue wounded soldiers. With overwhelming military superiority, the Republican Guard's lethal warfare forced thousands of Kurds to seek refuge in neighboring Turkey and Iran. Neither of those countries welcomed the Kurds, as both feared the political consequences of increasing the size of their already sizable Kurdish minorities.

At this point, French President Mitterand urged Bush and Britain's Prime Minister Major to take steps that would provide some protection for the Kurds. This led to the U.N. Security Council's resolutions of April 5 and 9, which condemned Iraq's suppression of Kurds and other dissidents and authorized the establishment of a 1,440-member U.N. observation team to oversee a "safety zone" for the Kurds north of the thirty-sixth parallel. The United States, Britain, France, and the Netherlands sent some nine thousand soldiers to that area to protect the Kurds from the Republican Guard and to permit safe return to their homes. The Western allies also undertook Operation PROVIDE COMFORT, a large-scale airlift of food, clothing, and medical supplies for the beleaguered Kurds. The allied forces remained in the safety zone until June 21, 1991, after which they kept a force in Turkey as a means of deterring a renewal of Iraqi warfare against the Kurds. Three months later, the allies withdrew those ground forces and decided to rely on the threat of air power to protect the Kurds.

In the United States, Saddam Hussein's survival and his suppression of the Shiites and Kurds led to much criticism, especially from conservatives, of Bush's leadership. They charged that he had ended the war too quickly, had failed to aid the Kurds and Shiites, and should now, in the words of a writer for the *National Review*, "finish the job we started." Recounting Saddam's "brutal carnage" that had made refugees of one-fifth of the population of Iraq, a writer in *Commentary* asked: "What is the limit before a regime is judged too reprehensible to be acceptable to us?" Capturing the sentiment of many Americans just ten weeks after the cease-fire, the *National Review* editorialized that "the full gains of a great victory are slipping from our grasp. The American people know this. Does President Bush?"

Public opinion polls underlined disillusionment with the war's outcome. Before launching DESERT STORM, Americans had equated victory with Saddam Hussein's overthrow; when the war ended with his military power presumably crippled, polls showed that a slight majority of Americans believed that the war could be considered a victory even if he remained in power. Within a few weeks, as Saddam suppressed the Shiites and Kurds, however, sentiment shifted decidedly in the other direction. By mid-April, 55 percent of Americans in a Gallup poll responded that Saddam's remaining in power meant that the war was "not a victory." A clear majority—57 percent—agreed with the contention that the cease-fire had been ordered too quickly and the war should have been continued until Saddam had been toppled. By the summer, 67 percent of Americans called the war a "partial victory" and 57 percent said they were "disappointed in Bush" because of Saddam's survival. Such sentiment was a long way from the heady euphoria of early March's display of yellow ribbons.

THE AMBIGUOUS LEGACY of DESERT STORM reflected the nature of limited wars. Leaving behind a crippled enemy is inherently dangerous, but the alternatives presented more serious long-term problems. Forcing the overthrow of Saddam Hussein or assisting the Shiite or Kurdish rebellion would have ruptured the U.N. coalition, which had been held together by the single objective of reversing the aggression against Kuwait. Supporting the aspirations of Shiites or Kurds would have been resented by Arab countries and, moreover, would have undermined the national integrity of Iraq. America's Western allies as well as the states of the Middle East, without exception, believed that regional stability would be undermined by the fragmentation of Iraq. More important, U.S. involvement in the internal affairs of Iraq would have led to a series of intractable problems. Arab peoples would have resented such an intrusion into the region, and nations around the world would have been critical of any semblance of a return to Western imperialism. American intervention would have taken on a life of its own, without a clear ending point. Certainly, any Iraqi leadership that took power with outside support would have been resented by a majority of Iraqis, not just Saddam's followers. And in the process, the United States would have converted the image of Saddam Hussein from a boorish and brutal dictator into that of a martyr.

So Bush practiced the careful realpolitik that had characterized his response to the Iraqi crisis since August 1990. As much as he abhorred Saddam Hussein and wanted his demise, Bush remained determined not to take steps that would undermine his leadership of the U.N. coalition. He relied on the punishing terms of U.N. Security Council Resolution 687 to prevent a resurgence of Iraq as a threat to regional stability. It was commonly assumed that the internal stress resulting from the sanctions would eventually weaken Saddam's position and bring about his overthrow, but that action, Bush wisely recognized, had to come from the Iraqis themselves. He also accepted the proposition that U.S. interest in the stability of the Middle East necessitated Iraq's survival as a political entity, meaning that, while he authorized some assistance to the beleaguered Kurds, he would not support their political aspirations.

The inconclusiveness of the war was followed by Saddam Hussein's endless efforts to subvert the terms of the United Nations–imposed peace. He quickly established a pattern of partial compliance and defiant testing of the United Nations's resolve. In April 1991, Iraq, as required by U.N. Security Council Resolution 687, provided information on weapons of mass destruction, but UNSCOM inspection teams subsequently discovered that the list was incomplete, and they found evidence of a much more fully developed nuclear program than either the Iraqis had conceded or U.S. intelligence had projected. The Iraqis then blocked the inspection teams from visiting a weapons factory and yielded only after Bush and the U.N. Security Council threatened military action (and after Iraqi trucks had been detected taking away machinery). By 1992, UNSCOM had supervised the destruction of Iraq's largest nuclear complex and thousands of chemical and biological weapons. Yet, at every step then and after, Saddam Hussein consistently engaged in obstructionist and delaying tactics before complying with U.N. demands. Also, his capacity to conceal weapons further frustrated UNSCOM. This behavior assured the continuation of sanctions and Iraq's isolation from the world of international trade and finance. Saddam Hussein was willing to subject his people to the resultant serious deprivations. His lack of cooperation, much less of any sign of contrition, was galling to Bush, his successor Bill Clinton, and the American public.

In November 1997, as Saddam Hussein continued his tactics of maneuver and threat to resist U.N. inspection, Bush was asked whether he now questioned his decision of six and a half years earlier not to march to Baghdad. His answer was clear: "No. What mother's son could I have asked to go beyond our mandate? We would have been an occupying army." The untidiness of the settlement notwithstanding, the rationale for restricting the war to its stated objective remains compelling.

Limited wars, by definition, end inconclusively, with an enemy, at best, seriously weakened. The U.N. coalition restored the prewar status quo through the liberation of Kuwait, battered the Iraqi infrastructure and army, and imposed a punitive settlement. Bush fulfilled the essential objectives. Iraq had been reduced to more of a nuisance than a threat to regional stability.

"Time is not on our side"

IN AN ADDRESS FROM THE OVAL OFFICE on the evening of March 19, 2003, President George W. Bush announced the beginning of "military operations to disarm Iraq, to free its people, and to defend the world from grave danger." Operation IRAQI FREEDOM blended the historic American sense of mission with a strategic imperative: "We have no ambition in Iraq except to remove a threat and restore control of that country to its people." "To remove a threat" underlined the distinction between this war and earlier ones. The United States was acting to eliminate a leader—Saddam Hussein—before he endangered international security: "The United States and its friends and allies will not live at the mercy of an outlaw regime that threatens the peace with weapons of mass murder."

The Iraq War was the culmination of a dramatic shift in strategic thinking. In the previous three wars, the U.S. objective was to curtail the territorial ambitions of the adversary: to repel the North Koreans and to restore the division of Korea; to intimidate North Vietnam into abandoning warfare in South Vietnam; to force the Iraqi Army out of Kuwait. In 2003, Iraq was not an aggressor, but it stood accused of being a potential aggressor, having allegedly failed to disarm after the Persian Gulf War and being poised to develop and use weapons of mass destruction (WMD). Moreover, in the aftermath of the terrorist attacks on the United States, the Iraqi government was accused of being a supporter, if not partner, of the al-Qaeda—a connection made more ominous by Iraq's potential capacity to supply WMD to terrorists. Thus Bush spoke of "meeting the threat now with our Army, Air Force, Navy, Coast Guard, and Marines, so that we do not have to meet it later with armies of firefighters and police and doctors on the streets of our cities."

That George W. Bush would lead a major reformulation of U.S. national security policy and take the country to war could scarcely have been imagined when he gained the presidency after the closest presidential election in more than a century. Bush's lack of foreign policy experience (his only public office had been that of governor of Texas since 1995), his limited overseas travel, and his seeming disinterest in international issues suggested a presidency focused on domestic problems.

Bush's unexpected leadership reflected in part the urgency resulting from the terrorist attacks, but the way that he would redefine America's approach to the world was in fact suggested during his 2000 presidential campaign.

In two major foreign policy speeches, Bush embraced the tradition of American exceptionalism. The cold war ended with American values triumphant, and Bush foresaw a continuing mission to build a democratic world. "Our nation is on the right side of history," he proclaimed. After a century of struggle through two world wars and the cold war, the United States had achieved "a vision of freedom and individual dignity . . . [a world] shaped by American courage, power, and wisdom now echoes with American ideals." Now the mission was to assure "a vision in which people and capital and information can move freely, creating bonds of progress, ties of culture and momentum toward democracy." Bush cast this role within a tradition of altruistic commitment to helping other peoples: "America has never been an empire. We may be the only great power in history that had the chance, and refused—preferring greatness to power, and justice to glory." While foreseeing America as the world leader, Bush promised that his presidency would lead in ways that "[did] not impose our culture" and that reflected "modesty . . . [and] humility." The United States would consult with and cultivate allies who were to be treated as "partners, not satellites." While his messages were short on specifics, Bush warned that the most serious threats to security now came from "unconventional and invisible threats of new technologies and old hatreds . . . . car bombers and plutonium merchants and cyber terrorists and unbalanced dictators."

One should not read too much into campaign speeches, but these glimpses into Bush's thinking suggest a leader of a strong ideological bent prepared to reassert American leadership boldly but not arbitrarily. His willingness to embrace a "vision" contrasted sharply with his father's aversion to the "vision thing"—the first hint of ways in which the new administration's foreign policy would depart from that of Bush I.

Reflecting his inexperience on foreign policy issues, Bush assembled an impressive national security team, drawing heavily on prominent Republicans who had served in his father's and earlier Republican administrations. James Mann, the author of *The Rise of the Vulcans*, which is the most complete study of the intellectual and political origins of Bush's national security policy, writes that the common experiences of his principal advisers meant that, "by the time the new administration's foreign policy team was assembled in early 2001, it had the feel of a class reunion."

Among the members of Bush's inner circle, Condoleezza Rice had exerted the most direct influence on the new president. She gained his confidence during the two years that she had been advising him on foreign policy as he pursued his presidential ambitions. An academic who held a doctorate in Russian studies from the University of Denver, Rice was provost of Stanford University—a position in which she earned a reputation as a decisive administrator. Earlier, during the Bush I administration, she had been a protégée of national security adviser Brent Scowcroft, serving on his staff and gaining the respect of Bush I, who was instrumental in bringing her to his son's attention. Like Scowcroft, she initially approached world problems from a realist perspective and was disdainful of allowing ideological considerations to influence policy. Eventually she became convinced that the United States had an important role to play in promoting democracy internationally. Rice's appointment as national security adviser (the first woman to hold that office) testified to Bush's confidence in both her counsel and her ability to integrate the political and military dimensions of U.S. policy.

Events would establish, however, the preeminence of Vice President Richard Cheney in the decision-making process. Respected for his work as secretary of defense under Bush I and earlier in the White House of Gerald Ford and as a member of the House of Representatives, Cheney had been asked by Bush to review potential vice-presidential candidates in 2000, only to conclude that he himself was the best qualified, so Bush named him as his running mate. Cheney became the most powerful vice president in American history. Often outspoken and secretive, he assembled a large staff of his own, including what amounted to his own national security council, but he enjoyed Bush's confidence and was careful (usually) not to challenge presidential prerogatives. Cheney, who believed that the executive branch had been weakened in the 1970s as a result of the Vietnam War and the Watergate scandal, was determined to strengthen presidential power. The historian Warren Cohen summarizes Cheney's thinking:

> No one surpassed him in conceiving of justifications for increasing American military power. And he had little use for the United Nations or any other multilateral organization that might restrict America's freedom to act as it chose anywhere in the globe. Like the president he served, he was very much

an assertive nationalist, but he was less committed to the vision of spreading democracy. . . . For Cheney, it would be enough to crush any state or organization that obstructed pursuit of the interests of the United States or threatened its security.

Cheney's belligerency surprised many former colleagues who regarded him as a realist. Brent Scowcroft, who as Bush I's national security adviser had worked closely with Cheney, remarked: "I've known Dick Cheney for thirty years. But I don't know Dick Cheney any more."

Cheney was influential in the selection of a man of similar world-view—Donald Rumsfeld—for a second tour of duty as secretary of defense. Indeed a quarter century earlier, Cheney had been a Rumsfeld protégé in the Ford administration in which Rumsfeld had served as the White House chief of staff before becoming secretary of defense in 1975; and at that time Cheney had replaced him as the president's chief of staff. Rumsfeld had also served four terms in the House of Representatives and had been the chief executive officer of two Fortune 500 companies. Utterly self-confident and frequently abrasive, Rumsfeld was determined to reshape the military into a more efficient fighting force. Like Cheney, as an "assertive nationalist," Rumsfeld was disdainful of democratic crusades and showed little concern about the opinions of other nations.

The most widely expected appointment was that of General Colin Powell as secretary of state. Powell enjoyed greater public stature than anyone else in the president's inner circle and for that matter than the president himself. He had been mentioned as a possible Republican presidential candidate in 1996—an opportunity that he did not pursue. His resumé from two tours of duty in Vietnam as a young army officer to service in the three previous administrations was impressive. As chairman of the Joint Chiefs of Staff during the Persian Gulf War and earlier as national security adviser under Reagan, Powell had earned respect as both a military officer, renowned for the so-called Powell Doctrine, which was intended to avoid the mistakes of the war in Vietnam, and an adept administrator with shrewd political skills. Powell's "star" quality—of which he was very conscious—and his concern with international opinion contributed to tensions with Cheney and Rumsfeld and hindered his interaction with Bush. That problem surfaced on the very day that the president-elect announced Powell's appointment. During the ensuing questioning from reporters, Powell dominated the responses in ways that showed no deference to Bush. It was a virtuoso performance meant in part to assure other nations of firm American leadership, but it came at the cost of an underlying and enduring tension in Powell's relationship with Bush. Working closely with Powell was another Vietnam War veteran, Richard Armitage, as under secretary of state; Armitage had been a colleague of Powell's in the Defense Department during the Reagan administration.

Among the members of the new foreign policy team, the strategic thought of Paul Wolfowitz was the best known. Another veteran of the Reagan and Bush I years, Wolfowitz became under secretary of defense. An academic like Rice, he held a doctorate in political science from the University of Chicago. In the earlier Bush administration, he had served as Cheney's under secretary of defense for policy and had been instrumental in the development of the 1992 Defense Planning Guidance statement (DPG). As the first such formulation of long-term defense planning after the collapse of the Soviet Union, it was prepared at a time when many members of Congress were calling for drastic cuts in the Pentagon's budget. Instead, the DPG called for the maintenance of high levels of defense spending, the continued development of more sophisticated weaponry, and the capability to prevent any unfriendly nation from dominating any region of the world considered vital to U.S. interest.

The 1992 DPG, which attracted a good deal of criticism when it was "leaked" to the media, reflected the thinking of the emerging neoconservatives—a label applied broadly to a group of officials, journalists, and scholars who influenced the Republican Party's criticism of Clinton's foreign policy and the direction of policy in the new Bush administration.

The leaders in the formulation of the neoconservative foreign policy agenda were mainly former liberal and hawkish Democrats who supported the Vietnam War as that conflict divided Americans and who were disenchanted by their party's move to the left and its seeming irresolution on national security. One neoconservative famously described himself as a "liberal mugged by reality." Strongly moralistic and nationalistic, the neoconservatives opposed accommodation with totalitarian regimes. Thus they were critical of Richard Nixon's policy of détente toward the Soviet Union and were dismayed by President Jimmy Carter's ineptitude during the Iranian hostage crisis, but they had thrilled to Reagan's call for strengthening the American military and to his denunciation of the Soviet Union as the "evil empire." Skeptical of the United Nations as an instrument of maintaining peace and of international cooperation in general, neoconservatives preached the importance of America's acting unilaterally to uphold its values and of maintaining a position of global military superiority.

Among the prominent voices of neoconservativism as it emerged during the last two decades of the twentieth century were the academic Jeane Kirkpatrick, who attracted much attention (including that of President Ronald Reagan, who named her U.N. ambassador) for arguing during the last years of the cold war that the United States needed to distinguish between communist and noncommunist authoritarian governments; Norman Podhoretz, the editor of *Commentary* and author of *Why We Were in Vietnam*, a strident postwar defense of that conflict; the journalist Irving Kristol, who edited the magazine *Public Interest*, and his son William Kristol, who edited the *Weekly Standard* and was a frequent guest on television talk shows; Richard Perle, a close associate of Rumsfeld and Wolfowitz, who had served as under secretary of defense during the Reagan administration; Lawrence F. Kaplan, who was executive editor of the *National Interest* and later senior editor of the *New Republic*; Elliot Cohen, dean of the School of Advanced International Studies at Johns Hopkins University; Robert Kagan, whose writings called upon the Republican Party to abandon a foreign policy of realpolitik associated with the policies of Nixon-Kissinger and Bush I and to support the promotion of democracy and human rights; Douglas Feith, who had worked on the National Security Council and as a Defense Department counsel to Perle during the Reagan years; and Frances Fukuyama, whose influential 1989 essay, "The End of History?" declared an irrepressible liberal democracy triumphant over not just communism but all ideologies.

During the 1990s, the neoconservatives looked with dismay on the survival of Saddam Hussein's regime in Iraq. They considered Bush I's failure to "march to Baghdad" in 1991 a mistake, which had enabled Saddam Hussein to suppress the Shiite Muslims and the Kurds and to reestablish his cruel control over the country. Moreover, Hussein had seemingly reneged on his commitment to disarm. And the Clinton administration's employment of military power to enforce the 1991 U.N. resolutions had been ineffective and had emboldened Saddam Hussein. Prominent neoconservatives established the Project for the New American Century (PNAC), which called for the vigorous pursuit of a global democratic foreign policy, beginning with the overthrow of Saddam Hussein. PNAC was in the vanguard of the movement that led Congress in 1998 to pass the Iraq Liberation Act, which made "regime change" a U.S. objective.

Bush's foreign policy quickly embraced the neoconservative agenda. This reflected the influence of Wolfowitz and Perle, who had met Bush during the presidential campaign and had found him receptive to their thinking, and of the prominent positions that neoconservatives held in the new administration. While neoconservatives were among new appointees to the National Security Council, the White House staff, and the State Department, their representation was especially visible at the Pentagon. Besides Wolfowitz as deputy secretary of defense, Feith became under secretary of defense for policy and Perle became chairman of the Defense Policy Board, a group of outside advisers to the secretary of defense, which he made much more influential than in previous administrations. Early in his term, Bush's campaign talk of cooperation with other nations gave way to a strident unilateralism. He abandoned Clinton's Agreed Framework plan with North Korea, which was intended to halt that country's nuclear development. He withdrew the United States from the 1997 Kyoto Protocol, the international agreement to reduce carbon dioxide and other emissions contributing to global warming. The repudiation of the Kyoto Protocol was widely criticized internationally, especially in Europe. Bush refused to submit to the Senate the agreement providing for U.S. membership in the International Criminal Court, which Clinton had negotiated, and then demanded that American allies on the court promise never to bring Americans before the body.

In taking these initiatives, Bush reflected dependence on his advisers and their neoconservative orientation. Cheney and Rumsfeld, while not sharing the neoconservatives' call for promoting democracy, found them useful allies in pressing for a unilateralist, muscular foreign policy. Powell, with his commitment to a multilateral policy that built on international cooperation and was sensitive to the opinion of allies, was isolated. It might have been different had Rice exerted herself and held to her earlier views. She proved to be ineffective in forcing careful consideration of policy options and, moreover, moved from being a realist to being an enabler, indeed an adherent, of neoconservatism. During the 2000 presidential campaign, she wrote an article in *Foreign Affairs* on Bush's foreign policy which sounded very much like that of the Bush I administration. Dismissive of ideology, she stated that, "to be sure, there is nothing wrong with doing something that benefits all humanity, but that is, in a sense, a second-order effect." Within months of taking office in the new administration, however, Rice became a fervent advocate of a pro-democracy foreign policy. Scowcroft, her onetime mentor, told a European diplomat, "I don't understand how my lady, my baby, my disciple, has changed so much." Given his lack of experience and the strong views and self-confidence of his principal advisers, Bush was to an extraordinary extent dependent on them. According to James Mann, "He could not have made decisions if the Vulcans [the name that Bush's foreign policy advisers devised to describe themselves] had not laid out the choices; he could not have formulated policy without the words and ideas they brought to him. That reality too increased the importance of the Vulcans."

The horrendous terrorist attacks of Tuesday, September 11, 2001, on New York City and Washington, D.C., shattered America's sense of security and accentuated the reorientation of national security policy. In the tense days that followed as the extent of death and destruction became known, as the media reported daily on the slow recovery from the rubble at the World Trade Center (WTC), and as the specter of other attacks loomed, Bush provided reassuring leadership. On the night of the attacks, Bush spoke briefly to the nation—"Today our Nation saw evil"—and promised that the United States would bring the perpetrators of the attacks to justice, making "no distinction between the terrorists who committed these acts and those who harbor them." With their allies, Americans would "stand together to win the war against terrorism." Among several talks that Bush gave over the next several days, especially dramatic was his September 14 visit to New York City, where he conversed with workers on the WTC site. When those assembled shouted that they could not hear the president as he began to speak, Bush shouted back: "I can hear you. I can hear you. The rest of the world hears you. And the people who knocked these buildings down will hear you." As he concluded, the audience was chanting: "USA! USA! USA!"

In that fervently patriotic environment, Congress, with virtually no debate and only one dissenting vote, on that same day passed a resolution granting Bush virtually unlimited authority to wage war against the perpetrators of the attacks. The president could "use all necessary and appropriate force against those nations, organizations, or persons he determines planned, authorized, committed, or aided the terrorist attacks of September 11, 2001, or harbored such organizations or persons." Although understandable in the context of an unprecedented crisis and the uncertainty of the enemy, the resolution gave, as Ivo Daalder and James M. Lindsay write in *America Unbound*, "stunningly broad latitude" to the president; "in effect, Congress declared war and left it up to the White House to decide who the enemy was."

The terrorist attacks stirred not only patriotism at home but sympathy and support overseas. To be sure, there were instances of crowds cheering news of the attacks, but overall Americans found reassurance in the international reaction. From Moscow, Russian president Vladimir Putin was the first head of state to call the White House and pledge help in finding those responsible for the attacks. In Paris, the left-leaning *Le Monde* proclaimed, "Nous sommes tous Americains." In London, the band at Buckingham Palace played "The Star Spangled Banner" throughout the day. In Seoul, South Korean schoolchildren prayed outside the U.S. Embassy. Thousands of Iranians held candlelight vigils, and the president of that country spoke of "disaster in the United States" as "tragic and grave." The German chancellor promised "unlimited solidarity" with the United States. The United Nations passed a resolution condemning those "responsible for aiding, supporting or harboring the perpetrators, organizers and sponsors of these acts" and authorized "all necessary steps" to respond to the attacks. For the first time in its fifty-two-year history, the North Atlantic Treaty Organization (NATO) invoked the provision in its charter obliging member nations to come to the assistance of another member that was under attack.

Within a few days, intelligence agencies confirmed that al-Qaeda, the terrorist organization under the leadership of Osama bin Laden, was responsible for the attacks. Based in Afghanistan with the tacit approval of the Taliban rulers of that country, al-Qaeda was known to have instigated earlier overseas terrorist attacks targeting Americans. Bush and his advisers thought that the United States had to act quickly and decisively against al-Qaeda not just in retribution but to disabuse Osama Bin Laden and his followers of any notion that the United States lacked the will and the capacity to use its military power against them. The failure of the United States to act forthrightly in response to earlier attacks, administration officials believed, had encouraged al-Qaeda to strike again and again, culminating in the September 11 assault. "Weakness, vacillation, and unwillingness to stand with our friends, that is provocative," Cheney said. "It's encouraged people like Osama bin Laden . . . to launch repeated strikes against the United States, and our people overseas and here at home, with the view that he could, in fact, do so with impunity."

Events moved quickly. In a televised speech to a joint session of Congress on September 20, Bush issued an ultimatum to the Taliban:

"Hand over the terrorists or . . . share in their fate." The crisis, however, demanded more than retaliation; it called for a broader mission: "Our war on terror begins with Al Qaida but it does not end there. It will not end until every terrorist group of global reach has been found, stopped, and defeated." Characterizing terrorists as a new and virulent form of a familiar enemy—totalitarianism—Bush summoned this generation of Americans to wage battle, as had previous generations, against evil men and institutions:

> We have seen their kind before. They are the heirs of the murderous ideolo-
> gies of the twentieth century. By sacrificing human life to serve their radical
> visions—by abandoning every value except the will to power—they follow
> the path of fascism and Nazism, and totalitarianism. And they will follow that
> path all the way to where it ends: in history's unmarked graves of discarded
> lies.

Speaking specifically to the nation's armed forces, he added, "I've called the Armed Forces to alert and there is a reason. The hour is coming when America will act, and you will make us proud." Finally, asserting American leadership, Bush defined a global struggle that allowed no room for hesitation or questions. "We will pursue nations that provide aid or safe haven to terrorism," he stated, "every nation, in every region now has a decision to make. Either you are with us, or you are with the terrorists." In sum, the United States would unilaterally set the agenda for this war.

Thus, nine days after the terrorist attacks, Bush called upon Americans to follow in the tradition of earlier generations by waging a struggle against an evil force. Reminiscent of President Harry Truman's March 1947 proclamation (what became known as the Truman Doctrine) of the imperative for a long-term commitment to combat totalitarian communism, Bush in 2001 asserted the necessity to prepare for a long-term conflict against totalitarian terrorism.

Yet, as America had learned during the cold war, there were problems in asserting a "with us or against us" position, for even allies, while supportive of America's overall objectives, could disagree on the specifics of policy (as, for instance, occurred when allies objected to broadening the Korean War and when very few of them supported the war in Vietnam). The importance of listening to the views of others, however, was conspicuously lacking in the neoconservative ideology and the policy that it spawned in the aftermath of September 11.

When the Taliban ignored Bush's ultimatum, American and British forces launched an invasion of Afghanistan on October 7. Within the international community Operation ENDURING FREEDOM was widely viewed as a legitimate expression of America's right of self-defense. The mission enjoyed broad support. At first, the United States had anticipated fighting with only British forces at its side, but it could not ignore the offers of assistance from other nations. In the end, twenty nations provided ground or air troops; these included Germany, France, Australia, Canada, Denmark, Greece, New Zealand, Norway, Pakistan, and Poland. Several other nations provided intelligence and logistical support and humanitarian assistance, and still others permitted the use of their air space and of their bases for bombing and surveillance missions.

This American-led international operation, assisted by anti-Taliban Afghan units, easily defeated the Taliban and placed a new government in power. The victory of ENDURING FREEDOM was tarnished, however, by the fact that Osama bin Laden and many followers fled to the remote mountains of Afghanistan and neighboring Pakistan. Also, the overthrow of the Taliban brought only a brief and superficial unity and stability to Afghanistan. A country long divided by the power of regional warlords and an economy based on the opium trade, Afghanistan proved to be a formidable challenge to nation building. Once the Taliban had been overthrown, moreover, Washington's focus shifted to Iraq.

The day of the terrorist attacks, Bush, Wolfowitz, Cheney, and others in the administration talked of possible Iraqi complicity with al-Qaeda and of the opportunity to attack Iraq. Bush insisted that the campaign against the known perpetrators had to be given precedence, but he never discouraged discussion on forceful "regime change" in Iraq. The shock of September 11 provided urgency to the determination of neoconservatives and their adherents, both inside and outside the government, to reconceptualize strategic thinking. They repudiated the longstanding assumption that the principal objective of U.S. military power was the containment and deterrence of prospective enemies.

This redefinition of U.S. national security policy emerged during the first nine months of 2002, beginning with Bush's State of the Union address of January 29 and culminating in the National Security Statement (NSS 2002) released on September 20. In the State of the Union address, Bush changed America's priority from retaliating against the September 11 terrorist attacks to preventing rogue states from developing WMD and supplying such weapons to terrorists. In the most memorable part of the speech, Bush stated that Iran, Iraq, and North Korea "and their terrorist allies constitute an axis of evil, armed to threaten the peace of the world. By seeking weapons of mass destruction, these regimes pose a grave and growing danger." The urgency of the threat necessitated a proactive American policy, not the historic reliance on containment: "We will be deliberate. Yet time is not on our side." The United States, Bush continued, "would not stand by while peril draws closer and closer . . . [for it could not permit] the world's most destructive regimes to threaten us with the world's most destructive weapons."

The indictment of three nations as the "axis of evil" blended two words drawn from the American tradition of fighting totalitarianism: the "Axis powers" had been the enemy during World War II and "evil empire" had been President Reagan's famed indictment of the Soviet Union. Implicit in the speech was that establishing a link between the "axis of evil" and terrorist groups was not necessary. Rather, it was assumed that their shared enmity toward the United States would lead rogue states to provide WMD to terrorists. So it was axiomatic that, if the United States permitted WMD to be developed, some day they would be used against Americans. The speech also shifted focus from the murky and frustrating task of fighting terrorists in the remote mountains of Afghanistan to confronting nation-states.

The "axis of evil" speech marked the beginning of the deterioration of relations with allies in Europe. The sympathy for the United States and unswerving support of the Afghanistan campaign gave way to criticism and resentment. Not only were European leaders annoyed by the failure of the Bush administration to consult with them on a major change in U.S. policy, they were offended by the lack of any mention of their support of the United States after the terrorist attacks. Although Bush saw fit to praise Pakistan, Russia, and China for their assistance, he conspicuously ignored NATO's resolution or the substantial troop commitments of European nations to Operation ENDURING FREEDOM.

In ensuing weeks, the Bush administration made clear that Iraq was the next military target. To clarify matters, Powell announced that, "with respect to Iran and with respect to North Korea, there is no plan to start a war with those nations." Administration officials and leading conservatives in the media talked openly of the imperative for regime change in Iraq.

Then, in his June 1 commencement address at the U.S. Military Academy at West Point, Bush introduced the strategy of preventive warfare.

While hinted at in previous speeches and remarks, Bush now made clear the commitment to this new doctrine: "We must take the battle to the enemy, disrupt his plans and confront the worst threats before they emerge." This essentially repudiated the provision in the United Nations Charter, which an earlier generation of Americans had helped to write, that nations should go to war only in self-defense. The United States would act unilaterally, Bush implied, for there was no mention in the speech of working with the United Nations. Essentially, Bush proclaimed a Pax Americana based on the nation's capacity to intimidate and if necessary destroy adversaries with its overwhelming military power: "Competition between great nations is inevitable, but armed conflict in our world is not. . . . America has, and intends to keep, military strengths beyond challenge, thereby making the destabilizing arms races of other eras pointless."

The "axis of evil" and West Point speeches, together with bellicose statements from other officials, triggered considerable criticism. Especially notable was that coming from prominent Republicans, including three leading officials of the first Bush administration. Scowcroft, writing in the *Wall Street Journal*, warned that war against Iraq would jeopardize the antiterrorist coalition, trigger widespread anti-Americanism in the Middle East, and undermine efforts to promote Israeli-Palestinian peace. Former Secretary of State James A. Baker, writing in the *New York Times*, accepted the objective of regime change but foresaw acting alone as generating anti-Americanism and undermining a postwar occupation for which the United States would need the assistance of other nations. Lawrence S. Eagleberger, who had served as under secretary of state and briefly as secretary of state, made much the same point: "I don't know why we have to do it now when all of our allies are opposed to it." Other Republicans also urged caution. In a lengthy essay in the *Washington Post*, Henry Kissinger, national security adviser and secretary of state in the Nixon-Ford administrations, challenged not so much preemptive war as the ensuing long-term commitment: "Military intervention should be attempted only if we are willing to sustain such an effort for however long it is needed."

From the halls of Congress, other Republicans—notably House Majority Leader Dick Armey of Texas and Senator Chuck Hagel of Nebraska—questioned the momentum for war. Armey criticized preventive war: "If we try to act against Saddam Hussein, as obnoxious as he is, without proper provocation, we will not have the support of other nation states who might do so. I don't believe that America will justifiably make an unprovoked war on another nation. It will not be consistent with what we have been as a nation and what we should be as a nation." Hagel, a Vietnam War veteran, doubted the evidence of Iraq's WMD development and shared Kissinger's concern about an extended commitment: "You can get the country into war pretty fast, but you can't get out as quickly, and the public needs to know what the risks are." These critics—Scowcroft, Baker, Eagleberger, Kissinger, Armey, and Hagel—were all conservatives writing from a realist perspective; this was an early indication that the assertive neoconservative agenda troubled many members of the Republican Party.

Although Bush and other officials assured Americans that no decision for war had yet been reached, in fact evidence suggests that, by the summer of 2002, Bush had concluded that war was necessary. A top-secret British memo (which was published in 2005) shows that Sir Richard Dearlove, the head of British intelligence, was startled, during meetings with U.S. intelligence officials in July 2002, to learn that they were planning for war: "There was a perceptible shift in attitude. Military intervention was now seen as inevitable. Bush wanted to remove Saddam through military action, justified by the conjunction of terrorism and WMD. But the intelligence and facts were being fixed around the policy. The [National Security Council] had no patience with the U.N. route, and no enthusiasm for publishing materials on the Iraqi regime's record. There was little discussion in Washington of the aftermath after military action." That terse report underlined that indeed war was inevitable, that intelligence was being "fixed" to justify it, and that the United States intended to ignore the United Nations.

Even though the advanced state of war planning was unknown beyond official circles, the administration still had many critics to whom it responded defiantly. In speeches on August 26 and 29, Vice President Cheney set forth an extended indictment of Saddam Hussein as an imminent threat, claiming that "there is no doubt that Saddam Hussein now has weapons of mass destruction . . . [and] is amassing [them] for use against our friends, against our allies and against us." Nothing less than the stability of the world was at stake. According to Cheney, "Armed with an arsenal of these weapons of terror and seated atop ten percent of the world's oil reserves, Saddam Hussein could then be expected to seek domination of the entire Middle East, take control of a great portion of the world's energy supplies, directly threaten America's friends throughout the region, and subject the United States or any other nation to nuclear blackmail." Dismissing further WMD inspections by the United Nations as being useless, Cheney's speeches marked the beginning of the administration's focus on WMD as the overriding reason for war against Saddam Hussein. Again, European criticism was strong, with France's president Jacques Chirac stating that Cheney was "legitimizing the unilateral and preemptive use of force."

The Bush administration added to domestic unease by asserting that the president did not need congressional authorization for war. This brought much criticism, again notably from Republicans. Senator Arlen Specter of Pennsylvania responded to Cheney: "It's a matter for Congress to decide. The president as commander in chief can act in an emergency without authority from Congress, but we have time to debate, deliberate, and decide." In an essay in the *Washington Post*, former senator and 1996 presidential candidate Robert Dole counseled that Bush "should seek congressional approval. . . . Consultations with Congress are essential, but not adequate when armed conflict is the issue."

Confronting criticism at home and abroad, Bush opted for modest accommodation but without compromising his prerogatives. Siding for once with Powell instead of Cheney, Bush agreed to take the WMD issue to the United Nations. It would be done, however, in an uncompromising mode, with the United States insisting that the international organization enforce disarmament resolutions.

Paralleling this concession toward the international community was acknowledgement of the need to build support at home. Like his father, Bush found that he could not risk the loss of public support that defiance of Congress entailed. As in 1990–91, polls underscored the public's caution. While a substantial majority (nearly 70%) supported military action to force Saddam Hussein from power, they wanted such an attack to have international and congressional support. Some 60 percent of Americans agreed that congressional approval of war was necessary and that the United Nations should resume weapons inspections.

So, in early September, Bush moved to the center of a campaign to cultivate both domestic and international support. On the home front, he operated from a position of political strength. Unlike 1990–91, when the majority of the Democratic members of Congress opposed war, in 2002 nearly all Democratic Party leaders supported a war resolution. This change reflected the party's vulnerability on national security, which had been accentuated by its opposition to the successful Persian Gulf

War. This played to a historic image of the Democratic Party as being irresolute on national security issues, which dated back to Truman's alleged "loss of China" to the communists in 1949 and the impressions of Truman and Johnson as ineffective leaders in the unpopular Korean and Vietnam wars, of Jimmy Carter as inept during the Iranian hostage crisis, and, most recently, of Bill Clinton as indecisive in the Balkans and Africa. These were simplistic versions of history, but they were powerful political impressions that left Democrats wary of confronting Bush. So the advice from Al From, the chief executive of the centrist Democratic Leadership Council, reflected political reality: "I hope the Democrats will support the president—period."

When Congress reconvened and Bush met with its leadership on September 4, he found the key Democrats—Senate Majority Leader Tom Daschle of South Dakota and House Minority Leader Richard Gephardt of Missouri—not only supportive of forceful regime change but encouraging him to become more aggressively involved in making the case for war. Thus assured of substantial majorities in Congress, Bush publicly promised to cooperate with Congress and "at the appropriate time to go to the Congress to seek congressional approval for [whatever is] necessary to deal with this threat." Soon the case for war was being made forcefully through congressional briefings on Iraq's WMD program by Rumsfeld and CIA Director George Tenet and through interviews with Powell, Rumsfeld, and Rice echoing the same theme on national news programs.

As he lined up domestic support, Bush moved to the international arena by addressing the U.N. General Assembly on September 12. He chided the United Nations to live up to its responsibilities to disarm Iraq and affirmed American determination to act unilaterally if necessary. For Bush, the U.N. speech served several political purposes. Critics of unilateral warfare were heartened by the decision to seek a Security Council resolution. Hawks responded favorably to the speech's belligerent tone and challenge to the international community. And more subtly, it shifted public attention away from questions about the necessity for war and the contentious issue of preemptive warfare to whether the United Nations would act; clearly Bush was stating that U.N. failure would in itself justify a unilateral war.

As the tone of the U.N. speech suggested, the United States was not modifying the belligerency of the "axis of evil" and West Point speeches—a point underlined with the September 20 release of the annual National Security Statement. The thirty-one page NSS 2002 stated the need for a many-faceted response at home and abroad to the threat posed by international terrorism, but its boldest passages pertained to preemptive warfare, American military predominance, unilateralism, and global democracy. Basically it maintained that a new threat necessitated a redefined strategy: "America is now threatened less by conquering states than by failing ones. We are menaced less by fleets and armies than by catastrophic technologies in the hands of the embittered few. We must defeat these threats to our Nation, allies, and friends. . . . [We must] prevent our enemies from threatening us, our allies, and our friends, with weapons of mass destruction." To meet this danger and to uphold international stability, the United States depended on overwhelming military superiority: "Our forces will be strong enough to dissuade potential adversaries from pursuing a military build-up in hopes of surpassing, or equaling, the power of the United States."

Addressing terrorism directly, NSS 2002 specified that the U.S. objective was to "disrupt and destroy terrorist organizations" by using military and other power against "any terrorist or state sponsor of terrorism which attempts to gain or use [WMD]." The United States would seek international support, but a lack of it would not be a restraint, for the priority was "identifying and destroying the threat before it reaches our border. . . . We will not hesitate to act alone, if necessary, to exercise our right of self-defense by acting pre-emptively."

Reflecting a longstanding neoconservative goal, NSS 2002 affirmed the commitment to the promotion of democratic values, which history had demonstrated were universal and were key to international peace: "The great struggles of the twentieth century between liberty and totalitarianism ended with a decisive victory for the forces of freedom—and a single sustainable model for national success: freedom, democracy, and free enterprise. . . . These values of freedom are right and true for every person, in every society—and the duty of protecting these values against their enemies is [the] common calling of freedom-loving people across the globe and across the ages." In sum, through its military and economic power, the United States would bring "free and open societies" into a union of values and interests embodying "a distinctly American internationalism." This vision of a world reflecting American values was not new; it was an embodiment of the concept of "American exceptionalism" that can be traced to colonial times and that was part of the country's political culture, but never before had it found such explicit expression as an overriding foreign policy objective.

NSS 2002 underlined the transformation in the Bush administration's strategic thinking during the year since the 9/11 attacks. Appropriately, the NSS 2002's vision became labeled the Bush Doctrine, for it marked a significant and far-reaching change in America's definition of its national security policy. Most immediately, it provided a broad rationale for war against Saddam Hussein.

Commenting on the magnitude of the changes in national security policy brought by the Bush administration and culminating in the NSS 2002 statement, Mann writes in *The Rise of the Vulcans:* "These developments represented . . . an epochal change, the flowering of a new view of America's status and role in the world. The vision was that of an unchallengeable America, a United States whose military power was so awesome that it no longer needed to make compromises or accommodations (unless it chose to do so) with any other nation or group of nations." In *America's Failing Empire,* the historian Warren Cohen underlines further the significance of the new doctrine: "Not since Woodrow Wilson had an American president or his Administration committed itself to the mission of remaking the world—and Wilson never imagined that the United States would use its military forces unilaterally. In the minds of many commentators, it was a revolution in American policy."

In different times NSS 2002 would have triggered a vigorous national debate. In Congress, committees would have held hearings on such a far-reaching change, bringing administration officials and experts to testify. Newspapers and television newscasts would have devoted attention to the document's significance. Not so in the political atmosphere a year after 9/11, when NSS 2002 had no discernible effect on Congress's support of Bush's war plans and when the media gave only scant coverage.

Among the points worthy of discussion was how Bush administration statements and NSS 2002 used the term *preemptive war* when what they were actually proposing was *preventive war.* In international law, "preemptive war" is considered a legitimate act of self-defense because it involves taking action against an enemy that is known to be about to attack. "Preventive war" has no such legitimacy; it involves destroying the war-making capacity of an enemy before it becomes strong enough to attack. For instance, during the early cold war, both Presidents Harry Truman and Dwight Eisenhower dismissed suggestions that the United States should attack the Soviet Union before it developed more sophisticated nuclear weapons. In the rhetoric of the Bush administration in 2002, such distinctions were ignored. Notably in the NSS 2002 passages quoted above, *preventive* and *preemptive* were used interchangeably as there is talk of "prevent[ing] our enemies from threatening us, our allies, and our friends, with weapons of mass destruction" and later of "identifying and destroying the threat before it reaches our border. . . . We will not hesitate to act alone, if necessary, to exercise our right of self-defense by acting pre-emptively." Lost in this imprecise language was the distinction between preemptive war against an *imminent* aggressor and preventive war against a *potential* aggressor.

The lack of debate over NSS 2002 was testimony to Bush's political strength, which he played skillfully in dealing with Congress on the war resolution issue. He controlled the timing and, to a large extent, the terms of the debate. First, he insisted, despite Democratic Party objections, that Congress vote on a war resolution prior to the midterm elections on November 5. It was risky for members of Congress, especially those who were in tight reelection races, to oppose the administration on an issue of national security. Second, Bush focused attention on the most emotional and understandable arguments for war—Iraq's alleged duplicitous development of WMD and its capacity to support terrorist groups. The administration benefited from the extent to which the public accepted the administration's contention of a connection between Saddam Hussein's regime and international terrorism. This "link" enabled the White House and its congressional supporters to respond to critics who contended that preemptive war against Saddam Hussein would detract resources from the war on terror, which, they argued, should be the nation's priority. Accepting the "link" argument, however, made Saddam Hussein's regime part of the terrorist enemy. Third, in response to those who argued that the United States should work through the United Nations, Bush claimed that a show of domestic resolve would enhance the prospects for U.N. action against Iraq. Promising to make additional efforts in the United Nations, Bush provided a rationale for support of the resolution that was seized upon by several Democrats, who regarded U.N. sanction of war as essential. By supporting the administration through a war resolution, the argument ran, Congress would strengthen the U.S. position in the United Nations, thus making an American war less likely.

In advancing that case, Bush made a virtue of his most notable weakness in comparison with the position of his father in 1991. The circumstances reflected a significant change in the U.S. relationship with the United Nations. While Bush I had first built a solid base of support in the United Nations, which strengthened his argument for a congressional war resolution, Bush II lacked substantial international backing. But he used that lack of support as a reason for Congress to vote for war. So, despite the difference between America's international stature in 1990–91 and in 2002, the president in both cases was able to use the United Nations issue to his advantage in dealing with Congress.

Perhaps most telling of Bush's political strength was the fact that nearly all prospective Democratic Party candidates for president in 2004 supported the war resolution. Senator Daschle was joined by his colleagues Joseph Lieberman of Connecticut, John Kerry of Massachusetts, and John Edwards of North Carolina. In the House of Representatives, Congressman Gephardt, who also had presidential ambitions, said "everything had changed" after 9/11 and went so far as to concede that his vote against the 1991 war had been a mistake.

The Bush administration's carefully crafted draft war resolution built on the president's position of strength and finessed constitutional issues. A series of sixteen "whereas" clauses built upon the record of Saddam Hussein's defiance of U.N. resolutions, Congress's commitment to regime change through its passage of the Iraq Liberation Act of 1998, and existing presidential power—including references to the 1991 war resolution and the 2001 terrorism resolution, as well as "the president['s] authority under the Constitution to defend the national security interests of the United States." The draft resolution "authorized [the president] to use all means that he determines to be appropriate, including force, in order to enforce the United Nations Security Council Resolutions, . . . defend the national security interests of the United States against the threat posed by Iraq, and restore international peace and security in the region."

Responding to reporters' questions on the resolution, Bush tacitly denied the necessity for congressional action and sounded much like his father nearly twelve years earlier: "This is a chance for Congress to indicate support. It's a chance for Congress to say, 'We support the administration's ability to keep the peace.' That's what this is all about."

Although most Democratic Party leaders in Congress supported the war resolution and tacitly accepted plans for preemptive war, a few prominent Democrats and much of the party's rank and file criticized what they saw as their leadership's sacrificing of principle to politics. Former President Carter denounced the doctrine of preemptive war, while Al Gore, former vice president and the 2000 presidential candidate, criticized war against Iraq as distracting attention and resources from the war against terrorism. In the Senate, a few Democrats—most prominently Ted Kennedy of Massachussetts, Carl Levin of Michigan, Dianne Feinstein of California, Joseph Biden of Delaware, and Bob Graham of Florida (the only prospective presidential candidate aside from Ohio's Dennis Kucinich in the House of Representatives to break ranks with the party's leadership)—were critical of the resolution's "blank check" authorization and the message that this sent to the United Nations. The notice that the United States was prepared to act unilaterally, Levin suggested, seemingly invited it by providing an incentive for the United Nations to do nothing. An editorial in the *Washington Post* castigated Democratic leaders in Congress: "[They] can't have it both ways: They can either face up to their momentous responsibility in deciding on war or abdicate their authority and join Mr. Bush in playing the short-term political angles."

By that definition, nearly all of the Democratic leaders chose "the short-term political angles." Bush and his bipartisan supporters in Congress defeated two substantial challenges. In the Senate, Daschle—together with Biden, as chairman of the Foreign Relations Committee, and the committee's ranking Republican, Richard Lugar of Indiana—proposed limiting the use of force to the destruction of Iraq's WMD, but the Bush administration, working with other Democrats, notably Gephardt and Lieberman, as well as Republican leaders, blunted that initiative. Still another alternative—similar to one proposed in the 1991 war debate—called for Bush to "return to Congress" for a war resolution if efforts at diplomacy failed. Senator Levin and a fellow Democrat, Congressman John Spratt of South Carolina, offered resolutions that supported the president's objectives, but they insisted that, should diplomacy fail at the United Nations, he would need to "return to Congress" with a request for explicit authorization to wage unilateral warfare. The war-making power of Congress would thus be preserved. That concern mattered little to most members of Congress, who voted down—as Congress had done in 1991—a "return to Congress" resolution. The senior member of Congress—the eighty-four-year-old Senator Robert Byrd (D.-W.V.)—criticized Congress's abandonment of constitutional responsibilities. In a *New York Times* essay, Byrd lamented the "rush to war" and Congress's failure to consider "the fundamental and monumental questions of whether the United States should go to war." Instead, by "being hounded into action on a resolution that turns over to President Bush the Congress's power to declare war," members of Congress were "walk[ing] away from their

Constitutional responsibilities . . . [and] giv[ing] away the authority to determine when war is to be declared."

Buoyed by congressional support, Bush, in a speech in Cincinnati on October 7, pressed his case for war. Drawing a parallel between the threats posed by Iraq and by the Soviet Union during the Cuban missile crisis forty years earlier that month, Bush quoted President John F. Kennedy's admonition on that occasion that "we no longer live in a world where only the actual firing of weapons represents a sufficient challenge to a nation's security to constitute maximum peril." Emphasizing the "link" between Saddam Hussein and the war on terror, Bush "linked" security with regime change: "Our demands are directed only at the regime that enslaves [the Iraqis] and threatens us. . . . If military action is necessary, the United States and its allies will help the Iraqi people rebuild their economy and create the institutions of liberty."

Normally such a strident speech would have triggered substantial questioning of what some observers saw as a virtual declaration of war, but it did not disrupt Congress's "rush to war." The war debate of 2002 lacked the drama of 1991. The Senate devoted three days to the issue, and the House of Representatives barely a half day. Democratic supporters repeatedly stressed the main resolution's bipartisan development and the administration's commitment to seek U.N. support before going to war. Congressmen and senators from both parties argued that the resolution, as an expression of national resolve, would increase the administration's capacity to gain international backing. Opponents reiterated the contention that Congress was again abdicating its war power, and a few, most forcefully Graham, warned of diverting attention from the war on terrorism. Byrd made an eloquent plea for the Senate not to compromise its war-making authority—"It isn't Robert C. Byrd that counts. It's the constitution"—but his effort to delay a vote failed. In the House, Minority Whip Nancy Pelosi of California—the most prominent Democratic Party leader to oppose the resolution—spoke for most Democratic members of that body when she warned of an unnecessary war that would divert resources from the war on terror and of an "interminable" postwar occupation that would cost lives and treasure: "If we go in we can show our power to Saddam Hussein. If we resolve this issue diplomatically we can show our strength as a great country."

On October 10, substantial majorities in both houses gave Bush the authority to wage war. The war resolution passed 296-113 in the House of Representatives and carried the Senate by 77-23. As in 1991, partisan differences were significant, but in 2002 a sharp division within Democratic ranks contributed to the much greater majorities than a decade earlier. Significantly, most House Democrats refused follow their party's leadership, as 126 of them voted against the resolution, but still 81 voted in favor. In the Senate, a majority of Democrats (28 to 21) supported the resolution. Thus, what stood out was the role of the leadership of the Democratic Party in giving the president substantial majorities. The congressional vote also reflected public opinion, as polls indicated that 62 percent of Americans favored military action against Iraq. The shadow of the congressional elections—little more than three weeks away—loomed over the vote. Among 11 senators in what were considered close reelection campaigns, 10 voted for the war resolution, and among 50 House incumbents in competitive races, 40 voted for it.

With the approval of the resolution that authorized war if he deemed it necessary, Bush combined a solicitous approach toward Congress with a reaffirmation of executive power. At a White House signing ceremony on October 16 with the Cabinet and congressional leaders at his side, Bush stated that, "with this resolution, Congress has now authorized the use of force." He went on to speak at length of Iraq's weapons of mass destruction program and closed by thanking Congress for "an overwhelming statement of support." Then later in the day, the White House issued a signing statement—modeled on Bush I's 1991 statement—which upheld the claim of absolute presidential war-making power, conspicuously speaking of congressional "support" but not its "authorization" of war.

Armed with support at home, Bush now relied on Powell, who enjoyed considerable international prestige, to carry America's case as the president fulfilled the promise to seek U.N. support. Playing a prominent role in negotiating with other members of the Security Council and in restraining the more hawkish elements of the administration, Powell managed after seven weeks of diplomatic give-and-take to gain what was widely regarded as a substantial victory with the unanimous passage of Security Council Resolution 1441 on November 8. In an atmosphere where France, Russia, and China as well as several nonpermanent Security Council members quietly questioned America's real interest in finding an alternative to war, Powell was able to build upon the willingness of the permanent Security Council members to support tougher inspections. Powell benefited from Iraq's message, which U.N. Secretary General Kofi Annan had encouraged, that it would comply with a resumption of inspections. The United States would have preferred U.N.

authorization for the use of force against Iraq if it defied inspections, but that recourse was unacceptable to other Security Council members. Resolution 1441, however, did stipulate that the Security Council would convene "to consider the situation" if Iraq was uncooperative and warned Iraq of "serious consequences" if it was found to be "in material breach" of U.N. resolutions.

Inspections resumed under the United Nations Monitoring, Verification, and Inspection Commission (UNMOVIC), whose head Hans Blix reported to the Security Council on January 6, 2003, that Iraqi officials were being cooperative and that no WMD had yet been uncovered. Inspections, Blix said, had to continue. Bush, however, was impatient. With a large force assembled in the Persian Gulf and mid-January to mid-March considered the optimum time to launch an attack, Bush remarked to Spanish Prime Minister Jose Maria Aznar in mid-December that the extended inspections were "like Chinese water torture. We have to put an end to it." In early January 2003, Rice told other high-ranking officials that "[Bush] really feels he has to do this." And shortly afterward Bush said to Powell: "I really think I'm going to have to take this guy out." Blix's January 28 report to the Security Council was upbeat: Iraqis were granting UNMOVIC full access to all sites; the inspections were proceeding and would be able to achieve verifiable disarmament within a reasonable period of time.

In this situation, Bush, Cheney and Rice—convinced that time was not on America's side—determined that the United States had to take the initiative by taking its case against Iraq to the United Nations. In so doing, it essentially dismissed the UNMOVIC inspections as irrelevant. On the day of Blix's second report, Bush summoned Powell: "We've really got to make the case, and I want you to make it. You have the credibility to do this. Maybe they'll believe you." Seeking U.N. authorization for war was necessary to retain the support of Britain and Spain and, of course, might win over the reluctant Security Council members. France remained the strongest critic; its foreign minister, Dominique de Villepin had said a few days earlier that "nothing justifies cutting off inspections to enter into war and uncertainty" and that a unilateral war would be a "dead end . . . perceived as victory for the law of the strongest, an attack on the rule of law and on international morality."

In the State of the Union address delivered on January 28, Bush thus focused on Iraq's putative nuclear weapons program. Among other claims, Bush said that the International Atomic Energy Agency "confirmed in the 1990s that Saddam Hussein had an advanced nuclear weapons program, had a design for a nuclear weapon and was working on five different methods of enriching uranium for a bomb." In what proved to be the most controversial (and later shown to be clearly unsubstantiated) part of his speech, he added, "The British government has learned that Saddam Hussein recently sought significant quantities of uranium from Africa." Declaring that Saddam Hussein "clearly has much to hide," Bush concluded that the United States would call upon the U.N. Security Council to convene on February 5 to consider Iraq's defiance of its resolutions.

Just as Secretary of State Baker had made the case on November 29, 1990, for the U.N. Security Council to set an ultimatum for Iraq's withdrawal from Kuwait, now Secretary Powell was called upon to make the case to that same body for a resolution calling upon members to authorize war again against Iraq. While Baker had operated from strength and had been certain of victory, Powell went to the meeting with the support of only one other permanent member (Britain) and two nonpermanent members (Spain and Bulgaria). After receiving a draft speech from the White House, Powell insisted on reviewing the evidence against Saddam Hussein. Wanting to make certain that he could support all allegations, Powell eliminated much of the original text. As he addressed the Security Council, Powell made certain that CIA Director Tenet sat directly behind him, thus giving the impression that the full resources of the nation's intelligence community were invested in the speech. In a virtuoso seventy-five minute performance, Powell charged, among other offenses, that Saddam Hussein had a "stockpile of between 100 and 500 tons of chemical weapons agent . . . enough to fill 16,000 battlefield rockets"; had since 1998 resumed his nuclear weapons program and was "determined to get his hands on a nuclear bomb," as was evident in covert attempts to acquire necessary components from other countries; and had developed a "covert force of up to a few dozen Scud-variant ballistic missiles" with plans for ballistic missiles with a range of 1,000 kilometers. "This is evidence, not conjecture," the secretary concluded, "this is true. This is all well documented."

Americans generally found Powell's speech to be persuasive, but it was met with skepticism in much of the rest of the world. Leaders of several key nations questioned whether Saddam Hussein had in fact been able to carry out such an ambitious and duplicitous WMD buildup and, even if he had, whether it posed such an imminent threat as to justify a multilateral invasion of Iraq and the overthrow of his government. France was unalterably opposed to the use of force "regardless of the circumstances." Germany and Russia followed France's leadership. With any U.N. Security Council resolution facing vetoes by France, Russia, and probably China, the United States found that it still had just four votes on the fifteen-member body. So the Americans abandoned their pursuit of U.N. authorization. Rather than being restrained by the embarrassing failure of diplomacy at the United Nations, a defiant Bush dismissed the lack of U.N. support: "We will lead a coalition of the willing to disarm him. Make no mistake about that."

The congressional resolutions of the previous October having given him authority to decide on the necessity for war, the administration prepared for the showdown. Saddam Hussein as a military threat remained the overriding rationale. Tenet told reporters, "We will find caches of WMD, absolutely." Delivering a final forty-eight-hour ultimatum to Saddam Hussein on March 17, Bush said that "intelligence gathered by this and other governments leaves no doubt that the Iraq regime continues to possess and conceal some of the most lethal weapons ever devised." Two days later Operation IRAQI FREEDOM began.

PRESIDENT GEORGE W. BUSH'S LEADERSHIP in moving the nation toward war in 2002–3 was ultimately based on the single rationale of urgency: the United States, acting alone if necessary, needed to disarm Iraq before it posed a direct military threat, an objective that could be accomplished only with the removal of Saddam Hussein from power. A decade of frustrating relations between his government and the United Nations demonstrated that he could not be trusted, but it was uncertain whether that duplicity had led to WMD production. Regime change in the interest of eliminating a tyrant, as an American objective, could, after all, have been achieved in ways other than reliance on military power. Other than the assumption that Iraq was steadily arming itself, there was no greater urgency for regime change in 2003 than there had been earlier.

Despite all the claims of Bush, Cheney, Rumseld, Rice, and Powell— presumably backed by the CIA and other intelligence sources—of impending development of WMD, many Americans and much of the international community remained skeptical. The timing was troubling: why was war necessary so long as U.N. inspections were making progress? By launching war, Bush's greatest risk was that the prewar claims of WMD development would be inconclusive or spurious. The "imminent threat" would thus be rendered an illusion.

On the home front, Bush gained impressive congressional majorities for the war resolution and support from the public. The bipartisan support in Congress reflected, to be sure, concern over WMD development, but it also owed much to political considerations—the vulnerability of Democrats, the impending congressional elections—and to Bush's commitment to seek another U.N. Security Council resolution (which provided a rationale for many doubters on the Democratic side to support Bush). In addition, the public's acceptance of the administration's dubious claim of a "link" between Saddam Hussein and al-Qaeda underlined the administration's ability to play on the emotions of September 11. Viewed another way, considering all the factors that contributed to a belligerent spirit, it is perhaps surprising that about one-fourth of the Senate and House members opposed the resolution. Without the support of virtually the entire Democratic Party leadership, Bush may still have prevailed in Congress, but it would have been a much closer vote.

Regardless of the reasons, Bush had achieved the essential public support, far surpassing that of his father in 1991 but not approaching that of Lyndon Johnson's nearly unanimous Tonkin Gulf resolution of 1964. Like Bush I, Johnson, and Truman, Bush II insisted that he did not need congressional authorization. The "blank check" authorization, like that in the two previous wars, troubled many constitutional scholars and a few political leaders who saw in it another step in the erosion of congressional war-making power. Senator Byrd railed against the spinelessness of Congress—on the constitutional issue he was unquestionably correct—but the new century began as the old one had ended, with presidential war power fundamentally unchecked.

On the international level, Bush squandered the immense good will after September 11 and embarked on a controversial unilateral course to achieve regime change and demilitarization of Iraq. To the leadership in Washington, the objectives in Iraq were so overriding and U.S. power was so overwhelming that the United States could risk international alienation. Wolfowitz had repeatedly offered assurances, however, that a show of resolve would lead reluctant allies and others to rally to America's side, but that did not happen. So the failure of the Powell-centered U.N. diplomacy in February 2003 had not been anticipated, and the administration talked now of having another international group at its side in Iraq, what became the "coalition of the willing." Yet, as it prepared to attack Iraq, the United States was perhaps more isolated diplomatically than ever before in its history. This was symbolized by the hastily called conference on March 16 of the leaders of United States, Great Britain, and Spain (which had emerged as the only other traditional ally at America's side) in the Azores, a small island group in the Atlantic. There the three leaders pledged their cooperation against Iraq. As Powell commented, "it was seen as a defeat and it was a defeat." And the much-trumpeted "coalition of the willing" was, aside from a few states that made troop contributions, little more than a list of forty-four nations that had promised nothing more than allowing their names to be included.

As Bush led the country to war on March 19, U.S. objectives were clear, but already differences had developed over the military requirement to achieve them. There was no question that the United States could easily defeat Saddam Hussein's army. A relatively small and mobile force could achieve that end after an intensive bombing campaign. Yet it was also obvious to military commanders and civilian officials that a much larger force would be necessary to secure and occupy Iraq. As is detailed in the next chapter, Bush tolerated, and was ultimately responsible for, an unconscionably delayed and woefully inadequate plan for the postwar occupation. That indifference reflected the assumption, perpetuated by neoconservative thought, that a representative, democratic Iraq state would emerge from the ashes of the Saddam Hussein regime.

That reflected the extent to which neoconservative ideology guided the decision for war. The WMD issue was integrated into the neoconservative demand for regime change, the vision of a democratic Iraq transforming the region, the faith in the unsurpassed military power of the United States, and the dismissal of international opinion. March 19, 2003, was a triumphant moment for the neoconservatives.

History Overpowers Ideology

ON MAY 1, 2003—just forty-three days after he announced the commencement of hostilities—President George W. Bush, attired in a naval pilot's flight suit, dramatically landed in a navy jet on the USS *Abraham Lincoln*, a carrier stationed thirty miles off the coast of California. A banner on the ship's tower proclaimed "Mission Accomplished." Although Bush never used that phrase in his remarks to the five thousand assembled sailors and the millions who witnessed the event live (and in endless replays) on television, his message conveyed the buoyancy of victory: "Major combat operations in Iraq have ended. In the battle of Iraq, the United States and our allies have prevailed." He went on to speak of remaining tasks: pursuing Saddam Hussein and other leaders of his government, finding weapons of mass destruction (WMD)—"we know of hundreds of sites that will be investigated"—and establishing a democracy. These goals "will take time, but it is worth every effort," for Operation IRAQI FREEDOM had far-reaching implications: "The battle of Iraq is one victory in a war on terror that began on September the eleventh, 2001." Reinforcing the May 1 sense of "accomplishment" was the announcement from Baghdad four days later by Lt. Gen. Jay Garner, who headed the postwar reconstruction and humanitarian office in Iraq, that political authority would be transferred to an interim Iraqi government by May 15.

The overwhelming military superiority of the United States had achieved a quick and decisive victory. The Iraqi Army offered little resistance as U.S. forces entered the country. It was only when the Americans approached Baghdad that they had to engage in several days of battle against the Iraqi Republican Guard units before capturing the Iraqi capital. Although scattered resistance continued and Saddam Hussein had fled and was in hiding, American armed forces were victorious. This had been achieved at nominal cost: American casualties totaled 139 dead and 542 wounded.

Bush soon discovered an inconvenient truth: defeating Saddam Hussein's armed forces would be the easy part of Operation IRAQI FREEDOM; stabilizing and rebuilding postwar Iraq would be the difficult part. As Bush stood on the USS *Abraham Lincoln*, he never anticipated that

Americans would still be fighting in Iraq five years later, that the war would become America's second longest foreign war surpassed only by that in Vietnam, and that, by the end of 2007, nearly four thousand American soldiers would have been killed in Iraq. Underlying the post–"mission accomplished" fighting was a failure to plan in a thorough or systematic manner for the problems that American forces would confront after Saddam Hussein was overthrown. Ideology, not realism, determined postwar thinking in the White House and Pentagon.

Bush staked his presidency on transforming Iraq. His wartime leadership continued, indeed exaggerated, the tight control of policymaking evident in the prewar period. Bush and Vice President Richard Cheney set the agenda, made the key decisions, and worked through Secretary of Defense Donald Rumsfeld, whose visible role helped to deflect criticism from the White House. Underlying the arrangement was a commitment to the neoconservative vision of a strong and democratic Iraq. Toward that end, Rumsfeld, with the White House's blessing, seized an opportunity to control planning not just for military operations but for the postwar administration. Traditionally, the occupation of defeated nations, like Germany and Japan after World War II or, more recently, Afghanistan in 2001–2, had been joint military and civilian operations, which made sense given the necessity of providing security while implementing political change. At the Pentagon, Rumsfeld's neoconservative deputies—Paul Wolfowitz, the deputy secretary of defense, and Douglas Feith, the under secretary of defense for policy—were instrumental in implementing occupation policy. Coordination between the Pentagon and White House occasionally faltered, but overall Bush and Cheney maintained control.

This system relegated Secretary of State Colin Powell and national security adviser Condoleezza Rice to secondary roles. Neither Cheney nor Rumsfeld ever showed much respect for Rice, who rarely challenged their positions, in any event. Cheney and Rumsfeld resented Powell because of his public stature and his concern with international opinion. Conspicuously lacking in policymaking was any effort to involve all appropriate agencies—no "interagency" communication as the executive branch officials called such interaction—which normally would have been Rice's function. Commenting on the lack of coordination, Richard Armitage, deputy secretary of state, observed that "there was never any [interagency] process to break. . . . There never was one from the start. Bush didn't want one, for whatever reason." In his book *Chain of Com-*

mand, the veteran investigative journalist Seymour Hersh describes the narrow base of policymaking:

> The perception persists that this was Rumsfeld's war, and that it was his assertiveness and his toughness that sometimes led to the bombing of the wrong target or the arrest of innocents. . . . George Bush talked about "smoking them out of their holes" and wanting them "dead or alive," and Rumsfeld was the one who set up the mechanism to get it done. The defense secretary would hold the difficult news conferences and take the heat in public . . . but the President and Vice President had been in on it, and with him, all the way. Rumsfeld handled the dirty work and kept the secrets, but he and the two White House leaders were a team.

While the Pentagon devoted more than a year to planning the invasion, Bush tolerated the deferral of postwar planning until two months before the war began. The delay reflected the facile assumption that planning was not necessary. Planning was not only tardy but hurried and superficial. It reflected the danger of applying ideology without regard for history.

Reflecting neoconservative thinking, Bush, Cheney, and Rumsfeld and his principal deputies believed that the occupation would be brief, for Iraqis would welcome the Americans as liberators. This would enable the Americans to turn over political power to a new Iraqi leadership that would quickly emerge. Cheney thus famously predicted: "The read we get on the people of Iraq is that there is no question they want to get rid of Saddam Hussein and will welcome us as liberators."

Such expectations had been encouraged by Iraqi exile groups, which had long been active in cultivating American support for Saddam Hussein's overthrow. The most prominent exile leader was Ahmad Chalabi, who headed the Iraqi National Congress (INC). Chalabi claimed that, once Saddam Hussein's tyranny ended, Iraqis would rally around his leadership. For months before the war, Chalabi and his colleagues, whose only hope of achieving political power was through American military intervention, provided American officials with information about Saddam Hussein's alleged stockpiles of WMD, offered assurances that an Iraqi democracy would quickly be established, and promised that oil revenues would finance postwar reconstruction (all of which proved false).

Born in Baghdad in 1945, Chalabi had fled with his family to the United States in 1958 when the military overthrew the monarchy. He did not return to Iraq until escorted by the U.S. Army in 2003. In the meantime, Chalabi, who earned a Ph.D. in mathematics at the University of Chicago, had been promoting the anti–Saddam Hussein cause among influential Americans. After the Persian Gulf War had left Saddam in power, Chalabi redoubled his cultivation of support from members of both major political parties, which included lobbying for the Iraq Liberation Act of 1998. He was the single most important Iraqi influence on the Bush administration as Operation IRAQI FREEDOM was being planned. He had become a favorite of the neoconservatives, to whom the overthrow of Saddam Hussein and the flowering of Iraqi democracy were high priorities. Chalabi had repeatedly assured his American benefactors that, after the overthrow of Saddam Hussein, the INC would seamlessly come to power and the United States could withdraw quickly from Iraq.

In fact, not all American officials were enamored with Chalabi. Bush was skeptical of his claims and promises, as were Powell and Rumsfeld; the Central Intelligence Agency (CIA) doubted his political stature within Iraq. Yet Bush did not act on his instincts and others did not push their concerns, so the American objectives in postwar Iraq became increasingly identified with Chalabi and the INC, despite the lack of any evidence (aside from Chalabi's claims) of substantial Iraqi support of (or even knowledge of) the INC. Chalabi remained the darling of the neoconservatives—notably Richard Perle, Wolfowitz, Feith—and prominent members of Congress, with Republican Senator John McCain of Arizona as an especially vocal supporter. So Chalabi and his followers gained in 2003 what they had long sought: the American overthrow of Saddam Hussein. In his book, *The End of Iraq*, Peter Galbraith, a former diplomat with considerable experience in the region, writes: "Ahmad Chalabi's role in the events leading to the American invasion of Iraq cannot, in my view, be overstated. If it were not for him the United States military likely would not be in Iraq today."

The vision of a brief occupation period under the military reflected not just the optimism of the "Americans as liberators" scenario, but the neoconservative prescription for effective nation building. Neoconservatives thought that they had learned from the "flawed" nation-building efforts of President Bill Clinton in Bosnia and Kosovo, which had relied heavily on the State Department. According to the neoconservatives, the State Department delayed transferring political responsibility, thus cultivating indefinite dependency on Americans. Clinton's "mistakes" would not be repeated in Iraq, whose peoples would quickly be granted political responsibility. Feith told Stephen Hadley, deputy national security adviser, that the Department of State had bungled the occupations of the 1990s and that, while the joint State-Defense occupation of Afghanistan had gone better, sole Defense responsibility would have been preferable and would be the key to success in Iraq.

So, confident that the Iraqis would see Americans as "liberators" and that the Defense Department's occupation policy would avoid earlier "mistakes," Bush tolerated the deferral of planning. It was not until January 20, 2003—a remarkably late date—that Bush signed a Feith-prepared directive that formally began planning for the postwar occupation under the direction of the Defense Department.

Despite the lack of any substantial planning, Rumsfeld on February 14 delivered a major speech—"Beyond Nation-Building"—which provided a vision for the future of Iraq. Criticizing implicitly the Clinton administration and the State Department, Rumsfeld said that the occupations in the Balkans provided examples of a policy that had led to a "culture of dependency." Bush, however, had done it correctly in Afghanistan by helping the Afghans rebuild their own country. However overstated his version of the success of the Afghanistan occupation may have been, Rumsfeld then foresaw an even easier assignment in Iraq:

> The effort in Afghanistan had to be planned and executed in a matter of weeks after September 11. With Iraq, by contrast there has been time to prepare. . . . We have set up a Post War Planning Office to think through problems and coordinate the efforts of coalition countries and the U.S. government agencies. General [Tommy] Franks [Combat Commander, Central Command] is in an interagency process that has been working hard on this for many months.

Rumsfeld's claims were simply false. He ignored the facts that Franks was absorbed with planning for the military phase, that Rumsfeld himself had only recently taken the first steps to plan for the occupation, and that there was no "interagency process." On January 20, the day of Bush's occupation directive, Rumsfeld had established the Office for Reconstruction and Humanitarian Assistance (ORHA) under the direction of retired Lt. Gen. Jay Garner, which seemed a questionable choice. Garner had no experience in postwar nation building, and his work in the Middle East was limited to the coordination of humanitarian relief in Kurdistan in 1991, but he had useful political connections with influential neoconservatives. He accepted the assignment on the assumption that his mission to Iraq would be brief.

It was not until the week after Rumsfeld's speech that Garner really began his assignment. He convened more than 150 experts from the departments of State and Defense, the National Security Council staff, and the CIA to engage in what amounted to preliminary discussion on the occupation. Participants pointed to several problems, the most important being that the United States and its allies lacked sufficient troops to provide postwar security. As one official stated, "Without sufficient troops, we risk letting much of the country descend into civil unrest, chaos whose magnitude may defeat our national strategy of a stable new Iraq, and more immediately, we place our own troops, fully engaged in the forward fight, in greater jeopardy." Another added that "security is far and away the greatest challenge, and the greatest shortfall. If we do not get it right, we may change the regime, but our national strategy will likely fall apart." Inadequate security, many conferees foresaw, would undermine civil administration, reconstruction, and humanitarian assistance. Moreover, the occupation would be very expensive, far beyond the levels contemplated by the Defense Department. Adding to the chaotic status of planning for the occupation, still other participants warned, was the "virtual state of war" (as one official called it) between the Defense and State departments.

The ascendancy of the Defense Department aggravated the bitter relationship between Powell and the trio of Rumsfeld, Cheney, and Bush. Rumsfeld pressed his advantage. Saying that the times required fresh thinking, he rejected Powell's suggestion that a few ambassador-level experts be included in the planning and postwar administration. When Garner included two State Department officials on his proposed planning staff, Rumsfeld (on the orders of Cheney) insisted that they be removed despite their qualifications (one of them had been working for a year, at Powell's behest, on postwar planning). Under Secretary of State Armitage saw the White House as unwilling to listen to potential dissenters: "[The dismissed State officials] were both inconvenient—you know, they wanted the facts to get into the equation. They were not people who stood up for the party line, that we'd be welcomed with garlands."

A very public rebuke of those who challenged the administration's position occurred in response to the February 25 testimony of army chief of staff Gen. Eric Shinseki before the Senate Armed Services Committee. Shinseki estimated that it would take several hundred thousand troops (300,000–400,000) to implement an effective occupation. This directly challenged the Rumsfeld insistence on a small-scale U.S. military operation then estimated at no more than 135,000 troops, so two days later Wolfowitz told another congressional committee that Shinseki's estimate was "wildly off the mark," asserting that it was "inconceivable" that it would require more troops to occupy Iraq than to conquer it. The occupation would be easy: "I am reasonably certain they will greet us as liberators, and that will help us to keep [troop] requirements down." And should more external forces be needed, the United States could look to other countries; even those that were objecting to the use of force would be eager to help once Saddam Hussein was gone. Wolfowitz asserted that there was "no reason to assume the US will or should supply" the bulk of military forces for the occupation; "I would expect that even countries like France will have a strong interest in assuring Iraq's reconstruction."

More than any other single event, Wolfowitz's dismissal of what the military leadership considered sound advice crystallized its estrangement from the civilian leadership in the Defense Department; many high-ranking military officers came to regard Rumsfeld, Wolfowitz, and Feith with disdain. Reflecting the military's disenchantment, army Col. Gregory Gardner, who served on the staff for the Joint Chiefs of Staff (JCS) and later in the occupation, put it bluntly: "Politically we'd made a decision that we'd turned it over to the Iraqis in June [2003] . . . so why have a Phase IV [occupation] plan?"

The result was superficial postwar planning, embodied in the Pentagon's brief Phase IV statement, which reflected the influence of the always optimistic Wolfowitz. It was based on tenuous assumptions: first, that a large number of Iraqi security forces would cooperate with the United States during the invasion and occupation (the "availability of significant numbers of Iraqi military and police who switched sides"); second, that an Iraqi government would quickly emerge, permitting a "quick handoff to an Iraqi interim administration with a United Nations mandate." The reference to the United Nations assuming responsibility underscored a third questionable assumption, that "the international community would pick up the slack from United States." Given the strong opposition within the United Nations to America's plan for unilateral war, why would any U.S. official have anticipated U.N. support? Two years later, a Rand Corporation study, based on classified prewar documents, underlined the bankruptcy of occupation planning: "Post-conflict stabilization and reconstruction were addressed only very generally, largely because of the prevailing view that the task would not be difficult."

Most striking was the inattention given to the tenuous nature of Iraqi nationhood. Among the nations of the Middle East, Iraq was the most lacking in terms of a "center" provided by a predominant ethnic group and a sense of cultural tradition and identity. Iraq had been created at the end of World War I by the British, who were given responsibility under the League of Nations mandate system to govern parts of the former Ottoman Empire. For administrative convenience, the British brought together three Ottoman provinces, each representing distinct groups with little in common: one in the Kurdish north, another in the Sunni Muslim center, and the other of Shiite Muslims in the south. The Shiites and Sunnis were Arab, but they embraced the two branches of Islam. The Kurds, although also Muslim, had their own culture and language and were alienated within this new state. The British placed a Sunni Arab prince as king in 1921, and that monarchy ruled Iraq, which became an independent nation in 1934, through a Sunni Arab–dominated bureaucracy and military. In 1958, the Iraqi Army overthrew the monarchy, but it continued the Sunni Arab control of the country through the Baathist Party. The dominant Sunnis, however, had always been a minority, constituting only 25 percent of the population; some 55 percent of Iraqis were Shiites, and Kurds comprised 20 percent. Repression and force, continuing to the reign of Saddam Hussein and his Baath Party, had been essential to the preservation of a reasonably stable Iraq. Hence, the overthrow of Saddam Hussein would almost certainly renew long-simmering sectarian and ethnic divisions. Indeed, after the Persian Gulf War, the Kurds had managed to establish a virtually autonomous Kurdistan state, which they were determined to preserve.

Americans appeared ignorant of, or indifferent toward, these divisions. In a meeting with three prominent Iraqi Americans in January 2003 about possible postwar problems, Bush became confused when they talked of Sunnis and Shiites. So the visitors devoted much of the meeting to explaining the two major sects of Islam. Bush's ignorance of a fundamental political problem within a country that he was about to invade is difficult to comprehend. Even the most cursory understanding of developments after the Persian Gulf War, which saw Saddam Hussein repressing the Shiites, would have provided a clue to the divisions within Iraq. Sparing that, it was reasonable that the National Security Council (NSC) might have prepared a summary of Iraqi political-cultural divisions for the president's review. Whether it would have made an impression, however, was problematic, for Bush came away from his meeting with the Iraqis convinced that Saddam Hussein's regime was responsible for the divisions and that its elimination would bring Iraqis together. In the end, Bush's indifference and misunderstanding represented the arrogance of his administration—an arrogance that ignored the forces of history within a troubled nation.

Had the White House chosen to listen, they could have heard from knowledgeable Americans, both inside and outside the government, who were troubled by the inattention to postwar planning. They foresaw a lengthy occupation whose success depended upon a substantial military presence. Frank Hoffman, a Marine Corps consultant, said a week before the invasion: "I don't see a lot of operational risks in the front end. I think the larger risks are the length and costs of postwar Iraq stability operations and opportunity costs we will be incurring." Drawing from the usually ignored history of Iraq, air force colonel John Warden wrote that the "biggest risk by far is strategic and is in the postwar period. When the British took over after World War I from the Ottomans, they found themselves being assassinated from almost the first day and saw the whole area in open rebellion within a year. . . . [The U.S. faces] a very high risk from the strategic side with years of difficult and very expensive occupation." Daniel Kuehl, a professor at the National Defense University, concurred: "I think the course of the war itself will be measured in a few weeks, but the Reconstruction (upper case intended, as a comparison to our own, 1865–76) will last years. It won't be a physical reconstruction as much as a political one."

Historical analyses pointed to the need for a substantial commitment. One study showed that the United States and its allies had invested twenty-five times more money and fifty times more troops into Kosovo in 1999 than into Afghanistan in 2001–2, and the results showed a significant difference: Kosovo's economic and political development surpassed that of Afghanistan, where the government controlled virtually nothing beyond the outskirts of Kabul and reconstruction was sluggish. When Powell asked a Middle East specialist to prepare a memo on "everything that could go wrong," the result was a projection of Shiite-Sunni clashes, influence from neighboring countries (Syria, Iran, and Saudi Arabia), and a failed economy and infrastructure. The State Department's thirteen-volume "Future of Iraq" project, prepared during 2002–3, reached the same conclusions in thoroughly documented detail. A study by Anthony H. Cordesman, a civilian expert on military strategy and the Middle East, bore the ominous title "Planning for a Self-Inflicted Wound," and said that planning was "uncoordinated and faltering" and based on ignorance about Iraq and the region.

Bush never addressed these concerns. The big issues of postwar Iraq—under what circumstances would a provisional government be established and how should it be constituted? how would a democratic constitution be written? what would be the status of the Iraqi military and the Baath Party? how would Kurdistan's determined autonomy or Shiite interest in an Islamic state be reconciled with the objective of a unitary secular Iraq?—were ignored.

The "liberation" of Iraq was accompanied by a breakdown of order. As many had foreseen, Iraqis refused to play the role scripted for them in neoconservative ideology. American forces were not welcomed and Iraqis had not rallied around Chalabi, whose six-hundred-man militia was flown to the city of Nasiriyah by the Americans. At Wolfowitz's urging, Rumsfeld bombarded the White House for permission to establish a government under Chalabi's leadership. Powell strenuously objected: how could the United States claim to be fighting for Iraqi democracy when it installed a government for the Iraqis? Cheney and Bush agreed, so Chalabi remained on the sidelines. In the meantime, Garner sought to work alongside State Department appointees (Powell having been given authority to include some personnel in ORHA), in particular a prominent neoconservative, the Afghanistan-born, Arabic-speaking Zalmay Khalilzad, who was given the title of special presidential envoy. Khalilzad sought to establish working relationships with representatives of various Iraqi groups, which Garner foresaw as leading to the "nucleus of a temporary Iraq government." The effort encountered resistance, as Shiite leaders refused to participate and Chalabi claimed that only the INC could represent Iraqis.

Whatever the prospects for the Khalilzad initiative, they were undermined by the chaos in Baghdad. As the undermanned American force stood by, Iraqis looted government offices (nearly two dozen government ministries were destroyed), civil servants fled their jobs, and the Iraqi police and army virtually vanished. One British official on the scene observed: "Garner's outfit . . . is an unbelievable mess. No leadership, no strategy, no coordination, no structure, and inaccessible to ordinary Iraqis. . . . Garner and his top team of 60-year-old retired Generals are well-meaning but out of their depth." That may have been accurate, but Garner, despite the shortcomings of his mission and the chaotic conditions in which it operated, was trying to reestablish order with the resources at his disposal and to fulfill his instructions for an early turnover of political power. With Khalilzad, Garner hurriedly planned for an interim government, one that would eliminate only the top-level Baath Party members from official positions. They essentially sought to rebuild a government from the remnants of the old while purging Saddam Hussein's most prominent followers. With much of the Iraqi Army in disarray and suffering from a high desertion rate, Garner anticipated recalling soldiers and rebuilding the army as an essential complement to the U.S. force in providing security; moreover, a visible Iraqi Army would reduce the impression of the U.S. forces as "occupiers." Toward that end Garner and CIA personnel had been meeting with Iraqi military officers to reconstitute the country's armed forces, envisioning a force of some 200,000–300,000 men. These considerations led to Garner's May 5 announcement that authority would be transferred to an interim Iraqi government within ten days.

In Washington, however, Garner's effort to salvage the objective of an early transition was rejected. The unexpected breakdown of order—which the Bush administration initially explained as the result of exuberance over Saddam Hussein's overthrow—combined with the Iraqi indifference, if not hostility, toward the Americans, forced reconsideration of the assumptions of a brief occupation. More than a caretaker "transitional" American administrator was needed. At Cheney's behest, Rumsfeld dismissed Garner and replaced him with Paul Bremer III, who became administrator of the Coalition Provisional Authority (CPA), as the occupation administration now became known. A career foreign service officer, Bremer had served as a special assistant to Secretary of State Henry Kissinger, as an ambassador-at-large for counterterrorism during the Ronald Reagan administration, and later as ambassador to the Netherlands. After leaving government service in 1989, he had been a managing partner in Kissinger Associates, a high-powered international consulting firm. Bremer's experience, however, had never taken him to Iraq and included no work in postwar societies or nation building. Nonetheless, when meeting with Bush and other officials on May 7, Bremer requested and the president gave him authority to exercise "all executive, legislative, and judicial functions" in Iraq.

That conferral of virtually dictatorial power meant that Bremer's appointment marked the transition of the role of American forces from that of "liberator" to "occupier." Seeing himself in a position comparable to that of Gen. Douglas MacArthur in reshaping Japan after World War II, the self-confident Bremer set out to make certain that Iraq would be transformed (as had been Japan) to reflect American values and institutions and would be linked politically, economically, and strategically to the United States. To some political observers, Bremer was "auditioning" to become the next secretary of state. From the beginning of his fourteen-month tenure in Iraq, Bremer operated largely on his instincts, with a certain flair for the dramatic, but the influence of Rumsfeld, Wolfowitz, and Feith was evident in his major decisions.

Convinced that the situation demanded bold leadership, Bremer announced on his arrival that, contrary to Garner's promise, there would be no interim government in the immediate future. Before there could be any transfer of power to Iraqis, Bremer was convinced, the remnants of the old regime had to be fully purged. He told Rumsfeld that "my arrival in Iraq must be marked by clear, public, and decisive steps to reassure Iraqis that we are determined to eradicate Saddamism." Insisting that there could be only one presidential envoy, Bremer demanded the dismissal of Khalilzad, the American official on the scene who was the most knowledgeable and most respected among Iraqis.

Within his first eight days, Bremer took the promised "decisive steps." He issued two far-reaching orders, both drawn up by Feith at the Pentagon. The first—"The De-Baathification of Iraqi Society"—banished the top four levels of Baath Party members (about thirty thousand persons altogether, or virtually the entire civil service) from ever holding government positions. The second order—"The Dissolution of Entities"—eliminated the entire security apparatus, dissolving the Iraqi army, air force, navy, secret police, militia, and Ministry of Defense. This order surprised nearly all officials in Washington (but not Wolfowitz and Feith), including the Joint Chiefs of Staff, Powell, and even Bush, who acknowledged that he had believed that the Iraqi Army was to be left intact. When he learned of Bremer's order, Garner, who was still on the scene in Baghdad, told Bremer that "you can get rid of an army in a day, but it takes you years to build one." Thousands of soldiers were left without a livelihood, triggering violent protests. The anti-American sentiment was fueled by a sense of betrayal, as many soldiers had refused to fight against the invading Americans and had believed promises of a role in a new army. As one Sunni told a reporter, "You Americans, you know you have created enemies here."

Indeed, Bremer's disbandment order reflected haste and ignorance.

If the objective was to eliminate Baathist influence in the military, the de-Baathification order would have been sufficient. Had the Pentagon or CPA investigated the situation, it would have learned that Baathists constituted only a small portion of the armed forces (about 8,000 of some 140,000 commissioned and noncommissioned officers), suggesting that Garner's effort to rebuild the military was on the right track. Coming on top of Rumsfeld's insistence on a relatively small U.S. force, Bremer's disbanding of the Iraqi army compounded the security problem.

The effect of Bremer's two orders was to end eighty years of Sunni Arab dominance of Iraq and the agencies that had preserved the unity of the country. Eliminating the military and police was an invitation for anarchy. According to Peter Galbraith: "Although he did not know it, Bremer had sealed Iraq's fate as a unitary nation. All the king's horses and all the king's men could not put Humpty Dumpty together again. This did not stop Bremer from spending the next fourteen months trying to do just that." In their massive history of the Iraq War, *Cobra II*, military correspondent Michael R. Gordon and Gen. Bernard E. Trainor concur: "In fact in their own way, Rumsfeld and Bremer each contributed to the security problem. Rumsfeld limited the number of American troops in Iraq, and Bremer limited the number of Iraqi forces that were immediately available. The two decisions combined to produce a much larger security vacuum."

Security was the obvious prerequisite for political change and economic rehabilitation. To replace the disbanded armed forces, Bremer initiated the New Iraqi Corps, which was to be "professional, non-political, militarily effective and representative of all Iraqis." This would fulfill Rumsfeld's instructions to Bremer that the "endstate is a viable force that is a source of Iraqi national pride, contributes to national unity and provides a model for ethnic cooperation." That American expectation, like others, clashed with Iraqi realities. The CPA recruited large numbers of men principally by offering public service salaries far higher than those under the old regime. Ethnic and sectarian differences, however, plagued the effort of the CPA and the American military to build the New Iraqi Corps and a police force. Training, moreover, was inadequate, so that the numbers of army and police were more impressive than was their capability.

As the American agenda was being undermined by the mounting insurgency in Baghdad and other areas, Bush and other officials dismissed the insurgency as a manifestation of the last remnants of Saddam

Hussein's regime. This explanation fit within prewar projections that such a "last gasp" would be the principal resistance to the American "liberators." Military commanders on the scene were not so certain, as they saw the insurgency becoming more widespread. Nonetheless, Wolfowitz assured a congressional committee that the insurgency lacked the essential ingredients of successful guerrilla warfare—popular support and external backing—and would soon atrophy. It was in that atmosphere of dismissing the insurgency as a "last gasp"—one that took forty-two American lives in the six weeks after the "mission accomplished" proclamation—that Bush told a press conference: "There are some who feel like the conditions are such that they can attack us there. My answer is bring 'em on. We've got the force necessary to deal with the security conditions." The "bring 'em on" challenge, which troubled many Americans as being unnecessarily bellicose, became widely known among the Iraqi insurgents and other anti-American elements in the region.

Indeed, "bring 'em on" came at a time when the prewar concerns voiced by numerous experts about insufficient planning for the occupation were proving prescient. In the summer of 2003, a government-commissioned study found that the serious situation on the ground required a force of about 450,000 (which was close to what General Shinseki had projected before being publicly rebuked by Wolfowitz).

The American capacity to provide security was undermined not just by inadequate troops but also by a lack of political-military coordination and an ill-conceived strategy. Bremer's appointment was paralleled by the designation of Maj. Gen. Ricardo Sanchez as commander of American forces in Iraq. Sanchez and Bremer never established an effective working relationship, a situation aggravated by the peculiar chain of command that had both of them reporting directly to Rumsfeld, and soon the top two Americans in Iraq were barely speaking to one another. Sanchez, moreover, seemed overwhelmed by the deteriorating military situation. He was unable to develop an effective means of combating the insurgents ("not a strategic or political thought," said one American officer), ineffective in working with Iraqis, and preoccupied with trivial matters. The retired army colonel-turned-historian Andrew Bacevich compares Sanchez to another ill-fated American general, one from the Vietnam War: "Historians will remember Sanchez as the William Westmoreland of the Iraq War—the general who misunderstood the nature of the conflict he faced and thereby played into the enemy's hands."

Bremer's questionable policies were made worse by the CPA's chronic mismanagement. He marginalized or dismissed the best-trained and most-experienced professionals, including several State Department men and women of ambassadorial rank, whom Garner had brought to Iraq. They were replaced by loyal Republicans, most of whom were inexperienced; these replacements were thrown into administrative positions, often with responsibility for considerable budgets, for which they were not qualified. A heavy reliance on private contractors further aggravated matters, for in several instances the contractors, too, squandered funds. In a country where the war had disrupted the economy and unemployment was widespread, the contrast between the hardships of most Iraqis and the largesse of the occupiers became conspicuous, if not notorious. The widespread mismanagement was instrumental in the failure of the CPA to rebuild Iraq's economic infrastructure. Most notably, electricity remained in short supply. Disrupted during the fighting, it was not restored to prewar levels (which had been inadequate because of Saddam Hussein's inattention to the infrastructure) because of insufficient funding, CPA inefficiency, and sabotage (a prime illustration of inadequate security). American firms, such as General Electric, which conscientiously tried to fulfill their contracts to rebuild the electrical grid, threatened to leave because of the dangers that their workers faced in just trying to get to their jobs in Baghdad. In this chaotic atmosphere, it was small wonder that CPA became commonly known among Iraqis to mean "Can't Provide Anything."

WITH EVENTS IN IRAQ CONFOUNDING prewar expectations, Bush seized upon the capture of Saddam Hussein to renew the American commitment. On December 13, Bremer announced, "We got him." U.S. soldiers pulled the filthy, disheveled former dictator from an underground hiding place near a farm north of Baghdad. Two days later Bush warned Americans that "terrorists in Iraq remain dangerous. . . . Yet it should now be clear to all that Iraq is on the path to freedom. And a free Iraq will serve the peace and security of America and the world." Indeed, he declared that 2003 had been the "year of accomplishment."

Undermining that claim were events in early 2004 that gave the lie to the justifications for war and contributed to the erosion of America's moral stature. The claim of Iraqi WMD, which had been the rationale for war, began to unravel in late October 2003 when David Kay, who had been named by CIA director George Tennet to head the 1,400-person Iraq

Survey Group (ISG), which was to hunt for stockpiles of weapons, reported to Congress. To the astonishment of the administration, Congress, and the public, Kay stated that, after three months of "remarkable progress," the ISG had found no WMD. When Bush was asked about Kay's conclusions, he skirted the question, saying only that the world was better off without Saddam Hussein. The WMD issue, however, could not be easily dismissed when, in January 2004, Kay reported that, with the work of the ISG nearly completed, the alleged WMD stockpiles did not exist. "We were almost all wrong," Kay said, "and I certainly include myself." Bush called for an investigation of the intelligence failure.

At the same time, Bush never conceded that the war was not justified. On February 8, 2004, Bush appeared on the television program *Meet the Press*. When Tim Russert, after quoting Bush's claims in his war message of March 19, 2003, that intelligence left "no doubt" of Iraq's possession of WMD, asked whether he had led the country to war under false pretense, Bush defended his position: "I expected there to be stockpiles of weapons. We thought he had weapons." He went on to place that assumption within the context of the 9/11 attacks and the knowledge that Saddam Hussein "had used weapons, which meant he had weapons . . . he was funding terrorist groups . . . he was a dangerous man in a dangerous part of the world. . . . I don't think America can stand by and hope for the best from a madman. . . . We [must] deal with those threats before they become imminent." Throughout the program, Bush, in sometimes confusing language, asserted that the absence of WMD, regardless of the faulty intelligence used by the administration, did not undermine the necessity of war.

While Bush was defending the war, Powell, who had staked his reputation on the claims of the WMD threat in his famed United Nations speech, was publicly questioning the justification of war. The renowned Powell's doubt attracted wide attention around the world and plainly annoyed Bush, Cheney, and the neoconservatives to whom Powell's apostasy provided evidence of his determination to put the protection of his image above the interest of the administration. Powell told reporters that he was "absolutely convinced" the invasion had been justified, defining the threat to American security in terms of Iraqi intent and capabilities; Saddam Hussein had been on the verge of "breaking free" and reconstituting lethal programs. From the White House perspective, so far, so good. Then, when asked if he would have recommended an invasion had the CIA told him there were no stockpiles, Powell replied:

"I don't know because it was the stockpiles that presented the final little piece that made it more of a real and present danger and threat to the region and to the world." After observing that intelligence agencies all assumed that the stockpiles existed, Powell concluded: "The absence of a stockpile changes the political calculus. It changes the answer you get to the little formula I laid out." So without saying so explicitly, Powell disassociated himself from the justification for war. Within a few hours, Rice was admonishing him to "get on board."

The realization that the vaunted WMD were nonexistent made the other justifications for war more significant. By early 2004, the vision of a democratic Iraq emerging from the ashes of the Saddam Hussein regime evaporated as the insurgency brought chaos to much of Iraq. It was no longer possible to talk of the insurgency as a "last gasp" of the old regime. Now strongly anti-American Sunni groups attacked U.S. forces through suicide bombings, car bombs, and other deadly means, and clashes between Shiites and Sunnis spiraled, making a mockery of claims that ethnic and religious groups were coming together. The fledgling Iraqi Army and police were undermined by differences among Sunnis, Shiites, and Kurds—each group with its own political objectives that did not give priority to Iraqi unity.

The American inability to control the chaotic situation became brutally evident in the spring of 2004, when an ambush of U.S. security guards in the city of Fallujah was followed by graphic television pictures of their mutilated bodies. Meanwhile, a six-thousand-man Shiite militia led an insurrection against the U.S. military presence in Sadr City, a part of Baghdad. In these and other clashes, the Iraqi Army performed poorly not just because of inadequate training but because it reflected the divisions within Iraqi society. Shiites refused to fight against Shiite militias, while many Sunnis refused to fight on behalf of a predominantly Shiite-Kurdish army and its American supporter. The Kurdish army, known as the *peshmerga*, of which six thousand men were contributed to the Iraqi Army, was the sole effective fighting force and the only one that was pro-American. But the Kurds had little loyalty to the Iraqi national army and were inclined to fight only when the interests of Kurdistan were at stake. Moreover, the Kurds were viewed with suspicion by the Sunnis as the political allies of the Shiites and the Americans, so Sunnis never trusted them as fellow "Iraqi" soldiers.

The third rationale for war—the "link" of Saddam Hussein to al-Qaeda and other Islamic extremists—was, like WMD, undermined by the lack of evidence. In June 2004, the bipartisan National Commission on Terrorist Attacks on the United States, established in the aftermath of the 9/11 attacks—commonly called the 9/11 Commission—released its report. It concluded that, while al-Qaeda had some contacts with Saddam Hussein's government, there was no evidence of a "collaborative operational relationship." Referring specifically to the claim of Cheney and others of a meeting in Prague in the Czech Republic between Osama bin Laden's lieutenant, Mohamed Atta, and an intelligence agent of Saddam Hussein, the 9/11 Commission stated that such a meeting had never taken place. There was an irony to the lack of prewar Iraqi connection with extremists for, within a matter of a few months, American intelligence agencies reported that the U.S. invasion had turned Iraq into a breeding ground for a new generation of Islamic extremist terrorists, thousands of whom were drawn to Iraq from other countries in the region.

As the justifications for war unraveled, America's mission in Iraq, and its moral stature throughout the world, was tarnished by the Abu Ghraib military prison scandal. In April 2004, the journalist Seymour Hersh, who had broken the story of the My Lai massacre during the Vietnam War, and the television programs *Nightline* and *Sixty Minutes* revealed that Americans had engaged in "sadistic, blatant, and wanton criminal abuses" of Iraqi prisoners. Abu Ghraib, which was located west of Baghdad and had been a notorious center of torture and killing under Saddam Hussein's regime, had been taken over by the American military to house captured Iraqis. Most embarrassing to the military leadership and most disturbing to Americans and people throughout the world were several dozen photographs—shown on television, on the Internet, and in the print media—of young American soldiers humiliating, degrading, and torturing Iraqi prisoners. Hersh describes the images:

> In one photograph, Private [Lynndie] England, a cigarette dangling from her mouth, is giving a jaunty thumbs-up sign and pointing at the genitals of a young Iraqi, who is naked except for a sandbag over his head, as he masturbates. Three other hooded and naked Iraqi prisoners are shown, hands reflexively crossed over their genitals. A fifth prisoner has his hands at his sides. In another, England stands arm in arm with Specialist [Charles] Graner, both are grinning and giving the thumbs-up behind a cluster of perhaps seven naked Iraqis, knees bent, piled clumsily on top of each other in a pyramid. There is another photograph of a cluster of naked prisoners, again piled in a pyra-

mid. Near them stands Graner, smiling, his arms crossed; Specialist Sabrina Harman stands in front of him and she too is smiling. Then there is another cluster of hooded bodies, with a female soldier standing in front, taking photographs. Yet another photograph shows a kneeling, naked, unhooded male prisoner, head turned away from the camera, posed to make it appear that he is performing oral sex on another male prisoner, who is naked and hooded.

Never had the United States suffered a more devastating blow to its claim of being a moral force in the world. The Bush administration hunkered down and blamed the crisis on an irresponsible media that exaggerated the actions of a few young soldiers in an otherwise upstanding army. Wolfowitz lashed out at journalists for misreporting the war generally and Abu Ghraib in particular, and Gen. Richard Myers, chairman of the JCS, lambasted coverage of Abu Ghraib in leading newspapers and on CNN; on the other hand, Cheney praised the reporting on the Fox network, which dutifully criticized the coverage on other news channels. Civilian leaders also contended that the Abu Ghraib incident was the action of men and women who did not reflect the military as a whole. Indeed, the official investigations fixed blame on the group of low-ranking soldiers and Brig. Gen. Janis Karpinski, who commanded all prisons in Iraq. To many observers, Karpinski had been made a scapegoat for the scandal, and other high-ranking officers, including Sanchez, who shared in responsibility for failing to act on early reports of the Abu Ghraib abuses, were unfairly exonerated. More generally, it seemed to many critics of the Bush administration that the incident grew out of a post-9/11 military culture, with its origins in the White House and Pentagon, which encouraged the brutal mistreatment of prisoners.

Still another casualty was the much-heralded "coalition of the willing." A defense analyst observed that the coalition partners "lacked the cohesion needed to respond effectively to the uprising." That had much to do with the hurried and superficial nature of the coalition. Aside from Great Britain, members had joined with the understanding that their troops would not be engaged in combat and would serve a peacekeeping function once the war was won. Instead, they were called upon to deal with insurgents, which nearly all refused to fight (some units being expressly forbidden by their governments to engage in combat). The commander of the 1,300-man Spanish unit complained: "We came for . . . security and stabilization operations. It has never happened. . . . All of a sudden, against our will, we find ourselves in the combat zone." By May

2004, Spain had withdrawn its forces. Units of only a handful of coalition members even went on patrols. One CPA official put it succinctly: "Except for the Brits, they're not there to fight." Having promised a peacekeeping operation that it could not deliver and then chastising members of the "coalition of the willing" for refusing to engage in combat, the United States lost stature with its partners. Marek Belka, the prime minister of Poland, said of the occupation: "It failed totally. Many mistakes, major mistakes, have been committed." Perhaps the best epitaph on the "coalition of the willing" was provided by a U.S. Marine colonel, who said: "The real 'coalition of the willing' that was in Iraq was the one of international jihadists flocking to Iraq to fight the Americans. These are people willing to fight.'"

In this situation, where a discredited American mission could provide neither security nor basic services, Bremer set out to reconstruct the Iraqi government. Operating against the Bush administration's deadline of June 30, 2004—four months before the American presidential election—to end the occupation and transfer authority to an Iraqi government, Bremer revealed both a distrust of the capacity of Iraqis to govern themselves and the conviction that his policies were in fact achieving national unity. At first, he was dismissive of the seven-member Iraqi Leadership Council, which had been established by Garner, as being insufficiently representative; when its members, who distrusted Bremer, ignored his request that they add more members, he appointed eighteen new members (thus minimizing whatever character it had as representing Iraqi interests) and renamed it the Iraqi Governing Council. To accommodate Bush's insistence on a transitional government, Bremer devised a complicated scheme of caucuses, which gave the United States indirect control over the Governing Council as it fulfilled its responsibility to write an interim constitution.

In an elaborate signing ceremony on March 8, 2004 (one designed to evoke comparisons with the constitutional convention of 1787), the CPA and Governing Council formally approved the interim constitution. Its provisions facilitated the development of a political alliance between the Shiites and Kurds to control the country. This left the Sunnis resentful of the Americans, who seemed determined, given Bremer's two orders of May 2003 and other actions, to deprive them of any political power. The Shiite-Kurdish alliance was one of convenience and did not reflect a common vision of Iraq's future: the majority Shiites sought political dominance, many envisioning an Islamic state; the Kurds wanted to preserve their control of Kurdistan. Despite the hurried and superficial political arrangements, Bremer proclaimed his mission fulfilled and announced that authority would be transferred on June 30, 2004, to an interim government headed by Ayad Alawi as prime minister. In a telling finalé to his duty in Iraq, Bremer secretly handed over power two days earlier than announced to assure that insurgents would not disrupt a formal ceremony. Bremer then departed Baghdad stealthily, with no ceremony at the airport; he appeared to depart on one aircraft only to be taken surreptitiously by helicopter to another plane to confound any potential suicide bombers. A CPA member spoke for many Americans on the scene: "This was embarrassing. He left Iraq in such an appropriate way, running out of town." Another CPA official, who thought highly of Bremer for his hard work, commitment, and sound instincts, provided perhaps the best analysis of his mission:

> Put bluntly, CPA never got on top of it, and they did not do their job to a passing grade level. . . . [Bremer] took bad advice and acted on it on a couple of big issues, and failed to see that he needed to clean out his staff. . . . [I]n the end you've got to hold him accountable and say, "Guess what: You guys did not get the job done."

Bremer's mission left behind the political framework that would be the basis of whatever emerged in the way of a new Iraqi government. With Bremer's departure, John Negroponte, a career diplomat who had been ambassador to the United Nations, became ambassador to Iraq, and Gen. George Casey replaced Sanchez as commander of U.S. forces. Negroponte and Casey, unlike Bremer and Sanchez, worked effectively together, and the presence of a career diplomat assured State Department involvement in policymaking.

The transfer of power notwithstanding, the deteriorating situation on the ground troubled several senior military officers. In September, Gen. William Odom, who had headed the National Security Agency under President Ronald Reagan, criticized a failing mission: "Bush hasn't found the WMD, Al Qaeda, it's worse, he's lost on that front. That he's going to achieve a democracy there? That goal is lost, too. It's lost. . . . Right now, the course we're on, we're achieving Bin Laden's ends." Retired Gen. Richard Hoare, the former marine commandant who had headed the U.S. Central Command, went further: "The idea that this is going to go the way these guys planned is ludicrous. There are no good options." In addition, Farnaz Fassihi, a Middle East correspondent for the *Wall Street*

Journal, wrote of her recent observations in Baghdad: "Despite President Bush's rosy assessments, Iraq remains a disaster. If under Saddam it was a 'potential' threat, under the Americans it has been transformed to 'imminent and active threat,' a foreign policy failure bound to haunt the United States for decades to come." Indeed, Iraq had become, as Fassihi wrote, a "barbaric guerrilla war."

In this atmosphere, Bush became the fourth incumbent president to seek reelection in wartime, the first since Franklin D. Roosevelt in 1944. Bush's approval ratings had dropped nearly 30 points from his "mission accomplished" high, and support for his handling of the war stood at only 45 percent. He enjoyed, however, the advantage of facing an opponent, Senator John Kerry of Massachusetts, who appeared vacillating on many issues, including Iraq. He had voted for the war authorization resolution in 2002, which led to Republican charges of "flip flop" when he later criticized the war. Kerry tried to play from his strength: his record as a decorated soldier in Vietnam. The contrast with Bush's avoidance of Vietnam War service ought to have given Kerry credibility on national security issues. Kerry's active role, after his discharge, in the Vietnam Veterans Against the War harmed him with conservatives and with hawkish fellow veterans, a group of whom engineered the well-funded "Swift Boat Veterans" smear campaign that questioned his war record. While Kerry failed to respond effectively to such charges, Bush hammered away at the importance of seeing through the mission in Iraq and warned that a Democratic victory would lead to abandoning of the country to the terrorists.

Bush benefited from the fact that, despite the insurgency and the revelations regarding the lack of WMD, al-Qaeda's noninvolvement with Saddam Hussein, and the Abu Ghraib abuses, most Americans supported the war even if they did not agree with Bush's handling of it: three-fourths of the public believed that Americans had made life better for Iraqis; more than 60 percent believed that Iraq had been a serious threat to the United States and that Saddam Hussein had "strong links to al Qaeda." On top of that advantage on the war, the Republicans also stressed moral values as a rallying point and a key to getting out the conservative vote on election day. Given all of Bush's advantages, what is perhaps most striking is that he won the popular vote by only 51 percent to 48 percent and the electoral vote by 286-251. The latter count and the distribution of "red" and "blue" states were almost identical with the results of the 2000 election.

In the aftermath of the election, Bush reshuffled his national security team in ways that strengthened the position of the neoconservatives. Powell was dismissed as secretary of state, thus eliminating a prominent, if rarely effective, voice of restraint. Powell's stature had been important in gaining support for the war at home and abroad, but Bush, Cheney, and Rumsfeld had always resented Powell and, with Bush reelected, Powell was no longer needed politically. As one prominent Republican said, "Colin has been used." Rice left the position of national security adviser to replace Powell, bringing with her to the State Department a reputation for deferring to Cheney and Rumsfeld. As national security adviser, Bush turned to Rice's former deputy Stephen Hadley, who was close to Cheney. Porter Goss, a former Republican congressman, replaced George Tenet as CIA director. Goss immediately made it clear that the CIA was not to provide independent intelligence estimates; he stated that the agency's function was "to support the administration and its policies in our work."

Shortly after Bush was inaugurated for his second term, the United States achieved a significant milestone in Iraq. On January 30, 2005, millions of Iraqis, defying threats of violence, went to the polls in elections for a national assembly. In his State of the Union address three days later, an exuberant Bush proclaimed that the corner had been turned in Iraq and beyond; the policy of the United States was the promotion "of democratic movements and institutions in every nation and culture, with the ultimate goal of ending tyranny in the world." The determination of Iraqis to vote was undeniably inspiring, but the election was not representative for, while the majority of Shiites voted in large numbers, the Sunnis, reflecting their resentment of American occupation policy, largely boycotted the election. They remained alienated as the elections resulted in a Shiite-dominated government under Prime Minister Nuri Kamal al-Maliki.

Indeed, the Sunni insurgency intensified, increasingly targeting the general population as well as American forces. The weeks after the election were marked by unprecedented bloodshed, as gunmen, car bombs, and suicide bombings took hundreds of lives in attacks on busses, in marketplaces, at Shiite mosques and religious festivals, and on other random targets. As the fighting continued throughout 2005, the United States redoubled efforts to train Iraqi security forces—to "stand up" so Americans could "stand down"—but this amounted in practice to equipping and training Shiites who saw the American-supplied weapons as useful for fighting against the Sunnis. As Craig Unger writes in *The Fall of the House of Bush*, "Unwittingly, America was spending billions of dollars to fuel a Sunni-Shi'ite civil war."

As the fighting in Iraq spread throughout the country and American-Iraqi forces proved incapable of providing security, the war divided Americans to an extent reminiscent of the "coming apart" years generated by the Vietnam War. Like the Johnson administration forty years earlier, the Bush administration proclaimed that American forces were making progress and victory was on the horizon. In May 2005, Cheney, speaking on CNN's *Larry King Live*, foresaw that the "level of activity that we see today, from a military standpoint . . . will clearly decline. I think that they're in the last throes, if you will, of the insurgency." Yet the insurgent attacks continued, and by the end of the following month, the total number of American deaths in Iraq reached seventeen hundred. In the midst of daily insurgent attacks, Baghdad suffered from shortages of electricity and drinking water; outside the Green Zone—which was the headquarters of American operations and the Iraqi government—security was nonexistent. The former interim prime minister, Ayad Allawi, who had welcomed the American invasion, was disillusioned; he said that "the problem is that the Americans have no vision on how to go about in Iraq."

The support that had carried Bush to reelection evaporated. By August 2005, Bush's overall approval rating had dropped to 38 percent. Regarding his handling of the war, it stood at 34 percent—about the same level as Johnson's Vietnam War approval rating after the Tet offensive of 1968. Bush's response to the loss of support differed from that of Johnson. Although Johnson had allowed himself to be seen as overwhelmed by an indecisive and unpopular war, had indulged in self-pity that blamed others for his plight, and had finally (if begrudgingly) accepted the imperative of disengagement, Bush remained serenely self-confident that the mission in Iraq was justified and was bound to succeed and that history would judge him favorably. Bush, in a revealing 2007 interview with the conservative *New York Times* columnist David Brooks, spoke of his unconquerable faith that he was part of a Divine-guided history moving humanity toward democracy. "It's more of a theological perspective," Bush said. "I do believe that there is an Almighty, and I believe a gift of that Almighty to all is freedom. And I will tell you that is a principle that no one can convince me that doesn't exist." Complementing that faith was Bush's conviction in the power of leadership to transform societies. Energized by the presidency, Bush retained a capacious view of the position and its possibilities and thrived on the exercise of leadership. As Brooks observes, "If Bush's theory of history is correct, the right security plan can lead to safety, the right political compromise to stability."

Bush's certainty in what he saw as his role in history accounts for his evident obliviousness to unfavorable information. David Kay, for instance, was perplexed by Bush's reaction when he briefed him and other high-ranking officials on the ISG's report that no WMD had been uncovered: "I cannot stress too much that the president was the one in the room who was the least unhappy and the least disappointed about the lack of WMDs. I came out of the Oval Office uncertain as to how to read the president. Here was an individual who was oblivious to the problems created by the failure to find WMDs." Speculating about the reasons for Bush's behavior, Kay suggested what seems the correct explanation: "Or was this an individual who was completely at peace with himself on the decision to go to war, who didn't question that, and who was totally focused on the here and now of what was to come?"

The chaotic situation in Iraq and the erosion of support for the war at home led to an initiative unprecedented in American history: the establishment in wartime of a bipartisan commission to advise the president on how to end the war. The fact that the necessity for the Iraq Study Group was widely accepted within the foreign policy elite and by both political parties was as important as its recommendations. The ISG underscored the extent to which Bush's war strategy was failing. Co-chaired by James Baker, the former secretary of state and Bush family confidante, and Lee Hamilton, a former Democratic congressman who had long served on the Foreign Affairs Committee in the House of Representatives, the ten-person ISG represented a cross-section of the country's most prominent foreign policy leaders.

The eighty-nine-page ISG report, released on December 6, 2006, portrayed a "grave and deteriorating state of affairs." The Iraq government lacked credibility among non-Shiites for it "is basically sectarian, and key players too often act in their sectarian interest." The police units "cannot control crime, and they routinely engage in sectarian violence, including the unnecessary detention, torture, and targeted execution of Sunni Arab civilians." The Iraqi Army lacked equipment, adequate training, and competent leadership. Moreover, ethnic differences undermined its capacity to unify the country: "Significant questions remain about the ethnic composition and loyalty of some Iraqi units—specifically, whether they will carry out missions on behalf of national goals instead of a sectarian agenda." Iraq's police force was no better, for its Shiite-dominated units "cannot control crime, and they routinely engage in sectarian violence, including the unnecessary detention, torture, and targeted execution of Sunni Arab civilians." The ISG report made seventy-nine recommendations, the most pertinent calling for (1) an expanded U.S. training program of Iraqi Army and national police that would enable the withdrawal of American forces by early 2008; (2) a Middle Eastern diplomatic initiative, including overtures to involve Iran and Syria, to reduce problems within Iraq, and to promote stability in the region; and (3) the deferral of U.S. aid until the Iraqi government met specific timetables for establishing a stable, representative democracy.

The ISG report was criticized on several points, including its refusal to acknowledge what many observers considered to be a "civil war" (the phrase never appears in the report) and a corresponding tendency to downplay the depth of the ethnic differences, especially the degree of Kurdish alienation. Moreover, many recommendations seemed irrelevant (notably proposed initiatives to deal with other Middle Eastern issues), misguided, or unattainable. Training more security forces did nothing to resolve ethnic differences within those units; in fact, it could make those differences even more lethal. Pursuing regional diplomacy ignored the fact that Iran and Syria benefited from America's being bogged down in Iraq and assumed that Iran in particular could be persuaded to reduce its historic interest in Iraq resulting from its affinity with fellow Shiites. Establishing benchmarks for the Iraqi government underestimated the impediments to a national "Iraqi" state. The uncritical acceptance of the Maliki government was difficult to reconcile with the ISG's dismay over his leadership when it had visited Baghdad in August. To Hamilton, Maliki "didn't give the appearance of being a confident, decisive leader." In meetings with members of Maliki's cabinet, the ISG found them illequipped to do jobs and profoundly divided along sectarian lines; they were not representative of the "unity government" that the Bush administration had been extolling. Most striking was that, after the ISG report was released, Iraqi groups, in a rare instance of political agreement, all found it objectionable: the Kurds feared the loss of their autonomy, the Shiites saw the "benchmarks" as unnecessarily accommodating the Sunnis, and the Sunnis found it difficult to accept any U.S. plan for the country's future.

Still, the ISG's acknowledgment of the conditions in Iraq and its recommendations, regardless of their flawed reasoning and shortcomings, constituted a major challenge to Bush's policy. During their deliberations, the ISG had met several times with Bush, who came across as more upbeat about the situation than the facts justified and (as one ISG member put it) determined to "convince us that we should be writing a report that would reflect *his* views." To the ISG, Bush expressed his conviction that history would judge the war a success and that his reputation, like that of Harry Truman, would improve with the perspective of time.

By December, stung by the Republican losses in the congressional elections that gave Democrats control of both the Senate and the House of Representatives and the criticism in the ISG report, Bush acknowledged that the time had come to reconsider strategy, but he treated the ISG recommendations with indifference. Perhaps any president, jealous of his prerogatives, would have been reticent to listen to a bipartisan report that was based on the assumption that his policy was failing. But presidents, especially one of Bush's self-confidence (so evident in his meetings with the ISG), do not *expect* to fail. It would have been entirely out of character for Bush to have embraced the ISG recommendations. So Bush changed strategy in a way that ignored the thrust of the ISG report.

Bush's principal initiative was to increase the number of U.S. forces by thirty thousand—a "surge"—intended to provide security. Increasing troops was an option that the ISG had specifically rejected as a recommendation, and that decision had been based on its meetings with U.S. military commanders in Iraq. When asked about more troops, General Casey had been emphatic: "We don't need it. You're not going to win this war at the point of a bayonet. You'll only win it when you meet the Iraqi people's basic needs—water, electricity, sanitation, jobs." One ISG member, former Defense Secretary William Perry, was so surprised by the commanders' views that he interviewed them individually, and they repeated the sentiment: more troops were not the solution to sectarian bloodshed. (Despite its rejection of more troops as a formal recommendation, the ISG had written in the text of its report a statement on which Bush and other officials seized: "We could, however, support a short-term redeployment or surge of American combat forces to stabilize Baghdad, or to speed up the training and equipping mission, if the U.S. commanders in Iraq believe that such steps would be effective." In a meeting with Bush after the release of the ISG report, Baker referred the president to this obscure sentence on page 73.) So Bush, in announcing the "surge," could relate it to the ISG, and his spokesmen could claim, however implausibly, adherence to the spirit of the ISG recommendations.

As military and civilian critics of the occupation understood, the political outcome of Operation IRAQI FREEDOM will ultimately depend on the Iraqis themselves. The American capacity to influence developments is limited. Bush's initiatives in early 2007 underscore the problems of trying to balance political forces without intensifying ethnic differences. The "surge" seemed to contribute to greater stability, with civilian deaths estimated to be down by 60 percent in 2007; the year was also the most deadly of the war for Americans, with 899 troops killed, bringing the total to 3,902 since the war began in March 2003. The cost of the war approached $400 billion.

Besides the influence of the additional U.S. troops, two critical developments reduced the level of fighting and civilian casualties. The main Shiite militia, al-Sadr's Mahdi Army, imposed upon themselves a cease-fire, and a large number of Sunnis, with American support, took action against extremist strongholds. The Sunni initiative was known as the Awakening, which Gen. David Patreaus, who became commander of U.S. forces, made the cornerstone of a pacification campaign. Throughout predominantly Sunni areas, "awakening councils," which claimed seventy thousand members, many of whom had fought earlier against the Americans, now joined Americans in fighting al-Qaeda and other extremists. To guard against "awakening council" members changing sides later, the Iraqi government—with American prodding and funding—offered them incentives: a promise of incorporation into the main Iraqi security force or army (expected not to exceed 20% of the "awakening" members) or job training through a joint American-Iraqi program.

The Awakening posed several problems. The Shiite-dominated government became wary of, and in some instances hostile to, a movement that armed Sunnis, who might turn against the government. Earlier in Afghanistan, Americans had bought the superficial loyalty of tribal leaders only to learn that they later turned against the central government and gravitated back toward the Taliban once American money ended. Col. Martin Stanton, chief of reconciliation and engagement for Multinational Corps–Iraq, said Americans had no illusions about the motivation of Sunnis joining the Awakening; as he observed, these were people who were being hammered by al-Qaeda and the Americans and who had to make a distasteful choice between the Americans, whom they still regarded as invaders, and the extremists. Americans on the scene, too, are wary. As America transfers more authority, its influence is bound to lessen. Maj. Gen. John E. Allen, deputy commander in Anbar Province, warned that "it's the case with any franchise organization. Sooner or later you lose control over the standards." The Awakening has caused problems in the U.S. relationship with the Iraqi government, whose leaders see it as dominated by former Sunni insurgents who have no loyalty to the government. The Awakening was a risky initiative. The United States was empowering a group of unelected leaders with the hope of integrating them into a democratic system new to them and creating a bond with a government that they see as working for the interests of Shiites and Iran.

The fragile security within Iraq led the Iraqi foreign minister to suggest in early 2008 that U.S. forces would be needed for another decade. Regardless of the duration of the American occupation, history suggests that Iraqis, whether united or divided, will determine the ultimate outcome of Bush's war.

Conclusion

Four Presidents and Their Wars

HARRY TRUMAN, LYNDON JOHNSON, and George H. W. Bush took the United States to war for similar reasons. Each acted to maintain a regional balance of power. George W. Bush's objective, however, was transformational: to disarm and overthrow Saddam Hussein's government and to establish a democracy in Iraq that would inspire political change throughout the Middle East. Thus, the thinking and calculations that guided the decision for war in 2003 differed fundamentally from those that led to the decisions of 1950, 1965, and 1991.

In the first three wars, Truman, Johnson, and Bush I were first and foremost convinced that military intervention against North Korea, North Vietnam, and Iraq was necessary to uphold international order. Failure to respond to acts of "aggression," they believed, would have resulted in the erosion of a stable world. In this way of thinking, the governments that Americans were protecting or restoring—South Korea, South Vietnam, Kuwait—were not critical to the United States per se (their loss alone would not have directly undermined American political-economic power), but rather their importance was derived from being part of the fabric of an international order that was considered fundamental to the security of the United States. In the Korean and Vietnam conflicts, U.S. intervention was intended to halt not just the communist armies in those countries but the extension of the power and influence of the principal communist powers. The Soviet Union and the Chinese People's Republic were seen as behind the North Koreans and the North Vietnamese, supporting, if not instigating, their expansion. In the Persian Gulf War, American officials calculated that Iraq—if allowed to keep Kuwait—would expand farther and thus undermine Middle Eastern stability, with disastrous consequences for the world's industrial powers.

Second, the preservation of that vital international order, the three presidents believed, depended to a large extent on the projection of American "credibility." Failure to support victims of aggression, it was reasoned, would not only embolden unfriendly powers but cause allies to lose confidence in American leadership. What was at stake was U.S. stature as a world power, a psychological dimension of international relations once described by Dean Acheson, who as secretary of state largely directed the response to the Korean crisis, as the "prestige of the United States . . . the shadow cast by power which is of great deterrent importance." In confronting the crises in Korea and Vietnam, leaders in Washington were convinced that placing American lives, resources, and prestige on the line would demonstrate resolve to vulnerable Asian allies, neutral countries, and the major communist powers. Dean Rusk, who served as assistant secretary of state for Far Eastern affairs during the Korean War and as secretary of state during the Vietnam War, wrote in 1965 that "the integrity of the U.S. commitment is the principal pillar of peace throughout the world. If that commitment becomes unreliable, the communist world would draw conclusions that would lead to our ruin and almost certainly to a catastrophic war." During the Persian Gulf crisis, intervention was considered essential to establishing American leadership in the post–cold war "new world order." Bush I foresaw that, "when we prevail, there will be a renewed credibility for the United States." So the imperative of upholding "credibility" constituted a fundamental goal of U.S. policy in Korea, Vietnam, and the Persian Gulf.

Third, all three presidents were guided by history, in particular the "lesson of the 1930s." They saw the crises in Korea, Vietnam, and the Persian Gulf as a test of whether democracies could respond to acts of aggression. The failure of the Western democracies in the 1930s to resist the early expansion of Germany, Italy, and Japan had presumably encouraged further aggression and an eventual major war. This "taught" the important lesson of "nipping aggression in the bud," which became a cornerstone of American foreign policy. In their memoirs, both Truman and Bush I wrote that word of aggression in Korea and the Persian Gulf immediately brought to their minds the challenge that the democracies had faced in the 1930s and the consequences of their failure. Johnson likewise saw the struggle in Vietnam as a test of the will and determination of democracies. The "lesson of the 1930s" thus reinforced the assumptions of the importance of upholding international order and American credibility. These three closely related assumptions meant that, in all three cases, presidents went to war convinced that it was essential to preventing a larger conflict.

The decision making in the Bush II White House had a very different context. Bush and his advisers spoke more of changing than of preserving the international order, more of intimidation than of credibility, more of the "lesson" of the Persian Gulf War than of that of the 1930s. This change resulted in part from the impact of the 9/11 attacks and the ensuing

proclamation of a "war on terrorism." The more significant factor, however, was the congruence of Bush's instinctive idealism with the assertive
nationalism of his principal advisers, Vice President Richard Cheney and
Defense Secretary Donald Rumsfeld, and the tenets of the neoconservative ideology. Iraq was the most immediate threat of the "axis of evil"—a
tyrannical regime that Bush I, neoconservatives believed, should have
eliminated in 1991. Allegedly, Iraq was covertly developing, if not maintaining stockpiles of, weapons of mass destruction (WMD) and was an
ally of the al-Qaeda. Containment no longer guided U.S. foreign policy;
waging "preventive war" and building democracy—embodied in the
Bush Doctrine—justified war against Iraq in 2003.

The decisions of Truman, Johnson, Bush I, and Bush II yielded different results. In Korea, the U.S. objective was ultimately achieved and the
prewar division restored but only after the painful and needless inter-
val when Truman permitted an ill-conceived pursuit of unification that
brought the intervention of the Chinese People's Republic. A war that
should have ended within a few months dragged on for three years.

In Vietnam, Johnson saw himself replaying the Korean War, "learning" from its "lesson." In particular, he sought to preserve the division of
the country and, recalling Truman's mistake, he was determined to avoid
any provocation of the major communist powers that would broaden the
war. He thus restricted U.S. warfare. While he managed to keep the war
limited in ways that Truman had not, Johnson dealt with a very different
kind of war than that Truman had faced in Korea. In this "war without
fronts," the Vietnamese communists were a resilient enemy, drawing on
a stable and determined base in North Vietnam, strength in the south,
the ability to largely control the fighting, and boundless supplies of arms,
equipment, and other materiel from the Soviet Union and the Chinese
People's Republic. Johnson searched for the combination of military
power and diplomacy that would conclude the war on acceptable terms,
but instead he found himself mired in a seemingly endless war that divided the people of the United States, destroyed his dream of the Great
Society, and drained the nation's resources.

In the Persian Gulf War, Bush I coordinated military operations with
political objectives. His actions reflected "lessons" that had been learned
from the Korean and Vietnam wars. He secured the only internationally sanctioned and congressionally approved objective: the liberation of
Kuwait. Unlike Truman, he avoided the temptation to expand the war,
which would have risked entangling the United States in intractable po-

litical problems and losing international support and stature in the process.

It became a doctrine of faith among neoconservatives that Bush I's failure to "march to Baghdad" in 1991 had been a mistake. Ironically, Bush II's leadership in the Iraq War floundered as he set about to remedy his father's "failure." The easy military victory was followed by U.S. inability to provide postwar security as Iraq plunged into civil war. Bush II learned that his father's apprehension about an American "occupying army" trying to administer Iraq reflected wisdom, not irresolution, as the neoconservatives had claimed.

In many ways, the differing outcomes were related to the quality of the decision making that took the country into these wars. Truman's decision to intervene in Korea was the most justifiable. All of his advisers, congressional leaders, and an overwhelming consensus of newspaper editorials and columnists agreed that the United States had to act quickly to halt the North Koreans. In the intense atmosphere of 1950, no one questioned that the North Korean invasion challenged U.S. security. Bush I's decision to launch DESERT STORM was less clear-cut, in that Congress and the general public were divided over whether sanctions against Iraq had been given a sufficient test. Differences, however, were only over tactics, not objectives, as the vast majority of Americans strongly supported the liberation of Kuwait. And after Bush I secured congressional backing for the military option, both sides considered the issue settled, and the public came together to support the war.

The decisions for the Vietnam War and the Iraq War were far more problematic. In confronting the intractable problems in Vietnam from November 1963 to July 1965, Johnson was surrounded mostly by civilian and military advisers who shared his conviction that upholding the integrity of South Vietnam was vital to the security of Asia and that U.S. military power, if properly employed, could force North Vietnam to accept the division of the country. He also, however, received conflicting counsel from officials within his administration and influential senators who questioned whether military intervention could prevent the disintegration of South Vietnam, whether the politically chaotic South Vietnam was important to U.S. security, and whether the United States could wage a successful counterinsurgency against a firmly based and determined adversary. In addition, critics turned the "credibility" argument on its head by warning that the United States risked losing international stature by embarking upon what much of the world, including many allies

and neutrals, considered a foolish military venture. Indeed, Johnson, unlike Truman and Bush I, lacked international backing for war. While the
Korean and Persian Gulf wars were waged in the name of the United Nations and justified by U.N. Security Council resolutions, Johnson could
not gain even minimal support from traditional European allies or any
major Asian country.

In the background to the Iraq War, Bush II was surrounded by advisers who supported the use of force against Iraq. The neoconservative
drumbeat for war against Iraq began the day of the 9/11 attacks. In the
Bush administration, no one questioned the assumption that the United
States needed to eliminate Saddam Hussein's regime. Secretary of State
Colin Powell, who was convinced that the United States should secure
international support and avoid unilateral action, was notably more cautious than were other officials. On the issue of WMD, which became the
rationale for war, the administration operated on the never verified assumption that Saddam Hussein had resumed production or possibly had
stockpiles that had never been uncovered by U.N. inspections. On the
postwar occupation, Bush never questioned the simplistic assumptions
of the neoconservatives that Americans would be welcomed as "liberators" and that an Iraqi leadership would emerge to foster a democratic
state. Bush and his advisers, perhaps most notably national security
adviser Condoleezza Rice, failed to consider the concerns of numerous
military and civilian officials who warned that the Pentagon's occupation planning was superficial and notably inattentive to Iraq's history of
ethnic and religious differences. So war was launched in what, despite
the overwhelming military superiority of the United States, was truly a
high-risk situation: perhaps Americans would not uncover WMDs; perhaps the flowering of democracy in the desert would be an illusion.

Adding to Bush's gamble was that, like Johnson in Vietnam, his war
lacked international support. In many ways America's isolation of 2003
was more striking than that of 1965 because of the military-diplomatic
U.N. involvement in Iraq since 1991 and because Bush II, unlike Johnson,
actually sought U.N. support. Bush made the effort, not because he and
most of his advisers believed it essential but because Powell consistently
pushed for working through the United Nations, Congress insisted upon
it as a condition of support for the war resolution, and most Americans
favored a multilateral operation against Iraq. Yet the Bush administration's attitude toward the United Nations underlined defiance rather
than solicitation. Bush's speech to the General Assembly scolded the

United Nations to live up to its disarmament obligations, and Resolution 1441 establishing renewed WMD inspections passed largely because of Powell's diligent diplomacy. When U.N. inspections went forward and Hans Blix reported Iraqi compliance, that no WMD development had been found, and that a few more months were needed to complete the process, Bush refused to delay invasion plans and ordered Powell to present the administration's case against Saddam Hussein to the Security Council. Powell's presentation failed to gain support for war. Never before or since has the United States been more humiliated in the United Nations than when it had to withdraw its Security Council resolution calling for military action against Iraq. Bush pasted together a "coalition of the willing," but it lacked substance and credibility.

Perhaps the key lesson to be drawn from charting the four paths to war is that, when presidents confront conflicting advice on fundamental issues, they need to make certain that the assumptions of policy are subject to a full and systematic debate. Instead, both Johnson and Bush II presided over highly personalized and idiosyncratic decision-making processes. Johnson's at least gave the appearance of thoroughness, but neither he nor Bush II insisted on it. Both presidents were impatient and showed scant concern with advice that challenged their predispositions. And in both cases they inclined toward a military solution as the best way of achieving a quick and decisive victory. From the early months of his administration, Johnson consistently maneuvered for a greater military role, which led inexorably to the open-ended commitment of July 1965. Once the overthrow of the Taliban in Afghanistan signaled a first victory in the "war on terrorism," Bush II pressed the case for war against Iraq. Beginning with the "axis of evil" label in the 2002 State of the Union address and culminating in the Bush Doctrine's rationale for preventive war, Bush left no doubt that he was preparing the country for the showdown with Iraq. Ignoring international opinion and the reservations of many Americans, Bush prepared in early 2003 "to take out this guy." In a sense, both Johnson and Bush II got the wars they deserved.

An integral part of the decisions for war was respect for constitutional processes, which directly affected the credibility of each president as commander in chief. Contrary to the letter and spirit of the Constitution and to traditional presidential respect for Congress's war-making powers, Presidents Truman and Johnson initiated wars without, in the judgment of many constitutional scholars, appropriate congressional authority. And Bush I & II, while seeking such authorization, contended that they did not need it. All four presidents claimed that the commander-in-chief clause provided a constitutional justification for the president to wage war.

Truman's decision to send troops to Korea without any semblance of congressional authorization was the most blatant disregard for the Constitution. During the week when he took the country to war, Truman twice formally consulted—only in the broadest sense of the term—with congressional leaders. Fundamentally, he acted and then informed them of his decisions. He contended that membership in the United Nations obliged the United States to support U.N. Security Council resolutions that called upon members to assist South Korea. As the first troops were being sent, Truman insisted that "we are not at war" and readily accepted the suggestion that intervention was "a police action under the United Nations." Truman never requested explicit congressional authorization, a decision that contributed to the initial ambiguity of the war's objective and to subsequence derisive characterizations of the war as "Mr. Truman's War" and the "police action."

Johnson sought to avoid Truman's mistake, but he did so in ways that brought criticism. In response to the purported clash of American and North Vietnamese ships in the Gulf of Tonkin during August 1964, he requested and gained congressional endorsement of an open-ended resolution authorizing him to use military power as he deemed necessary to "repel further aggression . . . [and] to assist any member or protocol state of the Southeast Asia Collective Defense Treaty requesting assistance in defense of its freedom." Critics subsequently charged Johnson with duplicity in his exaggeration of the incident that provided the pretext for the resolution and his reassurance of the public during the 1964 presidential campaign that Americans would not be sent to fight in Asia while he secretly planned for the large-scale involvement that came a year later. Johnson contended that the Gulf of Tonkin resolution provided all the authority that he needed to Americanize the war. Yet his private questions to advisers about whether he needed further congressional authority in 1965 and later suggest that he was not as confident on the constitutional issue as his public statements claimed.

Presidents Bush I and Bush II most clearly fulfilled their constitutional obligations. Bush I sought and gained explicit congressional authorization to commit U.S. forces to combat if Saddam Hussein failed to withdraw from Kuwait by the United Nations–established deadline date of January 15, 1991. Yet he was criticized for waiting until the last minute to request such approval; with 400,000 U.S. troops poised to attack and the ultimatum only days away, Congress had to debate hurriedly. Moreover, Bush complied reluctantly with the constitutional process, insisting that he did not need congressional authorization and would act without it. He could not, however, ignore the pressure from leaders in both parties, the media, and the public that he should go to Congress. Privately fearing that a prolonged debate or unfavorable outcome would weaken the international coalition and play to Saddam Hussein's advantage, Bush gambled that he could secure support for a war resolution. That proved a sound decision. The slender majorities in Congress effectively ended public debate and contributed to the high level of support for the war.

Bush II likewise gained a congressional resolution to use force against Iraq if it failed to disarm. There were differences, however, in the two presidents' domestic strength and the timing of the resolutions. Unlike his father, Bush II benefited from the fact that war was not controversial in 2002, as it had been in 1991. Public sentiment, strongly influenced by the terrorist attacks of a year earlier and the administration's claims of a link between Saddam Hussein and al-Qaeda, supported using force against the Iraqi dictator. Unlike his father, Bush II sought an early war resolution, insisting on congressional action in October 2002 in part for political reasons; with Democratic Party leaders reticent to challenge the president on an issue of national security, Bush wanted to force a war vote before the congressional elections. The early resolution was also justified as a means of strengthening the U.S. position as it presented its case at the United Nations. As a result, the war resolution of 2002 passed both houses of Congress by substantial majorities.

Once at war, the first three presidents faced the challenge presented by limited wars of asking the public to combine commitment with restraint. The presidents needed popular support, of course, but they had to avoid appeals that would stir demands for "victory" in the conventional sense. Despite their efforts to curtail the emotions of war, each had to respond to calls for "victory," which had some popular appeal given the immense power of the United States compared to that of its three adversaries. Truman, of course, blundered badly on this matter, and his mistake influenced the actions of Johnson and Bush. After the Inchon invasion, Truman moved from an initial "limited" objective and embraced the "victory" option, only to provoke the Chinese intervention that made it a "wholly new war." Afterward, Truman insisted that the war had to be again "limited," and this led to Gen. Douglas MacArthur's open questioning of the restraints that prevented him from unleashing military power against the Chinese People's Republic. His challenge to Truman—"war's very object is victory"—resonated with many Americans. Truman finally gained control over the war only by dismissing the insubordinate MacArthur, but by then the war had terribly divided Americans and his presidency was in disarray.

During the Vietnam War, "hawks" in Congress and the military chafed at presidential limitations and called for unleashing air power and expanding ground operations to achieve what they foresaw as an easily attainable victory. Johnson, almost obsessed with the fear of a larger war, stood his ground. Johnson may have done little that was right in the Vietnam War, but his insistence that the United States not risk a larger war was certainly correct.

In the Persian Gulf War, the liberation of Kuwait did not satisfy some Americans who, stirred in part by Bush I's emotional denunciations of Saddam Hussein, believed that the war should be continued to Baghdad to bring about his overthrow. Bush, who was determined to wage war only so far as it had been authorized by the United Nations and Congress, resisted the call for victory.

In the Iraq War, Bush II faced the problem of dealing with a defeated enemy. Contrary to neoconservative expectations, the Iraqis did not welcome Americans as liberators and no political leadership emerged to provide direction to a post–Saddam Hussein government. With an inadequate number of U.S. troops to provide security, centuries-old ethnic and religious differences plunged the country into civil conflict. The American occupation policy, promulgated by Paul Bremer and strongly influenced by neoconservatives, disbanded the Iraqi Army and security forces and largely eliminated the long-dominant Sunnis from political influence, thus ending the apparatus that had kept Iraq together for eighty years. In June 2004 Bremer turned political authority over to a new Iraqi government based on a coalition of Shiites and Kurds. U.S. forces, however, remained essential for internal stability. The capacity of the new Iraqi government to create a genuinely national state remained problematic.

Last, the wars largely defined each of these presidencies. As the wars in Korea, Vietnam, and Iraq dragged on, Truman, Johnson, and Bush II suffered declining popularity. Truman, who privately had decided not to seek another term before the outbreak of the war in Korea, had lost the confidence of the public by early 1952, when he announced his plans to retire. By that time, less than 30 percent of the public approved of his job as president. Johnson was even more emphatically a political casualty of war. His "approval" ratings precipitously declined, plunging, like those of Truman, to the 30 percent range. Criticized by "doves" for getting involved in Vietnam in the first place and by "hawks" for fighting too cautiously, Johnson was driven from office under the pressures of the tumultuous events of 1968, touched off by the Tet offensive. Bush II likewise lost support, with his approval ratings dropping into the 30–35 percent range as he began his last year in office. The failure to find WMD was devastating to his credibility. Never before had the rationale for an American war been demonstrably false. The persistent bloodshed within Iraq reinforced the misgivings of those who had opposed the war in the first place and led many hawks of 2003 to abandon the war. Bush's only hope for vindication in going to war was that eventually political leadership in Baghdad would be able to bring together the country's warring groups. This would involve political compromise in a country without such a tradition. Democracy seemed a distant goal, political stability perhaps a more realistic expectation.

Among the four presidents, only Bush I gained popularity as he waged a short and successful war. As his approval ratings soared to dizzying heights, Bush I appeared to be invincible politically, leading several prominent Democrats to withdraw from the contest for their party's 1992 presidential nomination and leaving the field to relatively obscure candidates, like Governor Bill Clinton of Arkansas. While the Bush I presidency will be best remembered for the skillful diplomacy and the military brilliance of the Persian Gulf crisis and conflict, the political consequences were deceptive. First, the patriotic fervor stirred by the war inevitably evaporated, contributing to a decline in Bush's popularity. Second, the revival of Iraqi power and Saddam Hussein's warfare against his opponents at home led more Americans to question whether Bush had ended the war too quickly. Third, Bush's very success in the Persian Gulf ultimately worked against him. Many Americans questioned why he failed to bring the same capacity for astute and committed leadership to address the problems of a sluggish economy. This inattention to domestic issues led to Bush's defeat in the 1992 election.

In the cases of Johnson and Bush I, the judgment of history, at least in the short run, parallels that of contemporaries. Both are usually regarded as "average" presidents. Johnson is criticized for waging an ill-conceived war that detracted from his historic civil rights legislation and the Great Society reform program. And Bush I is criticized for an indifference to domestic problems that undermined confidence in his leadership despite the success in the Persian Gulf War and his generally well-regarded diplomacy during the last months of the cold war. Truman's reputation over the years has improved, and he is now typically seen as a "near-great" president. He is given high marks especially for launching the containment policy in Europe. With respect to the Korean War, few scholars question the decisions to intervene and to keep the war limited, but the pursuit of "victory" is universally seen as one of great miscalculations in American history. Likewise, the image of Truman among the public is generally favorable; he is, in fact, far more popular among later generations of Americans than he was among his contemporaries. His reputation as a decisive, straight-talking leader—an image that Truman nurtured until his death in 1972 and that admiring biographers have since cultivated—has earned him much retrospective admiration. The extent to which Korea has become America's "forgotten war" helps Truman's reputation for it helps to obscure his mistakes and indecisiveness as commander in chief and the extent to which the public had lost confidence in his leadership. Bush II has repeatedly compared his presidency to that of Truman and expects that history will one day judge him as well as it now judges Truman.

The history of these wars underlines the importance of presidential leadership. In responding to an unfolding crisis, the president is called upon to relate it to broader national interests, to establish objectives, and to assess the nation's capacity to achieve them. Rarely are answers simple. In searching for decisions, a president is in many ways a "captive": of those whom he has selected as advisers; of the interests and recommendations, often conflicting, of various departments and agencies; of the quality of intelligence generated by the Central Intelligence Agency and other sources. A president must also be sensitive to international pressures and constraints, as well as congressional sentiment and public opinion. As on the battlefield, a "fog" envelops crises. The best that a president can do is to make decisions as "rational" as possible within the framework of the ongoing evidence, options, and recommendations. The quality of his decisions is enhanced by the fullness of his consideration of the assumptions of policy and the options at his disposal. In part, a president's decision is instinctive, as was the decision for war in each of these instances. The prospects for it being seen as a correct decision in the light of history are enhanced by the extent to which instinct is subjected to careful analysis by the president and his advisers. Overall, the quality of a president's leadership depends on sound judgment, having a sense of proportionality, and recognizing the potential and the limits of military power. Whatever faults they may have had, Truman's acceptance of a limited war, Johnson's determined avoidance of a larger war, and Bush I's stopping of a war once its objective had been achieved, were such judgments.

Bibliographical Essay

Introduction

There is a vast literature on the role of the president in taking the United States to war, much of it focusing on constitutional issues. The most authoritative works include Louis Fisher, *Presidential War Power* (Lawrence: University Press of Kansas, 1995); Arthur M. Schlesinger Jr., *The Imperial Presidency* (Boston: Houghton Mifflin, 1973); Edward Keynes, *Undeclared War: Twilight Zone of Constitutional Power* (University Park: Pennsylvania State University Press, 1982); Merlo J. Pusey, *The Way We Go to War* (Boston: Houghton Mifflin, 1969); W. Taylor Reveley III, *War Powers of the President and Congress: Who Holds the Arrows and Olive Branch?* (Charlottesville: University Press of Virginia, 1981); Gary M. Stern and Morton Halperin, eds., *The United States Constitution and the Power to Go to War: Constitutional and International Law Aspects* (Westport, Conn.: Greenwood, 1982); Francis D. Wormuth, Edwin B. Firmage, and Francis P. Butler, *To Chain the Dog of War: The War Powers of Congress in History and Law* (Dallas: Southern Methodist University Press, 1986); Ann Van Wynen Thomas and A. J. Thomas Jr., *The War-Making Powers of the President: Constitutional and International Law Aspects* (Dallas: Southern Methodist University Press, 1982); John Lehman, *Making War: The 200-Year-Old Battle between the President and Congress over How America Goes to War* (New York: Charles Scribner's Sons, 1992); Richard J. Barnet, *The Rockets' Red Glare: When America Goes to War* (New York: Simon & Schuster, 1990); Paul E. Peterson, "The International System and Foreign Policy," and Gordon Silverstein, "Judicial Enhancement of Executive Power," in *The President, the Congress, and the Making of Foreign Policy*, ed. Paul E. Peterson (Norman: University of Oklahoma Press, 1994), 3–45; J. Terry Emerson, "Making War without a Declaration," 17 *Journal of Legislation* 23 (1990); J. Gregory Sidak, "To Declare War," 41 *Duke Law Journal* 27 (1991); William Conrad Gibbons, "The Origins of the War Powers Provisions of the Constitution," in *Congress and United States Foreign Policy: Controlling the Use of Force in the Nuclear Age*, ed. Michael Barnart (Albany: State University of New York, 1987), 9–38.

On broader issues of presidential-congressional differences that relate to war making, the following are useful: Louis Henkin, *Constitutionalism, Democracy, and Foreign Affairs* (New York: Columbia University Press, 1990); Michael J. Glennon, *Constitutional Democracy* (Princeton: Princeton University Press, 1991); Thomas E. Mann, "Making Foreign Policy: President and Congress," and Robert A. Katzman, "War Powers: Toward a New Accommodation," in *A Question of Balance: The President, the Congress, and Foreign Policy,* ed. Thomas E. Mann (Washington: Brookings Institution, 1990), 1–69; John H. Sullivan, "The Impact of the War Powers Resolution," in *Congress and United States Foreign Policy: Controlling the Use of Force in the Nuclear Age,* ed. Michael Barnart (Albany: State University of New York, 1987), 59–76. The issues involved in the deployment of forces overseas are examined by Barry M. Blechman and Stephen S. Kaplan in *Force without War: U.S. Armed Forces as a Political Instrument* (Washington: Brookings Institution, 1978).

Much of the post–Vietnam War literature has been critical of presidential war-making power, and a useful counterpoint is Richard Neustadt's *Presidential Power and the Modern President from Roosevelt to Reagan,* rev. ed. (New York: Maxwell Macmillan, 1990), an updated edition of a significant book first published in 1960. Franklin Roosevelt's leadership in the face of crises in Europe and Asia in 1940–41 influenced the ways in which later presidents defined their powers. For good accounts of his actions, see Waldo Heinrichs, *Threshold of War: Franklin D. Roosevelt and American Entry into World War II* (New York: Oxford University Press, 1988); Robert Dallek, *Franklin D. Roosevelt and American Foreign Policy, 1932–1945* (New York: Oxford University Press, 1979); Robert A. Divine, *The Reluctant Belligerent,* 2d ed. (New York: Knopf, 1979); William L. Langer and S. Everett Gleason, *The Undeclared War, 1940–41* (New York: Harper & Row, 1953).

On the president as commander in chief in America's wars, there are two fine collections of essays: Ernest R. May, ed., *The Ultimate Decision: The President as Commander in Chief* (New York: George Braziller, 1960), which examines the military leadership of wartime presidents through 1960, and Joseph G. Dawson, ed., *Commanders in Chief: Presidential Leadership in Modern Wars* (Lawrence: University Press of Kansas, 1993), which has essays on wartime presidents from McKinley through Nixon. As the preeminent twentieth-century president whose leadership changed the office and influenced his successors, Franklin Roosevelt is the subject of much scholarly attention. To understand his wartime leadership, the following are valuable (in addition to the previously cited Dallek, *Roosevelt and American Foreign Policy):* Warren Kimball, *The Juggler: Franklin Roosevelt as Wartime Statesman* (Princeton: Princeton University Press, 1991); Eric Larrabee, *Commander in Chief* (New York: Harper & Row, 1987); Kent Greenfield, *American Strategy in World War II* (Baltimore: Johns Hopkins Press, 1963); James McGregor Burns, *Roosevelt: The Soldier of Freedom* (New York: Harcourt, Brace, Jovanovich, 1970); Thomas Parrish, *Roosevelt and Marshall: Partners in Politics and War* (New York: William Morrow, 1989).

Chapter 1. Harry S. Truman and the Korean Crisis

The most comprehensive source on the diplomacy of the Korean War generally and for the purposes of this chapter on prewar politics and tensions on the Korean peninsula and origins of the war is William Stueck's *The Korean War: An International History* (Princeton: Princeton University Press, 1995). General histories of the war are included in the bibliography for chapter 2.

Melvyn P. Leffler, *A Preponderance of Power: National Security, the Truman Administration, and the Cold War* (Stanford: Stanford University Press, 1992), and John Lewis Gaddis, *Strategies of Containment: A Critical Appraisal of Postwar American National Security Policy* (New York: Oxford University Press, 1982), are valuable for placing Truman's intervention in Korea within the context of evolving U.S. national security policy. To understand Truman and his administration, Alonzo Hamby's *Man of the People: A Life of Harry S. Truman* (New York: Oxford University Press, 1995), the definitive biography, provides a thoughtful appraisal. Robert H. Ferrell, *Harry S. Truman: A Life* (Columbia: University of Missouri Press, 1994), is also a fair-minded study. David McCullough, *Truman* (New York: Simon & Schuster, 1992), tells the Truman story colorfully but uncritically. Focusing on Truman as president are Donald McCoy, *The Presidency of Harry S. Truman* (Lawrence: University Press of Kansas, 1984); Michael J. Lacey, ed., *The Truman Presidency* (New York: Cambridge University Press, 1989); Robert J. Donovan, *Conflict and Crisis: The Presidency of Harry S. Truman, 1945–1949* (New York: Norton, 1977) and *Tumultuous Years: The Presidency of Harry S. Truman, 1949–1953* (New York: Norton, 1982). Donovan, a journalist, is especially effective at capturing the mood and personalities of the dramatic events of the era.

On the origins of the war in Korea, the following books analyze U.S. policy after 1945 and the political developments on the Korean peninsula: James Matray, *The Reluctant Crusade: American Foreign Policy in Korea, 1941–1950* (Honolulu: University of Hawaii Press, 1985); William Stueck, *The Road to Confrontation: United States Policy toward China and Korea, 1947–1950* (Chapel Hill: University of North Carolina Press, 1981); Charles M. Dobbs, *The Unwanted Symbol: American Foreign Policy, the Cold War, and Korea, 1945–1950* (Kent, Ohio: Kent State University Press, 1981). The scholarship of Bruce Cumings challenges conventional interpretations by stressing the war's Korean origins and the strength nationally of the communist movement. Emphasizing the widespead civil fighting on the Korean peninsula between 1947 and 1950, he contends that the North Koreans had little external backing for their attack of June 1950 and that they enjoyed widespread support when they invaded the south. See Bruce Cumings, *The Origins of the Korean War*, vol. 1, *Liberation and the Emergence of Separate Regimes* (Princeton: Princeton University Press, 1981), and vol. 2, *The Roaring of the Cataract* (Princeton: Princeton University Press, 1990). While not necessarily agreeing with all of Cumings's argument, several scholars have given greater emphasis to the local origins of the warfare and also the influence of major power rivalry. Good examples are John Merrill, *Korea: The Peninsular Conflicts of the War* (Newark: University of Delaware Press, 1989), and Peter Lowe, *Origins of the Korean War*, 2d ed. (New York: Longmans, 1997).

Disagreeing most sharply with Cumings are scholars who reassert the international origins of the war, an argument seemingly enhanced by the selected opening of archival sources of the Chinese People's Republic and the former Soviet Union. William Stueck argues along these lines in *The Necessary War*. The importance of Chinese or Soviet prewar backing of the North Koreans is stressed by several scholars: Sergei Gonncharov, John W. Lewis, and Xue Litai, *Uncertain Partners: Stalin, Mao, and the Korean War* (Stanford: Stanford University Press, 1993); Chen Jian, *China's Road to the Korean War: The Making of the Sino-American Confrontation* (New York: Columbia University Press, 1994); and Kathryn Weathersby, "New Findings on the Korean War," *Bulletin of the Cold War International History Project*, no. 3 (Washington, D.C.: Woodrow Wilson International Center for Scholars, fall 1993), and "The Soviet Role in the Early Phase of the Korean War: New Documentary Evidence," *Journal of American–East Asian Relations* 3 (1994): 1–33. A South Korean criticism of U.S. policy is that American prewar indications that the country would not be defended left them vulnerable; see Kim Chull Baum, "U.S. Policy on the Eve of the Korean War: Abandonment or Safeguard?" in *Korea and the Cold War: Division, Destruction, and Disarmament*, ed. Kim Chull Baum and James Matray (Claremont, Calif.: Regina, 1993), 63–94.

Truman's decisions of June 25–30 were first recounted by Glenn Paige in *The Korean Decision* (New York: Free Press, 1968), which is still useful, although inevitably dated in some respects. The documentary record of the meetings and communications is available in U.S. Department of State, *Foreign Relations of the United States, 1950*, vol. 7 (Washington: GPO, 1976). Pertinent documents at the Harry S. Truman Library are included in volume 18 of the *Documentary History of the Truman Presidency*, ed. Dennis Merrill (Washington: University Publications of America, 1997). After the publication of the State Department documents, Barton J. Bernstein wrote a critical account of Truman's actions: "The Week We Went to War: American Intervention in the Korean Civil War," *Foreign Service Journal* 54, no. 1 (1977): 6–9, 33–35, and "The Week We Went to War: American Intervention in Korea, part II," ibid., no. 2: 8–11, 33–34. Among recent works, Burton Kaufman, *The Korean War: Challenges in Crisis, Credibility, and Command* (Philadelphia: Temple University Press, 1986), and James Matray, "America's Reluctant Crusade: Truman's Commitment of Combat Troops in the Korean War," *Historian* 42 (1980): 437–55, provide substantial accounts, as do the previously cited *Reluctant Crusade* by Matray, *Man of the People* by Hamby, and *Tumultuous Years* by Donovan. The memoirs of Truman and Dean Acheson are also indispensible: Truman, *Memoirs*, vol. 2, *Years of Trial and Hope* (Garden City, N.Y.: Doubleday, 1956); Dean Acheson, *Present at the Creation: My Years in the State Department* (New York: Norton, 1969). Truman's public statements are available in *Public Papers of the Presidents: Harry S. Truman, 1950* (Washington: GPO, 1956).

The Acheson-Truman partnership in making foreign policy is analyzed by Cecil Crabb and Kevin Mulcahy in *Presidents and Foreign Policy Making* (Baton Rouge: Louisiana State University Press, 1986). Ronald McClothen, *Controlling the Waves: Dean Acheson and U.S. Foreign Policy in Asia* (New York: Norton, 1993), examines Acheson's approach toward Asian issues, stressing the priority given to the reconstruction of Japan.

Chapter 2. Harry S. Truman as Commander in Chief

For nearly thirty years after it ended, the Korean War inspired little popular or scholarly interest. This relative neglect resulted in part from the lack of primary sources, as well as from the American preoccupation with the conflict in Vietnam from the mid-1960s to the early 1970s. The standard early history was that of David Rees, *Korea: The Limited War* (New York: St. Martin's, 1964). Two American generals—Matthew B. Ridgway in *The Korean War* (Garden City, N.Y.: Doubleday, 1967) and J. Lawton Collins in *War in Peacetime: The History and Lessons of Korea* (Boston: Houghton Mifflin, 1969)—added insightful histories.

Beginning in the 1980s, writers began reexamining the war. This resulted in part from the availability of previously classified American and British documents. General interest in the Korean War was rekindled by pressures from the war's veterans, who resented the attention given to those who had served in Vietnam, by the ways that the Korean experience seemed instructive in understanding American frustration in Vietnam, and by the depiction of the war in popular culture, especially in the movie and long-running television series, *MASH*. So the 1980s witnessed several important histories of the war, including Max Hastings, *The Korean War* (New York: Simon & Schuster, 1987); Callum A. MacDonald, *Korea: The War before Vietnam* (New York: Free Press, 1987); Clay Blair, *The Forgotten War: America in Korea, 1950–1953* (New York: Times Books, 1987); Donald Knox, *The Korean War: An Oral History* (New York: Harcourt, Brace, Jovanovich, 1985); Donald Knox with Alfred Coppel, *The Korean War: Uncertain Victory* (New York: Harcourt, Brace, Jovanovich, 1988); Joseph C. Goulden, *Korea: The Untold Story of the War* (New York: Times Books, 1982); Bruce Cumings and Jon Halliday, *Korea: The Unknown War* (London: Viking, 1988).

The basic record of Truman's leadership can be traced through the documents published in the Department of State's *Foreign Relations of the United States (FRUS)* volumes pertaining to the Korean War: *FRUS 1950*, vol. 7 (Washington: GPO, 1976); *FRUS 1951*, vol. 7 (Washington: GPO, 1983); *FRUS 1952–1954*, vol. 15 (Washington: GPO, 1984). Volumes 19 and 20 of the *Documentary History of the Truman Presidency*, ed. Dennis Merrill (Washington: University Publications of America, 1997), add materials from the Harry S. Truman Library. The Office of Historical Division of the Joint Chiefs of Staff produced two volumes on the Joint Chiefs's role during the war: James F. Schnabel and Robert Watson, *The History of the Joint Chiefs of Staff: The Joint Chiefs of Staff and National Policy*, vol. 3, *The Korean War* (Wilmington, Del.: Scholarly Resources, 1979); Walter S. Poole, *The History of the Joint Chiefs of Staff: The Joint Chiefs of Staff and National Policy*, vol. 4, *1950–1952* (Wilmington, Del.: Scholarly Resources, 1979). The memoirs of Truman and Acheson and the Truman biographies by Hamby, Donovan, Ferrell, and McCullough, all cited in the bibliography for chapter 1, enhance understanding of the Truman presidency during the war. Truman's public statements regarding the war are included in *Public Papers of the Presidents: Harry S. Truman, 1945–1953*, vols. 6–8 (Washington: GPO, 1956–60).

The U.S. decisions to cross the thirty-eighth parallel and to reject calls for military restraint afterward are analyzed in several works including Stueck, *Korean War*, and Kaufman, *Korean War* (both cited in the section on chapter 1); James Matray, "Truman's Plan for Victory: National Self-Determination and the Thirty-Eighth Parallel Decision in Korea," *Journal of American History* 66 (1979): 314–33, Rosemary Foot, *The Wrong War: American Policy and the Dimensions of the Korean Conflict* (Ithaca: Cornell University Press, 1985); Rosemary Foot, "Anglo-American Relations in the Korean Crisis: The British Effort to Avert an Expanded War, December 1950–January 1951," *Diplomatic History* 10 (1986): 43–57; Peter Farrar, "Britain's Proposal for a Buffer Zone South of the Yalu in November 1950," *Journal of Contemporary History* 18 (1983): 327–51.

The conventional and still valuable study of China's intervention is Allen S. Whiting's *China Crosses the Yalu: The Decision to Enter the Korean War* (New York: Macmillan, 1960). The opening over the last decade of selected Chinese documents, however, has broadened knowledge of China's interests, decision making, and relations with the Soviet Union and North Korea. See Zhai Zhihai and Hao Yufan, "China's Decision to Enter the Korean War: History Revisited," *China Quarterly* 121 (1990); Chen Jian, "The Sino-Soviet Alliance and China's Entry into the Korean War," Cold War International History Project Working Paper, no. 1 (Washington, D.C.: Woodrow Wilson International Center for Scholars, 1992); Jonathon Pollack, *Into the Vortex: China, the Sino-Soviet Alliance, and the Korean War* (Stanford: Stanford University Press, 1990); Russell Spurr, *Enter the Dragon: China's Undeclared War against the U.S. in Korea* (New York: Henry Holt, 1988); Jian Chen, "China's Changing Aims during the Korean War, 1950–51," *Journal of American–East Asian Relations* 1 (1992): 8–41; Warren Cohen, "Conversations with Chinese Friends: Zhou Enlai's Associates Reflect on Chinese-American Relations in the 1940s and the Korean War," *Diplomatic History* 11 (1987): 286–92; He Di, "The Most Respected Enemy: Mao Zedong's Perception of the United States," *China Quarterly* 137 (1994): 144–58; Michael H. Hunt, "Beijing and the Korean Crisis, June 1950–June 1951," *Political Science Quarterly* 107 (1992): 453–78; Zhang Shuguaung, "'Preparedness Eliminates Mishaps': The CCP's Security Concerns in 1949–1950 and the Origins of Sino-American Confrontation," *Journal of American–East Asian Relations* 1 (1992): 42–72. Two works listed in the section on chapter 1—Gornncharov, Lewis, and Latai in their *Uncertain Partners* and Chen Jian in *China's Road to the Korean War*—are also valuable in providing context for China's intervention.

Zhang Shu Guang, *Mao's Military Romanticism: China and the Korean War, 1950–1953* (Lawrence: University Press of Kansas, 1995), provides the fullest account of China's overall warfare in Korea. Another account of the war after China's intervention is Edwin P. Hoyt's *The Day the Chinese Attacked, Korea 1950: The Story of the Failure of America's China Policy* (New York: McGraw-Hill, 1990). China's intervention and the subsequent warfare with the United States are cast within the broader context of Sino-American tensions in the following works: Gordon Chang, *Friends and Enemies: China, the United States, and the Soviet Union, 1948–1972* (Stanford: Stanford University Press, 1990); Zhang Shu Guaung, *Deterrence and Strategic Culture: Chinese-American Confrontation, 1949–1958* (Ithaca: Cornell University Press, 1992); Zhai Qiang, *The Dragon, the Lion, and the Eagle: Chinese-British-American Relations, 1949–1958* (Kent, Ohio: Kent State University Press, 1994); Harry Harding and Yuan Ming, eds., *Sino-American Relations, 1945–1955: A Joint Reassessment of a Critical Decade* (Wilmington, Del.: Scholarly Resources, 1989).

The differences over U.S. strategy, which came to center on the clash between Truman and MacArthur, were the subject of a contemporary study by Arthur M. Schlesinger Jr. and Richard H. Rovere, *The General and the President* (New York: Farrar, Straus, & Giroux, 1951), and, a few years later, by the more thorough work of John Spanier, *The Truman-MacArthur Controversy and the Korean War* (New York: Norton, 1959). In his memoir, *Reminiscences* (New York: McGraw-Hill, 1964), MacArthur defended his position. Biographies of MacArthur include Michael Schaller, *MacArthur: Far Eastern General* (New York: Oxford University Press, 1989), which is sharply critical of MacArthur, and D. Clayton James, *The Years of MacArthur*, vol. 3, *Triumph and Disaster* (Boston: Houghton Mifflin, 1985), which is more sympathetic toward its subject, although by no means uncritical. The Truman-MacArthur controversy is explored as part of overall strategic differences and decisions by D. Clayton James with Anne Sharp Wells in *Refighting the Last War: Command and Crisis in Korea, 1950–1953* (New York: Free Press, 1993). How the war affected the home front is explored by Ronald J. Caridi in *The*

Korean War and American Politics: The Republican Party as a Case Study (Philadelphia: University of Pennsylvania Press, 1968) and John Wilz, "The Korean War and American Society," in *The Korean War: A 25 Year Perspective* (Lawrence: University Press of Kansas, 1977).

The prolonged armistice negotiations have been treated most fully by Rosemary Foot in *A Substitute for Victory: The Politics of Peacemaking at the Korean Armistice Talks* (Ithaca: Cornell University Press, 1990). Also valuable in understanding the U.S. perspective are earlier books: Allen E. Goodman, ed., *Negotiating while Fighting: The Diary of C. Turner Joy at the Korean Armistice Conference* (Stanford: Stanford University Press, 1978), C. Turner Joy, *How Communists Negotiate* (New York, 1955). Barton J. Bernstein, "The Struggle over the Koren Armistice: Prisoners of Repatriation?" in *Child of Conflict: The Korean-American Relationship, 1943–1953,* ed. Bruce Cumings (Seattle: University of Washington Press, 1983), 261–307, assesses the prisoner-of-war issue. Eisenhower's nuclear threat is explored in several essays: Roger Dingman, "Atomic Diplomacy during the Korean War," *International Security* 13 (1988–89): 50–91; Daniel Calingaert, "Nuclear Weapons and the Korean War," *Journal of Stategic Studies* 11 (1988): 177–202; Edward C. Kiefer, "President Dwight D. Eisenhower and the End of the Korean War," *Diplomatic History* 10 (1986): 267–89; Rosemary Foot, "Nuclear Coercion and the Ending of the Korean Conflict," *International Security* 13 (1988–89): 92–112. Trygve Lie, *In the Cause of Peace: Seven Years with the United Nations* (New York: Macmillan, 1954), the memoir of the U.N. secretary-general, recounts efforts to restrain the belligerents.

For thoughtful analysis of the literature on the war, see Bruce Cumings, "Korean-American Relations: A Century of Contact and Thirty-Five Years of Intimacy," in *New Frontiers in American–East Asian Relations: Essays Presented to Dorothy Borg,* ed. Warren I. Cohen (New York: Columbia University Press, 1983); Rosemary Foot, "Policy Analysis of the Korean Conflict," in *America in the World: The Historiography of American Foreign Relations since 1941,* ed. Michael J. Hogan (New York: Cambridge University Press, 1995), 270–99. The basic reference work is *Historical Dictionary of the Korean War,* ed. James I. Matray (Westport, Conn: Greenwood, 1991).

Chapter 3. Lyndon B. Johnson and the Vietnam Crisis

The volume of writing on the Vietnam War surpasses that on the Korean conflict. This reflects the more extended prewar involvement of

the United States in Vietnam, the greater length of the war itself, and
the deeper controversies surrounding it. The contemporary disagreements about U.S. involvement have continued into the postwar literature.

Several general histories trace U.S. involvement in Vietnam. These
include George C. Herring, *America's Longest War: The United States and
Vietnam, 1950–1975*, 4th ed. (New York: McGraw-Hill, 2002); Paul M.
Kattenburg, *The Vietnam Trauma in American Foreign Policy, 1945–1975*
(New Brunswick, N.J.: Transaction, 1980); George Donelson Moss, *Viet-
nam: An American Ordeal*, 2d ed. (Englewood Cliffs, N.J.: Prentice-Hall,
1992); Robert Schulzinger, *A Time for War: The United States and Vietnam,
1941–1975* (New York: Oxford University Press, 1996); William S. Turley,
The Second Indochina War: A Short Political and Military History (Boulder,
Colo.: Westview, 1986); Stanley Karnow, *Vietnam: A History* (New York:
Viking, 1983); Gary R. Hess, *Vietnam and the United States: Origins and
Legacy of War*, rev. ed. (New York: Twayne/Simon & Schuster, 1998); Patrick J. Hearden, *The Tragedy of Vietnam* (New York: Harper Collins,
1991); Michael H. Hunt, *Lyndon Johnson's War: America's Cold War Cru-
sade in Vietnam, 1945–1968* (New York: Hill & Wang, 1996); Marilyn B.
Young, *The Vietnam Wars, 1945–1990* (New York: Harper, 1991).

Although varying in tone and emphasis, all of these works are critical of U.S. involvement; most stress the misapplication of containment
doctrine into a nationalist revolutionary struggle. The Hearden book
suggests economic imperatives behind U.S. policy, while the Young and
Hunt books are notable for stressing cultural and intellectual factors. In
strident critiques of American culture, both Loren Baritz in *Backfire: A
History of How American Culture Led Us into Vietnam and Made Us Fight
the Way We Did* (New York: Ballantine, 1985) and William Gibson in *The
Perfect War: The War We Couldn't Lose and How We Did* (New York: Vin-
tage, 1986) attribute U.S. involvement and warfare to an uncontrollable
technology. John Prados, *The Hidden History of the Vietnam War* (Chicago:
Ivan Dee, 1995), explores several important aspects of the war.

Thorough accounts of the war's complex origins through 1965 from
both American and Vietnamese perspectives are provided by Anthony
Short in *The Origins of the Vietnam War* (London: Longmans, 1989) and
George McT. Kahin in *Intervention: How America Became Involved in Vietnam* (New York: Knopf, 1986). For greater depth on the Vietnamese side,
see William J. Duiker, *Sacred War: Nationalism and Revolution in a Divided
Vietnam* (New York: McGraw-Hill, 1995), and his earlier book, *The Com-

munist Road to Power in Vietnam (Boulder, Colo.: Westview, 1981), and James P. Harrison, *The Endless War: Vietnam's Struggle for Independence* (New York: Columbia University Press, 1989).

Writing from a leftist perspective, Gabriel Kolko in *Anatomy of a War: Vietnam, the United States, and the Modern Historical Experience* (New York: Pantheon, 1985) casts the war in terms of an effort to control revolutionary movements in developing countries and provides a thorough analysis of the North Vietnamese political-military strategy and the reasons for U.S. failure. Also writing from a leftist viewpoint, Ken Post's multivolume *Revolution, Socialism, and Nationalism in Vietnam,* 5 vols. (Aldershot, England: Darthmouth, 1989-94), analyzes the communist movement's objectives, relationships with China and the Soviet Union, the North Vietnamese–Viet Cong interest, and the response to U.S. warfare.

For an understanding of the problems that Johnson inherited, the following works on U.S. policy under Presidents Eisenhower and Kennedy are instructive: David L. Anderson, *Trapped by Success: The Eisenhower Administration and Vietnam, 1953–1961* (New York: Columbia University Press, 1991); Ronald H. Spector, *Advice and Support: The Early Years* (New York: Free Press, 1985); Ralph B. Smith, *An International History of the Vietnam War,* vol. 1, *Revolution versus Containment, 1955–1961,* and vol. 2, *The Kennedy Strategy* (New York: St. Martin's, 1983-85); William J. Rust, *Kennedy in Vietnam: American Foreign Policy, 1960–1963* (New York: Scribners, 1985); John M. Newman, *JFK and Vietnam: Deception, Intrigue, and the Struggle for Power* (New York: Warner, 1992); Roger Hilsman, *To Move a Nation: The Politics of Foreign Policy in the Administration of John F. Kennedy* (Garden City, N.Y.: Doubleday, 1967); Lawrence Bassett and Stephen Pelz, "The Failed Search for Victory: Vietnam and the Politics of War," in *Kennedy's Quest for Victory: American Foreign Policy, 1961–1963,* ed. Thomas G. Paterson (New York: Oxford University Press, 1989), 223-52; Gary R. Hess, "Commitment in the Age of Counter-Insurgency: Kennedy and Vietnam," in *Shadow on the White House: Presidents and the Vietnam War,* ed. David L. Anderson (Lawrence: University Press of Kansas, 1993), 63-86; Orrin Scwab, *Defending the Free World* (Westport, Conn.: Praeger, 1998); Frederik Logevall, *Choosing War: The Lost Chance for Peace and the Escalation of the Vietnam War* (Berkeley and Los Angeles: University of California Press, 1999).

There are several valuable biographies of Johnson and studies of his presidency. The foremost biography is Robert Dallek's two-volume work, *Lone Star Rising: Lyndon Johnson and His Times, 1908–1960* (1991) and *Flawed Giant: Lyndon Johnson and His Times, 1961–1973* (New York: Oxford University Press, 1998); Dallek's fair-minded judgments acknowledge Johnson's considerable talents and tragic flaws, the latter being most conspicuous in his Vietnam policy. Highly critical of Johnson is Robert Caro, whose own multivolume work has not yet reached the presidential years; his devastating portrait of a power-driven, duplicitous Johnson in his formative years can be traced in *The Years of Lyndon Johnson*, vol. 1, *The Path to Power* (1982), and vol. 2, *Means of Ascent* (New York: Knopf, 1990). Doris Kearns Goodwin, *Lyndon Johnson and the American Dream* (New York: Harper & Row, 1976), based in part on conversations with the retired Johnson, provides insights into his leadership style and reflections on Vietnam. Paul K. Conkin, *Big Daddy from the Pedernales: Lyndon Baines Johnson* (Boston: Twayne, 1986), captures the essential Johnson.

Vaughan Bornet, *The Presidency of Lyndon Johnson* (Lawrence: University Press of Kansas, 1983), is a sound overview of Johnson's programs at home and overseas. An insightful introduction to Johnson's approach to international problems is provided by Waldo Heinrichs in "Lyndon B. Johnson: Change and Continuity," in *Lyndon Johnson Confronts the World: American Foreign Policy, 1963–1968,* ed. Warren I. Cohen and Nancy Bernkopf Tucker (New York: Cambridge University Press, 1994), 9–30.

Accounts by Johnson administration officials and advisers have offered valuable insights: Eric Goldman, *The Tragedy of Lyndon Johnson* (New York: Knopf, 1969); Richard N. Goodwin, *Remembering America: A Voice from the Sixties* (Boston: Little, Brown, 1988); Jack Valenti, *A Very Human President* (New York: Norton, 1975); Clark Clifford with Richard Holbrooke, *Counsel to the President: A Memoir* (New York: Random House, 1991); Hubert H. Humphrey, *The Education of a Public Man* (Garden City, N.Y.: Doubleday, 1976).

Johnson's memoir, *The Vantage Point: Perspectives on the Presidency* (New York: Holt, Rinehart, & Winston, 1971), is revealing on his thinking but is also self-serving and defensive on Vietnam matters. For Johnson's public statements on the war, consult *Public Papers of the Presidents of the United States: Lyndon B. Johnson, 1963–1969,* 10 vols. (Washington: GPO, 1965–70).

For an understanding of the key policymakers on Vietnam, still a good place to begin is with David Halberstam's *The Best and the Brightest*

(New York: Random House, 1972), which stresses the arrogance and self-confidence of the men who came to power in the 1960s. Secretary of State Dean Rusk is the subject of sympathetic studies by Warren I. Cohen in *Dean Rusk* (Totawa, N.J.: Cooper Square, 1980) and Thomas J. Schoenbaum in *Waging Peace and War: Dean Rusk in the Truman, Kennedy, and Johnson Years* (New York: Simon & Schuster, 1988). Rusk recounted some of his thinking in a quasi memoir: Dean Rusk, as told to Richard Rusk, *As I Saw It*, ed. Daniel S. Papp (New York: Norton, 1990). Secretary of Defense Robert McNamara is judged harshly by Deborah Shapley in *Promise and Power: The Life and Times of Robert McNamara* (Boston: Little, Brown, 1993). McNamara's controversial memoir, *In Retrospect: The Tragedy and Lessons of Vietnam* (New York: Times Books, 1995), recounts his role in policymaking and acknowledges the fundamental miscalculations that guided U.S. involvement. Under Secretary of State George Ball's dissenting position on Vietnam policy has been analyzed by David L. DiLeo in *George Ball, Vietnam, and the Rethinking of Containment* (Chapel Hill: University of North Carolina Press, 1991). Ball recounts his role in *The Past Has Another Pattern: Memoirs* (New York: Norton, 1982). The influence of Gen. Maxwell Taylor has been examined by Douglas Kinnard in *The Certain Trumpet: Maxwell Taylor and the American Experience in Vietnam* (Washington: Brassey's, 1981).

John son's decisions to intervene in Vietnam are the focus of several thoughtful studies, including Larry Berman, *Planning a Tragedy: The Americanization of the War in Vietnam* (New York: Norton, 1982), and Brian Van DeMark, *Into the Quagmire: Lyndon Johnson and the Escalation of the Vietnam War* (New York: Oxford University Press, 1991), both of which are sympathetic toward Johnson and the problems he faced in Vietnam but question the decisions he reached. Yuen Foong Khong, *Analogies at War: Korea, Munich, Dien Bien Phu, and the Vietnam Decisions of 1965* (Princeton: Princeton University Press, 1992), contends that policymakers looked to the past for guidance and believed that they had learned from the mistakes of the Korean War how to wage a successful limited war in Vietnam.

John P. Burke and Fred Greenstein, *How Presidents Test Reality: Decisions on Vietnam, 1954 and 1965* (New York: Russell Sage, 1991), is sharply critical of Johnson's essentially closed decision-making process. R. B. Smith, *An International History of the Vietnam War*, vol. 3, *The Making of a Limited War, 1965–66* (New York: St. Martin's, 1991), casts U.S. intervention within the framework of challenges presented by the major communist powers. Leslie Gelb with Richard Betts, *The Irony of Vietnam: The System Worked* (Washington: Brookings Institution, 1978), stresses the extent to which policymakers were aware of the obstacles facing the United States in Vietnam and how escalation driven by the objective of avoiding defeat led to stalemate. H. R. McMaster, *Dereliction of Duty: Lyndon Johnson, Robert McNamara, and the Lies That Led to Vietnam* (New York: Harper Collins, 1997), indicts Johnson and McNamara for pursuing a duplicitous gradual escalation in 1964–65 and isolating the Joint Chiefs of Staff from the process. Edwin E. Moise, *Tonkin Gulf and the Escalation of the Vietnam War* (Chapel Hill: University of North Carolina Press, 1996), provides the definitive account of the events in the Tonkin Gulf in 1964, concluding that the August 4 "encounter" was a product of American imagination.

The opening of American archival sources has stimulated much of the recent scholarship. The documents in the Department of State's *Foreign Relations of the United States (FRUS)* provide the basic source: *FRUS 1961–1963*, vols. 3 and 4 (Washington: GPO, 1991); *FRUS 1964–1968*, vols. 1–4 (Washington: GPO, 1992–98). Another important source is the Pentagon Papers, a classified study that documents U.S. involvement through 1967; its unauthorized publication in 1971 led to enormous controversy and a Supreme Court decision denying the Nixon administration's effort at prior restraint; of the several versions of the *Pentagon Papers* available in book form, the most useful is U.S. Congress, *The Pentagon Papers*, Senator Gravel Edition, 5 vols. (Boston: Beacon, 1971). An exceptionally valuable work, which makes exhaustive use of U.S. documents, is William Conrad Gibbons, *The U.S. Government and the Vietnam War: Executive and Legislative Roles and Relationships*, 4 vols. (Washington: GPO, 1984–89). Contributing to the documentary record on Johnson's early Vietnam policy is much of the material in Michael R. Beschloss, ed., *Taking Charge: The Johnson White House Tapes, 1963–1964* (New York: Simon & Schuster, 1997).

Chapter 4. Lyndon B. Johnson as Commander in Chief

Several of the works cited in the bibliographical essay for chapter 3 are also important as background for Johnson's wartime leadership. Specifically, the general histories of the war and the biographies and memoirs of Johnson and other officials provide useful insights into the way the war was waged.

Several thoughtful essays analyze Johnson as commander in chief.

Walter LaFeber, "Johnson, Vietnam, and Tocqueville," and Richard Immerman, "'A Time in the Tide of Men's Affairs': Lyndon Johnson and Vietnam," both in *Lyndon Johnson Confronts the World: American Foreign Policy, 1963–1968*, ed. Warren I. Cohen and Nancy Bernkopf Tucker (New York: Cambridge University Press, 1994), 31–98, are insightful; LaFeber casts the erosion of domestic support within the context of the difficulty of a democracy waging war, and Immerman criticizes Johnson for the failure to recognize the contradictions and limitations of his initiatives. George C. Herring, "The Reluctant Warrior: Johnson as Commander in Chief," and Sandra C. Taylor, "Lyndon Johnson and the Vietnamese," both in *Shadow on the White House: Presidents and the Vietnam War*, ed. David L. Anderson (Lawrence: University Press of Kansas, 1993), 87–129, add important perspectives. Herring attributes Johnson's shortcomings to his insecurity in dealing with military leadership and his penchant for compromise, and Taylor shows how Johnson created artificial images of the Vietnamese that reinforced his convictions and expectations. George C. Herring, "The Executive, Congress, and the Vietnam War," in *Congress and United States Foreign Policy: Controlling the Use of Force in the Nuclear Age*, ed. Michael Barnart (Albany: State University of New York, 1987), explores the ways that Johnson's leadership undermined relations with Congress. Frank E. Vandiver, "Lyndon Johnson: A Reluctant Hawk," in *Commanders in Chief: Presidential Leadership in Modern Wars*, ed. Joseph P. Dawson (Lawrence: University Press of Kansas, 1993), 127–43, sees Johnson's dedication to the Great Society contributing to uninspiring leadership and direction in Vietnam.

In addition, there are recent books on Johnson's wartime leadership Larry Berman, *Lyndon Johnson's War: The Road to Stalemate* (New York: Norton, 1989), stresses Johnson's failure to call for national commitment and his pursuit of strategy that he questioned. George C. Herring, *LBJ and Vietnam: A Different Kind of War* (Austin: University of Texas Press, 1994), likewise finds a flawed leadership contributing to incoherent military and political initiatives but also relates Johnson's problems to the inherent problems of limited warfare that were accentuated by the unique circumstances of the Vietnam conflict. Lloyd C. Gardner, *Pay Any Price: Lyndon Johnson and the Wars for Vietnam* (Chicago: Ivan Dee, 1995), sees Johnson victimized by the shallowness of advisers and his liberal vision that linked modernization in Southeast Asia with the Great Society. Frank Vandiver, *Shadows of Vietnam: Lyndon Johnson's Wars* (College Station: Texas A&M University Press, 1997), contrasts Johnson's self-confidence as a domestic leader and his hesitancy as a foreign policy leader and suggests that, had Johnson followed his instincts rather than recommendations of advisers, he might have succeeded in Vietnam.

Also see the valuable specialized studies on various aspects of Johnson's wartime leadership. On the pursuit of peace, Wallace J. Thies, *When Governments Collide: Coercion and Diplomacy in the Vietnam Conflict, 1964–1968* (Berkeley and Los Angeles: University of California Press, 1980), focuses on Johnson's futile efforts to negotiate with North Vietnam, which resulted from his persistent compromising on military strategy and the attendant inability to either force Hanoi's leaders to bargain or convince them of peaceful intentions. Kathleen J. Turner, *Lyndon Johnson's Dual War: Vietnam and the Press* (Chicago: University of Chicago Press, 1985), analyzes Johnson's unsuccessful effort to "sell" the war in ways that would be acceptable to both hawks and doves.

On the antiwar movement, Melvin Small, *Johnson, Nixon, and the Doves* (New Brunswick, N.J.: Rutgers University Press, 1988), concludes that Johnson (and Nixon), despite claims to the contrary, were influenced by the mounting protests and other aspects of public opinion. On policymaking, David M. Barrett, *Uncertain Warriors: Lyndon Johnson and His Vietnam Advisers* (Lawrence: University Press of Kansas, 1993), challenges the conventional criticism of Johnson for having an essentially closed advisory system. Henry F. Graff, *The Tuesday Cabinet: Deliberation and Decision on Peace and War under Lyndon B. Johnson* (Englewood Cliffs, N.J.: Prentice-Hall, 1970), is the standard account of the key group involved in determining Vietnam policy. Herbert Y. Schandler, *The Unmaking of a President: Lyndon Johnson and Vietnam* (Princeton: Princeton University Press, 1977), analyzes the debate within the White House in the aftermath of the Tet offensive.

Johnson's relationship with the military leaders and the limitations that he imposed on military operations have been extensively studied. Military leaders have contended that the limitations denied them the opportunity to achieve victory. The best-known proponent of this "if we had only been allowed to win" argument is Harry Summers, whose *On Strategy: A Critical Analysis of the Vietnam War* (Novato, Calif.: Presidium, 1982) indicts political leaders for forcing a strategy that violated long-established military doctrine. Other military leaders offering similar critiques include Bruce Palmer Jr., *The 25-Year War: America's Military Role in Vietnam* (Lexington: University Press of Kentucky, 1984); Philip

B. Davidson, *Vietnam at War: The History, 1946–1975* (Novato, Calif.: Presidium, 1988); Shelby Stanton, *The Rise and Fall of an American Army: U.S. Ground Forces in Vietnam, 1965–1975* (Novato, Calif.: Presidium, 1985). Some of these works are critical of Gen. William C. Westmoreland's search-and-destroy strategy; in his memoir, *A Soldier Reports* (Garden City, N.Y.: Doubleday, 1976), Westmoreland defends his actions while assailing the civilian leadership's restraints.

Several military officers and scholars, however, question the "if only we had been allowed to win" argument and contend that the military leadership itself contributed to failure because of its determination to wage a conventional war and its indifference to the importance of counterinsurgency and pacification. The best-known proponent of this viewpoint is the decorated veteran David Hackworth, who presented his argument most forcefully in *About Face* (New York: Simon & Schuster, 1989). Other expressions include Andrew Krepinevich, *The Army and Vietnam* (Baltimore: Johns Hopkins University Press, 1986); Larry Cable, *Conflicts of Myths: The Development of Counterinsurgency Doctrine and the Vietnam War* (New York: New York University Press, 1986) and *Unholy Grail: The U.S. and War in Vietnam, 1965–1968* (New York: Routledge, 1991). In an indictment of the military leaders' hand-wringing, Robert Buzzanco, *Masters of War: Military Dissent and Politics in the Vietnam Era* (New York: Cambridge University Press, 1996), stresses divisions within the military over strategy, the incessant interservice rivalry, and the Joint Chiefs' penchant for feuding with the White House while playing to hawks in Congress.

On the war itself, there are several valuable studies. The battle of Ia Drang Valley and its influence on the ways that both sides waged war are told by Harold Moore and Joseph Galloway in *We Were Soldiers Once . . . and Young: Ia Drang—The Battle That Changed the War in Vietnam* (New York: Random House, 1992). Operation ROLLING THUNDER is most fully analyzed by Mark Clodfelter in *The Limits of Air Power: The American Bombing of North Vietnam* (New York: Free Press, 1989), which argues that its ineffectiveness reflected the inherent limitations of strategic bombing, thus dismissing claims of air force leaders that all-out bombing could have brought victory. On the air war in the south, Donald J. Mrozek in *Air Power and the Ground War in Vietnam: Ideas and Actions* (Washington: Brassey's, 1988) sees it waged innovatively but bringing limited results. On the decisive events of 1968, the story of the Tet offensive is best told by Don Oberdorfer's *Tet!* (Garden City, N.Y.:

Doubleday, 1971), and the essential background is provided by James J. Wirtz, *The Tet Offensive: Intelligence Failure in War* (Ithaca, N.Y.: Cornell University Press, 1991). The often-ignored intensive fighting that followed the battles of Tet is superbly recounted by Ronald H. Spector in *After Tet: The Bloodiest Year in Vietnam* (New York: Free Press, 1993). The dramatic struggle at Khe Sanh is the subject of two books: Robert Pisor, *The End of the Line: The Siege of Khe Sanh* (New York: Norton, 1982), and John Prados, *Valley of Decision: The Siege of Khe Sanh* (Boston: Houghton Mifflin, 1991).

The war from the communist side has been studied by several scholars. John M. Van Dyke, *North Vietnam's Strategy for Survival* (Palo Alto, Calif.: Pacific, 1972), details the mobilization of resources in response to U.S. warfare. David Chanoff and Doan Van Toai, *Portrait of the Enemy* (New York: Random House, 1986), which is based on interviews with Vietnamese, shows how the communist leaders succeeded in gaining dedicated support. Also drawing heavily on interviews, Michael Lanning and Dan Cragg, in *Inside the VC and NVA: The Real Story of North Vietnam's Armed Forces* (New York: Fawcett, 1992), emphasize the effectiveness of communist recruitment and organization in building a mobile, committed, and disciplined army. Douglas Pike, *PAVN: People's Army of Vietnam* (Novato, Calif.: Presidium, 1986), and Greg Lockhart, *Nation in Arms: The Origins of the People's Army of Vietnam* (Wellington, Australia: Allen & Unwin, 1981), analyze the North Vietnamese army, but from different perspectives; Pike acknowledges its effectiveness while doubting its long-term political effects, but Lockhart contends that it was the key instrument in the communist drive for power.

For an understanding of the problems that Johnson encountered on the home front, there are three valuable studies: Charles DeBenedetti, assisted by Charles Chatfield, *An American Ordeal: The Anti-war Movement of the Vietnam Era* (Syracuse: Syracuse University Press, 1990), which analyzes the "movement of movements" and its influence; Terry Anderson, *The Movement and the Sixties* (New York: Oxford University Press, 1995), which captures antiwar protest within the context of broader social and cultural changes; and David Levy, *The Debate over Vietnam*, 2d ed. (Baltimore: Johns Hopkins University Press, 1995), which examines the arguments dividing hawks and doves and the ways in which the war touched a wide range of institutions and groups.

On the role of the principal congressional critic of the war, Senator

J. William Fulbright, the study by William C. Berman, *William Fulbright and the Vietnam War: The Dissent of a Political Realist* (Kent, Ohio: Kent State University Press, 1988), is illuminating; for an appreciation of Fulbright's entire career, Randall B. Woods, *Fulbright: A Biography* (New York: Cambridge University Press, 1995), is the definitive work.

On the role of the media, see Daniel C. Hallin, *The "Uncensored War": The Media and Vietnam* (New York: Oxford University Press, 1986), and two volumes in the Department of the Army's history of the war by William M. Hammond, *Public Affairs: The Military and the Media, 1962–1968* and *Public Affairs: The Military and the Media, 1968–1973* (Washington: Department of Army, 1988–96), which refute claims of antiwar sentiment in reporting and find that coverage was objective and implicitly supportive of U.S. objectives. Melvin Small, *Covering Dissent: The Media and the Anti–Vietnam War Movement* (New Brunswick, N.J.: Rutgers University Press, 1994), finds objectivity in reporting on the protesters. On the other side of the media debate, Peter Braestrup in *Big Story!* 2 vols. (Boulder, Colo.: Westview, 1977) criticizes the coverage of the Tet offensive as superficial and misleading.

The Nixon administration's Vietnam policy is thoroughly explored by Jeffrey Kimball in *Nixon's Vietnam War* (Lawrence: University Press of Kansas, 1998). Focusing on the last years of the war, Arnold R. Isaacs, *Without Honor: Defeat in Vietnam and Cambodia* (Baltimore: Johns Hopkins University Press, 1983), questions whether the damage inflicted on Indochina was worth the marginal gains at the negotiating table. William Bundy, *A Tangled Web: The Making of Foreign Policy in the Nixon Presidency* (New York: Hill & Wang, 1998), treats Vietnam policy within the context of the Nixon-Kissinger international initiatives. For a provocative insight into Nixon's instincts and actions, see Stephen E. Ambrose, "Richard Nixon: A Belligerent Dove," in *Commanders in Chief: Presidential Leadership in Modern Wars,* ed. Joseph P. Dawson (Lawrence: University Press of Kansas, 1993), 145–65. Two fine essays—Melvin Small, "Containing Domestic Enemies: Richard M. Nixon and the War at Home," and Jeffrey Kimball, "'Peace with Honor': Richard Nixon and the Diplomacy of Threat and Symbolism," both in *Shadow on the White House: Presidents and the Vietnam War,* ed. David L. Anderson (Lawrence: University Press of Kansas, 1993), 130–83—analyze Nixon's cultivation of domestic support and the interaction of his diplomatic and military initiatives in Vietnam.

Several essays examine the scholarship on the Vietnam War, the most recent being Robert J. McMahon, "U.S.-Vietnamese Relations: A Historiographical Survey," in *Pacific Passage: The Study of American–East Asian Relations on the Eve of the Twenty-First Century*, ed. Warren I. Cohen (New York: Columbia University Press, 1996), 279–312, and Gary R. Hess, "The Unending Debate: Historians and the Vietnam War," in *America in the World: The Historiography of American Foreign Relations since 1941*, ed. Michael J. Hogan (New York: Columbia University Press, 1995), 358–94. Also valuable in understanding the literature are Lester Brune and Richard Dean Burns, *America and the Indochina Wars, 1945–1990: A Bibliographical Guide* (Claremont, Calif.: Regina, 1990), and James S. Olson, *The Vietnam War: Handbook of Literature and Research* (Westport, Conn.: Greenwood, 1993). Basic reference guides include William J. Duiker, *Historical Dictionary of the Vietnam War* (Methucen, N.J.: Scarecrow, 1989), and James S. Olson (ed.), *Dictionary of the Vietnam War* (Westport, Conn.: Greenwood, 1988).

Chapter 5. George H. W. Bush and the Persian Gulf Crisis

There are sound histories of the Persian Gulf crisis and war. Lawrence Freedman and Efraim Karsh, *The Gulf Conflict, 1990–91: Diplomacy and War in the New World Order* (Princeton: Princeton University Press, 1993), is a thorough analysis of the diplomatic and military aspects of the United States–Iraqi clash and is notably balanced in its judgments. Michael R. Gordon and Bernard E. Trainor, *The Generals' War: The Inside Story of the Conflict in the Gulf* (Boston: Little, Brown, 1995), is also a very thorough account; while acknowledging the considerable accomplishments of Bush's diplomacy, Gordon and Trainor fault the U.S. military leadership on a number of points, particularly its role in the limitations of the U.N. victory. Dilip Hiro, *Desert Shield to Desert Storm: The Second Gulf War* (New York: Routledge, 1992), which casts the crisis within the history of Middle Eastern politics, stresses Saddam Hussein's miscalculations and their deleterious effect on his own people, the economic basis underlying U.S. policy, and the shrewdness of Bush's diplomacy. Lester H. Brune, *America and the Iraqi Crisis, 1990–1992* (Claremont, Calif.: Regina, 1993), provides a good overview and summary of the continuing debate over political and military issues. James Ridgway (ed.), *The March to War* (New York: 4 Walls 8 Windows, 1991), is a useful collection of documents.

The earliest history of the war, U.S. News and World Report, *Triumph without Victory: The Unreported History of the Persian Gulf War* (New York: Times Books, 1992), remains a reliable guide to official and behind-the-scenes developments. Burton I. Kaufman, *The Arab Middle East and the United States* (New York: Twayne/Simon & Schuster, 1996), sets U.S. policy in 1990–91 within the framework of interests in the region since World War II. Alexander L. George, *Bridging the Gap: Theory and Practice in Foreign Policy* (Washington: United States Institute of Peace, 1993), provides a thorough analysis of U.S. policy throughout the crisis.

U.S. policy has been criticized from various perspectives. How the actions of the United States during the 1980s contributed to the 1990–91 crisis is thoughtfully explored by Bruce W. Jettleson in *With Friends Like These: Reagan, Bush, and Saddam, 1982–1990* (New York: Norton, 1994). Majid Khadduri and Edmund Ghareeb, *War in the Gulf, 1990–91: The Iraqi-Kuwait Conflict and Its Implications* (New York: Oxford, 1997), details the history of the Iraqi claim to Kuwait and suggests that the Arab nations, freed from the intervention of the United Nations, might have resolved the dispute of 1990–91. More outspoken is Jeffrey Record, whose *Hollow Victory: A Contrary View of the Gulf War* (Washington: Brassey's, 1993) argues that the United States was slow to recognize Saddam Hussein's threat and compounded the problem by ending the war in a way that made him look invincible and that will lead to regional instability. Robert W. Tucker and David C. Hendrickson, *The Imperial Temptation: The New World Order and America's Purpose* (New York: Council on Foreign Relations, 1992), discusses the Persian Gulf conflict within the context of foreign policy changes brought by the end of the cold war and criticizes Bush for rejecting alternatives to war and then for failing to achieve a decisive victory. Michael J. Mazarr, Don M. Snider, and James Blackwell Jr., *Desert Storm: The Gulf War and What We Learned* (Boulder, Colo.: Westview, 1993), emphasizes that deterrence, diplomacy, and coercion necessitated warfare that, while successful, may offer little guidance in determining future strategy.

Bush's policy between August 1990 and January 15, 1991, triggered controversy that has continued into postwar scholarship. An early sympathetic account is that of Bob Woodward in *The Commanders* (New York: Simon & Schuster, 1991), which is based on extensive confidential interviews with policymakers and traces the development of policy and the personalities that shaped it. At the other extreme, Alex Robert Hybel, in *Power over Rationality: The Bush Administration and the Gulf Crisis* (Albany: State University of New York Press, 1993), criticizes Bush's decision making for misusing historical analogies, ignoring expert advice, and rushing to war.

Insight into the concerns of Americans on the eve of war is provided by *America Entangled: The Persian Gulf Crisis and Its Consequences*, ed. Ted Galen Carpenter (Washington: Cato Institute, 1991), which includes fifteen papers presented at a January 8, 1991, conference; among other points, participants frequently challenged the administration's assumptions that the U.N. coalition's warfare would build regional stability and would be a model for future crises. Last, several essays in *The Gulf War and the New World Order: International Relations of the Middle East*, ed. Tareq Y. Ismael and Jacqueline S. Ismael (Gainesville: University Press of Florida, 1994), find fault with Bush's policy, mostly for projecting U.S. power in ways that threatened long-term regional stability; these include Richard Falk, "Reflections on the Gulf War Experience; Force and War in the UN System," 25–39; Shibley Telhami, "Between Theory and Fact: Explaining U.S. Behavior in the Gulf Crisis," 153–83; and Enid Hill, "The New World Order and the Gulf War: Rhetoric, Policy, and Politics in the United States," 184–223.

The best source for tracing the day-to-day development of U.S. policy during the crisis is the joint memoir by Bush and Brent Scowcroft, *A World Transformed* (New York: Knopf, 1998), which includes excerpts from Bush's diary. Memoirs by two important officials provide insights into the response to unfolding events: James A. Baker III with Thomas M. DeFrank, *The Politics of Diplomacy: Revolution, War, and Peace, 1989–1992* (New York: Putnam's, 1995); Colin Powell with Joseph E. Persico, *My American Journey* (New York: Random House, 1995). For an understanding of Bush's career, Herbert S. Parmet, *George Bush: The Life of a Lone Star Yankee* (New York: Scribners, 1997), is the most complete biography and is fair in its assessments. Also noteworthy is the memoir of Admiral J. Crowe Jr., the former chairman of the Joint Chiefs of Staff who publicly questioned the Bush administration's offensive buildup; see his *The Line of Fire: From Washington to the Gulf, the Politics and Battles of the New Military* (New York: Simon & Schuster, 1993). An important element in the calculations of policymakers was public opinion, a topic that has been thoroughly studied by John Mueller in *Policy and Opinion in the Gulf War* (Chicago: University of Chicago Press, 1994), which documents and analyzes hundreds of polls taken on political and military issues throughout the crisis.

Chapter 6. George H. W. Bush as Commander in Chief

The general works cited at the beginning of the bibliography for chapter 5 cover the Gulf War as well as its origins; especially noteworthy on the ending of the war is Gordon and Trainor, *The Generals' War*. The Bush-Scowcroft, Baker, and Powell memoirs are valuable in recounting high-level decisions. James F. Dunnigan and Austin Bay, *From Shield to Storm: High-Tech Weapons, Military Strategy, and Coalition Warfare in the Persian Gulf* (New York: William Morrow, 1992), details the military strategy and operations of both sides, Saddam Hussein's miscalculations, and other factors behind the U.N. victory. Three valuable essays in *The Eagle in the Desert: Looking Back on U.S. Involvement in the Persian Gulf*, ed. William Head and Earl H. Tilford Jr. (Westport, Conn.: Praeger, 1996), present U.S. strategy within historical perspectives: Larry E. Cable, "Playing in the Sandbox: Doctrine, Combat, and Outcome on the Ground," 175–200; Michael T. Corgan, "Clausewitz's *On War* and the Gulf War," 269–89; Carline F. Ziemke, "A New Covenant? The Apostles of Douhet and the Persian Gulf War," 290–310. This book also includes important essays on the roles of the air force, army, navy, and marines in the war. Robert A. Pape in *Bombing to Win: Air Power and Coercion in War* (Ithaca, N.Y.: Cornell University Press, 1995) assesses the limits of air power as an instrument of "decapitation" in the Gulf War. Several of the essays in *The Gulf War and the New World Order: International Relations of the Middle East*, ed. Tareq Y. Ismael and Jacqueline S. Ismael (Gainesville: University Press of Florida, 1994), are critical of American strategy and diplomacy; these include Andrew T. Parasiliti, "Defeating the Vietnam Syndrome: The Military, the Media, and the Gulf War," 242–64; Ali A. Marzui, "Global Apartheid? Race and Religion in the New World Order," 521–35; and Richard Falk, "Democracy Died at the Gulf," 536–48. Bush's public statements are included in *Public Papers of the Presidents: George W. Bush, 1989–1993* (Washington: GPO, 1991–93).

Saddam Hussein's postwar policy is analyzed by Amatzia Baram in *Building toward Crisis: Saddam's Strategy for Survival* (Washington: Washington Institute for Near East Policy, 1998) and Andrew Cockburn and Patrick Cockburn, *Out of the Ashes: The Resurrection of Saddam Hussein*

(New York: Harper Collins, 1999). Scott Ritter, *Endgame: Solving the Iraq Problem Once and for All* (New York: Simon & Schuster, 1999), the work of a U.S. official in UNSCOM, criticizes the commission's work and the actions of the U.N. secretary-general. The Clinton administration's continuation of sanctions is discussed by John and Karl Mueller, "Sanctions of Mass Destruction," and F. Gregory Gause III, "Getting It Backward on Iraq," both in *Foreign Affairs* 78 (1998): 43–65. For an overview of U.S. intervention in foreign crises since the Persian Gulf War, see Lester H. Brune, *The United States and Post–Cold War Interventions: Bush and Clinton in Somalia, Haiti, and Bosnia, 1992–1998* (Claremont, Calif.: Regina, 1998).

The early scholarly writing on the war has been analyzed in two essays by Robert Divine: "Historians and the Gulf War," *Diplomatic History* 19 (1995): 117–34, and "The Persian Gulf War Revisited: Tactical Victory, Strategic Failure," ibid. 24 (2000): 129–38.

Chapter 7. George W. Bush and the Second Crisis with Iraq

and

Chapter 8. George W. Bush as Commander in Chief

The development of Bush's approach to the world can be traced through James Mann, *Rise of the Vulcans: The History of Bush's War Cabinet* (New York: Viking, 2004), an insightful series of biographical sketches of the "vulcans" who came together during the 2000 presidential campaign and who, after the election, dominated the formulation of Bush's national security policy. Ivo H. Daalder and James M. Lindsay, *America Unbound: The Bush Revolution in Foreign Policy* (Washington: Brookings Institution, 2003), is a critical and thorough account of the development of national security policy to the beginning of the war. On individual policymakers, there are several important books. Karen De Young's *Soldier: The Life of Colin Powell* (New York: Random House, 2006) is a sympathetic but balanced treatment of his difficult four years as secretary of state. On Condoleezza Rice, the most complete work is Elisabeth Bumiller's *Condoleezza Rice: An American Life, A Biography* (New York: Random House, 2007). Marcus Mabry in *Twice as Good: Condoleezza Rice and Her Path to Power* (Emmaus, Pa.: Modern Times/Rodale 2007) argues that she was ill-equipped temperamentally to be an effective national security adviser, and Glenn Kessler in *The Confidante: Condoleezza Rice and the Creation of the Bush Legacy* (New York: St. Martin's, 2007) focuses on her first two years as secretary of state, finding little accomplishment. On Cheney, Stephen F.

Hayes in *Cheney: The Untold Story of America's Most Powerful and Contro-versial Vice President* (New York: Harper Collins, 2007) underlines his mil-itancy and his determination to enhance presidential authority. Cheney's preeminent role in the most expansive definition of presidential power in U.S. history is traced by Charles Savage in *Takeover: The Return of the Imperial Presidency and the Subversion of American Democracy* (New York: Little, Brown & Co., 2007). Andrew Cockburn, in *Rumsfeld: His Rise, Fall, and Catastrophic Legacy* (New York: Scribner's, 2008), portrays the defense secretary as temperamentally and intellectually ill-suited for the chal-lenges of the war. Alan Weisman, *Prince of Darkness: Richard Perle; the Kingdom, the Power, and the End of Empire in America* (New York: Union Square Press, 2007), traces Perle's career from cold war hawk to leading neoconservative and his political agenda. For Perle's world-view in his own words, see Richard Perle and David Frum, *An End to Evil* (New York: Random House, 2003), which calls for the diverse use of U.S. power to overthrow or destabilize unfriendly governments: "A world at peace will be brought into being by American armed might and defended by American might, too."

The investigative journalist Bob Woodward has written three im-portant books related to the war. These rely heavily on confidential in-terviews with prominent officials and provide insight into the working of the Bush administration: *Bush at War* (New York: Simon & Schuster, 2002), which deals mostly with the response to the 9/11 attacks and the Afghanistan campaign; *Plan of Attack* (New York: Simon & Schuster, 2004), which details the decision for war and covers the early postwar prob-lems; *State of Denial: Bush at War, Part III* (New York: Simon & Schuster, 2006), which covers the continuing warfare through mid-2006.

Another well-known investigative journalist, Seymour M. Hersh, played a prominent role in uncovering the Abu Ghraib scandal. His book, *Chain of Command: The Road from 9/11 to Abu Ghraib* (New York: Harper Collins, 2004), includes much detail on the failures of intelligence and the ideological blinders of the Bush administration.

Besides Woodward's books, there are other important accounts of the Bush White House. Robert Draper's *Dead Certain: The Presidency of George W. Bush* (New York: Free Press, 2007) offers an anecdote-filled in-sight into the imprint of Bush's personality on policy, resulting from his leadership style and decision making. The subtitle of Craig Unger's *The Fall of the House of Bush: The Untold Story of How a Band of True Believers Seized the Executive Branch, Started the Iraq War, and Still Imperils America's Future*

(New York: Scribner's, 2007) tells it all, but it is still a well-told analysis, especially suggestive on the complex relationship of Bush I and Bush II. Sidney Blumenthal, *How Bush Rules: Chronicles of a Radical Regime* (Princeton: Princeton University Press, 2006), offers a balanced analysis. Ron Suskind, *The Price of Loyalty: George W. Bush, the White House, and the Education of Paul O'Neill* (New York: Pocket Books, 2004), uses the unhappy experience of the first Bush secretary of the treasury to underscore incompetent and disinterested presidential leadership. Other former Bush administration officials have written of flawed policymaking and intolerance of criticism: Richard A. Clarke, *Against All Enemies: Inside America's War on Terror* (New York: Free Press, 2004); Joseph Wilson, *The Politics of Truth: Inside the Lies That Led to War and Betrayed My Wife's CIA Identity* (New York: Carroll & Graf, 2004). Countering the critics, Bush's former speechwriter David Frum, in *The Right Man: The Surprise Presidency of George W. Bush* (New York: Random House, 2003), portrays a strong and decisive leader.

The neoconservative campaign against Iraq and call for a more militant foreign policy were stated in David Wursmer, *Tyanny's Ally: America's Failure to Defeat Saddam Hussein* (Washington: American Enterprise Institute, 1999); Robert Kagan and William Kristol, eds., *Present Dangers* (San Francisco: Encounter Books, 2000), which includes an important essay by Paul Wolfowitz, "Statesmanship in the New Century." Once war began, Lawrence F. Kaplan and William Kristol, in *The War over Iraq: Saddam's Tyanny and America's Mission* (San Francisco: Encounter Books, 2003), immediately cast it within a broader democratic role. On the important neoconservative link with Ahmad Chalabi, see Aram Roston, *The Man Who Pushed America to War: The Extraordinary Life, Adventures, and Obsessions of Ahmad Chalabi* (New York: Nation Books, 2008).

On the controversial use of intelligence in the Bush administration's case for war, see James Bamford, *A Pretext for War: 9/11, Iraq, and the Abuse of America's Intelligence Agencies* (New York: Random House, 2004); Frank Rich, *The Greatest Story Ever Sold: The Decline and Fall of Truth in Bush's America* (New York: Penguin, 2006); James Risen, *State of War: The Secret History of the CIA and the Bush Administration* (New York: Free Press, 2006); and Hans Blix, *Disarming Iraq: The Search for Weapons of Mass Destruction* (New York: Pantheon, 2004).

The promulgation of the Bush Doctrine triggered considerable debate among scholars. Robert G. Kaufman, *In Defense of the Bush Doctrine* (Lexington: University Press of Kentucky 2007), argues that it fit within the mainstream of a deep American tradition of "moral democractic realism." Mel Gurtov, *Superpower on Crusade: The Bush Doctrine in U.S. Foreign Policy* (Boulder, Colo.: Lynne Rienner, 2006), contends that it greatly expanded the rationale for U.S. militarism and imperialism. Two leading historians took brief, but cogent, differing positions on the Bush Doctrine: John Lewis Gaddis, *Surprise, Security, and the American Experience* (Cambridge: Harvard University Press, 2004), which reportedly became a favorite work of Bush; decidedly less favorable to the White House was Arthur M. Schlesinger Jr., *War and the American Presidency* (New York: W. W. Norton, 2004). The most scholarly rationale for war was provided by Kenneth M. Pollack in *The Threatening Storm: The Case for Invading Iraq* (New York: Random House, 2002).

Neoconservatism's development and influence have been traced in several works. Especially notable are Jacob Heilbrunn, *They Knew They Were Right: The Rise of the Neocons* (New York: Doubleday, 2008), which is a thorough study of the movement's intellectual and political origins, and Stefan Halper and Jonathon Clarke, *America Alone: The Neoconservatives and the Global Order* (New York: Cambridge University Press, 2004), which provides a full statement of its influence in the Bush administration. On the broader development of conservatism through the Bush administration, Kevin Phillips's *American Theocracy: The Perils and Politics of Radical Religion, Oil, and Borrowed Money in the Twenty-first Century* (New York: Viking, 2006) is thorough and provocative. Also useful is John Micklethwait and Adrian Wooldridge, *The Right Nation: Conservative Power in America* (New York: Penguin, 2004), which traces the contemporary "conventional wisdom" to the conservative "think tanks" of the 1970s.

Neoconservatism's ideology as an apology for empire has encouraged, and in some ways reflected, a renewed interest in American imperialism. The historian Niall Ferguson, in *Colossus: The Price of America's Empire* (New York: Penguin, 2004), argues that a "liberal empire" (like that of the British in the nineteenth century) would promote a global order reflecting America's values and preserving its interests. On the other side, two historians—Warren I. Cohen and Andrew J. Bacevich—are critical of imperial pretensions; see Cohen, *America's Failing Empire: U.S. Foreign Relations since the Cold War* (Malden, Mass.: Blackwell, 2005), and Bacevich, *American Empire: The Realities and Consequences of U.S. Diplomacy* (Cambridge: Harvard University Press, 2002). Bacevich, an army officer before becoming a historian, also has written *The New American Militarism: How Americans Are Seduced by War* (New York: Oxford University Press, 2005), which shows how, since the Vietnam War, Americans have become more militaristic and thus easily led into imperial adventures. Still another scholar, Chalmers Johnson, in *The Sorrows of Empire: Militarism, Secrecy, and the End of the Republic* (New York: Henry Holt, 2006), provides an angry but well-documented and thorough indictment of the contemporary American empire. Less scholarly than the other books, *America's Inadvertent Empire* (New Haven: Yale University Press, 2004), by William E. Odom and Robert Dujarrica, includes an excellent chapter by Odom, a retired general, on the military leadership's continuing failure to plan for the challenges that the United States faces as an imperial power.

The prolonged war in Iraq and occupation policy have been the focus of several works, which are critical of inept civilian and military policy. Peter W. Galbraith, *The End of Iraq: How American Incompetence Created a War without End* (New York: Simon & Schuster, 2006), the work of a former U.S. diplomat with experience in the region, focuses on American ignorance of Iraq's history. Much more detailed is the well-documented *Cobra II: The Inside Story of the Invasion and Occupation of Iraq* (New York: Random House, 2006), by Michael R. Gordon and General Bernard E. Trainor, the military historian and military journalist who also coauthored the most definitive work on the Persian Gulf War. Dilip Hiro, who also wrote a book on the earlier war, has contributed the insightful *Secrets and Lies: Operation "Iraqi Freedom" and After* (New York: Nation Books, 2004). Thomas E. Ricks, *Fiasco: The American Military Adventure in Iraq* (New York: Penguin, 2006), which is based on extensive interviews as well as available documents, provides a devastating portrait of strategic failure resulting from incompetent leadership. Charles Ferguson, *No End in Sight: Iraq's Descent into Chaos* (New York: Public Affairs Press, 2008), which is also based on interviews with officials and other participants, examines closely and dispassionately the American occupation.

Conclusion

Insightful analyses of presidential decision making and foreign policy are provided by Alexander L. George and Juliette L. George, *Presidential Personality and Performance* (Boulder, Colo.: Westview, 1998); Alexander L. George, *Presidential Decisionmaking in Foreign Policy: The Effective Use of Information and Advice* (Boulder, Colo.: Westview, 1980); Carnes Lord, *The Presidency and the Management of National Security* (New York: Free Press, 1988); Irving L. Janis, *Groupthink: Psychological Studies of Policy Decision and Fiascoes*, 2d ed. (Boston: Houghton Mifflin,

1982); Irving L. Janis and L. Mann, *Decisionmaking: A Psychological Analysis of Conflict, Choice, and Commitment* (New York: Free Press, 1977); Gregory M. Herek, Irving L. Janis, and Paul Huth, "Decision Making during International Crises: Is Quality Related to Outcome?" *Journal of Conflict Resolution* 32 (1987): 203–26; I. M. Destler, "National Security Management: What Presidents Have Wrought," *Political Science Quarterly* 95 (1980–81): 573–88. For an understanding of the problems presented by international crises, see R. N. Lebow, *Between Peace and War: The Nature of International Crises* (Baltimore: Johns Hopkins University Press, 1981).

Robert O'Neill, "Problems of Command in Limited Warfare: Thoughts from Korea and Vietnam," in *War, Strategy, and International Politics: Essays in Honor of Sir Michael Howard*, ed. Lawrence Freedman, Paul Hayes, and Robert O'Neill (New York: Oxford University Press, 1992), 264–78, addresses fundamental difficulties of waging limited warfare, drawing "lessons" from the Korean and Vietnam conflicts. A. J. Bacevich, "The Use of Force in Our Time," *Wilson Quarterly* (1995): 50–63, suggests that the success of the Persian Gulf War provides limited guidance in meeting future strategic challenges. Donald Kagan, *On the Origins of War and the Preservation of Peace* (New York: Doubleday, 1995), provides a broad historical overview of the ways that great powers since ancient times have tried to avoid wars but have also been compelled, often as a result of their mistakes, to fight them. In an interview with Frederic Smoler, Kagan relates his findings to recent American history; see "History's Large Lessons," *American Heritage* (1997): 59–67. Arthur M. Schlesinger Jr., "The Ultimate Approval Rating," *New York Times Magazine*, January 19, 1997, provides a recent historians' evaluation of American presidents.

Index